Social Development

Psychological Growth
and the Parent-Child Relationship

Under the General Editorship of

Jerome Kagan

Harvard University

Social Development

Psychological Growth
and the Parent-Child Relationship

Eleanor E. Maccoby

Stanford University

HARCOURT BRACE JOVANOVICH, PUBLISHERS

San Diego   New York   Chicago   Atlanta   Washington, D.C.
London   Sydney   Toronto

To Mac, Jan, Sarah, and Mark

Acknowledgments and Copyrights appear on pages 425 and 426, which constitute a
continuation of the copyright page.

Preface

MANY teachers of developmental psychology courses have been frustrated by the lack of suitable reading materials in social and personality development. Good materials are available on the development of language and cognition. But when it comes to such major topics as attachment, aggression, sex typing, moral development, and parent-child interaction, there is a gap. The handbook chapters are too technical, too long, and often dull. The treatment in the introductory texts is usually not in sufficient depth. In many writings, too, the effort to do justice to different points of view results in an "on the one hand, on the other hand" treatment that leaves the beginning reader confused and unable to form conclusions. What is needed is a thoughtful presentation of the important questions and the research designed to answer them—an account that does not get bogged down in methodological detail but that achieves readability without sacrifice of rigor. It ought to be possible, too, to present differences in viewpoints and contradictory findings without obscuring the substantial agreement that exists and the many valid conclusions that can be drawn from the existing evidence.

Filling the gap is a tall order, but this book makes the attempt. I have tried to minimize jargon and capture some of the vividness that is inherent in children's actions, thoughts, and feelings, while at the same time taking seriously the complexity of the processes that are described. The book is intended to be used as a core text in courses in social development, socialization, and family interaction. It can also be used in general child psychology courses, either as a supplement or jointly with a book on cognitive development. Instructors in education, home economics, human development, human services, family studies, and parent education may also find the book relevant to their students' interests. I hope that the book will also find readers among those most deeply involved with young children—namely, parents.

A central theme of this book is socialization—the process whereby children acquire the habits, values, goals, and knowledge that will enable them to function satisfactorily when they become adult members of society. More specifically, the book deals with the family's contribution to socialization. No one doubts that parents influence their children. Finding out what these influences are should be a simple matter. But when one attempts to discover whether some precise thing a parent does makes a child act in a certain way, the apparent simplicity melts away. Effects are sometimes delayed, sometimes disguised. Different children react in different ways to parental treatments that, on the surface, seem the same. The same child will react differently on one day than on another. Direct effects are sometimes accompanied by subtle and unexpected side effects. Most important, powerful growth forces within children make them more open to certain kinds of parental influences during some periods of childhood than during others. And to complicate matters further, the influence flows in two directions—children also influence their parents.

There have been many studies of the methods parents use to bring up their children and the relationship of these methods to the way the children behave and the personalities they develop. Much is known, and the available information is summarized and reported here. But the conceptualization of much of this research is not entirely satisfactory. Much of it has been done from the standpoint of social learning theory, which emphasizes the impact on children of other people's positive and negative reactions to their behavior and which also stresses the importance of the kinds of models adults provide for children to imitate. In my view, this concept of socialization is not wrong, but it is incomplete. It leaves out the developmental forces that determine how children will react to the socialization experiences they have. When I have tried to make this point to colleagues, the reaction has often been a blank stare or polite inattention. From such experiences I have come to realize that many people think of developmental change simply as an outcome of socialization experiences. It is by no means easy to convey the idea that development has dynamics of its own that intersect with the inputs from the environment to determine a child's response. One of my primary objectives in this book is to give substance to this interactive point of view.

The book is organized topically. Separate chapters deal with attachment, aggression, impulsiveness, sex typing, self-concepts, and moral development. The chapters have a rough chronological order. Attachment is treated first because it deals with the infant's initial social relationships and because it has been claimed that the attachments of infancy lay the groundwork for later interpersonal relationships. Aggression begins to be an issue in the third and fourth years, and problems of self-definition become paramount somewhat later. The chronological order should not be taken too seriously. Obviously, children's affectional relationships with their parents continue to be important after the peak period of clinging and proximity seeking has passed. In the same way, each behavioral domain has a time course that overlaps the others. As each domain is explored, we first consider the developmental pattern typical of most children. This information then serves as background for discussions of the parents' contribution to developmental change. It will be seen that under some circumstances parents can do little more than facilitate or impede developmental changes that inevitably occur. In other respects parental influence is deeper, impelling a child toward one developmental path rather than another. In most families, whatever the style of child rearing the parents adopt, there is a gradual transfer of the management and guidance processes from parent to child. We will consider the fact that parents manage this transfer in different ways and inquire whether this makes a difference in children's willingness to accept responsibility for their own behavior.

The title *Social Development* deserves some comment. The word *personality* might have been included, since the book is concerned with stable individual differences in the way children relate to other people and how such individuality comes about. The title cannot be *Child Development*, however, since the book does not attempt to encompass the large fund of theory and research about children's intellectual development, except in terms of the impact this development has on children's relationships with other people. Nevertheless, the close reciprocal link between social and cognitive development is repeatedly stressed. Clearly, children's ability to interact effectively with others depends on their understanding and interpretation of other people's knowledge, feelings, goals, and probable reactions. *Social cognition*, then, is a central theme.

Because the book focuses on development within the context of the family, the emphasis is on early and middle childhood rather than on later periods of the life span. Of course, socialization continues after children leave the family circle. And as the child grows older, forces outside the family, such as friends and school teachers, have a greater and greater influence. However, summarizing and analyzing what is known about the role of the family in children's social development is a sufficient task for a single book.

Although the words *mother, father,* and *parents* are used throughout, the discussion is meant to apply to all parent figures rearing children in nuclear families. At many points the need for information about a wider range of family types and a greater variety of cultural settings will be evident. To date, however, most studies have looked at the behavior of middle-class parents and children in Western industrialized societies. Wherever possible, reference is made to wider cross-cultural work, but the bias in available information cannot easily be overcome. It is not known how fully the conclusions apply to other populations. Much still remains to be learned about the urban poor, children in developing countries, the handicapped, and children whose care is extensively supplemented by day care or hired caretakers.

I would like to acknowledge the help of many people who have given generously of their time and brainstorming skills to help improve the quality of this book. First and foremost, my thanks go to Judith Greissman, editor *extraordinaire*, without whose encouragement, needling, and shameless flattery the book would probably never have been written. I cannot acknowledge sufficiently my intellectual indebtedness to Robert R. Sears and Pauline S. Sears and to John W. M. Whiting and Beatrice B. Whiting. My interest in the socialization pro-

cess and my respect for the importance and difficulty of devising rig-
orous methods to study it developed through their influence during
several years as an apprentice at the Laboratory of Human Development at Harvard. Another intellectual debt is to Lawrence Kohlberg.
Over the years, I have found his writings to be singularly provocative;
they have demanded considerable accommodation and change in my
earlier views. Repeated discussion sessions with several graduate students—Megan R. Gunnar, Catherine Lewis, John A. Martin, John U.
Zussman, Charlotte J. Patterson, and Janet DiPietro—helped to form
some of the ideas that have guided the structure of this book. Comments on the first draft of the manuscript by the publisher's two primary reviewers, Jerome Kagan and W. Andrew Collins, were
enormously helpful, as were those by Marian Radke-Yarrow and Tom
Lickona, who agreed to do somewhat more limited reviews. Other
colleagues have suggested source materials, reviewed early drafts of
individual chapters, or responded to appeals for discussion of issues,
and their helpful comments are gratefully acknowledged: S. Shirley
Feldman, John H. Flavell, Albert H. Hastorf, E. Mavis Hetherington,
Carol Nagy Jacklin, Mark R. Lepper, Zella Luria, Walter Mischel,
Jerry Patterson, and Robert Sears. Membership in two interdis-
ciplinary discussion groups at Stanford, one at the Boys Town Center
for Youth Development and the other at the Center for Research on
Women, has sharpened my awareness that the psychological perspective on socialization is only one of several possible perspectives. And
although the treatment in this book primarily reflects psychological
thinking and research, the viewpoint of other disciplines is not entirely ignored.

During the revision process, many muddy portions of the first
draft were greatly clarified by Phyllis Fisher, my manuscript editor.
My thanks go to her for her remarkably thoughtful attention to all
aspects of the substance and structure of the text. The book has also
profited from the skills of Sandra Lifland, copy editor, and Janou Pak-
ter, art editor.

Susanne Marie Taylor, Ruth E. Prehn, and Patricia D. Hallenbeck
have contributed more than their expert typing and their good cheer
under the pressure of deadlines. All three are parents, and their comments on the substance of the text have kept the parental perspective
in the forefront of my thinking.

Finally, my thanks go to my husband, Nathan Maccoby, for many
things: for the ongoing intellectual exchange that has spanned four decades; for full participation in the joint enterprises of rearing our own
family and managing our household; for his patience with my preoc-
cupation during the preparation of this book and his willingness to
discuss its substance at any hour of the day or night; and finally for
his strong and consistent support of the two-career family idea at a
time when this was uncommon.

Eleanor E. Maccoby

Contents

Social Development

Psychological Growth
and the Parent-Child Relationship

1

Introduction and

Historical Overview

How CAN we understand the development of a child? The fact that children undergo vast changes between infancy and adulthood is clear enough to the most casual observer. *Why* and *how* these changes occur, and the forces that make different children develop in different ways, are not so obvious. In popular wisdom there are different, contradictory viewpoints about the nature of childhood. Sometimes a young child is seen as a bundle of animal appetites in need of control, sometimes as a being whose fate has been preordained. On the other hand, a newborn child may be seen as an organism with few predispositions—a blank slate on which experience will write. The contradictory viewpoints lead to questions about how children should be raised. Should they be guided and carefully taught or left to grow with little pressure and control? The arguments are endless. The points of view have changed again and again over the centuries. The differences of opinion have been reflected in child-rearing practices, philosophic treatises, and, more recently, in the research and theories of child psychologists.

The following pages will survey early attitudes toward children and examine some child-rearing practices that developed from those

The brief historical account given here draws on the following sources: Aries (1965), deMause (1974), Kessen (1965), and Stone (1977).

3

views. Scholars' ideas about childhood will then be presented, starting with John Locke's and Jean Jacques Rousseau's. We will look at key issues in the development of the modern study of child behavior, focusing on the influence of past theory and research on child study today. The discussion will include the work of the behaviorists and psychoanalysts of the 1920s, the ideas of the learning theorists who dominated American psychology from the 1930s through the 1950s, the insights of the cognitive-developmental revolution of the past decades, and the contributions of other social and behavioral sciences.

THE CHILD AS VICTIM: EARLY IDEAS AND PRACTICES

> Bow down his neck while he is young, and beat him on his sides while he is a child, lest he wax stubborn and be disobedient unto thee, and so bring sorrow to thy heart. (passage included in Sir Thomas Bacon's catechism, 1550; quoted in Stone, 1977, p. 176)

Let us begin our story by looking at child-rearing practices that prevailed in England and in the American colonies from about 1500 to about the mid-1700s. The typical child living in England in the sixteenth and seventeenth centuries was frequently beaten. At home and at school, errors and infractions—large and small—provoked physical punishment. Schoolmasters felt justified in beating children (even those of college age) on the hands, lips, or buttocks for mistakes, laziness, or lack of deference. Children were supposed to stand when adults entered a room and remain standing silently until given leave to sit or speak. Not uncommonly, children had to kneel before their parents and ask their blessing at least once a day. John Calvin decreed the death penalty for juveniles who were chronically disobedient toward their parents, and laws with like penalties were passed in Massachusetts and Connecticut. Infants were tightly swaddled and hung like bundles on the wall while adults went about their tasks, and the swaddling cloths were not always changed regularly. Infants and young children were frequently given alcohol or opiates to keep them quiet. Some parents considered creeping or crawling to be animal-like. And from the time their children began to stand, some parents made them wear special garments reinforced with iron and whalebone, which forced the children into adult postures. In 1665, a two-year-old child died from such confinement. The physician told her father, "Her iron bodice was her pain, and had hindered the lungs to grow." A surgeon who examined her body said he found "her breast bone pressed very deeply inwardly. . . . two of her ribs were broken, and the straightness of the bodice upon the vitals occasioned this difficulty of breathing and her death" (quoted in Stone, 1977, p. 162). The use of these devices probably was most frequent among the more affluent middle and upper classes, but the attitudes that led to the practices were probably widespread.

Commonly at this time, children were sent away from home to work as servants when they were as young as six or seven years of age. Many such children were badly treated in their new households. In 1665 Samuel Pepys wrote, "I . . . made my wife, to the disturbance of our house and neighbors, to beat our little girl [a maidservant], and then we shut her down into the cellar, and there she lay all night" (quoted in Stone, 1977, p. 167). Adults were preoccupied with breaking the child's will, and the interesting question is, why? Three factors, specific to the period, probably affected parents' behavior and attitudes: widespread acceptance of Puritan religious values, limited medical knowledge, and lack of real understanding of children and childhood.

The Puritan influence

The Puritan fundamentalist religion of the time played an important role in adults' harsh behavior. Parents self-righteously believed that they were stamping out sin in their children. Consider the disciplinary action taken by an American Puritan father who was teaching his four-year-old son to read. The child could not read something the father expected him to know, and the father thought he detected defiance in the child. He took the child to the cellar, stripped him of his clothes, tied him, and beat him. He described the self-pity and suffering he felt as he carried out his duty.

> During this most self-denying and disagreeable work, I made frequent stops, commanding and trying to persuade, silencing excuses, answering objections. I felt all the force of divine authority and espress command that I ever felt in all my life. But under the influence of such a degree of angry passion and obstinacy that my son had manifested, no wonder he thought he should beat me out, feeble and tremulous as I was, and knowing as he did that it made me almost sick to whip him. At that time he could neither pity me nor himself (quoted in deMause, 1974, pp. 8–9)

Adults of this period saw their children's defiance, or even accidents that befell them, as punishment for the *parents'* sins. Cotton Mather, the evangelical New England Puritan preacher, said, when his small daughter fell into the fire and burned herself badly, "Alas, for my sins the just God throws my child into the fire" (quoted in de-Mause, 1974, p. 9). Lloyd deMause interprets these parental attitudes as examples of the psychodynamic defense mechanism of *projection*—that is, unconsciously, unacceptable thoughts and feelings were rejected by the parents and attributed to the children. The sins and weaknesses that these parents projected onto their children then justified the severe punishments they meted out.

The role of Calvinist beliefs should not be overemphasized, however. While less information is available about the situation in continental Europe at this time, there is reason to believe that the treatment of children was also highly punitive and authoritarian in countries like France, where Puritan ideas did not take root. It seems clear that by present-day standards, many—perhaps most—of the children growing up at that time were victims of parental abuse.

Infant mortality

If people in continental Europe did not share religious beliefs with people in England and in the American colonies, they did have in common a profound lack of knowledge about proper care and feeding of infants and control of epidemic diseases. Their ignorance resulted in a mortality rate among infants and children that was very high indeed. Before about 1750 an estimated 25 percent of children born in London survived to the age of five. The chances of survival were somewhat better in the villages and in the countryside, but even there early death was very common. In cities, survival was compromised by the unwillingness of most mothers to breast-feed their babies. Breast-feeding was considered vulgar, somehow degrading and animal-like, as well as being an interference with a woman's other activities. Safe substitutes for breast milk were not available, so mothers who could pay entrusted their infants to the care of wet nurses. Urban infants were generally sent to wet nurses in the countryside. As late as 1780, the police chief of the city of Paris estimated that 17,000 infants, out of about 21,000 born there each year, were sent to wet nurses in the country. Among those remaining in Paris, only a small minority were nursed by their mothers. Wet nurses were poorly paid and frequently attempted to nurse too many infants (including their own) or concealed the fact that their milk was giving out. Thus the food supply of many infants was inadequate.

Wet-nursing was not confined to the well-to-do. The poor left thousands of unwanted infants at churches and gates of foundling homes, and these children had to be fed. An enormous foundling home in St. Petersburg that took in 5,000 infants a year had 600 wet nurses on duty. After six weeks of nursing, the children were sent to peasant women in the countryside. About a third of these children survived to the age of six—a very good record for the time. In England in the 1700s, the survival rate for foundlings was much lower.

Aside from the problems surrounding the feeding of infants, there were the ever-present dangers of disease, which took a high toll of adults and an even higher one of children. During the late 1600s and early 1700s Queen Anne of England had eighteen children, *none* of whom survived into adolescence.

The very high rate of mortality among infants and children may have made adults fearful of forming strong attachments to their off-spring. Many parents certainly felt affection for their children, but parents had to cope with the possibility that they would suffer the pain of loss. Some historians have inferred that parents protected themselves by avoiding deep commitments and treating their young children as individuals only after they had survived the vulnerable early years.

Misinformation and its effects

Parents of this period knew very little about what was good for their children. People commonly believed that showing affection was bad for children. The Spanish writer Vives said, "Cherishing marreth sons, but it utterly destroyeth daughters" (quoted in Stone, 1977, p. 167). Needless to say, the children must have responded with mixed feelings. Believing they owed their parents obedience, respect, and even love, they nevertheless felt fear and hatred. Autobiographical writings of the times suggest that childhood was remembered as a time of terror. As Vives said, "There was nobody I did more flee, or was more loath to come nigh, than my mother when I was a child" (quoted in Stone, 1977, p. 167).

Of course, despite these injunctions many parents undoubtedly felt tenderness toward their children. A great deal of the ill-treatment was based on simple ignorance—ignorance about the natural course of sensory-motor development that leads children to crawl before they walk, ignorance about what children are capable of learning at different ages, ignorance about proper care and feeding. Witness the report by William Cadogan, a pediatrician, who wrote in 1749:

> The general practice is, as soon as the child is born, to cram a dab of butter and sugar down its throat, a little oil, spiced boiled bread and sugar, gruel, mixed with wine or ale. And it is the custom of some to give a little roast pig to the infant, which, it seems, is to cure it of all the mother's longings. (quoted in Kessen, 1965, p. 17)

Strangely, the punitive treatment of children—probably harsher than the treatment that prevailed during the Middle Ages—reflected a growing interest in children and a growing tendency to assign importance to the early years of life. In the sixteenth, seventeenth, and eighteenth centuries, debates about pedagogy flourished, and education increased in importance, at least for the well-to-do. Children began to be seen as needing training. Many contemporary writings compared the training of children to the training of horses, hawks, or dogs. And just as there were disagreements about whether horses ought to be broken or gentled, there were disagreements about the most effective approach to training children. While extreme harshness toward children was common, it was not universal, and voices were raised against it.

FOR GENTLENESS IN CHILD REARING: TWO INFLUENTIAL POINTS OF VIEW

The writings of two philosophers, Locke in England and Rousseau in France, were especially influential in changing people's attitudes toward child rearing. Both men were opposed to the use of physical punishment. Their ideas on the best way to raise children were very different, however. Locke was strongly in favor of careful structuring and guidance from the child's earliest years. Rousseau believed in allowing children considerably more freedom to grow and develop on their own. The controversy survives to the present day.

John Locke's views

Locke, writing late in the seventeenth century, opposed the idea that children are innately sinful. Although he believed in innate individual differences in intelligence and temperament, he opposed the notion, current at the time, that specific thoughts or ideas could be inborn. He saw the newborn child as being similar to a blank slate upon which experience would write. This view of human nature had an enormous effect on political and social philosophy, for it implied that human beings were perfectable through their own and others' efforts. Improving the environment of human beings could improve what they would become. In terms of child rearing, the doctrine assigned great importance to the early years and great power to parents, who could shape their children's futures in quite profound ways. In 1693 Locke said:

> The little, almost insensible impressions on our tender Infancies, have very important and lasting Consequences: And there 'tis, as in the Fountains of some Rivers, where a gentle Application of the Hand turns the flexible Waters in Channels that make them take quite contrary Courses, and by this Direction given them at the first in the Source, they receive different tendencies, and arrive at last at very remote and distant places. (1884, pp. 1–2[1])

[1]First published in 1693; citations refer to the Revised Edition, 1884.

He saw childhood as a time when life-long habits are formed. He urged parents to make children *practice* until desired social behaviors were nearly automatic:

> By repeating the same action the performance will not depend on memory or reflection, but will be natural in them. Thus bowing to a Gentleman when he salutes him, and looking in his face when he speaks to him, is by constant use as natural to a well-bred Man as breathing; it requires no thought, no reflection. Having this way cured in your child any fault, it is cured forever. And thus one by one you may weed them out all, and plant what Habits you please. (p. 38)

In Locke's view, the characteristic that distinguishes human beings from lower animals is their rationality—their ability to govern their own behavior by logical reasoning and coherent judgment. He said, "The great principle and foundation of all vertue and worth is placed in this, that a man is able to *deny himself* his own desires, cross his own inclinations, and purely follow what reason directs as best, tho the appetite lean the other way" (p. 21).

For Locke, then, the duty of parents lay in helping children control their appetites and become rational. To this end, he urged that "a Child should never be suffered to have what he *craves,* much less what he *cries for.*" Locke recognized that parents might misinterpret his injunction. He was not telling parents to avoid listening to their children. Just the opposite. He believed that children could only become rational if they were encouraged to express their curiosity. Indeed, he urged parents to thoughtfully and truthfully answer all their children's questions—a radical suggestion, indeed, for the times. At the same time parents were told to help children control their appetites and impulses. He elaborated:

> It is fit that they should have liberty to declare their Wants to their Parents, and that with all tenderness they should be hearken'd to, and supplied, at least whilst they are very little. But 'tis one thing to say, I am hungry; another to say, I would have Roast-Meat. Having declared their Wants, their natural Wants, the pain they feel from Hunger, Thirst, Cold, or any other necessity of Nature, 'tis the Duty of their Parents, and those about them, to relieve them. But Children must leave it to the choice and ordering of their Parents, what they think properest for them, and how much; and must not be permitted to chuse for themselves, and say, I would have Wine, or White-bread; the very naming of it should make them lose it.
>
> That which Parents should take care of here, is to distinguish between the Wants of Fancy, and those of Nature. (p. 84)

Locke believed that parents should serve as teachers from the time of their children's earliest infancy. In order to teach effectively, the parent must command the respect, attention, and affection of the child. Then punishment would not be needed, and simple approval or disapproval would bring compliance.

Jean Jacques Rousseau's views

Rousseau's writings came into prominence a half-century later with the publication in 1763 of *Emile*. In many ways Rousseau's views are diametrically opposed to Locke's. Rousseau thought that the child should be allowed to grow as the child's nature dictated, with as little pressure and guidance from adults as possible. He said, "Give the child no orders at all—absolutely none." And, "The most important rule of education is: do not save time, lose it. . . . Exercise the child's body, his limbs, his senses, his strength, but keep his mind idle as long as you can" (1974, pp. 55, 57, 58[2]).

While this kind of thinking might be interpreted as reflecting a respect for the natural wisdom of children, Rousseau meant something quite different. He felt that young children are not ready for instruction. He believed that it is pointless to try to teach children until they develop sufficiently to be able to reason, form judgments, and remember what they have learned. He wrote:

> The apparent ease with which children learn is their ruin. You fail to see that this very facility proves that they are not learning. Their shining, polished brain reflects, as in a mirror, the things you show them, but nothing sinks in. . . . Children are incapable of judging and they have no true memory. They retain sounds, form, sensation, but rarely ideas, and still more rarely relations. . . . All their knowledge is on the sensation level. Nothing has penetrated to their understanding; they always have to learn over again, when they are grown, what they learnt as children. (p. 72)

Rousseau was not suggesting that children be deprived of opportunities to learn. But he was opposed to parents acting as teachers. He urged a kind of freedom within clearly articulated limits, which he called "well-regulated liberty." He believed that children are capable of discovering for themselves certain of the laws of nature—that certain things can be while others cannot. But these "natural lessons" should not be supplemented by any extra sanctions imposed by parents. If the parent simply says, "There's no more left," children discover that they cannot have everything they want. The parent does not need to take the further step of saying that the child is not *allowed* to have more or that the child will be punished for trying to get more. Rousseau said, "It is in man's nature to bear patiently with the nature of things, but not with the ill will of another" (p. 56). Parental discipline, he thought, would be seen as hostility, and he advised against battles of will with children. He was *not* advocating total permissiveness with children, however, but rather a kind of neutral control

[2] First published in 1763; citations refer to the Foxley translation.

through the setting of unalterable boundaries. The following is a passage from *Emile*:

> If there is something he should not do, do not forbid him, but prevent him without explanation or reasoning; what you give him, give it at his first word without prayers or entreaties, above all without conditions. Give willingly, refuse unwillingly, but let your refusal be irrevocable; let no entreaties move you; let your "No," once uttered, be a wall of brass, against which the child may exhaust his strength five or six times, but in the end he will try no more to overthrow it. Thus you will make him patient, equable, calm and resigned, even when he does not get all he wants. (p. 55)

Evidently Rousseau believed that this kind of behavior would make the parent's "no" seem part of the nature of things to the child and would de-emphasize the element of authority. (In his emphasis on not yielding to children's whims, we see one similarity to Locke.) Rousseau recommended reasoning and teaching only after children had developed near-adult levels of logic and understanding.

Some of Rousseau's main ideas are:

1. Children are different from adults and are not just incomplete adults. Children are integrated beings, to be valued and understood for what they *are* rather than what they will become.

2. There is a natural order of developmental events. Development of true intellect—of understanding—comes rather late. Until this time, children are neither moral nor immoral.

3. Children actively take from the environment whatever is suitable for their stage of development. They are not just passive vessels into which knowledge is poured.

4. Parents should not disturb these natural processes by attempting to teach adult concepts and skills at a time when intellectual capacities are not sufficiently mature to profit from such teaching.

From our present perspective, Rousseau seems to underestimate young children's learning abilities. Nevertheless, the idea of readiness is still an important one in pedagogical thought. Other aspects of Rousseau's view were influential in the development of philosophies of education during the subsequent two centuries, but Rousseau did not have full possession of the field. Throughout the eighteenth and nineteenth centuries debate continued between his "teach later" position and Locke's "teach earlier" position.

THE DAWN OF SCIENTIFIC CHILD STUDY

We have been discussing views about children that grew out of religious beliefs, casual observation, and the theoretical writing of philosophers and pedagogues. A new and important step was taken in the middle of the nineteenth century when the child began to be seen as a possible object of scientific study. The publication in 1859 of Charles Darwin's *The Origin of Species* was the milestone that initiated this new phase in the understanding of childhood (Kessen, 1965). Darwin's 1877 paper describing the early development of his own child was also widely influential. Scientists began to draw analogies between the development of species and the development of individuals within a species from conception to maturity. The idea that *ontogeny recapitulates phylogeny*—that individual development repeats the development of the species—was proposed and debated. In the late 1800s and early 1900s academic programs for the study of child psychology were established. (The two notable figures of this period are G. Stanley Hall and James Mark Baldwin, and the reader is referred to Kessen, 1965, for a summary of their contributions.) The research of Ivan Pavlov was especially important for the future of psychology. Pavlov's work on *conditioned reflexes* offered scientists a new way to look at learning, and it had an enormous impact on psychology in general and developmental psychology in particular.

Behaviorism

As long ago as Locke, learning was seen as a process by which *associations,* or connections between events, are developed. Locke stressed the associations between sensations and images. Experimental studies of conditioning had a different emphasis. They dealt with observable behavior—with the associations between stimuli and responses. Following Pavlov's studies with animals, behaviorism was born, and its principles were quickly translated into doctrines concerning the proper rearing of children. In the 1920s John B. Watson conducted his famous experiment on the acquisition of fears in infancy. He worked with Albert, a nine-month-old infant, who at the beginning of the experiment was not afraid of rabbits but who was afraid of loud noises. On several occasions Watson made a very loud noise (by banging a steel bar with a hammer) just as a rabbit was brought into view. Little Albert quickly became afraid of the rabbit and would cry when it appeared, even when it was not accompanied by the loud noise. All kinds of advice to parents could be derived from this demonstration—for example, that children should not be brought to the table while they are upset or afraid, lest they learn to become upset at the sight of food.

The basic premise of behaviorism was that stimulus-response connections, forged through repeated experiences, are the building blocks of all knowledge, of all behavior. Parents, knowingly or not, have an important role in determining what the child's experiences shall be, and they should not leave the child's acquisition of associations to chance:

> All we have to start with in building a human being is a lively squirming bit of flesh, capable of making a few simple responses such as movements of the hands and arms and fingers and toes, crying and smiling, making certain sounds with its throat. Parents take this raw material and begin to fashion it in ways to suit themselves. This means that parents, whether they know it or not, start intensive training of the child at birth. (Watson, 1928, pp. 45–46)

Watson complained that parents not only fail to train the behaviors their children would need for later life, but that they often actively train the *wrong* behaviors. Specifically, Watson objected to *coddling*— hugging or kissing children, rocking them, holding them close. This kind of treatment, he thought, trains children to cling to their parents and to demand their attention, and it interferes with the development of independent competence. Watson commented:

> These love responses which the mother or father is building in by over-conditioning . . . are not constructive. They do not help [children] to conquer . . . [their] environment. Hence just to the extent to which you devote time to petting and coddling—and I have seen almost all of the child's waking hours devoted to it—just to that extent do you rob the child of the time which he should be devoting to the manipulation of his universe, acquiring a technique with fingers, hands and arms. Even from this standpoint alone—that of robbing the child of its opportunity for conquering the world, coddling is a dangerous experiment. (pp. 79–80)

What is the *right* way to treat children? Watson had ready answers:

> Treat them as though they were young adults. . . . Let your behavior always be objective and kindly firm. Never hug and kiss them, never let them sit in your lap. If you must, kiss them once on the forehead when they say good night. Shake hands with them in the morning. Give them a pat on the head if they have made an extraordinarily good job of a difficult task. Try it out. In a week's time you will find how easy it is to be perfectly objective with your child and at the same time kindly. You will be utterly ashamed of the mawkish, sentimental way you have been handling it. (pp. 81–82)

Psychoanalytic theory

The psychoanalytic movement, founded by Sigmund Freud at the same time that behaviorism was emerging, offered a very different view of human nature. The two viewpoints had one thing in common: Both held that events occurring early in children's lives could have important effects on the children's subsequent development. Speaking of infancy and very early childhood, Freud said:

> What poets and students of human nature had always asserted turned out to be true: the impressions of that remote period of life, though they were for the most part buried in amnesia, left ineradicable traces upon the individual's growth, and in particular, laid the foundations of any nervous disorder that was to follow. (1935, p. 55)

Here the similarity ended. The theories differed on which early experiences were thought to be important. Watson pointed to the effect of training by parents on children's habits, while Freud was concerned with the reaction of parents to children's intense emotions—their anger, fear, love, and (shocking to the puritanical view of the time) sexuality. In Freud's view, a natural sequence of events governs both the child's expression of these intense emotions and the acquisition of controls over them. He saw as a major task of early childhood the resolution of conflicts between strong inner needs and outside demands—that is, the erection of defenses against impulses, particularly sexual impulses. Indeed, he thought that children are essentially uneducable (in the intellectual spheres) until such defensive barriers against powerful emotions are erected. Although adults could help, a built-in developmental timetable plays a controlling role:

> We may gain the impression that the erection of these dams in the civilized child is the work of education; and surely education contributes much to it. In reality, however, this development is organically determined and can occasionally be produced without the help of education. Indeed education remains properly within its assigned realm only if it strictly follows the path sketched for it by the organic determinant and impresses it somewhat cleaner and deeper. (Freud, 1910, p. 40)

Thus, Freud was a developmentalist, while Watson was not.

Freud's analysis of the way children internalize adult standards of behavior was especially influential in later research. Particularly important was his concept of *identification*, the defense mechanism whereby children resolve inner conflicts by patterning themselves after those they admire. By identifying with the parent, children incorporate parental standards into their own psychic structures. A *superego*, or conscience, is formed, which enables children to perform some of the parents' controlling functions. One motivation underlying identification is fear—parental standards are accepted to avoid punishment. Another motivation is replacement of love—the child plays the role of the nurturant, comforting parent when the parent is busy, absent, or unwilling to give needed emotional support. An example given by Anna Freud will illustrate the process:

> A little girl, just two years old, had always been put to bed by her mother, and there was a familiar bed-time routine. For the first time, the mother was away over night, and the child was being put to bed by a baby-sitter. The child had great difficulty going to sleep, and even

though she was very tired, kept her eyes open after she was tucked in and the sitter had tip-toed out of the room. Through the open door, the sitter hears the child say, imitating her mother's voice: "Goodnight my dearest." (Personal communication)

Presumably this behavior reflected an early phase of the child's ability to incorporate the absent parent and exercise certain of the parent's functions.

According to Freud's theory, defensive identification (identification based on fear) develops somewhat later than identification based on replacement of love. Defensive identification was thought to be particularly important in the development of boys. As emotional involvement with the mother intensified, boys were thought to see their fathers as rivals. Exaggerating the threatening aspects of their fathers' presence, they would create a father image that merged with fantasies of threatening animals with big teeth, and they would imagine that the threatening figures wanted to bite, hurt, even castrate them. To cope with such fears, they would incorporate the dangerous figure, achieving some sense of control over the danger by pretending to *be* the threatening person. The result would be the formation of a superego. As Freud said, "The institution of conscience was at bottom an embodiment, first of parental criticism, and subsequently, that of society" (1914, p. 53). The formation of the child's superego was thought to have consequences beyond initiating self-monitoring and self-reward or criticism. A boy identifying with a powerful father would incorporate masculine sex-typed behavior. Both girls and boys identifying with their parents' values would experience guilt for deviations. Guilt was seen as a powerful force, motivating children to conform to parental strictures. Departure from these social codes would elicit painful, guilty self-criticism.

SOCIALIZATION RESEARCH AT MID-CENTURY

During the thirties, forties, and fifties, behaviorism dominated American psychology. The learning theories of Clark L. Hull and B. F. Skinner played a major role in the thinking and research of the scientific-academic community—including child psychology. Many studies demonstrated that children's behavior could be altered by changing the contingencies—that is, by changing the external events that regularly follow a given behavior. Smiling at or patting infants when they smiled could increase the frequency of their smiles. A shy, nonsociable child could be made more sociable by responding when the child was interacting with other children and by ignoring the child during periods of solitary play. The *acquisition curves,* or rates of learning, in such experiments closely resembled those found in animal studies. Parents were seen as having roles analogous to those of experimenters in animal research: As agents of reward and punishment, they were thought to be responsible for setting training goals, establishing reinforcement schedules, and thus *shaping,* or gradually modifying, their children's behavior. If the children were not behaving in ways the parents intended, the answer was simple: The parents must be accidentally reinforcing the wrong behaviors and failing to reinforce the right ones. Show the parents how to change the contingencies for their children's behavior and the behavior would change. Present-day research and clinical practice involving behavior modification are based on these same principles.

Serious efforts to integrate some of the ideas from psychoanalysis with the principles of learning theory were initiated in the 1930s by Neal E. Miller, John Dollard, and associates at Yale University's Institute of Human Relations. Subsequently, several Institute-trained people established their own research centers elsewhere, continuing and greatly expanding during the next two decades the work on socialization. Psychologists Robert and Pauline Sears and anthropologists John and Beatrice Whiting produced notable work, first at the Iowa Child Welfare Research Station and later at the Laboratory of Human Development at Harvard University. These researchers found in psychoanalytic theory a rich source of hypotheses about certain aspects of personality development. Ideas were developed that would never have been considered by researchers relying wholly on analogies from animal learning. However, the internal dynamics posited by psychoanalytic theory were difficult to put to empirical test. How was one to know whether a child had "identified" with a parent? Or whether a child was controlling his or her own behavior by means of a "conscience" that reflected an internalized parent? The research teams embarked on the task of finding observable, measurable behaviors that would serve as indices of the internal processes Freud talked about. And more important, they attempted to translate Freudian concepts into the language of learning theory.

This work was not easy, for there were some basic differences in the assumptions of the two points of view. Freud, after all, believed in *instincts,* or inborn urges. He thought that a child's tendency to form a powerful emotional attachment to the parents is built into the nature of the human organism. And he thought that the tendency to become angry—aggressive—toward parents in response to their restrictions and demands is built-in, as is, presumably, the tendency to resolve these intense emotional conflicts through identification. The learning theorist, on the other hand, wanted to explain how and why all these things happened by finding the set of contingencies, created intentionally or unintentionally by parents, that would bring them about. Learning theorists saw the process of identification as the outcome of a series of prior events, each of which involves learning. Identification was no longer seen as a virtually universal process occurring in nearly the same way and in roughly the same degree in all children. It became a *variable*—something that could take on different values under different conditions. Thus some children's identification with parents would be stronger than others, and variations in the intensity of identification would determine the strength or weakness of the developing conscience.

The learning theorist, therefore, had two questions: (1) What in children's learning history and in their relationships to their parents determines individual variations in the amount or kind of identification shown? and (2) What is the relationship between the intensity of a child's identification and the personality characteristics that are presumed to depend on it? In attacking the first problem, the researchers followed Freud's lead. Assuming that parental nurturance ought to be related to identification based on love and that the use of power and authority by parents ought to be related to defensive identification, they assessed these two aspects of parenting in a number of studies. They hypothesized that the events affecting identification must have something to do with both the child's intense attachment to the parents and with the resolution of conflicts about aggression and sexuality. And they looked at the conditions that determine variations among children in their attachment (called *dependency* at that time) and in their aggressiveness. Probably because the topic of sexuality in children was still fairly taboo, the "sexiness" of children was not measured, although parents' attitudes toward children's sexual behavior were assessed.

The researchers assumed that children become attached because their parents feed, warm, and soothe them and relieve their pain. These actions were believed to reinforce the child's tendency to remain close to the parents, cling to them, demand their attention, and resist separation from them. The explanation for variations among children in the intensity or frequency of their attachment behavior, then, was sought in variations among parents in frequency of reinforcement (that is, how nurturant they are) and in how contingent these reinforcements are on the child's dependent behavior. Similarly, aggressive tendencies were assumed to vary with the level of parental demands and restrictions (that is, the amount of frustration the child experiences) and with the way parents react to the aggression. If Freud were right, when parents react punitively, children are forced to inhibit aggression and, ultimately, to turn the aggression against themselves in the form of self-criticism and guilt. The studies focused on the frequency with which parents rewarded or punished aggressive behavior and the extent to which they forced the child to inhibit such behavior. Finally, these researchers undertook studies of children's sex typing, playing of adult roles in fantasy, ability to resist temptation, and manifestations of guilt following misdemeanors.

The research in child rearing that stemmed from this tradition was imposing both in conception and productivity, and it has been highly influential. (The reader is referred to the following major publications: Sears, Maccoby, and Levin, 1957; Sears, Rau, and Alpert, 1965; Whiting and Child, 1953; and Whiting and Whiting, 1975.) Major findings are incorporated in relevant chapters throughout this book. It will be seen that the importance of parental nurturance and of the way parents exercise authority have been amply demonstrated. Yet the yield of the work with respect to the theory of identification was disappointing. When relationships were found between parents' behavior and measures of children's guilt, self-criticism, or sex typing, they were small and not consistent from one study to another. In many instances the predictions from Freudian theory were not borne out. For example, no consistent relationships were found among characteristics that ought to have been linked by their common origins in the process of identification. The theory said that a young boy who was highly identified with his father would (1) be masculine, (2) take on adultlike values and behavior where appropriate, (3) be able to resist temptations to do naughty things, (4) experience strong guilt over any deviations from adult values that did occur. These traits should be more characteristic of the highly identified boy than of the boy who was not strongly identified with his father. As it turned out, the traits are virtually unrelated—a given child might be strong in one and weak in another.

What was wrong? Perhaps the problem was the methods of study. The researchers used objective behavioral measures of children's characteristics but relied fairly heavily on interviews to find out about parents. Perhaps parents simply could not report accurately on their own child-rearing behavior. Or perhaps the difficulty lay in the theory underlying the research. No one was ready to conclude that parental behavior has little or no influence on children, but it was clearly necessary for the researchers to rethink what the nature of the influence might be.

CHANGING VIEWS OF THE NATURE OF THE CHILD: INFLUENCES ON CURRENT RESEARCH

Several themes that greatly influenced socialization research and theory emerged in psychology and related sciences during the fifties and sixties. Psychologists, noting inconsistencies in individual responses from one situation to another, began to question the assumption that personality can be described in terms of individually consistent traits. Research in child behavior began to focus on developmental sequences—on the orderly changes that take place in growing children's ability to perceive, understand, and deal with the world around them. Studies of children's learning by workers with a number of different orientations suggested that reinforcement is not the only precondition for acquiring new behaviors. Research in animal behavior drew attention to the possibility that newborn infants come into the world predisposed to learn certain things. Anthropologists stressed the need to understand the effect of the social and cultural environment on the child's development.

Questions about traits

There were several themes emerging in psychological thinking during the late 1950s and through the 1960s that greatly influenced the reorientation that took place in socialization research and theory. One was an increasing awareness of how inconsistent behavior was from one situation to another and how difficult it was to differentiate children according to the *traits,* or personality characteristics, they possessed. The groundwork for questioning the consistency of personality traits had been laid in the 1920s and 1930s by Hartshorne and May. Their *Studies in Deceit* (1928) had shown the variability of individual children's trustworthiness. A child would be honest in some situations and cheat or tell lies in other situations. The identification of generally honest or generally dishonest children seemed impossible. Subsequent studies repeatedly encountered the same kind of problem. A child's aggressiveness might vary from day to day or from playmate to playmate or from situation to situation. Was it really possible or legitimate to say that one child is more aggressive than another, in any overall sense?

Walter Mischel's *Personality and Assessment,* published in 1968, brought together impressive evidence documenting the variability in individuals' behavior. Mischel questioned the usefulness of trying to label children according to traits such as aggressive, dependent, sex-typed, anxious, impulsive, or timid. Socialization research during the previous two decades had compared different children ranking them from high to low along a set of "trait" dimensions. The researchers had then tried to discover what child-rearing methods are associated with a given child's ranking. Mischel challenged this strategy. He argued against correlating parental behavior (or anything else!) with children's ranks since individual children really did not have a consistent position on a rank order. Because behavior differed so much from one situation to another, he proposed an experimental strategy that systematically varied situations and measured the impact of specific situations on specific behavior. An analogy could then be made from the experimental situation to the situations that parents created and maintained at home, and predictions could be made about how the children would behave at home. Mischel noted, however, that behavior at home might not generalize to other settings—the person, in other words, was "under situational control."

The cognitive revolution

During the sixties, American psychologists' commitment to behaviorism declined, and there was an upsurge of interest in *cognition*. Researchers wanted to know how human beings perceive the world and how they store, retrieve, and think about the information they have perceived. Increasingly, adults and children were seen as information processors. Child psychologists began to focus on age-related changes in information-processing abilities, and the work of Jean Piaget came into prominence. Since the twenties Piaget had been publishing prolifically on stages of development in children's thinking. Not all of his work had been translated, and it had attracted little attention (at least in the United States) until the cognitive revolution set the stage for a renewal of interest. Jerome Bruner and other scholars with ties to the European intellectual community had tried to alert American psychologists to the importance of the work by Piaget and Bärbel Inhelder, but existing translations of Piaget's work were obscure in style and concepts. The publication in 1963 of John H. Flavell's *The Developmental Psychology of Jean Piaget* made Piaget's theory and findings accessible to a wide audience who did not read French. Piaget's views were by no means universally accepted. Subsequent research has shown that the developmental sequences are not always as he had described them. Nevertheless, certain themes that have since been elaborated and basically confirmed by other researchers emerged from his work:

1. As children mature their conceptual abilities develop in certain fairly predictable sequences. At any given time an individual child may make use of several levels of thought and may not make use of the highest levels of which he or she is capable. Nevertheless, within this variability is a consistent thread of forward movement.

2. Most children go through sequences without skipping steps and without going backward. That is, progress is relatively irreversible.

3. The developmental changes in thinking are *structural changes*. That is, they represent changes in the way information is organized and in the mental activities, or *operations*, that the child performs with the information at hand. Structural change is not just a matter of accumulating more and more items of information.

4. The impact of any environmental event on a child will depend on what the child takes from that event—how the child interprets what has happened and how the new information is integrated with what the child already knows. Children are active participants in their own learning. Indeed, they set the pace.

There are echoes of Rousseau here, but with an important difference: Piaget's developmental timetable is not necessarily under complete biological control. For Piaget, the rate of development is not predetermined. He would not "leave the child's mind idle as long as possible." Children need stimulation from environmental events. Each new step in the developmental progression depends on new stimulation, as well as on the occurrence of previous steps. The developmental timetable may be linked to the physiological maturing of the brain, but brain growth is not a sufficient condition for taking developmental steps. Thus, although some people think that Piaget's system describes growth processes that are fully predetermined, this is far from the truth. Indeed, Piaget would probably decline to discuss the relative contributions of physiological maturation and experience to cognitive development, believing that the two kinds of determinants are intricately interwoven and not additive.

Piaget attempted to document the universals in the sequential development of thought processes. He paid little attention to individual differences in rates of progress through the developmental stages. Furthermore, he was not much interested in the emotions of children nor in their social behavior (apart from their acquisition of language). Nevertheless, his cognitive-developmental theory has implications for children's social-emotional development and for socialization research. Lawrence Kohlberg (1969), examining the research of the forties and fifties from the standpoint of cognitive-developmental theory, raises a number of critical issues:

1. Following Freud the earlier research assumed that certain adult behavioral tendencies are established early in life and remain relatively unchanged once established. This assumption was wrong. *Every* aspect of thought and behavior undergoes systematic developmental change, and therefore a characteristic of a child at age ten cannot be predicted from knowledge of this "same" characteristic at age four. No characteristic is ever the same across such an age-span, even though it goes by the same name.

2. By experimentally manipulating contingencies, the frequency of a given kind of behavior by a child of any age can easily be increased or decreased. But these demonstrations merely show

that such changes are trivial. They are momentary and under situational control, and they have little to do with structural change. Structural growth is not a simple outcome of reinforcement schedules, and therefore studies that examine the outcome of such schedules should not be taken as explanations of psychological development and should not be expected to yield predictions concerning future characteristics.

3. *Socialization* is the process by which the growing individual adapts and readapts to society and its requirements. The first step in any study of socialization should be to chart the normal developmental course of the social behavior that is of interest. If socialization studies are to deal with phenomena that are not transitory, they must try to understand and explain the normal structural changes that occur during development.

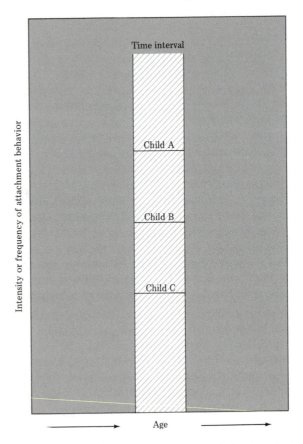

Figure 1-1.   Intensity or frequency of attachment behavior during one time interval. Three hypothetical children: The mother of Child A is most responsive. The mother of Child C is least responsive. Child B's mother falls in between.

And if the normal developmental steps have not been mapped out, the researcher is operating in the dark.

As will be seen in later chapters, there is reason to doubt Kohlberg's second point. Nevertheless, his distinction between structural changes and easily reversible changes is worth keeping in mind. And his complaint that the earlier research was not sufficiently developmental has major implications for the study of child behavior.

To underscore the implications of Kohlberg's critique, let us consider a question that has long interested students of socialization: Is the nature of children's attachments to their mothers related to the kind of treatment received from the mothers? In designing studies to answer this question, the researchers of the forties and fifties proceeded straightforwardly: They selected a group of children all the same age and assessed the frequency or intensity with which they showed attachment behavior. The researchers examined the mothers' treatment of the children. Figure 1-1 illustrates the approach. Suppose Mother A is found to be the most responsive to her child's signals, Mother C the least responsive, and Mother B somewhere in between. On the basis of the information shown in the figure, it is reasonable to conclude that children show more intense or frequent attachment behavior when their mothers are more responsive.[3]

Kohlberg's point was that developmental change has been left out of account. Attachment behavior is something that has a normal developmental time course. While it usually appears during the last half of the first year, increases to a peak usually during the second year, and then wanes gradually as children become more competent and independent, children differ in the rate with which they proceed through this sequence. The situation for different children might very well be the one depicted in Figure 1-2. Clearly, if this figure accurately portrays developmental differences, then the relationship between responsiveness and attachment depends on the time the measurements are taken. If attachment is measured at time 1, maternal responsiveness seems to be positively related to frequency and intensity of attachment. If measurements are taken at time 2, however, there seems to be no relationship. And if attachment is measured at time 3, then *lack* of responsiveness seems to make children intensely attached. In fact, none of these answers makes sense because there is no difference among children in the frequency or intensity of the attachment behavior portrayed in this figure. The only difference is the timing: Child A, whose mother is most responsive, peaks at about one year; Child B peaks at about eighteen months; Child C, whose mother is least re-

---

[3]The reader is asked to overlook for the moment whether a relationship between a maternal behavior and a child's characteristics means that the mother's behavior *caused* the child's behavior. This question will emerge repeatedly in later chapters, but it is not the issue here.

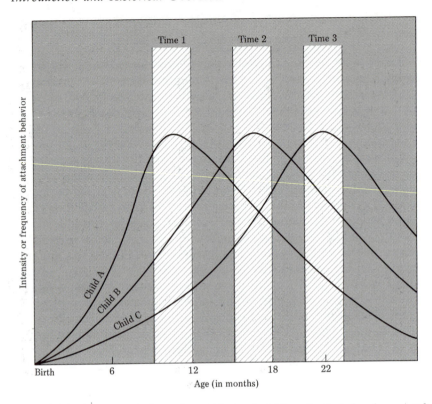

Figure 1-2.   Occurrence of attachment behavior. Hypothetical developmental sequences in three children: The mother of Child A is most responsive. The mother of Child C is least responsive. Child B's mother falls in between.

sponsive, peaks a few months later. The researchers might reasonably have examined the relationship between maternal responsiveness and age at onset of attachment. Or they might have examined the relationship between maternal responsiveness and age at peak intensity of attachment. By studying maternal responsiveness and intensity of attachment at a fixed point in time, they would be asking a meaningless question.

Kohlberg and others of a cognitive-developmental persuasion (for example, Emmerich, 1968) believe that in order to know what are reasonable questions to ask about causes and consequences of changes in children, it is necessary first to know what the normal developmental sequence is. And before asking questions about stable individual differences among children, we must first show that there *are* stable differences that persist across time. We may discover that *something* persists across time, but it is not necessarily the "same" behavior. Most likely it is qualitatively different, having grown out of earlier patterns. We may also discover that very little persists across time, so that the real focus of interest should be the changes that occur with growth in all children—the differences consisting of the timing or the ultimate level reached.

Imitation

Kohlberg's suggestions about how research on socialization ought to be reformulated were not the only ones being made in the sixties. Some critiques proceeded from an entirely different point of view— namely that the earlier work had moved too far away from behaviorism. The argument was that the studies of the forties and fifties were overloaded with too many unnecessary inferences about unobservable processes, such as identification. What did we really mean when we said that children "internalize" a parent's values or "identify" with a parent? The critics emphasized that the only reliable indicator of the occurrence of any such processes is simply that children can be seen to act like their parents—to say many of the same things, adopt their mannerisms, and so forth. Why not, then, simply study imitation itself and put aside the unanswerable questions of whether imitation is a reflection of deeper, internal processes?

With this point of view in mind, an extensive program of research on imitation was undertaken during the sixties and seventies, led by Albert Bandura and his colleagues (Bandura, 1969, 1971). Of course, there was a history of earlier work on imitation. James Mark Baldwin (1906) considered imitation to be a central process in socialization. Miller and Dollard had done experiments on imitation to determine whether children would acquire a tendency to imitate widely if imitative actions were reinforced (*Social Learning and Imitation*, 1941). Studies of adult role taking focused on children's imitation of adult activities during imaginative play (Sears, Rau, and Alpert, 1965). Bandura's work grew out of the earlier tradition but represented a considerable narrowing of the concept of identification. Also, Bandura set up innovative research procedures that brought out many clear instances of imitative behavior in children—something previous researchers had found difficult to do. Looking at the conditions that foster imitation, he found (1) that previously unfamiliar adults are more likely to be imitated by preschool children if the adults first are nurturant toward the children and (2) that imitation is also increased if the model is powerful—that is, if the model has control over toys and snacks that the child wants. The reader will note in Bandura's focus on love and power the influence of psychoanalytic theory on his research.

While these findings were important in their own right, their impact was broader. In conjunction with the cognitive revolution, Bandura's work weakened the foundations of the reinforcement theories that motivated much previous research. If children were not actually performing actions at the time they learned them, their behavior could not be reinforced. Bandura and others provided many demonstrations that reinforcement has less influence on initial acquisition of a given bit of behavior than on whether children choose to perform the action at a later time. This work opened a new line of thought concerning the role of parents in children's learning. Parents were no longer simply agents of rewards and punishments: They were also seen as *models* whose behaviors could serve as patterns for children to follow. Sometimes parents could even be seen unintentionally to countermand their own orders. That is, while demanding one kind of behavior from their children and attempting to enforce their demands with rewards and punishments, parents might simultaneously exemplify something quite different. The investigators considered this problem and also examined the conditions under which an adult is likely to be imitated by children.

In retrospect, the failure to attribute to children a greater role in their own socialization is a curious omission. In light of the increasing prominence of work on cognitive development (particularly the information on language acquisition), the research on imitation could have been interpreted as showing that children *select* certain aspects of adult behavior to imitate. The research program could have moved toward studying the influence of developmental level on the child's choice of what adult behavior to imitate or how children incorporate new material into previously acquired repertoires. These developments did not occur, however.[4] Socialization was still viewed as a one-way process with the parents shaping the child's behavior. As model, the parent was now even more influential than before. In addition to setting requirements for social behavior and enforcing them with rewards and punishments, parents now were assumed to teach by setting a positive example. Furthermore, the nurturant, powerful, and available parents would easily command their children's attention, and the children would imitate what they saw. Imitation would be a powerful element in socialization, relieving parents of some of the burden of constant monitoring and repeated sanctions. Children would spontaneously learn how they were supposed to behave, and rewards and punishments would only be needed to support the *performance* of their learned behaviors.

Instinct

Socialization research was also influenced by *ethology*, the branch of biology that studies animal behavior and, more specifically, un-

---

[4]In his recent work, Bandura has focused strongly on cognitive factors influencing performance in many situations. Here we refer to the earlier work and the impact it has had on viewpoints about socialization.

learned behavior patterns in relation to an organism's adaptation to its environment. The publication in 1951 of Niko Tinbergen's *A Study of Instinct* made a considerable impression on students of animal behavior. Subsequent publications by Konrad Lorenz (1957) served to underscore the same major points that Tinbergen made: that genetically controlled behavior is not necessarily a rigid chain of reflexes and that learning can play a role in the unfolding of instinctive patterns of behavior. Their demonstration of *imprinting* was especially important. They found that during a brief period shortly after hatching, young ducklings form a strong attachment to the first large, moving organism they see. The moving figure need not be the mother duck or even another bird. Indeed, Lorenz himself became their mother object by being present at the right moment, moving appropriately, and preventing the ducklings from seeing the mother duck. Lorenz liked to demonstrate the ducks' attachment by walking around his yard or swimming in his pond, followed closely by a fleet of quacking ducklings. This work raised the possibility that other organisms might have built-in biases that predisposed them to *learn* certain things. Thus, special sensitivity to certain kinds of environmental stimuli might have evolved in a species, and certain response systems might be in a state of readiness to become connected, through learning, to these particular stimuli.

This kind of thinking had obvious implications for human socialization. After all, children are unable to function independently for a long period after birth. Was it not possible that human infants have built-in tendencies to be especially attracted by human faces and voices, ensuring closeness to people who have these attractive qualities? And was it not also possible that adults have a built-in attraction to certain qualities of infants, ensuring that caretaking skills are learned more rapidly than behavior patterns that have no instinctive component? The ethologists had drawn attention to the intricate interweaving of learning and instinct. It became clear that both factors can influence the same behavior and that human beings, who can learn more than lower animals and are less controlled by rigid patterns of inherited behavior, may nevertheless have inherited biases toward certain kinds of learning. Psychological thinking began to move from Watson's view of the newborn as a "squirming bit of flesh" toward acceptance of the idea of inborn competencies that facilitate an infant's acquisition of behaviors needed for survival. The imprinting work was especially important for thinking about parent-child interaction since it suggested that there might be reciprocal biases predisposing adults and infants to relate to each other in ways that would support the protection and care of infants. The work by John Bowlby, Mary Ainsworth, and Harry Harlow, discussed in Chapters 2 and 3, has been especially influenced by the ethological viewpoint.

Temperament

Newborn infants are not all alike. Some are more irritable than others, some more active, some more interested in the events around them, some more easily soothed once they become upset. Furthermore, certain temperamental differences may have a genetic component, and some may have sex-linked determinants. Research findings suggest that some temperamental qualities are fairly enduring (Buss and Plomin, 1975; Kagan and Moss, 1962; Thomas et al., 1971). Obviously, such inborn temperamental differences ought to influence children's responses to their caretakers and caretakers' responses to children. Certain methods of child rearing will work better with some types of children than others. Furthermore, a given method may have different outcomes for children with different temperaments. Most studies of socialization have attempted to find universal themes that apply to the development of most or all children, but we will find that it is necessary to complicate the picture at a number of points by taking individual temperament into account.

Social structure

The cross-cultural work begun by the Whitings in the forties and fifties continued thereafter with a shift in focus and method. Their earlier research had relied on parent interviews—an inadequate source of information about child rearing, the Whitings thought, because parents do not always notice significant events in the parent-child interaction. Believing that nothing would take the place of reliable observation, they sent teams of trained anthropologists to various field settings throughout the world. The initial objectives were: (1) to widen the range of parental behaviors that were studied and see whether effects on children could be more clearly identified when their parents' treatment varied more greatly than is usual within a single culture, (2) to determine whether relationships between parental treatment and the characteristics developed by children are ever truly universal, or nearly so—that is, whether the basic relationships predicted by Freud and by learning theory can be detected in widely different cultural settings, and (3) to see how variations in family structure, cultural history, and politico-economic organization modify the processes and effects of parent-child interaction.

As the work continued into the sixties, interest focused on the third objective. While no one doubted the usefulness of concepts from both learning theory and psychoanalytic theory, it became more and more evident that parent-child interaction is greatly influenced by such factors as (1) whether the society is polygamous or monogamous,

(2) whether the society depends on hunting, agriculture, fishing, herding, or has a more complex form of economic organization, (3) how work is distributed between men and women, and (4) whether there is a system of universal education. These factors determined whether children were assigned chores and, if so, what kind. And the work that children did in turn influenced—among other things—their helpfulness to one another and the kinds of demands they made on their parents. Clearly, the child-rearing process is embedded in a network of other social processes. Parents rear their children within a social system. Their behavior can only be understood within the context of the society as a whole.

WHERE DO WE STAND TODAY?

Current studies of parent-child interaction are influenced by all the schools of thought described in this chapter, and the studies to be reported in the following chapters reflect these varied points of view. Current researchers continue to investigate the effects of parents' treatment on their children, but the approach is more sophisticated. For one thing, awareness of the influence of momentary situations on children's behavior has led researchers to obtain information about the child in a variety of situations and at a number of different times in order to identify a stable set of characteristics that distinguish individual children from one another. In addition, it is now widely understood that developmental change is the rule rather than the exception and, therefore, that the characteristics a child has at a given age will not be the same characteristics the same child has later on, even though the two may be connected. Considering these developmental transformations, it now seems unlikely that the parents' primary contribution to the child's long-range development comes from teaching specific behaviors. Rather, the parents' most lasting influence probably comes through establishing modes of interacting with other people and teaching certain modes of adaptation to changing life circumstances. Recently, interest has revived in the parental contribution to the child's developing sense of identity or *self*. The assumption is that a coherent self-concept may function as a child's gyroscope, keeping the individual to a relatively steady course and producing long-term consistencies in behavior. Because this possibility seems promising, a chapter on the development of self-concepts has been included in the present volume.

The concept of identification is not dead. Freud's original formulation included much more than imitation of the parents' actions—it involved the incorporation of parental values as well. As more is learned about the development of children's capacity for self-regulation (see Chapter 5), it becomes evident that children use a set of standards as the basis for monitoring their own behavior. These standards can vary from detailed, task-specific norms to comprehensive ideologies. The standards may or may not resemble the parents' own. Rapid social change limits the degree to which direct transmission of parental values is possible or even desirable. Nevertheless, an important issue is the determination of the way children's standards and values develop and the role parents can play in shaping them.

Identification also includes the extensions of the ego, or self, to other persons. Psychoanalytic thinkers have claimed that at certain points in children's development, the children participate vicariously in the parents' power and competencies by merging their own egos with those of their parents, at least to some extent. We now understand that identification, in this sense, is a two-way process: Parents also make their children part of their own egos. A process of mutual empathy within families enables each member to take pride in the others' accomplishments and suffer vicariously when the others are unhappy. Investigation of these empathic reactions is just beginning to be included in studies of family relationships.

The objectives in current studies of socialization are somewhat more modest than those of the earlier work because researchers understand that they are exploring a constantly changing relationship. Parents undoubtedly affect what the child will be like during the immediately ensuing period of time, and what the child becomes influences the parents' behavior at the next point in time. Each influences the other in a series of feedback loops. Each partner in the interaction is also influenced by forces outside the relationship, and it is now clear that the interaction itself may be modified by these outside conditions. Locke may have been right when he said that the river of a child's life could be deflected at its source by the parent's hand in such a way that its ultimate destination would be greatly affected. But there are mountains and valleys encountered along the route to the sea that also determine the river's course. With this analogy in mind, the child's life may be seen as a series of decision points along a continuous path. The path taken at each point is determined by the forces acting at that point—parental forces as well as other environmental influences. And each new segment of the path is, of course, crucially affected by the child's position when the new decision is made. Thus there is a cumulative effect of earlier decisions and thus of earlier parental influences.

Figure 1-3 illustrates this conception—the figure is, of course, oversimplified. Assuming that children all start at the same place is undoubtedly unrealistic. In any case, the implications of this view of development are clear: The effect of parents and children on one another can best be studied over a series of relatively short time-intervals.

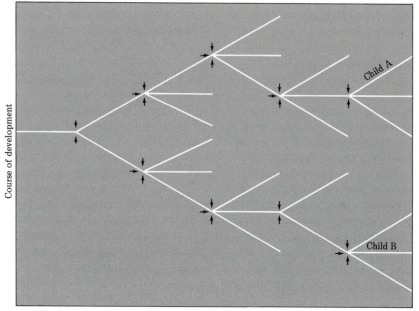

Figure 1-3. Two possible developmental paths. Starting together, two children's lives continuously diverge at a series of decision points. The arrows represent parental and other environmental influences.

This book, then, is devoted to the study of many decision points in children's social development and many moments of parental influence. The following pages offer a cumulative record of many years of study by people with very different points of view who have asked very different questions about the nature of the child. The author's own bias toward the cognitive-developmental position will be evident at many points. But it is a limited bias. While the strengths of cognitive-developmental theory will be stressed, it will be evident that the theory is too "cold" and does not give enough weight to the role of emotions in social development. Another weakness of the theory is the overcommitment to the idea that all children go through the same series of stages, albeit at different rates. The possibility of divergent paths is ignored. Surely, some children acquire certain patterns of behavior and other children acquire *different* patterns. Surely, some of these differences can be maintained over fairly long periods of time by the continuation of the very conditions that led to their adoption in the first place, despite the developmental changes that co-occur.

The developmental patterns shown in Figures 1-1, 1-2, and 1-3 need not be mutually exclusive. If they can exist side by side, it is no longer meaningful to ask which represents the truth about development. Rather, we must find out which applies to which behaviors under which conditions over what period of time.

Clearly, an effort to bring about some integration of the various points of view is called for. Modest attempts at this integration will be made in the chapters that follow. Readers are invited to join the enterprise.

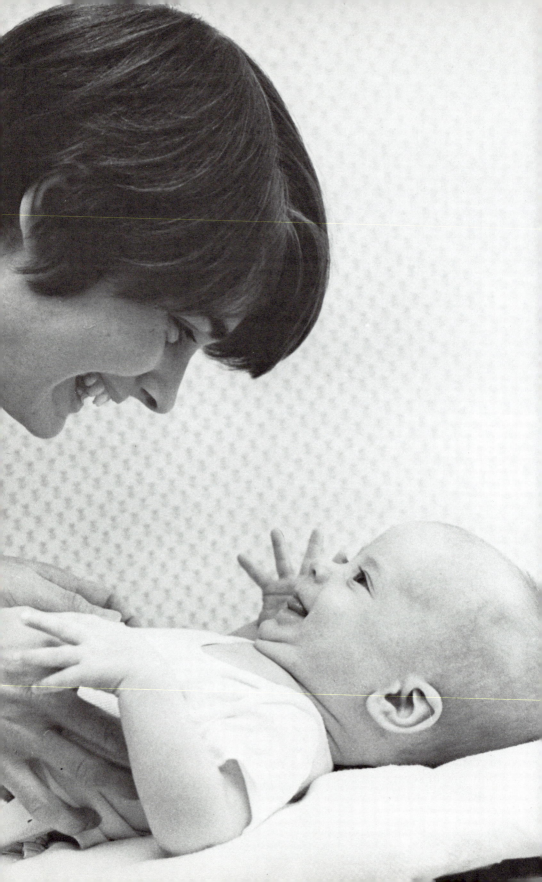

CHAPTER 2

The Development
of Attachment

Human beings share with many other mammals the inability to function independently immediately after birth. Species differ in the relative immaturity of their newborns. The pouch-young opposum is still fetal—it is capable only of finding its way into the mother's pouch, where it attaches itself to her nipple and completes its development in its warm, soft haven, as though still in the uterus. The wildebeaste, by contrast, must be able to run with the herd only moments after birth—it seems much like an adult, except that it gets its food by suckling. The maturity of the human infant is midway between these two extremes. Human babies have a great deal of developing and learning to do before they can sustain themselves without adult help.

The immature young of many species share a tendency to form strong attachments to certain mature individuals. Attachments, of course, are usually formed to an adult of the infant's own species, although there are recorded cases of cross-species adoptions. The infant's attachment takes the form of staying close to the adult and showing distress on separation. Adults, in turn, form strong attachments to infants and try to keep them close. Adult female mammals feed their young from the secretions of their own bodies, but this is only one of several functions that they perform to sustain the lives of their offspring. From the standpoint of evolution, a strong attachment bond between the nurturant adult and the helpless infant clearly has survival value and seems likely to have become a built-in tendency through the processes of natural selection.

In this chapter we will look at the formation of attachment bonds in several species. The focus of our interest will be the built-in systems that both mother and infant bring to the attachment process, as well as the learning that takes place as the parent-child relationship develops. We begin the discussion with a description of the attachment process in certain animals lower than humans. This way of organizing the topic is meant as a reminder that human beings have a biological heritage and that we need to understand this heritage in order to understand our own behavior. We will then examine attachment between human parents and their infants, considering similarities and differences between human beings and other mammals.

ATTACHMENT IN LOWER ANIMALS

The genetic programming that enables parents and their infants to respond immediately to one another is particularly clear in lower animals. Ethologists' studies of the rapid and relatively inflexible attachment mechanisms of birds were an early example for the behavioral sciences of the variety and complexity of parent-child linkages. In many mammalian species attachment also begins as soon as the infants are born. The young animal quickly comes to know its own mother and stays with her specifically. The mother selectively feeds, retrieves, grooms, and protects her own young. The mechanism drawing the mother and child together varies from species to species. At the same time, the qualities that attract the parents of a given species to their infants are not necessarily the same as the qualities that attract the infants to their parents, but the two appear preprogrammed into a smoothly operating joint behavioral system. In birds the attachment process seems to grow mainly out of instinctive responses to visual cues. In animals such as the rat, chemical bonds appear to be the primary attractant.

Instinctive linking between parents and their young: birds

Ethologists' studies of birds first drew attention to the intricate behavioral meshing between parents and offspring. The behavior of the herring gull provides a good illustration. The adult birds have a red dot on the side of their beak. Newly hatched herring gull chicks have a built-in tendency to peck at a red dot (they will peck at a red dot painted on a block of wood). The parent, when its dot is pecked, opens its mouth and regurgitates well-chewed but only partly digested food, and the chick is fed. Other aspects of a chain of instinctive behaviors bring the parent back to the nest when it has eaten enough to feed the young. The herring gull chicks do not instinctively recognize their own parents. Recognition is found only in birds whose young leave the nest. Young ducks, for example, are able to be selective. They will follow only their mother; they will not join the ducklings trailing after another nearby adult bird. Studies of this species have revealed that for a few hours after birth the newly hatched birds will follow the first moving object they see. After this period they avoid unfamiliar moving objects and stay close to the individual to which they became attached before their capacity for being afraid developed. Eckhard Hess (1959) suspected that fear is the mechanism that prevents the diffusion of a duckling's attachments to other adult birds. As a test of the hypothesis, he administered tranquilizers to ducklings so that they did not become afraid of unfamiliar moving things according to the usual timetable. For the tranquilized ducklings the period during which imprinting took place was extended. For an ethologist discovering the effect of timing on the onset of fear, a logical new step in research would be to look for a matching behavioral pattern in mother ducks—some tendency to keep their ducklings in relative isolation from other birds during the normal period of imprinting.

Chemical attractants: rats

Among certain mammals odors play an important role in binding mothers and infants together. An odorous substance that is produced by one animal and influences the behavior of other animals is called a *pheromone*. The functioning of pheromones has been demonstrated in studies of mother and infant rats. If a nursling rat is separated from its mother and the mother is placed in one hidden chamber and a virgin female is placed in another, the infant will find the mother only if currents of air blow from the adult toward the infant and not if the air blows the other way. Is the infant attracted by the smell of the mother's milk? Michael Leon (1977) has shown that the attractant is a different odor. In addition to the excreta that are the normal products of an animal's digestive processes, a mother rat excretes *cecotrophe*—a partly digested food substance marked by a distinctive odor that young animals find attractive. While the rat pups are very young the mother rat excretes very little cecotrophe, and the pups, if they happen to be exposed to the substance, are not very interested in it. However, the production of this pheromone gradually increases to a maximum on the sixteenth day following the birth of a litter, and Leon has shown that as its quantity increases, so does maternal attractiveness. When mother rats of different postpartum ages are placed in an olfac-

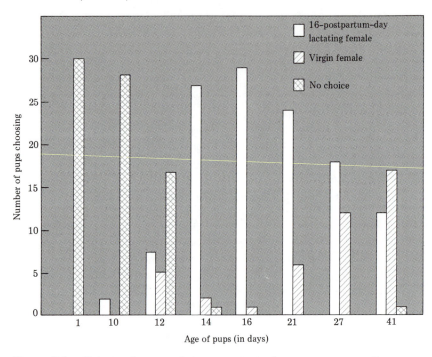

Figure 2-1. Rat pups' approach to a constant pheromone source. Pups were given a choice between a lactating female that was sixteen days postpartum and a virgin female. The pups were tested on the different postpartum days indicated, and each pup-female pair was tested only once. Note that pups do not begin to approach the lactating female until day 12 and that this response peaks at day 16. (From Leon, 1977)

tory discrimination apparatus along with a virgin female, pups of a given age go most quickly and most reliably to a female that is sixteen days postpartum—provided that the air currents are blowing in the right direction! The same pattern of response is elicited if the ceco-trophe of a female who is sixteen days postpartum is in the compartment, rather than the female herself.

Leon has also found a matching developmental change in the pups' sensitivity to a given amount of the pheromone. When tested with a maternal animal who is sixteen days postpartum, pups ten days old or younger are not very sensitive to the maternal pheromone, but their interest in the odor increases rapidly thereafter, reaching a maximum when they are sixteen days old (see Figure 2-1). These changes in the mother's attractiveness and the infant's ability to be attracted are nicely geared to changes in the infant's ability to move about. Until ten days of age the pup remains in the nest. Thereafter, it ventures farther and farther away from the nest, and stronger and stronger attractants are needed to help it find its way back. The sixteen-day-old animal is nearing the age of weaning. The decline in both the output and the response to the pheromone is synchronized with the pup's developing ability to find its own food and survive without nursing.

Leon has been able to trace in fine detail the largely hormonal physiological mechanisms that cause the mother to excrete the requisite amounts of cecotrophe at specified times following the birth of the litter. In most of Leon's experiments, pups over ten days old were attracted by the cecotrophe produced by any maternal rat. The question, then, is how a pup finds its own nest when there are other nests in the vicinity. Actually, free-living rats do not build nests close to one another, so there is not much danger of pups going to the wrong nest. Perhaps for this reason rats are a species in which mothers and pups are not very selective: Mothers will accept substitute pups quite readily, and infants will suckle from a number of different mothers. Strictly speaking, therefore, we should not use the term *attachment* for the mutual attraction between mother rats and their pups since the term is more properly used for a relationship that is specific between certain individuals. Rat pups, in approaching adult females, show *some* selectivity based on the distinctive odor of the cecotrophe. If the mother's diet is varied, her pups tend to approach only cecotrophe excreted by any mother whose diet is the same as their own mother's. Evidently the odor of cecotrophe is affected by what the mother eats. And since mothers in a free-living state are likely to eat somewhat different things, a basis exists on which pups can identify their own mothers. But a pup's preference for cecotrophe of a specific dietary flavor surely cannot be instinctive—the pup must have become familiar with this specific odor during its early days with its mother. Thus, *experience,* or learning, plays a role in what so far have seemed to be purely instinctive arrangements. Perhaps the young animal finds the mother's cecotrophe attractive because the odor is associated with nursing. We do not know for sure, but clearly something about the infant's early experience marks certain pheromones as special attractants.

While both mother and infant appear to be operating according to a built-in timetable, the normal timing of developmental change can be altered. Most mothers lose interest in their young at about the time the infants can fend for themselves. However, maternal interest declines sooner if a mother is separated from and then reunited with her litter. She will no longer retrieve and suckle her infants as she would have done if contact had been maintained. She is also likely to resume her estrous cycle sooner (Rosenblatt and Lehrman, 1963). On the other hand, maternal behavior can be extended considerably beyond its normal duration by continually supplying the mother with new batches of very young pups. The presence of the young, then, powerfully stimulates the mother's maternal behavior. What qualities in the infant intensify the mother's caretaking? Does the pup make a specific sound, emit a specific smell, or is it appearance (for example, hairlessness) that matters? This question has one answer for rats and a different answer for other species, but the point is that in every species *some* pattern of characteristics makes very young animals especially strong elicitors of caretaking behavior during the limited period of time when the young possess the characteristics and need the care.

Very different mother-infant systems exist between the rat and the herring gull. The newly hatched herring gull chick instinctively pecks at a red dot. This behavior would be useless in a rat's nest since the rat mother has no red dot, and (even if the chick could survive on milk) the rat mother lets down milk in response to sucking, not pecking. Similarly, a rat pup in a herring gull's nest would find its instinctive reflexes useless. A rat cannot see red; but even if it could see the dot and did find it interesting, sucking would not release the food carried by the adult bird, and pecking is not part of the rat's response repertoire. In addition, the pup would perish from cold. A rat needs the warmth of its mother's and littermates' bodies to keep its own temperature within viable limits, and adult herring gulls spend much time away from the nest and will not crouch on top of their younglings to keep them warm. The point is that the instinctive behaviors of the adult and infant animals of a given species must *match;* they are intricately *coordinated*, even from the very beginning. Processes of learning, of course, make the coordination smoother during the time the two generations live together and depend on one another.

ATTACHMENT IN SUBHUMAN PRIMATES

We do not know how large a part pheromones play in the attachments of higher animals. In dogs, sheep, and a number of other species, licking the newborn infants or consuming the placenta primes the mother for lactation and caretaking and plays a role in allowing her to recognize her own offspring. The mother's licking also helps the newborn youngling to find a nipple and begin to nurse. If a ewe's head is restrained so that she is prevented from licking her lamb, the lamb does not begin to suckle as soon as it would with an unrestrained mother and it is slow to gain weight (Alexander and Williams, 1964). Body warmth is also important as a mutual attractant. In a number of mammalian species, the young cannot maintain their own body temperature at a level needed for survival. They must be nested in soft material that will hold body heat, or they must be clustered together with littermates. They also need to be warmed periodically by the mother's body. In such species the young instinctively move toward warm places, and the maternal animals respond to young animals by crouching over them and retrieving them if they wander out of the nest.

In monkeys and apes the precise nature of the attractants and the physiological processes underlying them have not yet been traced in detail. It is clear that sound plays a part. A monkey infant utters a distinctive peeping cry when separated from its mother. The mother retrieves the infant at once when she hears this cry, but she makes no sound herself in the process. An even more important role is played by the sense of touch. Mutual grooming, clinging, mounting, body-contact play, even kissing are probably equally or more important than odors in building attachments in these advanced species. In short, all the senses interact in the complex set of behaviors that characterizes attachment in monkeys and apes. And as in all higher species, attachment depends on experience as well as on instinct. In a free-living natural environment, the attachment between a mother and her infant develops in the context of a troop, a herd, or some other social group. As we shall see, the nature of the social context influences an infant's attachments; but across a wide variety of contexts, a strong mother-infant bond is universal, and the behavior in the wild is not much different from that seen among animals in captivity.

The intensity of attachment

The attachment between any mother and infant animal can be extraordinarily strong, and both partners can resist separation with all the varieties of intense behavior at their command. Lambs that have been separated run about frantically, bleat, and repeatedly butt the sides of their cages with their heads. As for infant monkeys, anyone working with them is well aware of the turmoil that attends a separation. Jensen and Tolman give the following report concerning rhesus monkeys:

> Separation of mother and infant monkeys is an extremely stressful event for both mother and infant, as well as for all other monkeys within sight or earshot of the experience. The mother becomes ferocious towards attendants and extremely protective of her infant. The infant's screams can be heard over almost the entire building. The mother struggles and attacks the separators. The baby clings tightly to the mother and to any object which it can grasp to avoid being held or removed by the attendant. With the baby gone, the mother paces the cage almost constantly, charges the cage occasionally, bites at it, and makes continual attempts to escape. She also lets out occasional mooing-like sounds. The infant emits high-pitched shrill screams intermittently and almost continuously for the period of separation. (1962; cited in Bowlby, 1973, pp. 61–62)

Humans who have adopted and raised young monkeys or apes uniformly comment on the infant's intense insistence on maintaining body contact. Some years ago, a couple, both psychologists, raised an infant chimpanzee, Viki, from the age of three days. Viki's clinging was notable:

> From the moment she left her crib until she was tucked in at night: . . . she sat on my lap while I ate or studied. She straddled my hip as I cooked. If she were on the floor, and I started to get away, she screamed and clung to my leg until I picked her up. If some rare lack of vigilance on her part let a room's length separate us, she came charging across the abyss, screaming at the height of her considerable ability. (Hayes, 1951; cited in Bowlby, 1973, p. 58)

More than twenty years before Viki's adoption, a psychologist and his wife had adopted a seven-month-old chimpanzee and raised her along with their young son—who was two months older—in order to identify similarities and differences between the early development of a human child and a young ape (Kellogg and Kellogg, 1933). They too reported that the chimp, named Gua, was extraordinarily unwilling to be left alone for even the briefest period. Her resistance to separation was considerably more intense than that of the human child. It is now known that when rhesus monkey mothers and infants are separated, both show an elevation of *cortisol*—a hormone that is a sensitive indicator of stress (Mendoza et al., 1979). Furthermore, when the two are reunited, *both* show a drop in cortisol, and it returns quickly to normal levels. If animals are taken out of their cages, handled, and returned to cages from which their attachment object has been removed, they do not show a similar drop in cortisol. However, they may cling to other animals or to a cuddly object (such as a blanket), and they may seem to be somewhat comforted by this contact. Thus, there is physiological evidence of the power of mothers and infants to soothe one another following a stressful experience, and clearly it is contact with a *specific individual* (the infant's own mother or the mother's own infant) that has this effect.

Excellent descriptions of recent work on the development of attachment in monkeys and apes are available from several sources: Bowlby, 1969; Bowlby, 1973, Chapter 4; Rheingold and Eckerman, 1970; Rowell, 1972, Chapter 7; Simonds, 1977. Some of their main points follow.

Young monkeys and most apes can cling firmly to their mothers' fur as soon as they are born, and they spend all their early infancy in direct contact with their mothers' body. As they grow older, they begin to spend more and more time away from their mothers, and they begin to travel greater and greater distances. If some threat arises or if the troop moves, infant and mother quickly reestablish contact. The infant's curiosity about new objects and events and its interest in playing with other young monkeys are the magnets that draw it away from its mother. Hunger and the need to be soothed when alarmed are the magnets that draw the infant back. The mother plays an active part, retrieving her infant and restricting its movements when she perceives danger. In captivity, a mother caged with other adults is more restrictive than a mother caged only with her infant (Hinde and

Spencer-Booth, 1967), and her restrictions can be related to threats she perceives from specific other animals. In one caged group a juvenile female repeatedly kidnapped two infants, and the mothers had difficulty getting them back because the young female was backed by the dominant male of the group. These two mothers restricted their infants' movements to a very narrow range.

The mother also plays an active part in the weakening of the attachment relationship. At a certain point she begins to refuse to carry or nurse the infant and, in some species, actively pushes the older infants away and may bite or slap them when they approach. In other species the detachment process is gentler. In some species the mother's loss of interest is apparently triggered by a change in the infant's color. Among baboons, for example, the infants change from black to the normal adult color at about six months, and when this occurs the adults in the troop no longer accord them a special, protected status.

As we saw earlier, primate infants and mothers strongly resist separation. How quickly they recover from separation seems to depend on whether they are alone or with other animals and on their treatment by the other animals. Among monkeys that do not quickly adopt newly abandoned infants (rhesus and pigtail macaques, for example), the infant usually frantically searches for its mother and then seems depressed. It withdraws from its cage mates and huddles in a corner, sometimes rocking its body rhythmically, and is silent or moans softly. Infant bonnet macaques, on the other hand, do not show such profound reactions to separation, at least not overtly. They are accepted quickly by other cage mates and cling to them, appearing to derive thereby some of the comfort necessary for a resumption of normal social behavior.

Social organization and attachment patterns

The nature of the attachment between an infant and adults depends greatly on the social organization of the group into which the infant is born. This point is best illustrated by considering savannah, hamadryas, and forest baboons, three subspecies with different attachment patterns (see Kummer, 1968, and Simonds, 1977, for additional details).

The savannah baboon troop consists of adult males, who have strong attachments to one another and a fairly stable dominance hierarchy, and adult females with their young, who are loosely organized into mother-lineage groups and stay mainly in the center of the troop. No long-lasting, exclusive mating bonds exist between individual adult males and females, and adult males, particularly those of high status, show protective behavior toward all the infants of the troop.

The infant forms a strong attachment to its mother but also has contact with other adult and juvenile females that are close by in the center of the troop. These females gather near to touch and sniff a newborn and inspect its genitals. They hold or groom the infant fairly often, at least until its fur changes color. The infant's mother spends a good deal of time grooming the males of the troop, and thus the infant comes into frequent contact with a number of adult males. The infants, especially the males, are allowed to take liberties with the adult males—climbing on them and sometimes pulling their hair or playfully biting them and then scampering off to a safe distance. The infants of those females who stay near each other form a play group. The play gets rougher as the infants grow older, and the female infants tend to withdraw to the sidelines and remain with the adult and juvenile females while the young males continue to roughhouse together. Thus, an infant has tactile contact with many members of the troop in addition to its own mother, and these contacts form the basis for the social relationships the infant will have as it grows into full membership in the troop.

The hamadryas baboon troop is made up of several fairly autonomous units consisting of an adult male with one or more female consorts and the offspring of these females. A juvenile male starts his own harem by kidnapping an infant female. He carries this infant, protects her, grooms her, corrals her (tries to keep her away from other members of the troop), and when she is old enough, she becomes his first consort. A juvenile male sometimes carries and grooms an infant male, but such relationships are short-lived. The growing young female focuses her grooming exclusively on her abductor, thus forming an intense and exclusive bond in advance of mating. Under the watchful eyes of her male consort, a female forsakes all others and cleaves only unto him until he becomes too old to maintain his dominant position, at which time a young, stronger male succeeds in kidnapping her for his harem. An infant's initial attachment is to its mother, of course, and for the first six months (until it loses its black color) she carries, nurses, and retrieves it when it strays. There is one adult male nearby—the infant's putative father—and this male allows the infant to climb on him with impunity. The infant's play contacts are primarily with the infants of the other females who are consorts of the infant's father. No troopwide male play group exists to form the basis of an adult social structure. When the infant changes color, its social situation changes drastically as well. Its father rejects it and refuses further tactile contact. Its mother no longer retrieves it when it strays and no longer tries to interfere when another animal carries it away, though she will nurse it when it returns to her. Growing up as a hamadryas baboon, then, involves a narrowing of the young animal's range of social contacts, rather than the widening that occurs among the savannah baboons. The young hamadryas male may have a close relationship with one or two other young males, but some are fairly solitary until they begin to acquire females. Female infants are not rejected quite so quickly or thoroughly by their parents and maintain some relationship with them until they move into a male's orbit.

The social organization of the forest baboon troop is midway between the rather extreme patterns of the savannah and hamadryas troops. Their habitat is safer than the savannahs, and the adult males do not play a protective role for the females and infants of the troop as a whole. Large troops have subgroups made up of several adult males and several adult females with their infants. Relatively enduring bonds are formed between pairs of males and females. The infant has social contact with the adult males in its subgroup, but it usually develops an especially close bond with the mother's male consort, who shows considerable interest in his offspring—he carries, grooms, and protects them. The infant also has grooming relationships with older sisters and aunts, and it plays with the infants of those females. Females tend to give birth to infants every year (as distinct from the two-year spacing characteristic of the other subspecies), and often a mother will continue a close relationship with an older infant after her new infant is born. Thus, two or more infants of the same mother come into contact. The forest baboon, then, develops through the female something that approximates an extended family relationship, and siblings, cousins, and aunts remain in contact for considerable periods of time. A curious element in the life of the forest baboon is that anyone carrying an infant is less likely to be threatened or attacked by dominant animals. A juvenile male will sometimes pick up an infant and then go closer to a dominant adult male than he otherwise would dare to do. This "insurance value" of an infant serves to extend its social contacts.

The lessons to be learned from these vignettes are these: Some aspects of the formation of attachments in subhuman primates are still under the control of built-in releasing mechanisms, and some depend on the animals' life experience. Just as the mother in a lower-order mammalian species is bound to her offspring through the action of the chemicals she ingests when she licks her newborn young, so maternal behavior in apes can be triggered by specific releasers, such as the color of the infant's coat. Undoubtedly other releases exist as well, probably including pheromones to which both mother and infant are responsive. And while infant apes, like less advanced mammals, form their first and strongest attachment bond with their biological mothers, the pattern of additional attachments—the number and identity of other individuals with whom the infants form bonds—depends on the social organization of the troop. The social structure of the group either brings the infant into intimate, tactile contact with other animals or prevents such contact. In other words, familiarization—experience—plays a large role.

It is tempting to use these different attachment patterns as evidence that instinct plays a smaller part and learning takes over as the major factor in development as we go up the phylogenetic scale. I am here using *instinct* to refer to rigid chains of behavior in which each action is triggered either by its preceding action or by an external event whose power to trigger the action is preprogrammed in the organism. Instinctive behavior-chains are very similar from one member of a species to another. *Learning* permits individuals to adapt to their environments in individual ways, depending on their unique experiences. Can we say that the three kinds of baboons, with their three different forms of social organization, are showing learned adaptations to their different environments? And that the differences in the attachments formed by their infants have not evolved genetically but are taught to each new generation? The question is difficult to answer. There is some evidence that the herding and harem-building behaviors of the hamadryas male are inherited rather than learned (Simonds, 1977). In order to determine what is learned, it would be necessary to introduce several male hamadryas infants into a troop of savannah baboons. If they were successfully adopted and raised, it would then be possible to determine whether they take on the usual social behavior of a savannah male or attempt to import the hamadryas pattern. In the absence of such evidence, we can only note the possibility that forms of social organization can be affected by inherited behavioral tendencies. Meanwhile, I believe the view that best fits our existing information is that social organization in apes has grown up as a form of adaptation to a given environment. If a troop's environment changed, the troop would probably change its social organization—perhaps not immediately, but over a number of generations small enough that the change could not be a product of evolutionary selection. And the pattern of attachments formed between infants and adults would be heavily influenced by the social organization that developed in the new environment.

To say this is not to deny that instinct continues to play a role. Rowell (1972) notes that young monkeys learn very quickly to recognize other individual monkeys, but they have more difficulty distinguishing among abstract shapes. Thus, they are primed to pay attention to the features of their environment that are most relevant for forming attachments. And adults, on their part, also have built-in tendencies to respond to signals that emanate only from young infants. I mean only to imply that as we go up the phylogenetic scale, the role of cultural transmission in the individual's social behavior becomes progressively greater. We have argued that this role is greater in apes than in dogs and rats. Now we come to human beings.

ATTACHMENT IN HUMANS

Humans are primates and share with other primates the characteristic of having a very long period of infancy. It would be surprising had infants and adults not inherited a tendency to learn quickly the system of mutual signaling and mutual gratification that we see as the attachment bond. Without strong mechanisms keeping infants close to adults and motivating adults to care for and protect infants, our species would not have survived. And humans, like monkeys but not like rats, live in social groups, so there should be some mechanism that fosters the development of bonds between specific mothers and specific infants. Despite the inevitable presence of some inherited mechanisms, however, human beings are the most adaptable of all known species, and a vast and complex culture is passed on by each generation and must be learned by the next. As a result, considerable variations in the nature of parent-infant attachments are found among human groups and even among individual families within the same society. Many similarities also exist—behavioral patterns that are found in virtually all human parent-infant relationships. These, of course, are the aspects of attachment that reflect any inherited tendencies our species possesses.

In the remainder of this chapter, we will consider the *universals*—the characteristics of human attachment that develop in all or most children. In Chapter 3 we will consider the variations in attachment patterns among families, and we will focus on the nature of the conditions that determine these variations.

Children's attachment to their parents is a passionate thing. When a two-year-old is frightened, the child's small arms cling to the parent's body with surprising strength. When the parent has been away and the two are reunited, the child's smiles and enthusiastic hugs are among the unalloyed pleasures of parenthood, signaling that the child returns the parent's love. On occasion children will protest with all the vigor at their command a separation from their parents. Yet, the quality of a young child's affection is not the same as an adult's—it is more demanding and less giving, and it is built on the child's needs and the parents' ability to gratify the needs.

Beginnings and early change

Both human mothers and newborn infants are equipped with reflexes that support their mutual adaptation. The infants have a sucking reflex—they will suck vigorously on any object that is placed in their mouths. The stimulation of the mother's nipples by the infant's sucking releases a maternal hormone called *prolactin,* which facilitates the production of milk. Thus, the actions and responses of mother and child support the development of an interactive system that results in the infant's being fed. This system of reciprocal reflexes is quickly transformed into an integrated system of mutual behaviors. When we discuss attachment in human beings, it is important to remember that the relationship is a two-way process. Parents become attached to children as well as children to parents. Much less is known about parental attachment than is known about infant attachment, and consequently the discussion that follows will be relatively one-sided, emphasizing the development of attachment bonds in the infant. The reader is asked to bear in mind, however, that there are reciprocal developments going on in the adults who are caring for the children.

The development of attachment takes place more gradually in human children than in subhuman mammals. Human infants cannot cling effectively or crawl to adults until some months after birth. Initially they cannot even distinguish their own caretakers from others. Although newborns are capable of certain actions that attract caretakers and are themselves attracted by certain features possessed by other human beings, this behavior is not focused on specific individuals and therefore does not represent attachment in the technical sense of the term.

What are the earliest elements of mutual attraction that later form into a fully developed specific attachment? The newborn's capacity to cry—and to stop crying when rocked, warmed, or fed—is of course one of the main attributes that binds a child's caretakers to the child. An infant's crying is a penetrating, disturbing sound to most adults. The strong sense of relief that most adults experience when they are able to soothe a crying infant suggests that a built-in system exists for reinforcing nurturant actions. But infants are equipped with other, more positive attractants. Their skin is soft to the touch. Their smiles are gratifying. A newly bathed, freshly diapered infant has a delightful smell. Perhaps something about their appearance—the shape of their body, the ratio of head to body size—is attractive to adult humans in precisely the same way that a coat of black fur is attractive to adult baboons (Tinbergen, 1951).

The newborn infants, for their part, are also equipped to be especially attracted by certain kinds of stimuli. Newborns do not look indiscriminately at all objects—they can only briefly coordinate the movements of both eyes, and they can focus only on certain distances. Nevertheless, they show visual preference for objects that are large, distinctly contoured, strongly contrasted, and in motion—and human faces possess at least some of these characteristics. Perhaps more important, infants are capable of being soothed by certain events that occur primarily in the presence of caretakers. Being fed when hungry is of course a prime example, but there are others that are not so obvious. Experiments with crying newborns have shown that their crying will abate when they are rocked, warmed, or lifted and put to the shoulder. Also—strangely—being wrapped in material that is furry or has a fuzzy surface is more soothing than being wrapped in something smooth (here something seems to have gone wrong with the system; human parents lost their fur a very long time ago!). Evidently the tactile aspect of comforting is important to young humans just as it is to young monkeys. Furthermore, amplified rhythmic sound, including the sound of a human heartbeat, will reduce the amount of crying in a newborn's nursery (Brackbill and Adams, 1966), and young infants tend to become both alert and quiet at the sound of human voices.

New mothers also seem to be predisposed to respond to certain stimuli. Close contact with the newborn apparently stimulates maternal feelings and behavior. The human mother does not lick the birth fluids from her newborn infant, but other forms of stimulation probably do serve to initiate mother-infant bonding. In order for such bonding to develop, of course, the mother and newborn must have an opportunity to be together.

In many industrialized societies the usual hospital practice allows a mother only a few moments to look at her infant after the infant is born. The infant is then taken to a nursery, brought back for a short visit eight hours or so after birth (usually without any attempt at feeding), and only on the following day is the infant brought to the mother at regular intervals for feeding sessions, which last twenty or thirty minutes. A group of pediatricians (Klaus et al., 1970) were concerned about the possibility that the postpartum separation of mother and infant might interfere with the mother-child relationship. If human mothers *were* equipped with any instinctive tendencies to stimulate their infants in certain ways that would foster mutual attachment, hospital routine might entail too much separation to permit such behavior to occur and serve its function.

With this issue in mind, the physicians varied the postpartum setting. For the experimental group, each mother had a private, quiet, warm place to rest after giving birth, and her infant was placed nude against her nude body for approximately an hour. A comparison group of mothers and infants was treated according to the normal hospital routine. The researchers reported that the extended-contact mothers rapidly increased the amount of time spent looking closely at their babies' faces, and they touched the babies extensively. In the researchers' words, "The mothers started with fingertip touch on the infants' extremities, and proceeded in 4 to 8 minutes to massaging, encompassing palm contact on the trunk. . . ." (Klaus et al., 1970, p. 191).

In a second study the interaction between a different group of fourteen extended-contact mothers and their babies was compared with the behavior of a group of fourteen mothers with normal hospital experience. The infants were all firstborns. The observations, by people who had no knowledge of the mothers' hospital experience, were made on several occasions after mother and child had left the hospital. It was found that during a physical examination when the infants were one month old, the extended-contact mothers were more likely to stand next to the examination table and soothe their infants if they cried. The mothers who had not had such contact were more likely to remain seated at some distance. Furthermore, the experimental mothers showed their infants more physical affection during feedings, had more eye-to-eye contact with them, and expressed more concern about leaving them in anyone else's care. Similar differences between the two groups of mothers were reported when the infants were a year old (Klaus and Kennell, 1976).

The authors have interpreted their findings to mean that there is a critical period immediately following birth when it is important for mother and infant to have close bodily contact. This important issue needs to be studied with additional samples of mothers. The exact timing of the critical period (or indeed, whether there *is* a period of optimal readiness) is yet to be substantiated. And observers disagree on the long-term effect of early separation. One group asserts that the separation disrupts for a long period of time the closeness of the mother-child relationship and that the child may be less able to have close affectional ties later in life. Others point out that whole generations of Americans and Europeans have experienced standard hospital separations, and the children have nevertheless grown into reasonably normal, healthy adults. Unless one wants to claim that whole populations are impaired in their capacity for affectional bonding, it must be the case that any handicaps created by immediate postpartum separation are usually overcome in the course of normal caretaking. The information that would answer these important questions is simply not now available. For our present purposes, the main point is that human mothers as well as infants are probably predisposed to form an attachment and to respond to one another's signals and that early body contact with the infant (along with the infant's crying, nuzzling, and sucking) may activate maternal responsiveness.[1]

The first social responses: looking, smiling, crying

The nature of the visual stimuli that infants find most attractive changes during the first two months of life. Attractiveness is no longer a matter of well-defined contours, but is a matter of complexity. That is, the infant increasingly prefers to look at things that have a good deal of contour, have many different angles or lines, and are made up of many rather than few elements. And the preference for more complex displays is followed by a preference for certain configurations—certain shapes. The infant especially likes patterns that are concentric. Perhaps this preference is related to infants' interest in

[1] So far there have been no studies in which fathers have had close body contact with their newborn infants, so we do not know whether adult male bonding to an infant is stimulated by such contact.

eyes. If given a choice among drawings of human faces that have various features missing, infants prefer to look at drawings that have *eyes*, no matter what else may be missing. (For a full discussion of the early development of visual preferences, see Fantz, Fagan, and Miranda, 1975).

If infants are shown incomplete drawings of faces, eyes alone are enough to get them to smile. But they become more selective, and by the fourth month they need more features. By the fifth month they smile most readily at faces with *all* the features represented, and they soon come to prefer three-dimensional rather than flat representations. The infant's visual concept of a human being is undergoing refinement. The final step in this progression is reached when the baby smiles most consistently at pictures of *familiar* faces.

Infants not only grow more discriminating during their first six months of life, but also smile more frequently. Why do these changes occur? Research findings suggest that infants smile when they manage to solve a challenging visual problem—that is, when they recognize something that initially seems strange (Kagan, Kearsley, and Zalazo, 1978). The increase may thus reflect a growing sophistication in the *schemata*, or mental representations, that an infant has built up and uses for recognition of objects and events. In addition, babies get positive reactions from their caretakers when they smile. Adults find infants' smiles highly attractive, and they pay more attention to a smiling infant than to a sober one. They smile in return, talk, or pick up the child. If an experimenter systematically responds in these ways to an infant's smiles, the frequency of smiling increases quite substantially (Brackbill, 1958). Of course, the fact that social reinforcement by an experimenter *can* increase smiling does not prove that this kind of behavior in normal family life *does* produce increasing readiness to smile. More convincing evidence for a causal relationship comes from studies of groups of infants reared in different settings. Children living in orphanages are slower to develop social smiling than are children reared either in their own families or the family-like environment of a communal children's house on an Israeli kibbutz (Gewirtz, 1965). This work suggests that the rate of development of the child's social responsiveness, as shown by smiling, depends on the responsiveness of the child's caretakers.

Parallel developmental changes take place in infants' crying—in the conditions that make them cry and in what will soothe them. Detailed analysis of tape recordings of the crying of very young infants has shown that three kinds of infant cries can be distinguished: hunger cries, anger cries, and pain cries (Wolff, 1969). The pain cry is different from the others—it has a sudden, rather than a gradual, onset, and individual cries are followed by fairly long silences while the baby is holding her or his breath. Most mothers can distinguish between the three kinds of cries and report being most upset by a tape recording of a pain cry. If the long, silent periods of breath holding are short-ened, mothers find the sound more tolerable. Thus, from the beginning, a baby is equipped with a differentiated signal system to which most mothers rapidly become attuned. Furthermore, detailed analysis of the sound patterns produced by individual infants shows that each baby has a distinctive crying pattern, so that a basis exists for caretakers to recognize their own infant's cry.

Newborn infants do more crying when they are in a cold rather than a warm room, when their clothing is removed (regardless of room temperature), and when they are hungry. As mentioned earlier, they can be soothed by being warmed, wrapped, rocked, fed, or given a pacifier. As infants progress into their second month, the causes and cures for crying begin to change. If a person disappears from sight or touch, the infant is now more likely to cry than if an interesting non-human object is taken away. Being rocked by a mechanical device is no longer as soothing as being rocked in human arms. At this stage of development, however, the infant does not care which person leaves or which person does the rocking.

Hundreds of times during the first half-year of life, the infant cries and someone comes to relieve the distress. There can be little doubt that the baby learns the connection between the two events. When do infants begin to cry on purpose or cry to get attention rather than sim-ply because they are cold, hungry, or in pain? It is difficult to know exactly, but the transition does take place. Schaffer (1971) provides an excellent review of the developmental changes in smiling, crying, and proximity seeking during infancy. He puts the matter clearly:

> In the early weeks, crying and smiling serve as signals only in the sense that other people will almost invariably be impelled to react to them. They are not yet signals in the sense that the infant uses them purposely in order to summon help and attention. They tend to be triggered off by certain primitive stimuli, with no foresight involved on the part of the infant as to the likely consequences of his actions. The realization that these responses have quite predictable effects on others comes only with time and will depend on the learning opportunities that an infant en-counters in his particular social environment. (1971, p. 79)

How can one tell whether crying has become purposeful? Timing is one indication. After a familiar person has left the infant alone, quite young infants will cry and then calm rather quickly by them-selves. Older infants are likely to continue crying until something very specific happens—the return of the person whose departure started the crying in the first place.

During the first six months of life, then, infants develop many components of what will soon become a true attachment. Their visual attention, crying, and smiling increasingly become linked to the pres-ence of other human beings. But the key to the process is the dawn of infants' ability to recognize their own parents—the *specific* persons who will become the objects of their first focused attachments. Exactly when does this recognition first begin? Probably not during the first two months of the infant's life. Infants of this age seem unable to tell one face from another. By the third month some infants frown more when approached by a stranger than when they are approached by their mothers and fathers. Some infants also stop crying more quickly when picked up by their mothers than when others attempt to soothe them. By the fourth month most infants clearly show that they know and prefer the familiar members of the household—by smiling and cooing more on seeing their faces or hearing their voices (see for example, Bower, 1974)—but they are still fairly friendly to strangers. They may show signs of not wanting to be left alone, but they usually do not protest the departure of a familiar caretaker any more strongly than they do the departure of a relative stranger. By six or seven months, however, these protests begin to become differentiated, and separations from familiar caretakers become especially distressing.

The first attachment object

As infants move into the second half of their first year, some dramatic behavioral changes take place. Crying and smiling are no longer the primary methods for achieving or maintaining contact with a caretaker. Many infants begin to make calling sounds to attract their mothers' attention. They begin to crawl and can now actively approach another person and follow if that person moves away. An infant of this age clearly enjoys staying close to a specific person—usually the mother. The child is especially pleased when the mother approaches and especially distressed when she leaves, and no one can comfort the child as effectively as she. The infant takes obvious pleasure in body contact—climbing on the mother, exploring her face, hair, clothes. As children become able to move around more freely on their own (by eight months and later), they use their mothers as a haven, moving directly to them in preference to others in case of any alarm. When this begins to happen, children have become truly attached.

Up to now we have been using the term *attachment* without giving a formal definition. By *attachment* we mean a *relatively enduring emotional tie to a specific other person*. In infancy and in early childhood attachment is shown primarily by the child's (1) seeking to be near the other person, (2) showing distress on separation from that person, (3) showing joy or relief on reunion, and (4) being oriented toward that person even when not in close proximity—listening for the person's voice, watching the person's movements, and directing actions toward that person (for example, calling or showing objects to that person).

What determines children's choice of attachment object? Clearly, the person need not be the biological mother: Adopted children become firmly attached to their adoptive mothers. Almost always, the first and strongest attachment is to the mother or other primary caretaker. But attachments to other family members develop very quickly. Children soon begin to seek proximity to the father and show pleasure at his approach—in fact, the two attachments quite often develop at the same time. Children may also become attached to a grandparent, an uncle, or an older brother or sister—someone who may have no role in caretaking but who is an engaging playmate. Schaffer and Emerson (1964), in their longitudinal study of sixty Scottish infants, report that by eighteen months most of the infants had become attached to at least three people.

Shortly after children have developed their first specific attachment, they rather suddenly become wary of strangers. Seven- or eight-month-old children who previously allowed strangers to hold them now may retreat or protest when a stranger tries to cuddle them. Most children are highly interested in strangers and quite often will make friendly overtures toward them. But the days of indiscriminate acceptance of sudden, intimate contact are clearly over, and by the last half of the first year, most children will avoid strangers on at least some occasions.

Between the ages of seven and twelve months, then, infants become increasingly focused on the specific people to whom they have become attached, and they begin to change their behavior toward the attachment objects. Younger infants are happy in the presence of their principal caretakers and distressed in their absence. Older infants take a more active role in bringing about the contact they want or need at the moment. Bowlby (1969) notes that before the age of about eight months, most infants seem to make few organized, planned efforts to achieve contact. After this age infants not only follow their mothers and select a comfortable degree of proximity to them, but the infants begin to try to influence their mothers' behavior. These early efforts at influence take the rather primitive form of direct, physical pushing and pulling. If the mother is reading, the child may pull the book off her lap; if she is telephoning, the child may try to grab the receiver out of her hand. As children grow older, they develop more acceptable means of achieving contact—means that fit in better with their mothers' ongoing activities but that nevertheless satisfy their own needs for help or comfort.

Attachment and emotional security

Newly mobile infants use their attachment objects in a variety of ways. And while they frequently approach them for fun and games, a more important function is served by the attachment object's ability to provide a sense of security. Children who are tired or who are upset by an unexpected loud noise or the presence of a stranger will move close to their attachment figures and then show signs of feeling more comfortable. A child who is crying will usually become calm when picked up and will stop clinging tightly after a few moments of being held. Recordings of infants' heart rates show the same calming effect: Upset infants' heart rates return to normal more quickly when they are held by their mothers than when they are held by strangers (Main and Londerville; cited by Sroufe and Waters, 1977). The idea that infants' proximity seeking is based on their need for security and that attachment figures can provide this security and soothe them was suggested many years ago by Blatz and colleagues (Blatz, Bott, and Millichamp, 1935). The view has been reaffirmed in more recent work (Blatz, 1966; Flint, 1959). Harlow's work with monkeys (1961) of course gave added impetus. In more recent years, Bowlby (1969, 1973) and Ainsworth and her colleagues (Ainsworth, Bell, and Stayton, 1971; Ainsworth and Wittig, 1969) have been especially influential in presenting this view and in mobilizing research support for it. In fact, the issue of attachment and emotional security has been a major area of interest with researchers considering such issues as the growth of the child's capacity to tolerate separation.

The effect of separation in a strange setting

Ainsworth and her colleagues (1969, 1971) used a research procedure called the *Strange Situation* to study the ways in which the mother's presence or absence affects the child's behavior and emotional security. A mother and her infant are brought into an observation room that is well stocked with toys. The mother puts down the infant and goes to a chair. After a few minutes an unfamiliar woman enters and soon engages the mother in conversation. The stranger then attempts to play with the child, and the mother quietly leaves the room, leaving her handbag on her chair (as a signal to the infant that she will return). While she is gone the child's reaction to the stranger is noted, and when the mother returns the reunion is the focus of observation. At a subsequent point in the scenario, the mother leaves the child alone in the room for a few minutes, giving the observers an opportunity to see whether the child protests her departure and giving a second opportunity to see how the infant greets her on her return.

Hundreds of infants and young children of various ages have been observed in this situation or in situations with a slightly altered sequence, and some characteristics of children's reactions are now clearly established:

1. A child usually stays fairly close to the mother during the first few moments in the strange environment but soon leaves her side to explore the room and the toys, occasionally returning to reestablish contact.

2. When the stranger enters the room, the child usually goes closer to the mother. The child may cling to her or retreat behind her, peering at the stranger, or may simply take a toy close to the mother's feet and play there, covertly glancing at the stranger. Many children stare openly or smile at the stranger, but they usually begin their visual contact with her from a safe haven at the mother's side.

3. Most children warm up to the stranger fairly quickly and soon respond to the stranger's efforts to engage them in play. Some children, however, continue to cling warily to their mothers.

4. Children interact with a stranger more comfortably when the mother is present than when she is not.

5. When the mother leaves the room, most children immediately become less involved in play. Many children cry, and those who do not cry usually show signs of disturbance. Some children go to the door and wait there for the mother's return, while others remain immobile at one spot on the floor, holding a toy but not playing with it. Their reactions make it seem as if their normal functioning had been suspended.

These stressful responses are not just typical of the artificially contrived laboratory setting. A similar situation often prevails at home, although there are some differences. Most infants in their own homes with no stranger present do not show signs of disturbance as the mother goes about her normal activities and moves in and out of the room where the infant is playing. Infants old enough to follow will sometimes do so, but quite frequently they do not, especially if they are intensely involved with toys. The child's play does not usually stop or slow down when the mother is out of sight. Nevertheless, the child derives some comfort from the sounds of the mother's activities, and too long a silence may send the child looking for her. Any small upset or frustration is likely to bring the child to her side. And quite often the child protests when she signals by putting on her coat or picking up her car keys that she is about to leave the house.

The age of maximum separation protest

The response to separation undergoes considerable change as the child grows older. Protest over the mother's leaving usually reaches its greatest frequency and strength during the first half of the second year, but it commonly remains quite strong through the second birthday. The waxing and waning of separation fears seems to be very similar for most children regardless of the setting in which they are growing up. Kagan (1976) and his colleagues studied a group of 100 children—half of whom spent five full days each week at day-care centers and half of whom spent their days at home. The children and their mothers visited a laboratory playroom at two-month intervals, starting when the children were three-and-a-half months old and continuing until they were thirteen-and-a-half months; then they were seen again at the ages of twenty and twenty-nine months. The children's reactions were observed when their mothers left the room. The incidence of fussing and crying was similar for the two groups and showed nearly identical age changes (see Figure 2-2).

It is surprising that protesting was not more common in the home-care children than in the day-care children considering that the day-care children had experienced daily separations from their mothers throughout the period of study. Do children of this age simply never get used to being separated from their mothers? Actually, they do—the day-care children were quite comfortable when their mothers left them at the familiar center each morning. The testing situation, however, was unfamiliar, and the children were not certain where their mothers had gone and when they would return. Under these conditions, both day-care and home-care children became distressed.

Kagan (1976) presents information from several different cultures, ranging from children of the !Kungsan Bushmen of Botswana to apartment-reared children in highly urbanized Western settings. He shows that in each of these diverse settings, children show little separation

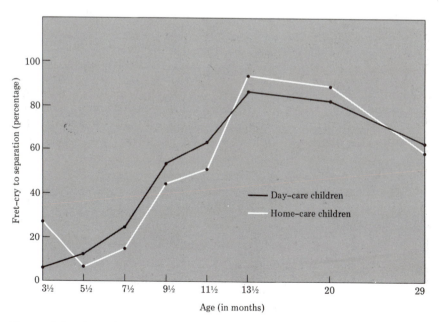

Figure 2-2.   Age changes in day-care and home-care children's distress response to separation. Note the similar patterns in the two groups. (From Kagan, 1976)

protest before the age of eight months. The incidence and intensity of protest then increases, reaching a peak early in the second year and declining thereafter. We can only conclude that the disruptive effects of separation seem to be governed by a cognitive-developmental time-table that is similar in widely different life situations. This timetable seems to determine whether children are old enough to organize voluntary protest behavior and to perceive the uncertainties of a situation and whether they are young enough to feel helpless in the face of these uncertainties. The role of uncertainty in determining the strength of the infant's protest can hardly be overestimated. A familiar setting and familiar people make all the difference in a child's comfort. Strange as it may seem, a mother's use of an exit door other than the door through which she usually comes and goes is enough to increase the likelihood of her fifteen-month-old infant's protest (Littenberg, Tulkin, and Kagan, 1971).

Accepting comfort from others besides the mother

Other persons besides the mother can provide security in the Strange Situation. When three people are present—mother, father, and stranger—the child usually stays closer to the mother than to the father and closer to the father than to the stranger (Cohen and Campos, 1974). When an infant in the observation room is alone with the father, the infant reacts to his presence or absence in ways similar to those described for mothers. Kotelchuk (1976) observed in the Strange Situation children ranging in age from six to twenty-four months; they were left with either (1) their mothers, (2) their fathers, or (3) a stranger. When the adult briefly left the child alone, the child's reaction depended on who had left. As Figure 2-3A shows, when either the father or mother left, the child's play was disrupted. When the stranger left, the child actually played more actively, indicating more comfort alone than in the presence of the stranger. Parallel effects on other aspects of the child's behavior were also observed. When the mother or father left, the child was likely to stand by the door waiting for the adult's return, and this seldom happened when the stranger left. The mother or father's return was followed by a period of touching and clinging, and this was not seen with the stranger. Thus, the father also serves as a source of security and comfort, although the child's ability to use the father as such develops somewhat more slowly. The year-old child clearly plays less and cries more when the mother leaves, while such a response to the father's departure is not evident until the age of fifteen months (on the average). Furthermore, the child usually protests the mother's departure somewhat more strongly and clings somewhat longer to the mother on reunion (see Figure 2-3B).

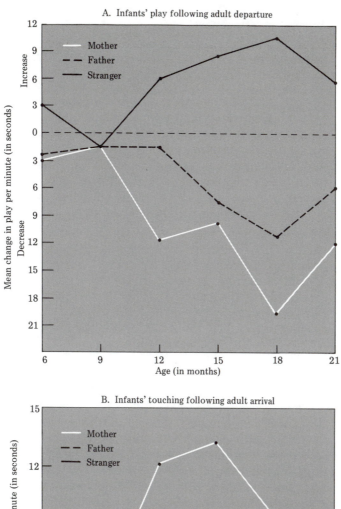

A. Infants' play following adult departure

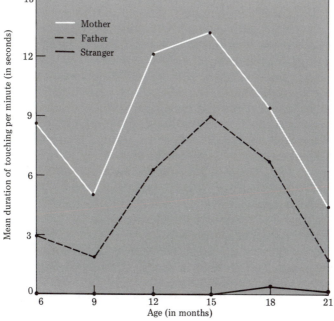

B. Infants' touching following adult arrival

Figure 2-3. Age changes in infants' responses to mother, father, and a stranger. (From Kotelchuk, 1976)

Kotelchuk makes an additional point about the role of fathers: When fathers were actively involved as caretakers, children were more comfortable when left alone with a stranger. The period during which children strongly protested separation from their parents was shorter for children who were cared for by both their mothers and their fathers (by comparison with families where the mothers did almost all the caretaking). Thus, caretaking by more than one family member appears to help insulate the child against separation distress or at least to hasten the normal developmental decline in this reaction.

By the age of two-and-a-half, children can derive some security from the presence of a person they have known only briefly. Feldman and Ingham (1975) had a female research assistant play with children for an hour or so in the comfortable surroundings of the children's homes. Then the new acquaintance (the baby sitter) functioned in the mother's role in the Strange Situation. The children stayed close to her when the stranger entered, played vigorously in the sitter's presence, slowed down or abandoned their play when she left the room, and so forth. It appears, then, that children of two-and-a-half (and presumably older) need not be attached to a person in the same way that they are attached to family members in order to make use of the person for security-giving purposes. Year-old children, however, could not transfer their trust to the new acquaintance and were inconsolable in the Strange Situation. Their willingness to explore the toys was not facilitated by the baby sitter's presence. The infants in this study lived in fairly traditional homes in Australia and were accustomed to almost exclusive maternal care. While the children might have been more responsive to the baby sitter if they had been used to a variety of caretakers, Kagan's work makes this seem unlikely. Most year-old children are unwilling to be left with briefly acquainted strangers whether they are accustomed to several caretakers or not. The important factor is the relative familiarity of the substitute caretaker. A different group of infants, aged ten to fourteen months, were left with a baby sitter for several hours on each of three days. They were quite comfortable with the sitter and quite distressed when she left the room (Fleener, 1973). Children as young as twelve months apparently require a fairly long acquaintance period before they can find security in the presence of non-family adults.

Children's increasing willingness to accept substitute caretakers on short acquaintance is further illustrated in work by Maccoby and Feldman (1972). A group of children was seen in the Strange Situation at the ages of two, two-and-a-half, and three. No change with age was observed in the pattern of play when the stranger joined the mother and child—at each age children consistently played less in this situation. And at each age, play declined quite markedly when the child was left entirely alone. But when the stranger joined a child who had been alone, an age difference was evident. The three-year-olds were able to resume normal play, while the two-year-olds' play remained as fragmentary as if the children were alone.

The waning of separation fears

We have stressed the sense of security provided by mothers' closeness, and it almost might seem that children have everything to gain by constantly staying near their mothers and nothing to gain by moving away. Nevertheless, on their own initiative children gradually play comfortably at greater and greater distances from their mothers. In other words, as children grow older, they seem to be attached to their mothers by a longer and longer leash. Rheingold and Eckerman (1970) clearly demonstrated this change by measuring the distance children traveled in an L-shaped grassy yard along two sides of a house. The mother sat at the end of the long arm of the L, the child was set down on the grass near her chair, and the mother remained seated while the child explored. The yard contained some trees, two birdbaths, some planted terraces, and a paved patio—but no toys. Observers stationed inside the house noted the greatest distance each child moved away from the mother's chair. The average distance increased regularly with the child's age—from 6.9 meters at one year and 15.1 meters at two years to 17.3 meters at three years and 20.6 meters at four years.

The counterweight to attachment is curiosity. Children are positively attracted by novel elements in their environment as long as security-giving elements are also present. As they grow older and spend more time at a distance from their mothers, they begin to substitute other, more distant forms of contact for the immediate physical contact that they seem to require when they are younger. Carr, Dabbs, and Carr (1975) found that children aged eighteen to thirty months played more comfortably if they could see their mothers than they did if their mothers were behind them or behind a screen. Curiously, the children did not look at their mothers more frequently when they were in view. Apparently just knowing they *could* see their mothers was enough to provide security. When the mother was behind the screen, the child vocalized more, evidently substituting this kind of contact for visual contact.

During the time children are increasing the distance they can comfortably put between their mothers and themselves, they continue to cling or follow their mothers closely when tired, ill, or emotionally upset. They also go through this kind of *regression* (return to earlier patterns of behavior) if they have been separated from their mothers and showed disturbance during the separation (Heinicke and Westheimer, 1966).

We have been reviewing a series of changes that a child's attachment behavior undergoes during the first few years of life. John Bowlby (1969) has conceptualized these changes as a series of phases that normal children go through in a predictable sequence:

> *Phase 1.* (About eight to twelve weeks of age.) *Orientation and signals without discrimination of figure.* Infants respond socially to nearby people by orienting toward them, following them with their eyes, grasping them if they are within reach, and smiling or vocalizing, but they orient with about equal frequency and intensity to any person who approaches.

> *Phase 2.* (About three to six months of age.) *Orientation and signals directed toward one or more discriminated figures.* The social responses just listed increase in intensity and are increasingly directed toward the infant's mother figure. However, strangers are still reacted to in a fairly friendly fashion.

> *Phase 3.* (Six months to about two-and-a-half years.) *Maintenance of proximity to a discriminated figure by means of locomotion as well as signals.* The infant now takes an active part in maintaining proximity to the attachment figure and uses this person as a base from which to explore. Certain other persons are selected as subsidiary attachment figures. Friendly responses to others wane and are replaced by wariness or, under certain circumstances, withdrawal. Feedback from the child's own movements and those of the mother is now used by the child to determine whether the desired degree of proximity has been attained. Proximity seeking thus becomes more accurate and is adapted to the mother's movements as well as to the child's own.

> *Phase 4.* (Little is known about the age when this phase normally begins, but for many children the onset is probably sometime in the third year.) *Formation of a goal-corrected partnership.* The child begins to conceive of the mother as a separate person with goals of her own and begins to infer what these goals are and how they can be influenced by the child's own actions.

So far we have been discussing phases 1 through 3; more will be said about phase 4 later. First, however, we turn to a discussion of the reasons the developments represented in the first three phases occur.

WHY DO INFANTS AND YOUNG CHILDREN BECOME ATTACHED?

Attachment is so universal in young children that it seems almost pointless to ask why it occurs. Surely it is simply something natural—

something built into human nature. But as we saw in the case of the mother rat and her pups, instinct works through certain mechanisms (primarily odors, in the case of the rat), and it is interesting to try to discover what the mechanisms might be in the case of human children and their parents. Judging by what we know about subhuman primates, whatever attachment instinct human beings have probably takes the form of *readiness to learn* a mutual reaction system very quickly. Let us consider what forms this readiness and the associated learning might take.

Feeding and the comfort of contact

The primary factor in attachment was once thought to be feeding. A very young infant is fed five or six times a day and sometimes even more often, and always it is the helpful actions of an adult that appease the child's painful hunger. The infant has hundreds of opportunities to learn that the appearance of the mother (or other caretaker) signals the end of discomfort and the beginning of pleasure. No wonder the child comes to feel that the caretaker's presence is comforting.

We now know that hunger and feeding are only one element, and perhaps a minor one, in the development of attachment. The experiments of Harlow and Harlow (1965, 1969) are the classic demonstration of this fact. The Harlows separated infant monkeys from their mothers at a very early age and raised them with artificial surrogate mothers. (The infants were fed by means of a feeding bottle fastened to the side of the cage.) The surrogates were dummies, about the same size and shape as real monkey mothers, with wooden heads and faces. Some surrogate mothers had bodies made of a wire mesh, and others were padded with foam rubber and covered with soft terry cloth. The preference of the young monkeys was startlingly clear: When given a choice, they always clung to the soft, padded mother, and they spent a good deal of their time clinging to its body. When a frightening object was introduced into the cage, the infant would run screaming to the soft mother, throw its arms around "her" neck, and bury its own face in the mother's covering. It would cling there until less afraid and then gradually venture out, making little trips of exploration toward the suspicious object and returning repeatedly to the soft mother as home base. The behavior of the infants raised with only a wire mother was remarkably different: They did not become attached to it and did not spend time in contact with it, but would huddle in the corner of the cage. These infants often clutched parts of their own bodies and rocked themselves rhythmically. When a frightening object was introduced, they would go to a corner, curl up into a ball, and scream. If a piece of cloth were available in the cage, they would pull it over their heads, but they would not go to the wire mother.

The importance of the mother's soft body surface was strongly underlined in a later phase of the Harlows' work, when mothers with feeding mechanisms were constructed (the nipple of a feeding bottle projected through each dummy's upper torso). Even when the infants could feed from a wire mother, they did not become attached to it, but would drink their milk quickly and leave, returning only when hungry. Some effect of feeding was noted, however. Comparing the infants' responses to cloth mothers with nipples and cloth mothers without nipples, there were indications that the infants became somewhat more strongly attached to the feeding mothers—that is, they spent somewhat more time clinging to the feeding mothers' body. Still, the differences were small. The ultimate proof of the relative importance of the mother's body surface was found in the behavior of an infant that had both cloth and wire mothers available, with only the wire mother having a nursing bottle. This infant worked out a method of sitting on the cloth mother and clinging to it with one hand while leaning over to nurse from the wire mother!

For human infants too, the contact comfort provided when an infant clings and a mother pats, rocks, and holds her infant close is of crucial importance in developing a mutual attachment. Of course, feeding and holding are usually combined in a single ministration. In breast-feeding, contact comfort is guaranteed while the infant is being fed. And bottle-fed infants are usually held during all or most of a feeding. Clearly, however, human infants can become attached to people who never feed them, and we must conclude that although feeding is usually a contributing part of the interaction pattern that builds attachment, it is not a necessary part.

Lest we overemphasize the role of contact comfort in the development of attachment, we should note that surprisingly strong attachments can be found between animals who are prevented from having physical contact with each other but who can nevertheless see, hear, and smell each other. This fact was discovered accidentally in the process of attempting to raise a lamb in the presence of an ewe that was not its mother. Sheep normally refuse to adopt a strange lamb—indeed, they will batter the young animal if it attempts to approach. Cairns and Johnson (1965) attempted to circumvent this rejection by constructing a wire fence that separated the lamb's enclosure from the ewe's. Under these conditions the lamb developed a close attachment to the ewe: It approached her as closely as the fence permitted, moved back and forth along the fence synchronously with the ewe's movements, and was distressed when the ewe was taken out of the enclosure. Cairns (1966) even found that isolated lambs developed strong attachments to a television set that provided visual and auditory stimulation! While the importance of seeing and hearing the attachment object undoubtedly varies from species to species, the point is that sight, hearing (and, no doubt, smell) do play a large role in the development and maintenance of attachments.

Surprisingly, both animals and human infants become strongly attached to caretakers who punish them. An early experiment by Fuller (cited in Scott and Fuller, 1965) illustrates the point. From the time of weaning a group of puppies was cared for exclusively by an adult experimenter who fed the puppies and played with them frequently. Another group was treated in the same way by the same experimenter except that occasionally, at random, the experimenter would rap a puppy sharply on the nose as the puppy approached. The experimenter wanted to know which group of puppies would stay closer to him during a test period when neither feeding, play, nor punishment occurred. The answer was clear: The randomly punished group showed the most proximity seeking.

The same kind of response to punishment was seen when some of the female monkeys raised in isolation by the Harlow group were mated and gave birth. These maternal animals rejected and were abusive toward their infants (see Chapter 3 for further discussion), but the infants nevertheless persisted strongly in their efforts to cling. Strong attachments have also been found in human children who have been severely abused by their parents.

A study in the Harlow laboratory looked at attachment to a cloth mother that at unpredictable random intervals would blast the clinging infant monkey with a strong current of compressed air (Rosenblum and Harlow, 1963). Infants treated in this way spent more time on the surrogate mother than did infants raised on surrogates that never "punished" them. Two explanations have been offered for this paradoxical effect:

1. Abusive mother monkeys tend to be most abusive when their infants are trying to leave them (or when someone else attempts to remove the infant). Perhaps the infants learn that the way to avoid abuse is not to attempt to leave (Seay, Alexander, and Harlow, 1964).

2. The natural response in the infants of species that form attachments is to seek proximity when afraid or distressed. Punishment distresses a young animal and distress causes it to cling. Thus, punishment intensifies the very behavior for which the infant has been punished!

The second explanation fits the results of both the monkey and the puppy experiments better than the first does. But quite possibly both processes operate in certain situations.

Mutual reactiveness as a causal factor in attachment

In a well-functioning relationship between child and caretaker, the adult knows the meaning of the child's signals, and only certain people can be counted on by the child to do what the child expects—to integrate their behavior with that of the child so that their mutual activities can run smoothly. In effect, the caretaker is acting *for* the child and *with* the child in fulfilling the child's needs and by doing so provides a predictable environment in which the child can feel comfortable. An example will illustrate the point:

> A little girl of twenty-two months had been taken care of almost exclusively by her mother. On one occasion an aunt came to take care of her while the mother was away for the day. The aunt prepared lunch and brought the child's highchair close to the table. She swung the highchair's tray into place and set out the child's utensils and bib on the tray. Then she lifted the little girl to put her into the highchair. The child stiffened her body, curled up her feet, and refused to be put into the highchair. The puzzled aunt set the child down on the floor. The child pointed to the tray of the highchair and cried. Finally the aunt held the child on her lap to feed her her lunch, but the child was clearly upset and the feeding did not go well. A few days later the aunt was present to watch the child's mother give her lunch. The mother brought out the highchair *without* setting the tray in place. The little girl lifted up her arms to be picked up. Her mother set her in the highchair. The child held her head back so the mother could swing the tray over her head into place. The child lifted her chin and the mother fitted the bib under it. The child leaned forward and put her head down on the tray while the mother tied the bib behind her neck. Then the child sat up with a big smile, banged the tray with her hand, and said, "Milk!" She was ready for lunch.

Here we see the well-practiced integration of two people's activities. The sequence of behaviors is like a ballet. The participants know their own moves and they know the other's moves. It is as though each member of the pair possessed one-half of the same habit.

The fulfillment of the young child's daily needs requires the close integration of child's and caretaker's activities. The child cannot eat, dress, or go to the toilet alone—the cooperation of a partner is needed for all these activities. If the partners are accustomed to the details of each other's ways of doing things, the interaction goes well and the pair's mutual objective can be accomplished efficiently. Unfamiliar partners are upsetting because the child does not know how to start the interaction and keep it going to the desired conclusion. As a matter of fact, if the infant and a stranger *do* know their respective parts in a familiar routine—such as in a game of peek-a-boo—the child interacts comfortably with a stranger and does not show fear (Morgan and Ricciuti, 1969). Usually, however, individual children have worked out with their parents interactive routines that strangers do not know, and so they feel immobilized with a stranger. In other words, children need adults as their agents, and children's sense of control depends on the adults' noticing and understanding the children's signals and on their carrying out the necessary reciprocal actions. The child wants to be close to the person or persons with whom dependable interaction patterns have been established. The presence of these people is the guarantee that the child's own part of many activities can be carried out effectively.

The relationship between attachment and mutual signal-response systems is evident in extreme form in the case of deaf infants. Sadly, parents and pediatricians often do not recognize a child's deafness until well into the child's second year of life. The attachment of these undiagnosed children to their parents is often slow to develop and may be weak. In some cases, however, deafness is diagnosed early, and the mother and child can be taught a sign language that will facilitate communication. The process is laborious at first. The child's attention must be focused on the object being named (for example, a bottle of milk) while the adult makes a hand sign for *milk*. Usually, the adult also makes the appropriate lip and mouth movements. Thus, in the process of learning, the child receives three simultaneous pieces of visual information: the object to be named, the hand sign, and the correlated mouth movements. Many repetitions are necessary, and this is particularly true when the object—such as a clock on the wall—is not in the same field of vision as the trainer's hand and mouth and the child must look back and forth from object to trainer. Nevertheless, patient repetition does finally take effect, and once the connection between the object and the sign is understood, the child shows great excitement. By the end of the first year, the child is using signs to communicate. Surprisingly, a deaf child who is carefully taught can learn at least as many, and probably more, signs by the age of one year as can a hearing child who is learning vocal speech.

The people experimenting with teaching sign language to deaf infants (Schlesinger, 1980) faced a difficult issue: Should they have professional trainers spend an hour or so a day teaching the infant signs, or should they use the slower approach of teaching the mother to use sign language and having her teach the infant? The answer emerged quite quickly. When professional trainers were used, the infants became attached to the trainers! When the researchers changed their training methods so that the mothers learned sign language and became the teachers of their children, normal attachment bonds developed between the children and their mothers, and this relationship played an important part in the later successful socialization of the children. In the work of the Schlesinger research team, we see a clear demonstration of the importance of a mutually understood signal system in the development of attachment.

Roedell and Slaby's (1977) study of the factors that make a child either accept or reject the advances of an unfamiliar person illustrates the same point. Five-month-old infants were brought to the laboratory observation room on eight different occasions over a period of three weeks. On each visit three young women came in (one at a time) to be with an infant. Each stayed with the infant for eight minutes, but each interacted with the infant differently. One of the women interacted only in the *proximal mode*—that is, she patted, rocked, and carried the infant around the room; she did not smile or speak to the infant or play eye-contact games, but she did make sure that the infant could see her face. Another of the women interacted only in the *distal mode*— that is, she did not touch the infant, but smiled at, talked to, played peek-a-boo with, and in the other ways kept eye contact with the infant at a high level. The third experimenter was simply present, facing the infant, and did not interact either proximally or distally. For any given infant, the same woman played the same role in all eight sessions, but each woman played the other roles with other infants so that any differences in the infants' behavior toward them could not be attributed to some special characteristic of the particular women involved in the study.

On each of the eight days of the experiment, the infant's preference among the three strangers was measured by placing the infant in a specially designed wheeled walker and recording the infant's movement toward or away from the strangers. All the children previously had demonstrated at home that they knew how to use the walker for proximity-seeking purposes—they would consistently move it close to their mothers in the presence of a stranger. In the laboratory room the three strangers sat passively in front of the infant, at an equal distance from the child's starting point, and records were made of the infant's movements. The results are shown in Figure 2-4. Over eight sessions the infants showed an increasing preference for the *distal* interactor. Their interest in the noninteractor changed very little, and as the number of encounters increased, they showed less and less interest in the proximal interactor.

Does this experiment mean that contact comfort is not, after all, very important in building an infant's interest in being near a particular adult? We must remember that in real-life situations contact comfort is often initiated by the infant. The infant shows signs of distress and is then picked up and patted, or something frightening happens

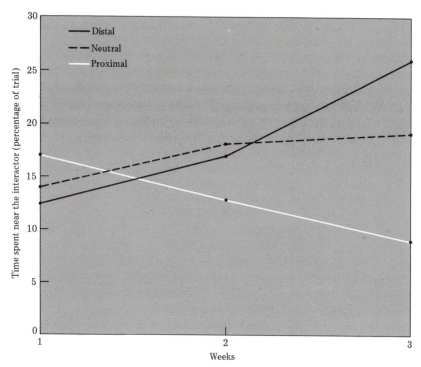

Figure 2-4. Infants' social preferences. Note the increase between weeks 2 and 3 in preference for the stranger who played eye-contact games, smiled, and talked and the decrease in preference for the stranger who interacted only with body contact. (Adapted from Roedell and Slaby, 1977)

and the infant goes to the adult, in whose arms fear is lessened. In the Roedell and Slaby experiment, the proximal interactor presumably initiated a good deal of the interaction—for example, by picking up a baby who had not signaled readiness for this intervention. In fact, by not responding in kind to the baby's vocalizations, smiles, and visual regard, the experimenter prevented the development of a signal system that would have allowed the infant to let the adult know whether the infant was ready to be picked up. From the infant's point of view, the interactor may have seemed to swoop down and move the infant about unpredictably in a way that left the infant little control over his or her own movements. This experiment does not show, then, that contact comfort is something infants usually avoid. Nor does it show that physical contact is unimportant in developing infants' relationships to others. It does show, however, that distal interaction— eye contact and responsive facial expressions—is important in establishing another person's attractiveness to an infant. We assume that this attraction rests on the development of a signal system. The experiment suggests, further, that infants prefer people who allow them to have a role in setting the pace of the interaction (see Ross and Goldman, 1977, for additional research demonstrating this point).

The sense of mastery as a causal factor in attachment

Let us return for a moment to the matter of *uncertainty* in a young child's life and the adult's role in assisting the child to function in unfamiliar situations. Every adult has experienced the feeling of disorganization that occurs on entry into an unfamiliar environment. The first day in a new school or college, the first few days in a new job, being a stranger in a foreign country and unable to understand the language that others are speaking—these are experiences that may be interesting and exciting but also often leave one feeling tense, tired, insecure. Infants are, in a very real sense, perpetual strangers, at least outside the narrow confines of their own daily routines in their own homes. They do not understand the language, and they do not know what kind of behavior to expect from others. They do not know the signals that might make it possible to anticipate and interpret the bewildering events occurring in the complexity of the vast spatial layout that surrounds them, and they are likely to get lost moving from one place to another. No wonder, then, the close presence of a familiar person becomes important.

Cairns (1966) has suggested that familiarity is, indeed, the key to attachment. We organize our own behavior around the familiar, he says. We can cope with moderate amounts of unfamiliar stimulation so long as the stimulation occurs in a context that is largely familiar. A parent is a highly salient stimulus to a little child, according to Cairns, so that in the parent's presence a large portion of the complex set of stimuli impinging on the child is automatically familiar. Is the young child willing to explore a novel environment only in a parent's presence because the parent's presence makes the situation as a whole seem largely familiar, as Cairns suggests? Or does the parent's presence perform some additional function? We cannot be sure, but it seems likely that the parent provides something beyond sheer familiarity. The child may learn to trust the parent's competence in dealing with aspects of strange situations that are beyond the child's own comprehension and control. So long as the child can *control* the parent—that is, know how to signal distress and be able to count on the parent's protective response—the child may not feel so helpless in the face of novel situations.

In the preceding discussion we have shifted the emphasis from familiarity to control because the two are related. Familiar sequences of events are predictable, and knowing what is going to happen gives us some sense of control over events. We can at least get set for oncoming events, and sometimes we can even avoid unpleasant consequences if we know how to read warning signals. Furthermore, in familiar situations with familiar people, we know how to alter the sequences of events by asserting our own objectives and getting others to take them into account. Considerable research now shows how important a sense of control is for optimum development (see Seligman, 1975). Recent work by Gunnar (1978), described in more detail in Chapter 7, has shown that children who could activate a potentially frightening mechanical toy by pressing a panel were less afraid of the toy than were children who saw it activated an equal number of times but who had no control over its onset. The relevance of this experiment for an infant's attachment behavior is at present a matter of speculation, but it may mean this: An infant will be less afraid of interacting with another person if the infant can control the other's movements. In fact, the mere presence of such a person will moderate fears of other aspects of the situation. Thus, the infant is more readily soothed by such a person. When we say that an infant can control an adult, we mean, in part, that the adult's actions are contingent on those of the child. The adult is predictably responsive. If the child does a given thing, the adult will do a given thing. The sense of being able to influence the actions of the caretaker is one of the developmental achievements of the first year of life—one of the factors that consolidates and organizes a child's attachment to those specific persons who are responsive.

Whether or not control and its fear-reducing properties are the key to the development of attachment, it has been demonstrated that *responsiveness* by the attachment object is a major factor. More will be said about this in the next chapter. For the present we will refer to an experiment by Cairns and Scholz (reported in Cairns, 1979). A wastebasket was suspended from the ceiling of a compartment where a lamb was isolated. The wastebasket was wired so that it would beep softly whenever it was jostled or pushed. At first the lambs that were tested with this contrivance were distressed by it and would occasionally attack it. After the first day they began to stay close to it and press their bodies against it. They would even show considerable distress if it were taken away. Thus, the simple fact that an object is perceptibly responsive to a young animal's movements can be the basis for the formation of an attachment.

To summarize the main points so far: We have been exploring several factors that are involved in the development of attachment. One factor is the adult's provision of comfort when the infant is distressed. And while a common form of distress in infancy is hunger, feeding is only one of the many ways in which adults can soothe children, and it is apparently not as important for the development of attachment as are holding, patting, rocking, and other forms of contact comfort. Infants find these kinds of body contact soothing when they are afraid, tired, in pain, cold, or distressed for any other reason. In addition to providing body contact, certain adults become familiar interaction partners. Through joint action with these individuals, infants can accomplish many things they cannot manage alone, and they come to seek the close presence of the people who provide this predictable, coordinated interaction.

Play as a causal factor in attachment

In completing our chronicle of factors underlying attachment, we must not overlook the sheer entertainment value of adults and their activities. Life can be boring for an infant or a toddler. The rate of a child's pestering for attention has repeatedly been shown to depend on whether there are toys or other interesting, novel objects available to absorb the child's interest. (Monkey infants also demand attention when bored: If they are alone with their mothers they make more bids for attention—more attempts to get their mothers to play—than if other monkey infants are also in the cage [Suomi, 1976].) People are the primary resource when a child has no toys or other interesting activities. And when given a choice, some children always seem to prefer people over objects. Not surprisingly, the people whom the child prefers are the ones who like to play with the child and provide interesting fun and games that are well adapted to the child's age-related capacities for joining in (Ross and Goldman, 1977). The adult who reads an inappropriately complex book to a child will not be a preferred playmate. But an adult who plays pat-a-cake with a six-month-old, rolls a ball back and forth with an eighteen-month-old, plays hide-and-seek with a two-year-old, and lets each child discover the elements in each new game without rushing is the person who will be greeted with excited anticipation and swarmed over with demands for action.

It is in the area of play that fathers come into their own. As we have seen, fathers are used by infants as a source of comfort when distressed, and they can serve as a secure base for exploration in a novel situation. Recent studies of fathers and newborns also suggest that fathers do not differ from mothers in (1) sensitivity to the infant's signals, (2) skillfulness in holding the newborn in a comfortable position, and (3) success in getting a baby to take a given amount of milk at a bottle feeding (Parke, 1978, presents an excellent summary of work on father-child interactions). In most families, however, the mother assumes primary responsibility for infant care and has more opportunities to comfort the baby and learn to interpret the baby's needs. The father usually sees less of the child during the day, and he often sets aside a period when he comes home from work for playing with the child. At this time the mother usually withdraws and leaves the father and child to their play while she does other things. Perhaps as a consequence of these patterns, the child commonly develops during the second year of life different relationships with the two parents. If both parents are present the mother becomes the source of comfort when the infant is distressed, and the father becomes the chosen person when the child is in the mood for play. The father's style of play is usually somewhat different from the mother's: He chooses rougher, more physical play, while she is likely to play conventional games like pat-a-cake, join the child in playing with a set of toys, or read to the child. More than one kind of satisfaction can be derived from an attachment object, and a given child will develop qualitatively different attachment relationships with several significant people in her or his life.

WHY ATTACHMENT GROWS LESS INTENSE

The infant's attachment is built primarily on two factors: the comfort provided by contact with the attachment figure when the child is distressed and the role of the attachment figure as a communication partner who may be relied on to understand the child's signals and to carry out (or to help carry out) the actions that the child needs to have performed and cannot perform alone. The child's intimate reliance on the attachment figure's ability to carry out these functions lessens during the third and fourth years of life. The child spontaneously ventures farther and farther away from the parent and is less and less upset over brief separations. What specific aspects of the child's growth permit this attenuation, this distancing, to take place?

First, the child's environment comes to seem less uncertain and fear provoking. The child's widening experience means that progressively more situations are familiar. Furthermore, cognitive growth enables the child to *classify* situations so that their relationship to previously encountered events can be seen. Classification is not an unmixed blessing, of course. Once a child has been frightened by a dog, the child is likely to transfer this fear to all objects classified as dogs—thus familiarity may *increase* and widen fear. But classification of new events into familiar categories generally mitigates strangeness and gives the child less reason to seek the security of contact with the attachment figure.

Second, the acquisition of language increases the infant's choice of communication partners. The signal system worked out between infant and mother can be quite an individual, personal thing (as we saw in the case of the two-year-old's preparation for lunch). A firm command of language, however, permits the child to participate in the signal system that is general for the culture. Other people besides familiar caretakers can now understand the child's needs. With some hope of success, the child and the stranger can merge their activities through the mediation of mutual verbal requests and explanations. The child has less need for the familiar caretakers as exclusive interaction partners or exclusive *agents* for the pursuit of the child's goals.

And finally, of course, the child can accomplish more and more without the cooperation of a partner. Dressing, eating, toileting, organizing for play, going from one place to another—all are increasingly under the child's own control.

Does all this mean that the child's need and love for others gradually dies away? Certainly not. Many of the child's needs and objectives continue to be social and can only be accomplished with a partner. We never outgrow the capacity for taking pleasure in touching and holding the people we love, but the need for the comfort of body contact does diminish rapidly after the age of about three. Children continue to need more distant forms of reassurance, however, and they do not stop needing to know that their attachment figures are available in situations that are frightening or beyond their capacity to handle. As one three-year-old said indignantly, on finding his mother after having lost sight of her in the grocery store, "Mom, I want you handy!"

Later transformation of the attachment relationship

We saw earlier that Bowlby postulates a fourth stage in attachment, beginning between the ages of two and three, when children begin to conceive of the attachment objects as separate selves. Robert Marvin (1977) expands on this point, arguing that during these years the attachment relationship is not weakened but rather is *transformed*:

1. By the age of about one year children have started trying to influence their caretakers' behavior. By certain direct actions they attempt to get their caretakers to act on their behalf. In short, children are attempting to insert their own plans into the caretakers' ongoing plan of action.

2. During the second and third years, children learn to modify their own plans—adapting themselves to their partners' plans. In other words, they weave the caretakers' plans into their stream of behavior at the same time that they attempt to insert their plan into the adults'. Thus, for example, a mother may ask her little boy to wait for her to read him a story until she finishes a telephone call. His inhibition of demands and temporary cessation of attempts to climb onto her lap represent his acceptance of her plan and the integration of it with his own. The development of a verbal communication system

facilitates such mutual adaptation. The boy can tell his mother what he wants her to do; she can tell him what she wants him to do; then they can develop a joint, integrated plan.

3. Even though the child learns to take account of the mother's demands in the process of making his or her own demands, this response does not mean that the child views the mother as a person with separate plans and thoughts. The child is responding to the mother's actions, not to her *intentions*. Not until about the age of four will the child begin to understand that the mother is a separate self, with her own patterns of thoughts and motives.

When this third step occurs, the nature of the relationship changes. The child no longer needs to find security through physical contact or proximity. A shared set of ideas, goals, and plans now permits the child to be confident that even when the mother is out of sight, she is acting in ways that are integrated with the child's own plans of action. The child is not upset by separation if the reasons for leaving and the plans to return at a certain time are clear, for the child's own plans can then conform to the mother's. But if the mother's departure seems capricious, unexplained, and unrelated to the child's needs and activities, the balance of mutually integrated plans is disturbed.

Marvin illustrates in fascinating detail the difference between the reactions of four-year-olds and those of three- or two-year-olds to the mother's leaving a Strange Situation. The scenario calls for the mother to say that she has to make a phone call and will be back soon. Among a group of four-year-olds, nearly half immediately agreed to the mother's departure. When the mother returned, these children greeted her cheerfully but did not show any marked tendency to go close to her or to hang on to her. There was another group, however, who did not agree to her departure. The children in this group asked her why she had to go, followed her to the door, begged to be taken along, and cried when she left. Their crying did not have the frightened, helpless quality of younger children left alone; it was angry and seemed somehow more deliberate. When the stranger came in, these children were willing to calm down and play with her, but they seemed to harbor some resentment toward the mother, for when she returned they moved close to her and became insistent and strangely demanding. Here is a rather extreme example of one of the children's behavior on the mother's return:

Child: I want a glass of water.
Mother: Pretty soon, as soon as we leave.
Child: I want it now!
Mother: They don't have any water in here.

Child: Yes they dooo! (It was quite obvious that we didn't.)
Mother: Well, you can have some as soon as we leave.
Child: Noooo, now!
Mother: We can't just go wandering around this building looking for water.
Child: But I need a drink of waterrrr!
Child: I want to get up on you.
Mother: But look at all the toys to play with.
Child: But I want to get up on you. Help me! (Mother helps the child up.)
Mother: O.K., you can sit on my lap.
Child: No, I wanna glass of water!
Mother: You can have some as soon as we leave; it'll only be a minute.
Child: I want some beer!
Mother: Beer? Beer isn't for little girls.
Child: Yes it is.
Mother: No it isn't.
Child: Yes it is.
Mother: No it isn't.
Child: Yes it is. (Marvin, 1977, pp. 44–45)

This interchange reminds us of the unreasonable demands that children sometimes make when they are put to bed against their will. What was happening, at least according to Marvin's interpretation, was that the mother's behavior had upset the equilibrium—the mutual understanding about each other's activities—that usually permitted mother and child to integrate their plans. The mother had refused to listen to the child's reasons for wanting to come along and had not been willing to adjust her own behavior to the child's. When she reappeared, the child appeared to be attempting to restore the balance by directing controlling actions toward her. Evidently, the little girl wanted to prove to herself that the mother had resumed her willingness to listen, negotiate, and comply.

We have been describing a change in the nature of the objectives in the child's relationship with the primary attachment figure. Of course, simply being near the loved person—which was the child's first goal—continues to be a source of satisfaction throughout life. But as the child matures the attachment partner begins to be conceived of as a person, and the relationship becomes a reciprocal meshing of two individual streams of behavior, such that each partner takes account of the other's needs, actions, and plans. The child's goal becomes the maintenance of the relationship, and this is now possible over at least brief periods of separation. However, frequent communication is required so that the partners can adapt themselves to changes in each other's plans of action. Physical proximity is no longer of paramount importance, except for its role in guaranteeing communication.

A child who is able to enter such a relationship has moved into a realm that is strictly human (so far as we know), and the close similarity between young children and young monkeys breaks down. While the vastly more sophisticated linguistic communication system among human beings probably makes the transition possible, other cognitive abilities also facilitate the change. What must the young child be able to do in order to enter into an attachment relationship that involves coordination of the activities of two *selves*? Marvin suggests two possibilities:

1. Inhibition and taking turns. When two people integrate their behavior they must take turns, and taking turns involves inhibition. In conversation, for example, people speak successively, not simultaneously, so each inhibits her or his own speech while the other person is speaking. In a simple ball game, one person throws the ball and then waits while the other person retrieves it and throws it back. Similarly, when a mother must finish a telephone call before attending to her child's needs, she promises to play in a minute, and the child inhibits the seeking of contact. After the telephone call, the mother postpones (inhibits) whatever other action she might have intended in order to fulfill her agreement and play with the child.

2. Conceptualizing another person. When children are very young they have little understanding of what other people know, what they intend, what they want. For a mature attachment relationship, each person must construct a schema of the other person. Such a schema involves knowledge of how the other person will probably react to one's own actions, what the other person likes or dislikes, how the other person normally organizes his or her time. In other words, attachment requires each partner to see events from the other person's perspective.

In later chapters we will discuss the development of children's ability to inhibit ongoing action (Chapter 5) and to take the perspective of others (Chapter 8). For the present it is sufficient to note that these and other relevant changes do occur and that they affect the nature of the child's attachment relationships. And of course, as the child changes, so must the parent. No longer is the parent's reciprocal role primarily to reach out and offer comfort or to serve as the child's agent in satisfying the child's moment-to-moment needs. The parent increasingly plays an organizing role—setting up situations so the child can function well. And the parent also increasingly makes demands and insists that the child take the parent's needs into account.

Clearly, a great deal of variation is possible from one parent-child pair to another in the way the early attachment relationship develops and how (and *when*) it is transformed as the child grows older. These variations are our topic in Chapter 3.

SUMMARY AND COMMENTARY

We began this chapter by examining the formation of attachment bonds between newborns and adults in several animal species. We found that the primary attachments are almost always formed between the infant and the biological mother, although there are species in which both the maternal animals and the newborn young will fairly readily accept substitutes for one another.

Major themes are:

1. Mother and infant have coordinated biological systems that predispose them to be responsive to one another. Within a given species these instinctive behaviors *match*. If the infant has a built-in reflexive response to certain stimuli produced by the mother, the mother will have a matching instinct that causes her to respond to the infant's behavior and to the sight, sound, smell, or touch of the infant in such a way that the two will be drawn together and their actions will be coordinated.

2. The close attachment between mothers and infants follows a predictable developmental course that is quite consistent among the animals of a given species. Attachment wanes when certain growth changes take place in the infant and when certain physiological changes (for example, the resumption of estrous cycles) take place in the mother. However, the period of strong attachment may be shortened or prolonged under certain conditions.

3. The instinctive behaviors of mother and infant are quickly modified or consolidated through learning. Among higher animals the social organization of the group determines the nature of the social contacts a young animal will have and the kinds of attachments it will form. And social organization depends, at least in part, on the habitat in which the group lives.

Thus, among higher mammals it is correct to say that attachment behavior is instinctive and also that it is learned. Instinct and learning are not antagonistic or mutually exclusive processes—they depend on one another.

The development of mutual attachments between human parents and their infants shows many similarities to the patterns found among subhuman primates. But there are differences as well. Major aspects of developmental change are:

4. While newborn infants are initially highly attracted by certain features that adult human beings possess and are soothed by certain things they do, the infant does not immediately become attached to specific adults. By about the fourth month,

infants clearly show that they recognize and prefer their mothers and perhaps one or two other persons as well. By the age of seven months, they usually protest separation from specific attachment figures and show wariness toward strangers.

5. Attachment as shown by protest and distress over separation usually reaches its peak intensity and frequency somewhere between the ages of fourteen and eighteen months. The peak is quite similar in different cultures and does not appear to be affected substantially by variations in rearing conditions.

6. At about the age of three-and-a-half or four years, the goal of attachment shifts for most children from simply maintaining proximity to maintaining more distant contact through the coordination of plans and mutual agreements.

The development of the infant's attachment to specific persons is based on several aspects of the interaction between them. While feeding plays a role, it is overshadowed by two other processes:

7. Body contact between an infant and an adult is a strong factor in producing a specific attachment and has been shown to calm both infants and mothers (for example, physiological indicators of stress, such as rapid heart rate or high levels of blood cortisol decline with such body contact).

8. More distant forms of communication also build specific attachments. Infants seek proximity to persons with whom they frequently achieve eye contact and who respond contingently and reciprocally to the infant's own smiles and vocalizations.

For a very young child, the familiar adult caretaker is the child's agent and cooperating partner in action sequences that the child cannot yet carry out alone. The suggestion was made that children need to have some degree of control over important events in their lives and that this includes a sense of control over the actions of the adults with whom they must interact to achieve their objectives. In a sense, the responsive adult has agreed to be predictable and to allow his or her actions to depend on what the child does—and it may be this aspect of contingent responsiveness that binds the child close. The responsiveness of adults, however, has its limits, and as children grow older, adults are less and less willing to be their always-available servants. As children begin to understand the purposes of others, how to fit their own objectives into other people's plans, and how to be responsive as well as how to demand responses from others, the attachment relationship between the adult and child is transformed into a more balanced partnership.

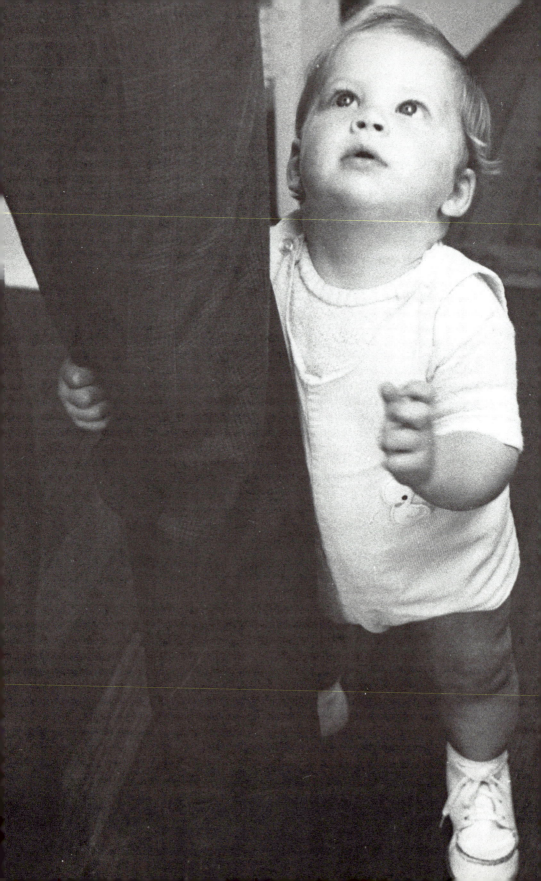

CHAPTER 3

How Children Differ in

Their Attachments

W E have been tracing the development of the uniform attachment patterns that characterize the behavior of most
children in most living situations. Now we turn our
attention to differences—to the considerable variations that exist
among children. Children progress at different rates through the developmental changes we have been describing. Mother-child pairs
also differ in the quality of their attachments. In this chapter we
will first describe some of these differences. Then we will consider
how the differences come about and the effect of these differences
on other aspects of the child's development.

SECURE AND INSECURE ATTACHMENT

Children show very different reactions to separation—some seem
intensely upset, others appear scarcely bothered by the absence of
their mothers or other principal caretakers. A great deal of what we
know about the differences in the quality of children's attachments
derives from short-term observations of small samples of children participating with their mothers in experiments like Ainsworth's Strange
Situation. We must therefore ask whether the differences that are reported are persistent behavioral characteristics that continue to charac-

terize individual children over time. We must also ask as we look at securely and insecurely attached children not only what the mother brings to the attachment interaction, but what the child contributes.

The consistency of individual children

Anyone observing a group of children in the Strange Situation is struck by the differences in the way mother-child pairs relate to one another. Most children, if they are young enough, are distressed by their mothers' departure, especially when the mothers leave them alone in the strange room without any other adult caretaker. But not all children show joy and relief when their mothers return. While some are comforted by their mothers' presence and quickly return to play, others seem anxious and stay close to their mothers for considerable periods, ignoring the toys. Can we describe some children as more attached than others? Schaffer and Emerson (1964b) scored the intensity of their Scottish infants' attachments during each monthly home visit (judgment of attachments was based on the infants' response to separations). They found that starting from the age at which a specific attachment first appears in each child, individual infants show moderate consistency from one month to the next in attachment intensity. The consistency does not last very long, however. For example, from knowing how strongly attached a child was at twelve months, the researchers could not predict whether attachment would be strong or weak (compared with other children) at eighteen months.

Other studies have attempted to trace consistencies over time in such behaviors as how often individual children look or smile at their mothers, how close they stay to them, and how upset they are over separation. We saw in Chapter 2 that these aspects of attachment change a good deal as children grow older. Nevertheless, individual children conceivably could maintain a high or low rate of these behaviors relative to other children even if the level of the behavior was changing in the group as a whole. In fact, however, little consistency can be seen over intervals of several months (Masters and Wellman, 1974). On the basis of this evidence alone, we might conclude that from one age period to another, no children continue to be exceptionally clingy, exceptionally resistant to separation, or exceptionally likely to look and smile at their mothers. And indeed, such a conclusion should not be too surprising in view of the growth changes that we know take place.

There is another possibility, however. Perhaps consistency does exist—perhaps children do remain strongly or weakly attached over relatively long periods of time—but we have been looking at the wrong indicators of the attachment. Changes in the frequency of a behavior like smiling may not mean that the child's attachment needs are different, but may mean only that the child can satisfy these needs in new ways. A child who cannot yet talk may achieve contact with the mother by crawling after her from room to room or by climbing onto her lap and turning her face in the child's own direction. But once this child can talk (even a little), she or he may be quite satisfied to maintain more distant contact. Perhaps over considerable periods of time, the strength or weakness of attachment remains relatively constant, but changes take place in the way the attachment is expressed, so the continuity is not revealed by correlating specific behavioral indicators. In short, perhaps we need to look for continuity in the meaning of certain behaviors, rather than in the behavior itself.

Determining what a bit of behavior means is difficult, in part because meaning is not constant. A child who is playing happily ten feet from the mother in an experimental room may be (1) only weakly attached (or even unattached), (2) so comfortably attached that immediate physical contact is not necessary for reassurance, or (3) reassured by distance contact (looking or speaking). We can only determine the meaning of a proximity score by considering it in conjunction with other related behaviors. Furthermore, proximity seeking is so much influenced by other factors—the familiarity with the elements in the situation, the immediately preceding events, the age of the child—that simply measuring the distance between a mother and child without taking these factors into account tells us little about the child's enduring characteristics. To understand attachment—or any other behavior—observations must be analyzed *in relation to context and age* (see Sroufe and Waters, 1977, for an excellent discussion of the issues involved in looking for "meaning" or functional equivalence in specific behavioral indicators).

A typology of attachment behaviors

Ainsworth and her colleagues have attempted to take account of age and context, and they have achieved considerable success. In a study of Ugandan infants, Ainsworth (1967) made a series of visits to the homes of a group of infants and observed the infants' interactions with their mothers over several months of development. Ainsworth was struck by the consistencies during this time in the behavior of individual mother-child pairs. Most pairs seemed to have a comfortable relationship from which the infant derived security, but certain infants seemed to be *insecurely* attached. These children showed a good deal of tension in their interactions with their mothers and could not be easily comforted by their mothers when they were upset. Nevertheless, they clung strongly to their mothers when upset and were greatly distressed on separation. Since the completion of the African study, Ainsworth and her colleagues have observed many American infants with their mothers and have refined the classification. They use the Strange Situation as their primary method for assessing the quality of an infant's attachment. With this information, they are able to identify three types of attachment:[1]

> Type A. *Avoidant.* In the preseparation phase of the experiment, exploration of toys by an avoidant infant is relatively unaffected by the mother's whereabouts in the room. When the mother reappears following separation, this type of infant usually ignores her. If the infant greets the mother at all, the approach is tentative: After starting to approach, the child may turn or look or move away. The avoidant infant is not particularly distressed by separation from the mother and is as easily comforted by a stranger as by the mother.
>
> Type B. *Securely attached.* The securely attached infant plays comfortably with toys, usually reacts positively to strangers, and does not stay particularly close to the mother in the preseparation phase of observation. Play is considerably reduced during the mother's absence, and the child's distress is obvious. When the mother returns, the securely attached child goes to her immediately, seeking contact, calms quickly in her arms, and then is able to resume play. These children show neither avoidance or resistance toward the mother.
>
> Type C. *Resistant.* The resistant child is likely to be fussy and wary in the preseparation episode and to have difficulty using the mother as a secure base for exploration. Upon reunion after separation, the resistant infant seeks contact with the mother but simultaneously resists contact and shows anger. For example, the child may go quickly to the mother and reach out to be picked up and then, when picked up, struggle to get down. These children do not return readily to play, but remain uninvolved and direct frequent glances toward the mother.

Type A and C children are sometimes grouped together as anxious or as insecurely attached. Subgroups within these major types have been identified, but the classification into the three broad groups is adequate for the purpose of searching for individual stability and investigating the home conditions that underlie variations in the quality of attachment.

Ainsworth and others have found that Type B is by far the most common pattern. Type A, while rare, is especially interesting because it seems to imply the *absence* of an emotional relationship between mother and child. There are reasons to be cautious about this conclusion, however. Sroufe and Waters (1977) have monitored infants' heart

---

[1] These descriptions are a composite, taken from Ainsworth, Bell, and Stayton (1971) and Sroufe and Waters (1977).

rate during the Strange Situation, and they report that Type A infants maintain accelerated heart rates during reunion with their mothers, even while they are avoiding them—a finding that indicates that the infants are responding emotionally, even while seeming to ignore their mothers.

The Ainsworth classification makes it possible to show stability in the quality of a child's primary attachment, at least during the relatively short time spans over which the matter has so far been studied. Waters (reported in Sroufe and Waters, 1977) classified fifty infants at the age of twelve months and saw the same group of infants again (with their mothers, in the Strange Situation) at the age of eighteen months. At twelve months, nine children were classified as As (avoidant); nine were classified as Cs (resistant); and the remainder were Bs. Six months later the infants were again observed in the Strange Situation, and an independent classification placed forty-eight of the fifty in the same group as before. In short, almost all the individual infants maintained the same qualitative pattern of attachment over a six-month period. Securely attached infants remained so, at least for six months, and disturbances in the attachment relationship also remained constant over the same period.

The infants studied by Waters were being raised by middle-class parents, and their family environments were generally quite stable. Recent work with a group of impoverished families, in which there was considerable stress and instability, has shown more change in infants' attachments (Vaughn et al., in press). This finding suggests that children's early attachment patterns do not become permanent characteristics. If important aspects of their life situation (such as maternal responsiveness—see the following section) change, the children can shift from secure to insecure attachments, or vice versa.

The mother's contribution to attachment

We have seen that most infants become securely attached to their mothers (and often to other people as well) by the age of one year. But some infants do not. How can we explain these differences? There can be little doubt that the nature of the attachment is related to the way in which parents respond to their infants. Ainsworth and her colleagues have studied the mother-infant interaction to see whether patterns prevailing during the first year will predict the strength or weakness of attachment to the mother at the age of one year.

In the first study (Ainsworth and Bell, 1969), twenty-six mother-infant pairs were observed in their families' homes at least every three weeks during the first three months of the infant's life. Detailed records were made of feeding behaviors: the timing of feedings, how quickly the mother responded to the infant's hunger cries, how much the mother coaxed or attempted to force the infant to eat, whether the baby was overfed or underfed, and whether the mother allowed the baby to reject a new food.

Feeding an infant can take a long time;[2] mothers need rest and have other things they must do. Most mothers attempt to move their infants toward some sort of schedule and try to get them to take enough food so they will not be hungry again too soon. Infants, however, do not always cooperate in these efforts: They dawdle, lose interest before their mothers think they are really finished, and sometimes take brief naps. A mother may attempt to keep her infant aroused and feeding by tickling or slapping the infant's feet, shaking the infant, or stimulating the infant's mouth by moving the nipple back and forth. Another mother may let her baby set the pace. Many mothers take an intermediate path, making brief efforts to keep the feeding going, but not persisting in these efforts if their babies seem too unwilling.

When offering solid foods, mothers vary greatly in their responsiveness to their infants' reactions. A mother may time her approach with the spoon, carefully waiting until the baby's mouth is open. Another mother may thrust the spoon into the baby's mouth before the previous bite has been swallowed. When introducing a new food, some mothers watch to see their baby's reaction and govern the next move accordingly. If the baby makes a face and spits out the food, the mother will try a different food or offer the rejected food on another occasion, when the baby may be more willing to take it. Other mothers persist, and some perceive the infants' lack of compliance as stubbornness and feel they must win this early battle of the wills. If a mother yields to her baby's resistance, she fears the baby will have established a pattern of not respecting parental authority.

These variations in feeding patterns are not entirely due to the sensitivity or lack of sensitivity of the mothers, of course. Some infants are much easier to feed than others. Some infants become voraciously hungry, others have delicate appetites. Some infants quickly consume fairly large quantities of food, and then sleep a long time; others eat or drink slowly, lose interest quickly, and then quickly become hungry again, presenting incessant demands that require a great deal of patience on the part of the caretaker. When we detect differences between mother-child pairs in the feeding situation, we cannot be sure whether the source of the differences lies in the mother, in the child, or in both.

Ainsworth and Bell identified nine feeding patterns, which could be arranged roughly along a continuum reflecting degree of maternal responsiveness to the infant's signals and states. They then asked whether knowing the kind of feeding pattern that developed during

---

[2] An extreme case: One mother of premature twins reports that for several weeks the infants became hungry every two hours. It took an hour to feed each child—the round-the-clock demands on the exhausted parents defy imagining!

the first three months would make it possible to predict whether the child would be securely or insecurely attached at the age of twelve months. Prediction was possible. They observed in the Strange Situation twenty-three of the original twenty-six infants and they found that every one-year-old whose mother's feeding patterns reflected relatively high sensitivity showed secure (Type B) attachment. Among the twelve one-year-olds whose mothers were relatively insensitive in feeding, ten showed either avoidant (Type A) or resistant (Type C) attachment behavior, and only two showed secure attachment. Thus, the kind of pattern that develops during early feeding interaction seems to persist and show up later in situations quite unrelated to feeding.

The same mother-infant pairs were observed at home during the last half of the first year, and once again the relationship of the mother's caretaking style to the security of the child's attachment at twelve months was studied. The mothers were rated on four dimensions (these descriptions are condensed from Ainsworth, Bell, and Stayton, 1971):

1. *Sensitivity-insensitivity*. This scale deals with the mother's response to the infant's signals and communications. The sensitive mother is able to see things from the baby's point of view, and she interprets the baby's signals correctly. The sensitive mother makes her responses temporally contingent on the baby's signals and communications. In contrast, the insensitive mother's interventions and initiations of interaction reflect, almost exclusively, her own wishes, moods, and activities. This mother may distort the implications of her baby's communications; often she does not respond at all.

2. *Acceptance-rejection*. An accepting mother may occasionally feel irritated by her baby. But in general she cheerfully accepts being tied down to some extent by baby care; she shows relatively little irritation over the baby's bad moods; and she enjoys the good moods. The rejecting mother has feelings of anger and resentment that outweigh her affection for the baby. Her feelings may be shown by openly saying that she finds the child an irritating nuisance, frequently opposing the child's wishes, maintaining an atmosphere of irritation and scolding, or all these things.

3. *Cooperation-interference*. The cooperative mother respects the baby's autonomy and tries to avoid situations in which she will have to interrupt the baby's activities or exert direct control. If she must exert control, she tries to get the baby into a good mood so that her direction will seem congenial. The interfering mother imposes her will on the child with little concern for the child's mood or current activity. She attempts to

shape the child to her own standard, and her efforts toward this end can be quite abrupt or forceful.

4. *Accessibility-ignoring.* The accessible mother is tuned in to the baby's signals so that she notices them even at some distance and when other things are going on. The ignoring mother is preoccupied with her own activities and thoughts—she often fails to notice the child's signals and seems to forget about the child except at the times she has scheduled a caretaking task or when there is an intensification of the child's signals.

These four dimensions of behavior are, of course, interrelated: A mother who is sensitive is usually also accepting, more cooperative than interfering, and more likely to be accessible than to ignore the baby. Many mothers were not consistent: Sometimes they would respond sensitively to the babies' signals and at other times they would not. Most mothers in this and other studies by the Ainsworth group can be classified as either highly responsive or somewhat inconsistent in responsiveness; a small minority, however, are consistently insensitive.

How do these patterns of mothering relate to the type of attachment the child displays in the Strange Situation at the age of twelve months? The securely attached (Type B) infants had mothers who were above the midpoint on all four responsiveness scales; that is, these mothers had been sensitive, accepting, cooperative, and accessible during the preceding three months. The mothers of the two types of insecurely attached infants were differentiated in the following ways: Type A (avoidant) infants had mothers who had been rejecting and insensitive; Type C (resistant) infants had mothers who had been rejecting but had tended to be either interfering or ignoring.

In interpreting their findings, Ainsworth and her colleagues argue that different styles of mothering have important consequences for the child's development. The researchers clearly imply that certain patterns represent good mothering—mothering that enables a child to become securely attached and to take subsequent developmental steps more readily. In this study they observed a small sample of mother-child pairs and they found relatively few cases of inadequate mother-child interaction. Are their findings too limited to form a basis for generalizations about the effects of maternal behavior on children's development? Valid generalizations require confirming evidence from other samples of children.

Clarke-Stewart (1973) has found evidence that supports some of the Ainsworth group's ideas. She conducted seven home visits to each of thirty-six infants from the time the infants were one-and-a-half months old until they were eighteen months old. At the age of twelve months the infants and their mothers participated in a replica of Ainsworth's Strange Situation. The information of interest for our present purposes was obtained from observations of mother-infant interaction during the home visit when the infants were eleven months old. Mothers were scored on several dimensions, including:

1. *Responsiveness.* The proportion of the child's bids (calls, cries, vocal demands, and so forth) to which the mother responds.
2. *Expression of positive emotion.* The frequency of affectionate touching, plus smiles, plus praise, plus social speech, all divided by the amount of time the child is awake.
3. *Social stimulation.* The frequency with which the mother comes close to, smiles at, talks to, or imitates the child, divided by the amount of time the child is awake.

These dimensions are not precisely the same as those described by the Ainsworth group but the similarities are sufficient to permit a search for consistencies in findings.

From observations in the Strange Situation, Clarke-Stewart classified children into attachment categories that are similar (but not identical) to those used by the Ainsworth group. The results are shown in Figure 3-1. The mothers of securely attached infants had high scores on all three behavioral dimensions. Children who were labeled *unattached* (similar in several respects to Ainsworth's Type A, avoidant group) and those labeled *malattached* (like the Type C, resistant children) had mothers who (on the average) received low scores on these dimensions. The mothers of Type A and Type C children were not clearly different from each other.

Clarke-Stewart also used an additional measure of attachment—children were not classified into types, but rather were arranged along a scale of attachment intensity. This measure was based on observations of interaction in the home. Infants who were rated as strongly attached (they frequently looked at, smiled at, stayed close to, followed, and gave objects to their mothers) had mothers who had received high scores on responsiveness, positive emotion, and stimulation. Thus, the two methods of measurement yielded similar results.

In both studies maternal sensitivity and responsiveness appear to be the central elements in the formation of secure attachment. And a finding from Ainsworth's early (1967) work with Ugandan mother-infant pairs gives further support to this view. In interviewing the African mothers, Ainsworth found that some were able to report minute details about their babies' reactions and progress, while others seemed quite vague about their infants' characteristics and often could not answer questions about the infants' preferences and reactions. The well-informed mothers were the ones whose infants developed the most secure attachments during the time that the home visits took place. We may assume that the well-developed information store reflects the mother's history of attentiveness and sensitivity to her child.

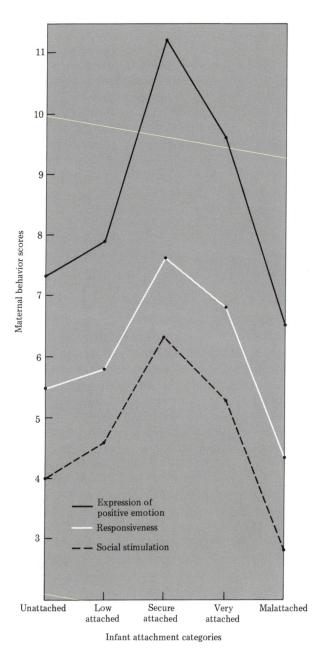

Figure 3-1. Relation between maternal behavior and infants' attachment. Note that the mothers of securely attached infants had the highest scores on all three dimensions of behavior. (From Clarke-Stewart, 1973)

The mother of a securely attached child, then, is a mother who *notices* what her child is doing. When the child signals her, she is concerned about interpreting the signals accurately. In short, she is a good communications partner.

The child's contribution to attachment

We have been discussing studies of secure and insecure attachment as if the mother's behavior were solely responsible for the extent of the child's attachment. In fact, attachment grows out of an interaction pattern between two individuals, and insecurely attached infants may be children whom no mother could easily relate to. Would a given mother have developed a more responsive pattern with a more responsive infant? Perhaps some infants invite and others resist the maternal behavior that leads to attachment.

In the longitudinal study by Schaffer and Emerson (1964a and b), mothers reported that from their first days of life certain infants seemed to resist being held and cuddled. In home visits these non-cuddlers seemed restless, and they resisted the restraints imposed by clothing and bed covers. Schaffer (1971) suggests that these children may simply have been exceptionally active. In any case, they were somewhat slow in developing specific attachments to their caretakers. Although they did develop normal attachments, contact between the mother and child took the form of mutual looking and talking, with less than the usual amount of body contact. Temperamental characteristics of infants, then, can shape the form of the mother's responsiveness. Beyond this, we can only speculate that infants who are difficult to soothe when crying (colicky babies, for example) may not support their mothers' responsiveness, but may instead discourage interest in helping them.

Some suggestive trends regarding the child's role in the interaction have recently emerged from studies of mothers and infants who are handicapped in some way. We saw earlier that deaf infants are often slow to develop normal attachments to their mothers. Jones (1977) worked with children who have Downs' syndrome (popularly called mongolism), and he found abnormalities in the pattern of interaction between the mother and child. He compared a group of these retarded children, aged thirteen to twenty-three months, with six younger infants of normal intelligence who were matched with respect to scores on developmental tests. He then made detailed, moment-to-moment observations of the interactions between the infants and their mothers. He distinguished between interchanges in which the mother was inviting the child to do or say something and those in which the child initiated the interchange and the mother merely responded. In most of the Downs' syndrome mother-child pairs, the balance of the initiative lay with the mother, while with normal children it was usually with the child. Furthermore, the normal infants were more likely than the retarded infants to glance at their mothers—this *referential* glance seemed to be making some reference to the child's ongoing activity and inviting some sort of reaction from the mother. Jones gives this example: "Child bangs drum, looks up, pausing in activity, mother nods, smiles and says 'Yes, that's right! You banged it, didn't you?' Child continues banging drum. It was almost as if the look meant 'Look at me, aren't I clever?' " (p. 394).

If we may hazard a generalization from Jones's small sample, it seems likely that normal infants tend to take the initiative in inviting maternal response, while retarded infants (who are at the same level of development in other respects) do not take initiative. We may suspect, further, that when infants take the initiative, their mothers are more likely to be classified as responsive by observers, but when mothers take the initiative they appear to be more intrusive and less sensitive to their infants. Thus, the finding that mothers of securely attached infants are more responsive may reflect a circular process: The mother's responsiveness is partly an outcome of characteristics of the child (as well as the mother's own preexisting tendencies), and at the same time the mother's responsiveness has an effect on the nature of the child's attachment.

THE CONSEQUENCES OF EARLY ATTACHMENT

How much does the nature of early attachment matter in a child's subsequent development? This is a controversial issue. Kohlberg (1969) questions whether early relationships have any important effect on an individual's capacity for forming relationships later in life unless interpersonal traumas are so extreme in infancy that they produce serious retardation in cognitive growth. He raises this question because he believes that the quality of relationships is so greatly transformed during cognitive growth that it is difficult to imagine how there could be any continuities between an infant's attachments and the affectional ties formed at later stages by the more mature individual.

Others—specifically, Erikson (1950) and Bowlby (1969)—strongly believe that the nature of the mother-infant bond is important for later development. Erikson says:

> Mothers create a sense of trust in their children by that kind of administration which, in its quality, combines sensitive care of the baby's individual needs and a firm sense of personal trustworthiness within the trusted framework of their culture's life styles. This forms the basis in

the child for a sense of identity which will later combine a sense of being "all right," or being oneself, and of becoming what other people trust one will become. (p. 249)

The issue is a profoundly important one. Does the quality of the mother-infant bond really affect the social and nonsocial competencies of later life, when activities extend beyond the narrow confines of the home? If the mother-infant pair gets off to a poor start, can the situation later be rectified? Two types of research have supplied some answers to these questions: (1) studies of both monkey and human infants who have experienced what is called *maternal deprivation* and (2) long-term studies of children with different early attachments. The deprivation studies assess two types of infants: those who have had no opportunity to form a close attachment with any one parent (due to isolation from adults or residence in institutions in which personnel changed frequently) and those whose early attachments were disrupted by separation from their attachment figures. The long-term studies follow the development of children with different kinds of attachments to see whether the children's later personality development is related in any way to their early attachment patterns. We will first briefly summarize some of the work on maternal deprivation and then turn to a fuller consideration of the development of children who have different patterns of early attachments.

Maternal deprivation in monkeys

In Chapter 2 we discussed the work of Harlow and his colleagues, pointing out that their young monkeys seemed able to use a soft but inanimate surrogate mother for purposes of gaining contact comfort and that this comfort enabled the infants to explore a strange environment. This account provided no information on the young monkey's subsequent development. As it turned out, they were not normal in their social behavior. As juveniles some of the surrogate-reared animals were placed with normally reared age mates, but they were notably defective in their ability to interact with the normal monkeys. They either withdrew in fright, were unusually aggressive, or were both by turns. When they reached sexual maturity they did not engage in normal sexual activity, appearing not to know the necessary pattern of reciprocal behaviors. The males never bred successfully. A few of the females, caged with experienced normal males, were eventually mated, but when their infants were born the new mothers proved to be as deficient in normal maternal behavior as they had been in sexual behavior. They would sit on their infants, hold them upside down by one foot, push them away, and, on occasion, attack them. They were much more competent with a second infant—the first ones had apparently educated their mothers to a considerable extent.

Is interaction with an animate, reacting mother necessary for normal social development in monkeys? Harlow and his colleagues allowed infant monkeys to have the company of other infants while continuing to be deprived of interaction with adult animals. Exposure to age mates in infancy seemed to counteract a number of the effects of maternal deprivation. Animals reared without mothers but with age mates are more timid about exploring their environment than are normally reared animals (Meyer et al., 1975). However, they show normal patterns of sexual and maternal behavior in adulthood. Apparently, the important element in social development is interaction with at least one other reacting species member.

Could the damage done by total isolation during infancy be reversed by any later form of social contact? Initial attempts at "therapy" with these animals did not have very encouraging results. Providing extended social contact with normal monkeys was difficult because the isolated monkeys' excessive aggressiveness disrupted the normal social life in the cage. However, some of the isolated animals have been rehabilitated by caging them with normal infants (Novak, 1979; Novak and Harlow, 1975; Suomi and Harlow, 1972). The isolates do not usually initiate interaction with their small cage mates and may threaten them and push them away when they approach. However, they are less aggressive than they would be toward older monkeys, and the infants persist in approaching and clinging. The infants also attempt to initiate bouts of play. Although the isolates are slow to respond at first, they do eventually warm up and begin to hold the infant close when it clings, and they even begin to initiate play. After a period of such experience they can be introduced with good success into a normal cage-living group. Brandt and Mitchell (1973) succeeded in rehabilitating young monkeys after six months of isolation by placing them with older (but still preadolescent) females, who accepted their initially provocative behavior. Preadolescent males were not such successful therapists: They tended to counteraggress. Thus, the formation of normal social attachments by a previously isolated animal seems to depend very much on the receptiveness and tolerance of the host.

Rehabilitation is possible but difficult, and early social deprivation may have long-lasting effects. One interpretation of the effects is that monkeys become adapted to whatever living conditions they find themselves in and, therefore, isolated animals become adapted to isolated living and socially reared animals, to social living (see Cairns, 1979, for a forceful exposition of this viewpoint). However, the problem seems to be more complicated than this. Isolated young monkeys develop bizarre behaviors: They huddle in corners, rock themselves, suck their own fur, even bite themselves. Such behavior can hardly be described as adaptation to the isolated environment. It might more reasonably be interpreted as the outcome of the evolutionary history of the species. Monkeys have evolved as social animals, and they do not readily adapt to a nonsocial environment. Their own patterns of behavior go astray because in the absence of matching behavior from a social partner, they attempt to be their own social partners. The attempt is not very successful since they cannot calm and soothe themselves as effectively as a social partner could. Thus, the exploratory behavior that would normally promote adaptation to a new situation is impaired.

What are the effects of separating an infant monkey from a mother to whom it has already become attached? After the two have been reunited, is there any evidence of subsequent effects? Kaufman and Rosenblum (1967) studied four pigtail monkeys that were separated from their mothers for four weeks when they were five or six months old. The mother was removed from the cage, leaving the infant in a familiar environment with other familiar companions. Initially the infants' behavior was considerably disrupted, but toward the end of the month the infants showed much recovery. Our concern here, however, is with the infants' behavior after the mothers' return. Most striking was the amount of mutual clinging and proximity between reunited mother and infant: Even as long as three months after the separation, the pair spent much more time together, and the infant spent much less time exploring away from the mother, compared with unseparated monkeys.

Spencer-Booth and Hinde (1971) studied longer-term effects in rhesus monkeys. They, too, separated the mothers and infants by taking the mother out of the home cage and leaving the infant with other familiar animals. They worked with three groups of infant monkeys: five animals that were separated from their mothers for six days at about seven months of age, eight animals that were separated for two six-day periods, with the separations also occurring at about seven months; and a control group of eight animals that were not separated. The monkeys were observed with their mothers at the ages of twelve, eighteen, and thirty months. At twelve months the mother-infant pair was placed in an unfamiliar cage that had a tunnel big enough for the infant but not for the mother to go through. The tunnel led to a filter cage where food or a strange object had been placed. The previously separated infants had stayed somewhat closer to their mothers in the home cage than had nonseparated infants, but the differences were small. In the filter-cage test, differences were more apparent: The previously separated monkeys were less adventurous in leaving their mothers, in going through the tunnel, and getting the food or playing with the strange object. Figure 3-2 shows some of the results from this test.

By the age of thirty months the differences between the three groups were no longer detectable in the home cage, and few differences were evident even when the animals were tested alone in a strange cage. However, some effects could still be seen under solitary test con-

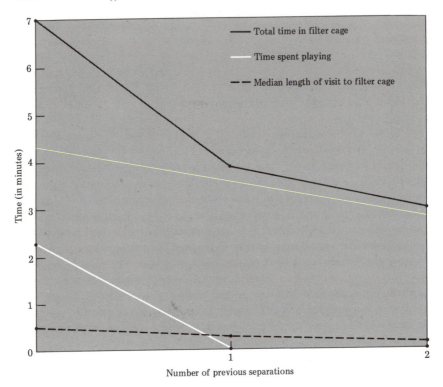

Figure 3-2.   Effect of earlier maternal separation on the exploratory behavior of twelve-month-old monkeys. Note the relative lack of adventurousness in the previously separated animals. (Adapted from Spencer-Booth and Hinde, 1971)

ditions: The previously separated monkeys were less willing to come to the experimenter to receive vitamin pills, which normally they liked; they took longer to begin trying to reach a piece of food that was out of reach; and they gave up sooner when they did not succeed. This work offers an important lesson: Long-term effects of early separation may not show up under normal living conditions, but they may take the form of a *greater vulnerability to stress.*

Maternal deprivation in human children [3]

Fortunately, a human child rarely experiences full-scale maternal deprivation—in the sense of being brought up in isolation—without the opportunity to form attachments to anyone. A few cases of children who have been hidden away and isolated from human contact are on record (see Clarke and Clarke, 1976, for a full account of the

[3] See Rutter (1972; 1979) for a review and summary of relevant research.

known cases), and the attempts to rehabilitate them make a fascinating story. The most tenable generalization from these cases is that rehabilitation is unlikely unless the child has had the company of at least another child during all or some of isolation from normal social contacts.

One important study describes the rehabilitation of a group of young children whose parents were killed by the Nazis during the Second World War (Freud and Dann, 1951). These children were hidden in basements and attics and were moved repeatedly at night from one location to another. They had frequent changes of caretakers but were always kept together. Thus, they were the only constant element in one another's lives, and they formed very strong mutual attachments. When at the end of the war they were rescued, they were very poorly developed, both physically and mentally. Normal speech was almost entirely missing, and they were fearful of and resistant toward adults.

At the age of three or four the children were brought to a house in rural England for rehabilitation. At first they clung together desperately, showing great distress when one of them was isolated from the group because of an infectious illness. They were also hostile toward and suspicious of adults. Gradually, however, they began to form attachments to specific caretakers. As the attachments progressed, the children became intensely possessive toward their favorite adult, jealous of this person's attentions toward any other child, and despairing when the person was absent. Curiously, their intense clinging was also occasionally mixed with shows of anger toward "their own" caretaker. Ultimately the attachments moderated and became more normal in their intensity. At this stage, the children began to show great progress in becoming socialized: There was a spurt in their language development, and they became responsive to adult efforts to teach them acceptable social behavior. We do not know the ultimate fate of these children. What we do know is that they were able to make the transition from their initial child-oriented attachments to adult-oriented attachments, although the transition was a painful one. The new attachments were of sufficient quality to permit the children to explore their new environment and begin to learn to cope with it. Most important: They began to accept the adults as teachers and models. These children provide an example of the formation of attachments to adults at a later-than-normal time. The example shows that when late attachment occurs, it can serve the usual security-giving functions. The children's prior attachment to one another may have been the essential element making possible the new attachment.

The Freud and Dann study raises an important question: How plastic are the attachments of young children? That is, how readily can they shift from one attachment figure to another? This question is important because it bears on public policy regarding children. When awarding custody in divorce and deciding on adoption or foster care for children who cannot be cared for by their natural parents, the courts must make decisions about the primary caretakers in children's lives. It is important to know whether such children can readily form new attachments if they are transferred to a caretaker who has not been the primary attachment figure and whether the experience of disrupting one attachment and forming another leaves any scars that will show themselves later in the children's lives.

Some writers have argued that the disruption of an early primary attachment leaves the child emotionally insecure, even if new attachments are formed. Bowlby (1973) has said that the early disruptions will show their effects in later life in the form of sudden depressions or anxieties that seem unrelated to current life stresses. His position has been taken to mean that children should be allowed to remain with their accustomed caretakers under all possible circumstances—that *continuity* of an attachment relationship is the most important consideration in making decisions about children's lives. This view has had worldwide influence on policies affecting the placement of children who come under the jurisdiction of the legal system (see Goldstein, Freud, and Solnit, 1973, for an application of this view to legal policy). For example, in the interests of maintaining existing attachments, children have sometimes been allowed to remain in abusing or neglectful homes instead of being placed elsewhere.

More recent work, while not invalidating the finding that separation from an attachment figure is extremely distressing to young children and should be avoided if possible, has indicated that children *can* recover from separation quite fully if their new circumstances are adequate. This point is illustrated by the work of L. Yarrow and colleagues (Yarrow and Goodwin, 1973; Yarrow et al., 1973), who studied children who were placed in permanent adoptive homes before the age of sixteen months. Children placed as newborns, of course, never experience separation from an attachment figure. Children placed at a later age had had foster mothers, and some had formed close attachments to these women. As might be expected, the infant's distress over separation from the foster mother and resistance to the new parents depended on the infant's age at the time of adoptive placement. A majority of infants older than six months of age showed various forms of distress: disrupted eating and sleeping patterns, excessive clinging to the new mother or outright rejection of her—pulling away, stiffening when she approached, and refusing to be comforted by her when crying. Children under six months of age seldom showed such reactions. Again, not surprisingly, an infant's distress was greater following a close, satisfying relationship with the original caretaker.

For our present purposes the important issue is the later effects of the separation, particularly in the cases where the separation caused great distress. At the age of ten years children were tested and interviewed, and their adoptive mothers were also interviewed. Each child was scored on forty personality dimensions, which were grouped into twelve summary scores. Several findings are of interest: Children adopted after six months, compared with children adopted before that age, were found to be somewhat less likely to score high on *social discrimination*—that is, their relationships with different people tended to be at the same level of intimacy. But *there were no differences among the three groups on any of the other eleven summary dimensions,* nor on an overall rating of adjustment, nor on any of the measures of intellectual ability. Perhaps more important: The child's adjustment at ten years of age was not related to the degree of disturbance at the time of adoption. Thus, we see that although the experience of being shifted from one primary caretaker to another was clearly upsetting to children older than six months of age, lasting effects could not be detected ten years later. Of course, the researchers may not have measured the crucial indicators, but they did focus on the child's anxiety reactions, especially anxiety over separation. Or perhaps the children sampled were too young at the time of the separation to be permanently affected—only a very few were over twelve months of age, and we know (see Chapter 2) that the most intense distress over separation normally occurs at a later age than this.

Only a few other studies have followed children who have undergone extensive separation in childhood (see Cairns, 1979, Chapter 7; Maas, 1963) and more work on this highly controversial issue is badly needed. Meanwhile, we can hazard a tentative conclusion: The child's later adjustment will be primarily determined by the quality of the relationship with the new caretakers, not by the experience of separation. If the child is distressed and either resistive or excessively clingy at the time of entrance into the new home, the new relationships may get off to a bad start. Adoptive parents may find it difficult to cope with the child's disturbance and still remain responsive and loving. Thus, lasting damage may grow out of the difficulties separation can create in the early phases of a new relationship. However, if the new parents persevere, and a close, comfortable relationship is established, the child is likely to survive the experience without deep scars.

A final word about separation: Prior separations can sometimes *help* a child cope with a new separation. This point is illustrated by a study of a group of Welsh children who went to the hospital for tonsillectomies (Stacy et al., 1970). At the time and place the study was done, tonsillectomies were postponed until children were four years old. Then if the operation was needed, children were kept in the hospital for at least four days, and the parents were allowed to visit but could not stay overnight. In this situation the stress of hospital procedures added to the stress of separation, and understandably, many of the children were highly distressed. Surprisingly, however, some children coped quite well, and these children, it was found, had previously been separated at least briefly from their parents. Most of the less-disturbed children had been away from home overnight, staying with grandparents or family friends. Presumably their prior separation experiences had been pleasant and constructive on the whole, and had protected them against the damaging effects of a subsequent stressful separation.

Early attachment and subsequent development

Researchers have begun to accumulate evidence that security of attachment at the age of twelve or eighteen months does have an effect on the way in which developmental tasks are dealt with during the next year or so. A first piece of evidence comes from the work of Mary Main (1973). Main observed forty mother-infant pairs in the Strange Situation when the children were twelve months old, and she classified the children into Ainsworth's A, B, and C attachment types. When the children were twenty months old she gave them the Bayley Scale of Infant Development in order to assess their ability to understand simple words and to carry out certain simple tasks. Children's relationships with the examiner were noted, as were their responses to test items. At twenty-one months the infants had a play session with an unfamiliar adult. In this session the adult attempted to get the child to roll a ball back and forth. At this time the children also were given the opportunity to explore a set of unfamiliar toys. The people who did the latter assessment did not know what kind of attachment behavior each infant had shown at twelve months. At twenty and twenty-one months:

1. Type B (securely attached) children had higher scores on the Bayley Scale. Their play with toys was more intense and involved: They stayed longer with a toy and paid more attention to its specific features, and they showed more enjoyment in their play. They willingly approached the adult playmate in the play session, and they entered freely into the game of ball.

2. Type A (avoidant) children stayed away from the adult playmate and would not enter the game of ball. They showed anger more frequently than did the children in the other groups. They showed normal levels of exploratory play.

3. Type C (resistant) children had lower developmental quotients than Type B children. They showed less intense involvement with toys: shorter bouts of play, more restless flitting from one activity to another, and less enjoyment of play.

Work by Matas and colleagues (1978) adds to our understanding of the developmental differences among children who show different patterns of early attachment. Matas assessed the quality of attachment at either twelve or eighteen months. Then, when her young subjects were two years old, Matas presented them with fairly complex problems involving the use of tools—problems that were difficult for children of this age. Those who had been rated securely attached approached the problems with enthusiasm, interest, and pleasure. They followed directions easily, and when they encountered difficulties they seldom cried, fussed, or became angry. When help was needed they comfortably asked for it from the adults who were present. The behavior of children who earlier had shown disturbances in their attachment relationships (Type A or Type C children) presented a striking contrast. These children tended to ignore or reject directions from adults; they became frustrated easily, manifesting frustration reactions that ranged from foot stamping to outright temper tantrums; and they quickly gave up trying to solve the problems. They seldom asked for help even when they clearly needed it. Some of them (usually Type Cs) hung on to their mothers, retreating from the task; others (Type As) avoided their mothers and occasionally showed unprovoked anger toward them.

A recent report on a group of nursery-school children further amplifies our understanding of the relationship between attachment and later development. Waters, Wippman, and Sroufe (1979) assessed children's attachment at fifteen months of age and then observed them in nursery school at the age of three-and-a-half years. In terms of the way the children played with other children, those who had been securely attached were very different from those who had been insecurely attached. Children who had been securely attached at fifteen months tended to be social leaders—other children sought them out, and they were likely to be the initiators of, as well as active participants in, activities. When other children were distressed, they showed empathy. Teachers rated these children as more forceful, self-directed, and eager to learn. Insecurely attached children tended to be socially withdrawn and hesitant about participating in interactions and activities. Teachers found them less curious about new things and less forceful in pursuit of their goals than their more securely attached schoolmates. We see then that children who had been securely attached as infants were socially quite well adjusted. They were active in initiating play, while the insecurely attached children tended to remain on the sidelines and to withdraw when other children attempted to play with them. Teachers' ratings confirm the differences between the two groups.

It seems clear that children who are securely attached by the time they enter their second year of life are better equipped to cope with the new range of challenging experiences they encounter during the following two years or so. Of course, we still cannot be sure that the early attachment relationship is directly responsible for the success or failure of a child's later problem-solving attempts. For one thing, children who were securely attached at twelve or fifteen months probably were receiving sensitive, responsive mothering at that age and probably were continuing to receive the same kind of mothering as they grew older. The mothers of these children probably continued to respect their autonomy and support their efforts to cope independently with new experiences, while standing ready to give direct help when needed. Thus, the well-adjusted social behavior of these children at three-and-a-half might reflect the current healthy state of the parent-child relationship, rather than being an outcome of the relationship that existed two years earlier.

There is a further problem in interpreting these "delayed-effects" studies: Certain children may develop good relationships with their parents and, later, with teachers and other children, despite anything their parents do. And at the risk of boring the reader, we must again note that certain difficult children may resist forming normal attachments and may have difficulty coping with new tasks, even with parenting that would be quite satisfactory for most children. If we were able (1) to intervene in the families of insecurely attached children and help the parents to change the patterns of interaction, and (2) if these changes produced normal attachments, and (3) if this intervention resulted in improved problem-solving behavior on the part of the children a year or two later, we would have developed solid evidence about the precise way in which early events lead to later ones. In the absence of such demonstration, we can only say that it seems likely that the early patterns of parent-infant interaction do influence the child's approach to the following set of developmental tasks.

DIFFERING ATTACHMENT PATTERNS DURING THE PRESCHOOL YEARS

In Chapter 2 we saw that attachment undergoes considerable qualitative change during the third, fourth, and fifth years of life. The clingy, proximity-seeking manifestations wane. On the average children become much more willing to tolerate separations from the people to whom they are attached. They also seem much less oriented toward their caretakers when the caretakers are present and more able to maintain an integration of their own and other's behavior without constant contact and reassurance. Some children manage these changes much more quickly than others and with less conflict. Indeed, even at four or five years of age, some children still cling to their mothers in the ways that average children of a much younger age do.

Studies of preschool and kindergarten children document these variations. Of course, older children, like younger ones, differ from time to time and from situation to situation in how much parent contact they seem to require. Nevertheless, individual consistencies do exist, and they permit us to describe some children as being slower than others in giving up immature forms of attachment behavior (although these consistencies have not been as well documented as they have been for younger children).

A word should be said here about terminology. For a considerable period (from about the mid-1940s to the mid-1960s), a good deal of research was done on the development of *dependency* in children. Included in this category was all behavior that could be interpreted as an effort by the child to obtain help, comfort, caretaking, or attention. Dependency was thought of as behavior that a child might show toward any adult or even another child—it did not imply a relationship with a specific other person, as the term *attachment* does. Individual children were thought to differ from one another rather consistently in how intensely or in how frequently they showed such behavior, and research efforts were designed to discover the reasons why some children were more dependent than others. As it turned out, children who "showed off" to get attention were not the same children who frequently stayed close to adults, sought physical contact with them, or asked for help. And children who were quite clingy toward their parents might not show similar behavior toward other adults or toward children of their own age. Thus, the characteristics that defined dependency were not useful in identifying consistent, stable characteristics of individual children. Partly because of these discoveries, researchers turned toward the concept of attachment, which offered a different way of viewing some of the same behaviors. This concept helped shift the focus of researchers' attention to affectional bonding between the infant and one or more specific other persons. In addition, the researchers looked for the qualitatively different forms such bonds could take. These changes in focus have been very productive, but as we attempt to understand individual differences in attachment behavior among children aged four through six, we encounter a problem. Most of the research on children of this age was done at the time when people were using the concept of dependency. Thus, the relationship of their work to the more recent work on attachment is unclear. We do not know, for example, whether children labeled *dependent* at age four or five are children who, from an Ainsworth-Bowlby point of view, would have been labeled *insecurely attached* at a younger age. We will return to this question. Meanwhile, we turn to some of the work on individual differences in dependency during the preschool years, selecting material that seems to have certain continuities with early attachment patterns.

In an interview study conducted in the Boston area with families of five-year-olds (Sears, Maccoby, and Levin, 1957), mothers were asked whether their children seemed to want a great deal of attention, how their children reacted when they left them with someone else, whether their children seemed to want to stay close to them and hang on to them, and so forth. The following comments by mothers illustrate the range of behavior typical of children at this age (all examples in this section are from Sears, Maccoby, and Levin, 1957):

> Mother A: "John is kind of—well, he could be loved and kissed constantly, and I'm not like that myself as much as probably I could be. A little bit is all right, but Johnny could just sit there. . . . He would like to have you hold him constantly. Like looking at television, he wants to sit in your lap, and have you bill and coo and love him, and all this stuff. I don't think in the first place it's healthy, and yet I don't know why he should be that way." (p. 144)
>
> Mother B: "He doesn't play too well alone. He likes to be around me. He used to follow me around in every room—in fact, even now, if I am in the bedroom making beds, he is in the bedroom too; or if I am in the living room, he is in the living room. He follows me around." (p. 149)
>
> Mother C: (When asked about going out of the house and leaving the child with someone else): "That's really a problem. She'll screech her head off. She doesn't like it. They all—as a matter of fact, they'll cry if I go away and leave them. Even if I go out and leave someone in the house to mind them, they'll want to go with me. 'Don't go out, Mommy, stay home with us.' " (p. 152)

By contrast, another mother reports:

> Mother D: (How much attention does Peter seem to want from you?) "Very little. He can be left to his own devices for two or three hours at a time, except occasionally to show me or ask me something." (How about following you around or hanging on to your skirts?) "Never." (Did he ever go through a stage of doing that?) "Nope." (p. 144)

There is a considerable range in parental reactions to clingy, helpless, or attention-demanding behavior on the part of children. Some parents become quite irritated and employ various sanctions if the child does not leave them alone:

> Mother E: (How do you feel about it when she hangs on to you and follows you around?) "It depends on what I'm doing. If it's sewing, something that I'm sitting down doing and she can participate in it, too, to some degree, I don't mind. But if I'm trying to get something done—for instance, the hours before dinner, I'm feeding the baby and so forth—I get exasperated and just tell her to get out and let me get this done." (How do you generally react if she demands attention when you're

busy?) "I realize that I shouldn't react. I try to save myself from reacting antagonistically, but I do. I become peeved and I think she feels that. But at this stage, though, she seems to have become antagonistic herself. At that stage—just the both of us, we both become very antagonistic. And my voice rises and finally I threaten her with having to stay in her room."

(So when she does want attention when you are busy, you generally ask her to wait or what?) "Yes, I ask her to wait. Or if it's a serious attention, I mean that she needs something buttoned or something she can't do for herself, ask her to wait. She, however, is soon impatient about it and doesn't want to wait. She'll ask me every minute until it's done."

(How about if it's something she could probably do by herself?) "Then I tell her she should be able to do it by herself, and if it's a question of conflict of wills, which it often is, well, it's just that, and finally one or the other of us wins out. It often takes ten minutes, fifteen minutes." (p. 162)

By contrast, another mother doesn't find irritating her child's demands or contact seeking, and this mother complies quite readily:

Mother F: (How did you feel about it when she hung on to you and followed you around?) "Well, I didn't think too much about it. I mean I wouldn't say that it was an aggravating situation by any means, because, after all, a mother's love is pretty strong. It never bothered me." (How do you generally react if she demands attention when you're busy?) "Well, if I'm busy I'll just say I'm busy, that's all. When I get through doing what I am doing, I'll see what she wants or what her demand is. And usually then I'll take care of it." (How about if she asks you to help with something you think she probably can do by herself?) "Well, in a case like that, I usually ask her if she can do it by herself, and if she says that she can, but she isn't sure, I tell her I'll help her. . . ." (How about the little things, such as putting things away, putting things on? . . .) "Well, we've always waited on them hand and foot—the both of us have. Some people say it's a very bad habit to get into—waiting on your children and having your children depend upon you so much. As for putting on their things, why if they ask me to put on a coat or anything like that, I gladly stop what I'm doing and do it for them." (pp. 163–64)

Still another mother expects her five-year-old to be quite self-reliant:

Mother G: (How did you feel about it when she wanted to be with you all the time?) "I had to teach her that she had to be alone at times, and not have me around." (How do you generally react if she demands attention when you're busy?) "I don't pay much attention to her." (How about if she asks you to help her with something you think she could probably do by herself?) "I tell her she's supposed to do it herself and I'm not going to help her." (And then does she do it?) "Oh, yes if she feels like it." (Otherwise, what do you do?) "Otherwise, I just let her alone, let her have one of her stubborn streaks, or just take things away, and tell her she can't play any more if she's going to be like that." (p. 164)

In Chapter 2 we described a transition that normally takes place in the mother-child attachment relationship during the preschool years. In the infantile form of attachment, the child wants the mother nearby, available to cling to for reassurance in uncertain situations and available as an "executive" or at least as a partner in satisfying the child's needs. The more mature form of attachment is a cooperative linking of the two streams of behavior. Such a linkage, which is necessary if the child is to function adequately when out of the mother's presence, requires: (1) a good level of communication, so that each knows a good deal about the other's plans and movements, and (2) mutual trust, so that each can count on the other person doing what is expected. Furthermore, the child must trust the mother's affection and good will, believing that she will act to protect the child's own interests at all times. The transition to this form of attachment is not complete by the ages of four and five. The young child still needs the comfort of physical affection and the physical presence of the parent a good deal of the time. The relationship is still one-sided in that the parent has to be much more active in serving the child's interests than vice versa. Still, progress in the direction of a mature, more equal relationship is being made, at least in some families.

We see from the preceding comments by mothers that the transition is not always easy. In the case of Mother E, the mother and child have not found a successful way to integrate their activities. The child has not yet learned to inhibit demands in return for the mother's promise to help later. Perhaps the arrival of the new baby has distracted the mother so that she has too often forgotten to attend to the needs of the preschool child (also, of course, the older child may be showing jealousy of the mother's attentions to the baby). In this family a coercive cycle of interaction seems to be developing (to be discussed further in Chapter 4), and the issue of the mother's helping or not helping has become fraught with tension.

Another way of looking at the relationship between Mother E and her child is to say that the child is engaging in controlling efforts (see Marvin's hypothesis, Chapter 2) in an attempt to restore an integration of plans that she feels her mother has broken off inexplicably. Whatever the explanation, it is clear that the communication between them is inadequate.

Mother G's report would lead us to believe that there is less tension in the family. (We do not know how this situation would look from the child's point of view!) However, this case may represent a process of *detachment*, rather than transition to continued attachment at a more mature level. The mother appears to be breaking off (or at least minimizing) the relationship. She does not want to integrate her activities with a child's any more than is absolutely necessary. If she is a good judge of what the child is actually capable of doing without help, she may succeed in getting her daughter to be quite independent so that her daughter actually does live a good deal of her life without "bothering" her mother. However, this child will probably spend a good deal of time away from home as soon as she is old enough, and the family may not be able to exercise as much control over her future activities as they would wish. We will return to the issue of control in Chapters 7 and 10.

Mother F continues to have a close, integrated relationship with her five-year-old. Indeed, it might be alleged that she is babying the child. The mother herself fears that she and her husband may be responding too readily to the children's demands for help. Does such treatment by parents retard the development of independence in their children? Sears and his colleagues found that parents who usually responded quickly and easily to their children's requests for help had children who were not more likely to make excessive demands for attention and help than were children whose parents did not wait on them. Indeed, if parents gave help and attention on demand without feeling or showing irritation in the process, their children tended to make demands infrequently (at least according to their mothers' report). The key factor seemed to be whether the mother reacted negatively at the same time that she yielded to her child's importuning and gave help. Reactions like those of Mother A were associated with the highest levels of dependency in the children.

What is there about a mother's irritation with a child's clinging or demands for attention that seems to make the problem worse rather than better? We surmise that from the child's viewpoint, the mother is not only denying help but also denying affection and emotional support. Actually, this is more than a surmise. Parents do, on occasion, imply or even say explicitly that children's nagging (or other undesired behavior) makes it hard to love them. (See Chapter 4 for a discussion of withdrawal of love.) Here are some examples (again taken from Sears, Maccoby, and Levin, 1957):

> Mother H: "Most of the time I say to him 'Tommy, now stop it. You're a bad boy. And Mommy doesn't like bad boys.' And he'll turn around and ask me if I love him. I'll say: 'Yes, I love you, but I don't like you.' He tries to figure that one out, but he can't."(p. 343)
>
> Mother I: (What do you do when he acts like that?) "Well, I'd probably yell good and loud and just simply open the door to his room and throw him in bodily and leave him there. I'd tell him he

was terrible, just a mean boy and I'm not proud of him. I might say I hate him the way he is acting." (p. 343)

Mother J: (What do you say to her when you are scolding her?) "Well, we usually start with 'Why?' . . . and 'You just go up to your room and stay there and I'll talk to you later about it.' Or 'I don't want to talk to you; I just don't want to have anything to do with you, that's all.' " (p. 344)

We saw in Chapter 2 that any stimulus or event that produces uncertainty (insecurity) causes the infant to seek contact with an attachment figure. In fact, animal studies demonstrate that punishment by an attachment figure increases proximity seeking by the infant, and we interpreted this behavior as a response to the insecurity engendered by the punishment. The connection between the kind of scolding illustrated above and a four- or five-year-old child's excessive clinging may not be so immediate or so obvious, but it is there. A parent's threat to withdraw affection from the child arouses strong anxiety in children, as witnessed in these reports from Sears and his colleagues:

Mother K: "After she's done something bad, she's very sorrowful and needs to be reassured that you love her. She'll say many times 'I love you, I love you,' and wants obviously to be reassured that you love her too." (p. 168)

Mother L: "There was one period when he would go out to play, and he would suddenly come in the house and throw his arms around me, and he would ask: 'Do you love me?'—and then I would assure him I did love him, and he would go out again, but he would keep coming in." (p. 169)

Thus, when parents' behavior raises doubts in children's minds about whether they are loved, the children will want to reassure themselves. Quite often their efforts will take the form of clinging or making demands for attention. As we noted earlier, these may be the very behaviors that caused the parents to react unaffectionately in the first place, and so a vicious cycle is established. It is worth noting that in the study by the Sears group, parents who reported occasional withholding of affection as punishment for naughtiness had children who (on the average) were somewhat more dependent than usual for their age.

Evidence of the kind just cited is not very satisfactory. Parents may not realize that they are withholding affection as a form of control, and consequently, it is risky to rely on parental reports in obtaining data on how frequently this method of control is used. Furthermore, correlations between parental descriptions of their own behavior and their evaluation of the characteristics of their children may be biased. We saw that parents who are not irritated by dependency demands report that their children do not make many of them. Perhaps this relationship reflects the fact that such parents do not consider their children's bids for help and attention to be especially frequent. Parents with less tolerance for the behavior might consider the same number of demands to be "quite a lot." We need detailed observations of parent-child interaction—and they need to be of the sort that have been provided by students of infant attachment—before we can be sure that there is a real connection between withdrawal of affection and children's continuing to show immature, clingy forms of attachment at the ages of four and five.

Assuming for the moment that the connection *is* real, we can see some parallels with work reported earlier in this chapter. Avoidant infants, it will be recalled, had mothers who tended to be rejecting; resistant infants had mothers who tended to be inattentive (inaccessible). In the report of Mother E, we may certainly be seeing a continuation of an inattentive-mother, resistive-infant pattern that was established sometime earlier. Possibly maternal rejection in infancy later takes the form of withdrawing affection frequently in order to discipline and control. But this is speculation. Currently no group of preschool or older children whose attachment patterns were studied in infancy has been observed interacting with their mothers. We do not know how enduring the early patterns are nor what transformations they undergo with growth. Until such evidence is available, we can only speculate. But it seems highly likely that the behaviors crucial to secure attachment in infancy—sensitivity, acceptance, cooperation, and accessibility—continue to be important in supporting a smooth transition to mature forms of attachment. Children's successful development in this respect depends not only on whether the children feel secure about their parents' affection, but also on whether they have developed the competencies that allow them to continue to function as close parental involvement in their activities is gradually withdrawn. The aspects of parenting that underlie the development of these competencies are discussed in Chapter 5.

SUMMARY AND COMMENTARY

In this chapter we have discussed the different attachment patterns adopted by different children and have asked whether children maintain these patterns consistently over considerable periods of time. We have looked at the conditions that underlie differences in quality of attachment and have considered both the parent's and child's contribution to the relationship. Finally, we have asked whether the history of a child's early attachments affects the child's subsequent development.

With respect to the existence of stable individual differences, it has been shown that:

1. Children can be reliably classified according to whether their attachment is secure or insecure. Two subgroups of insecurely attached children can be identified; these categories have been labeled *avoidant* and *resistant.*

As to the origins of these differences:

2. Certain maternal reactions seem to foster the development of secure attachment during the child's first year. These behaviors include sensitivity, acceptance, cooperation with the infant's ongoing behavior, accessibility, sociability, and ability to express positive emotions. In sum, *responsive* mothering is related to secure attachment.

3. Certain preexisting characteristics of the child are also believed to contribute to the attachment pattern that develops.

A comment on point 3: Students of secure and insecure attachment have assumed that the quality of mothering is primary in determining how secure a child's attachment will be. Consequently very little attention has been paid to the child's personal qualities that may determine the parents' response. The meager evidence available indicates that children do contribute to the nature of the attachment. For example, congenitally retarded children less often initiate interaction with their mothers than do normal children and hence receive less response, and from early infancy some children seem to be more easily soothed than others by body contact.

Does the history of a child's early attachments have any bearing on later personality development? It has been alleged that failure to become attached, disruption of a primary attachment, or the formation of an insecure attachment will distort the child's ability to form close emotional ties. Lack of opportunity for attachment (maternal deprivation) has been studied primarily in animals, where infants can be experimentally isolated. The animal studies have shown:

4. Isolating monkeys in infancy produces serious deficits in their later social behavior. Monkeys reared in isolation are aggressive toward other monkeys when caged with them, their sexual behavior is impaired, and they are timid in exploring novel environments.

5. Rehabilitation is difficult, but adult isolates can acquire relatively normal social behavior by being caged with infants. And young monkeys isolated in early infancy can be rehabilitated by being caged with adolescent females. However, the effects of even one week of separation in infancy can still be seen a year later.

6. Infants reared without mothers but with several age mates grow up to be normal in most respects but are timid about exploration.

With respect to the effects of disruptions of attachments that were already formed:

7. In monkeys, while both infants and mothers react strongly to separation, the infants adapt quite quickly to their new social environment if there are animals there who will adopt them.

8. Human infants who are moved from one home to another after the age of six months find separation distressing, but subsequent adjustment appears to be determined primarily by the nature of the new family situation. The meager evidence currently available suggests that intense initial distress does not prevent children from forming a close tie to the new parents.

With respect to the later effects of secure or insecure primary attachment:

9. In their second year infants who are securely attached at twelve months have the following characteristics: They focus attention well in play; they interact willingly with a friendly stranger; they undertake new tasks enthusiastically, are persistent, follow directions easily, and ask for help when needed, but are not overly reliant on adult help. Insecurely attached children are less interested in undertaking new tasks, give up easily, are easily frustrated, and avoid interaction with unfamiliar adults.

10. By the age of three, when observed in nursery school, children who were securely attached as infants interact smoothly with other children; they undertake new tasks readily and are described as "self-directed."

Conclusions 9 and 10 must be interpreted cautiously. We cannot be sure whether the early secure attachment enabled the children to be socially outgoing and task oriented or whether the children who form secure attachments easily also get along well with other children when they are old enough for social play. Perhaps attachment has no real connection with sociability and self-directedness. Or perhaps the attachment *does* make a difference, but the *current* parent-child relationship, not the earlier one, is what matters. In spite of these questions, existing evidence suggests that some children develop more secure relationships with their parents, and while this may reflect inborn characteristics of the child, it probably also reflects the parental sensitivity—being tuned in and responsive to the child's signals. Paradoxically, the children with the most *insecure* relationships seem most closely bound to their parents. That is, they have difficulty moving away from them to explore novel environments, undertake new learning experiences, and interact with new people. However, insecure relationships need not remain so. They can change if the quality of the parental response is changed.

CHAPTER **4**

Children's Aggression
and Parents' Responses

It is difficult to know exactly what people mean when they say that someone has acted *aggressively*. Some people call the person who starts a fight aggressive but would not use the term for the person who fights in self-defense. Some people reserve the term for actions that injure others, while other people use it more broadly, to include behavior that is merely assertive—as in "he's an aggressive salesman."

We encounter definitional problems in studying animal behavior, too. In a litter of puppies, rough play begins at about the age of three weeks when the puppies start to mouth and bite one another. By the fourth week the play has become rougher. The puppies begin to growl and snarl when they bite, and the victim may yelp. Are the puppies still playing, or are they being aggressive? The puppies' teeth appear, their muscles grow stronger, and they become more and more capable of hurting one another. Meanwhile, their actions are increasingly focused and organized into patterns that we recognize as fighting, although play continues too. By the seventh week, if the littermates are left together, they begin genuinely injurious attacks on one another. Quite often attacks are concentrated on the smallest animal in the litter. In certain breeds, (for example, fox terriers) the smallest animal will be attacked so fiercely that it may be killed if it is not removed. (For good descriptions of the development of fighting in puppies, see

Cairns, 1979; Rheingold, 1963; and Scott and Fuller, 1965.) Following the onset of attacks that are serious enough to inflict real injury, a social structure usually emerges. Certain animals become dominant, others subordinate. Now the dominant animal only needs to threaten to make another animal give way when there is a contest over a bit of food. The frequency of fighting diminishes and is largely replaced by signals and a mutually accepted social hierarchy.

In animals as well as in humans, then, drawing the exact line between play and aggression is difficult, but the distinction can be made, and the shift clearly does occur. Definite patterns of aggressive behavior distinguish aggression from an accidental injury inflicted by one animal on another (a thing that seldom happens). Aggressive threats take different forms in different species. In bulls, pawing the ground and bellowing are part of the pattern. In monkeys and apes, threats are expressed by a direct stare, a distinctive threat cry, a square-shaped mouth, bristling hair on the back of the neck, and (sometimes) drumming on the ground with the hands. Dogs snarl, show their teeth, growl, and stiffen their hair. From these patterns of behavior we infer that the animal is preparing to be aggressive in the truest sense: It is signaling that it is about to injure its victim.

Nothing that human infants do during the first year can properly be considered aggressive if we use the term to mean actions directed toward a specific other person that are intended to hurt or frighten. During the first few months of their lives, infants are capable of very little in the way of either direction or intention. At first they cannot accurately direct the movements of their arms and hands or even their eyes. They begin to show intention when they are able to coordinate the movements of eyes and hands, first looking at an object and then directing a grasping movement to the specific spot on which their eyes have fixated. Directing action toward a specific other person comes later and is probably most clearly seen when young infants hold out their arms to be picked up by familiar persons but fail to do so with strangers.

As infants develop cognitively, they begin to understand that one event can cause another and that other people can be the agents of frustrating events. A good example of the dawning of this understanding is given by Jean Piaget (1952), who with one hand offered a matchbox to his six-month-old son Laurent, but held his other hand in front of the matchbox so that the child could not reach it:

> Laurent tries to pass over my hand, or to the side, but he does not attempt to displace it. As each time I prevent his passage, he ends by storming at the box while waving his hand, shaking himself, wagging his head from side to side, in short, by substituting magic-phenomenalistic "procedures" for prehension rendered impossible. . . .

> At 6 months 17 days I present a rattle to him while placing my hand in front of it, so that only half the object is visible. Laurent tries to grasp it directly, but not set aside my hand.
>
> At 7 months 10 days, Laurent tries to grasp a new box in front of which I place my hand. He sets the obstacle aside, but not intentionally; he simply tries to reach the box by sliding next to my hand, and, when he touches it, tries to take no notice of it. . . .
>
> Finally at 7 months 13 days Laurent reacts quite differently. . . . I present a box of matches above my hand, but behind it, so that he cannot reach it without setting the obstacle aside. But Laurent, after trying to take no notice of it, suddenly tries to hit my hand as though to remove or lower it. I let him do it to me, and he grasps the box. I recommence to bar his passage, but using as a screen a sufficiently supple cushion to keep the impress of the child's gestures. Laurent tries to reach the box, and bothered by the obstacle, he at once strikes it, definitely lowering it until the way is clear. (p. 217)

We see here the beginnings of a child's understanding that other people may be obstacles and that it is necessary to act in two stages in order to achieve one's objective: first removing the obstacle and then moving toward the object itself.

The infant who pulls off an adult's eyeglasses because of an interest in a shiny object, then, is not behaving aggressively. How about Laurent, who pushed away his father's hand in order to reach a toy? The action was specifically directed toward the father, so it passes the first test for being aggressive. But was the action intended to hurt or frighten the father? It is doubtful that this child treated his father's hand any differently from the pillow that got in his way. He was much too young to know that another person but not an inanimate object could experience pain.

Aggression in the sense that adults know it is a cognitively complex act. Children only gradually approach adult levels of sophistication in these matters. At first they are not even aware of the effect of their own actions. When they have achieved some understanding of the relationship between their own and others' behavior, they then move on to attempts at controlling what others do.

This chapter begins with a look at the development of young children's capacity to be intentionally aggressive: what they must understand about themselves and others in order to carry out genuinely aggressive acts. Age-related changes in aggression are then considered in the light of these understandings. The effect of the family and other environmental factors is discussed in terms of both encouragement and control of aggressive behavior. The chapter ends with an examination of (1) changes in the purposes for which school-age children use aggression and (2) the balance between aggressive and nonaggressive means of self-assertion.

EARLY DEVELOPMENT

Knowledge and intention

What kinds of understanding must a child master in order to be able to carry out an intentionally hurtful act? The aggressor (whom we will call A) must know:

1. that another person can help or get in the way of A's own objectives, know what A wants him or her to do, and experience distress;
2. that A's own actions can cause distress;
3. *which* actions can cause distress in *which* other people;
4. how to carry out distress-producing actions;
5. that distress can cause other people to act the way A wants them to;
6. that the distressed person's action can be in A's interests.

The word *know* is used here rather loosely. Obviously the aggressing child need not consciously say, "Aha! If I shake my fist at that other boy, he will be afraid I am going to hit him; he knows that if I hit him it would hurt; if he knows I want the toy, he'd rather give it to me than get hurt; so I'll reach out for the toy so he'll know what I want, and I'll shake my fist at him so he'll know he'd better give it up." The aggressive child may be only dimly aware of all these elements in the situation. But in early childhood an awareness of each of these elements gradually develops, although some are understood much earlier than others. With a view toward obtaining a clearer picture of when and to what degree children become capable of being aggressive in the fullest sense of the word, let us consider the developmental course of some of the elements of aggression.

First steps

The knowledge that other people can serve as obstacles that block one's own intended course of action probably comes very early— witness Piaget's infant son. Between the ages of one and two years this knowledge is extended. W. Bronson (1975), as part of a longitudinal study of children in this age group, observed the behavior of groups of three or four children playing in a room that was well stocked with toys. (The mothers were present to provide the children with a sense of security, but they were asked not to initiate any play.) Children of this age do not typically engage in sustained interactive play. Most of their encounters consist of brief disagreements over toys—one child trying to take a toy from another child.

Bronson found no change in disagreements over toys during first, second, and third trimesters of their second year. The emotional intensity of children's reactions to the situation did increase, however; as they progressed through their second year, children showed more intense frustration and more anger over having a toy taken from them. Bronson notes that this is the time when children increasingly tailor their play to the specific characteristics of the toy. If a toy is taken away, substituting a different object and continuing to play becomes more difficult, and the loss becomes progressively more frustrating. Something else is also happening. Bronson observes that the loss of a toy gradually becomes an offense to the child's very self, and she suggests that the discovery of the concept of ownership enables the child to develop an understanding of "I" and "mine."

The behavior of one of Bronson's subjects illustrates how the child is preoccupied with the issue of ownership: "A few moments after entry Linda—not yet engaged in anything beyond a thorough survey of the scene—mutters repeatedly 'Mine! Mine!' and remains where she is, continuing her survey. There was no response by the other children to Linda's declaration" (Bronson, 1975, p. 146). More often, of course, a child's assertion of "mine" comes during a tug of war over a toy. Bronson noted that fairly often the children were struggling over a toy that neither child played with before the encounter or after the tug of war was over. The children seemed to be struggling over the fact of possession rather than over the toy itself.

What we see, then, between the ages of one and two years, is an increase in the intensity of involvement with objects, a staking out of claims, and an increasingly intense emotional reaction to encounters over possession. During these struggles, Bronson observed, the children's attention is usually entirely directed toward the toy; the children seldom look at one another. What we do *not* see is an increase in what may legitimately be called aggression. The children are not trying to force another child to withdraw by hurting or frightening the other child; they are merely trying to remove an obstruction.

The other as the focus of anger

As the child matures there seems to be a gradual shift from undirected anger to true aggression—that is, anger focused on a specific person. A classic piece of research charting this shift was done many years ago by Florence Goodenough (1931). She asked forty-five mothers to keep daily diaries of the angry outbursts of their children, recording instigating circumstances as well as adults' responses. The children ranged in age from seven months to seven years; most were

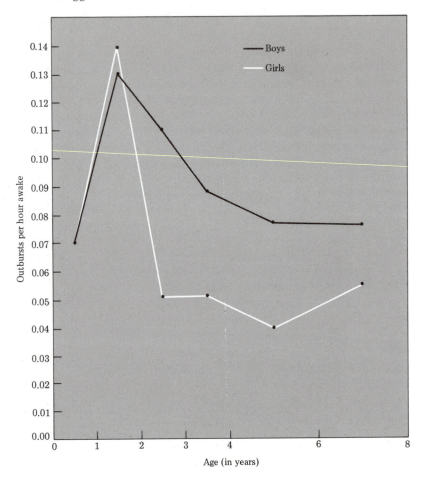

Figure 4-1.   Age and sex differences in frequency of angry outbursts. Note the peak in outbursts between the ages of one and two. (Adapted from Goodenough, 1931)

two or three years old. The mothers varied widely in the number of days for which they kept records, the modal number being thirty-one daily records for each child. In all, the mothers recorded a total of 1,878 outbursts. The children differed greatly in the frequency of their outbursts: The highest rate was shown by a boy aged nineteen months, who averaged nearly 4 outbursts a day; the lowest was a girl of four years eleven months, who had only 4 outbursts of anger in 381 hours of observation (a rate of 0.13 per day). Figure 4-1 shows age and sex differences in frequency of outbursts. We see that the frequency declines after the second year, but more rapidly in boys than in girls. The sex difference will be discussed more fully in Chapter 6.

Goodenough reported age changes in the type of outburst as well

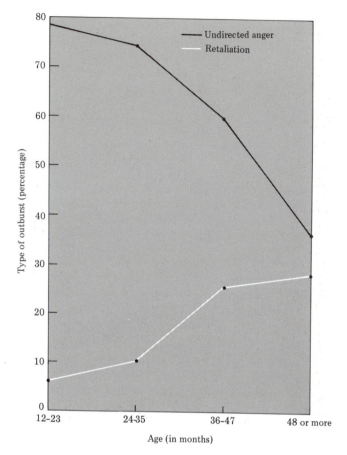

Figure 4-2. Age changes in focused and unfocused anger. Note the reciprocal relationship between the two types of anger. (Adapted from Goodenough, 1931)

as in the frequency. Most of the outbursts of the youngest children were undirected tantrums, while after the age of three such behavior diminished greatly (see Figure 4-2). At the same time, there was an increase in the proportion of outbursts that occurred as retaliation for perceived injury from someone else. Thus, the proportional frequency of true (directed) aggression shows a marked increase over this age range.

Anger and parental demands

The circumstances that provoke anger also change with age. During the second and third years of life children find that parents expect more of them. Anger occurs most commonly over parental attempts to establish routine physical habits—that is, toilet training, washing, and going to bed. These expectations represent profound changes in the child's life experience. Up to the first birthday, most parents believe that their infants are too young to be disciplined and that they are almost entirely helpless when it comes to meeting their own basic needs. Parents take it for granted that adults should respond to an infant's signals for help. Of course, infants inevitably suffer some frustrations; they may have to wait while the bottle is being warmed or the mother answers the phone. But by and large, parents demand very little in return for their many services, although there are differences among parents in whether they respond to *all* the child's signals and in how quickly they respond.

About the time the child starts to walk, or perhaps a few months sooner, things begin to change. The wider range of movement means that the child can get into a lot of mischief. Actions seem more intentional; the parent begins to think of naughty behavior as being deliberate—at least sometimes—rather than accidental. Furthermore, children now seem more capable of changing their behavior on the basis of adults' reactions. Children begin to understand adult language; their memories are better, and there is hope that current experiences will carry over to future occasions. So mild discipline is inaugurated, and parents begin to issue prohibitions: "No, No!" "Stop that!" "Don't touch!" Parents are also not quite so ready to act as servants. When the child makes a demand, the mother may ask the child to wait or refuse altogether if she thinks the demand is unreasonable.

All this comes as a shock to the infant, who has been blissfully confident about being the center of the world. *Infantile omnipotence* is the term Sigmund Freud used to describe the feeling that the world is peopled by adults who exist to serve the child's needs. It may seem strange to think that a creature who is so completely dependent on others for survival can feel so powerful and independent. In discussing this seeming paradox, Ausubel (1958) distinguished between *executive* and *volitional* independence. Children have volitional independence if they can get their wishes fulfilled by other people. Although they do not have executive independence (that is, they cannot do things for themselves), Ausubel believes that most infants have enough volitional independence to generate a sense of omnipotence. The day of reckoning does eventually come, however, and the omnipotent phase is followed by what Ausubel calls the *ego devaluation crisis*.

Assigning the onset of this crisis to a precise age period is difficult. All through the second year and even beyond, parents do continue to indulge and wait on their children. They think of them as babies, and they recognize how many things the children cannot do for themselves and how rudimentary their powers of understanding are. Nevertheless, socialization pressure in some degree does begin in the second year and is considerably augmented in the third and fourth years.

What is the essential nature of the ego devaluation crisis? Ausubel notes several important features:

1. Children begin to realize that parents are satisfying their needs because the parents want to, not because they have to.

2. Having *volitional* independence—getting what they want—no longer seems possible to children unless they also have the power to do things for themselves. Thus, children begin to understand that adults, not young children, have volitional independence and that this independence is a result of adults' executive competence.

3. Points 1 and 2 imply that children must be subject to their parents' will, not vice versa. Children thus become aware of their real lack of power in the family constellation.

In short, children's growing cognitive capacities enable them to appreciate that adults are independent agents who may have objectives different from their own. Furthermore, when objectives conflict, the reality is that adults have a considerable power advantage. In the usual family situation, the child must ultimately yield.

The child does not accept without a struggle this reorientation of the perceived power relationships within the family. A period of negativism begins, and the child tests the limits of adult authority.

The Ausubel view is persuasive, although it is difficult to muster solid evidence that infants do in fact feel omnipotent. Surely there must be many infants who never come to feel that they are the center of the world; indeed, there are some who are seldom played with and whose wishes are frequently ignored. One wonders, too, whether the sense of self develops sufficiently during the first year of life for the child to experience a sense of loss of the power of the self. One thing is certain however: The onset of socialization pressure does frustrate the child, sometimes quite acutely. And the frustration shows itself in anger and resistance.

The self as cause of others' distress

We have been considering the nature and occurrence of undirected anger. The process of converting at least some of this anger into aggression involves several cognitive achievements, among them the knowledge that others can feel distress and that one's own actions can cause that distress.

It is not clear just when young children come to understand that others can experience distress just as they themselves experience it. By the end of the first year—probably sooner—infants can distinguish between sad and happy faces. In this sense the children know something about other people's emotional states, and they are capable of a kind of sharing of others' feelings—that is, they may cry when someone else cries or laugh when others laugh. But at least at the youngest ages, this response may simply be a conditioned reaction: The sound of their own crying has accompanied their own distress states, and therefore the sound of any child's crying makes them feel distressed and makes them cry. This kind of participation in others' emotions remains with human beings all their lives, but as children develop it is complicated by awareness that others have separate identities and can feel distress at different times and for different reasons. This awareness that one's own and other people's feelings are separate is presumably a necessary prerequisite to understanding the connection between one's own actions and other people's emotional states.

When do children discover that their actions can cause distress in others? Parents begin to teach this when their children are very young. When a child as young as one year bites, scratches, or pinches, adults say "no," and they may also show signs of anger or pain or say, "that hurts." When children are old enough to understand language more fully, parents say, "you hurt your sister's feelings," or "you're making me angry." The adult's intention, of course, is to inhibit the child's aggressive behavior, partly by appealing to the child's natural sympathy. Parents seem to assume that children will feel distressed when others—at least, those emotionally close to them—are distressed and that if children are told when their actions are hurtful, they will want to inhibit this kind of behavior. Parents are surely right most of the time in this assumption. In addition, of course, there may be the implied threat that if the child continues in hurtful behavior, retaliation from others will follow. In any case, if children are to be taught to avoid hurting others, they must be helped to make the connection between their own actions and the impact of these actions on others. But this knowledge can cut both ways—it can provide one of the building blocks for becoming intentionally aggressive.

In fact, children have plentiful opportunities to learn which actions cause distress and how to carry them out. Most young children watch television shows in which they see such actions modeled, and they also see aggressive actions within their own families. Albert Bandura (1973) and G. R. Patterson (1976) have made the point that children in modern Western societies can scarcely fail to acquire an extensive repertoire of aggressive actions. Some of what they see is beyond their comprehension: They cannot understand that a delicately worded insult *is* an insult or that such an insult can hurt worse than a blow. No doubt these limits have led producers of animated cartoons to exaggerate both the size of the objects with which their characters hit one another and the clues to the fact that the characters have been injured—for example, the victim may be flattened like a pancake. But in spite of limited understanding, children four years old and older do know a variety of ways to hurt others. Whether a child carries out these actions depends not so much on what the child knows as on whether the child chooses to use the elements in his or her repertoire.

As children reach the ages of three and four they usually spend much more time than they did as toddlers playing with other children. And their play becomes more and more interactive—that is, each child's actions depend more on what other children do and how they respond, and children even begin to construct joint plans of action. Increased social play involves hitting, pushing, and grabbing toys, as well as imitation, sharing toys, mutual smiling or laughing, and other signs of pleasure in the interaction. It is important at this point to distinguish aggression from other patterns of playful interaction that, on first glance, may look much like it. Witness the following episode:

> Jimmy, a preschooler, stands observing three of his male classmates building a sand castle. After a few moments he climbs on a tricycle and, smiling, makes a beeline for the sand area, ravaging the structure in a single sweep. The builders immediately take off in hot pursuit of the hit-and-run phantom, yelling menacing threats of "come back here, you." Soon the tricycle halts and they pounce on him. The four of them tumble about in the grass amid shouts of glee, wrestling and punching until a teacher intervenes. The four wander off together toward the swings.

Although the teacher reacted as though the children were fighting (or were about to), there are good reasons for not calling this kind of play aggression. Blurton-Jones, an ethologist, has made unusually detailed records of the bodily movements involved in children's social behavior (1972). For example, *fixate* is differentiated from a friendly glance and is defined as "looking directly at the eyes of the other child for more than about two seconds, with rapid onset of this position and with no smile." Blurton-Jones identified two separate behavioral clusters:

1. *rough-and-tumble play*—laugh-playface, run, jump, hit-at, and wrestle

2. *aggression*—fixate, frown, hit, push, and take-tug-grab

The clusters were independent in that the items included within each cluster tended to occur together, and items in one cluster tended not to occur with items in the other. Blurton-Jones found that aggression tended to occur in the context of disputes over toys, while rough-and-tumble play did not.

Returning to the incident just depicted: We can surmise that Jimmy wanted to generate some action in which he could have a part.

He risked starting a fight, but instead a bout of rough-and-tumble play ensued. The incident illustrates the point that when one child intrudes on another the intrusion may or may not escalate into an aggressive sequence, depending on the reaction of the other child. In view of this, it is not surprising that socially active children tend to become involved in both positive and negative encounters. Several observers (Emmerich, 1964; Jacklin and Maccoby, 1978; Murphy, 1937; Patterson, Littman, and Bricker, 1967) have found it difficult to disentangle aggression from other forms of social behavior. Children who are most actively engaged in social play show more positive and negative behaviors than do children who prefer to play by themselves. At least between the ages of about two-and-a-half and four, the children who are most frequently aggressive tend to be the children who also play happily with other children and show frequent friendly, sympathetic behavior toward them. Apparently then, sociable impulses lead a young child to be both aggressive and unaggressive—the nature of the interchange depends on such circumstances as the toys that are present and the responses of other children.[1] This situation appears to change during the later preschool years, as sociable children acquire more skills in getting what they want without fighting (Emmerich, 1964). After about age four-and-a-half or five, the most sociable children no longer exhibit the most aggression. But earlier, at the age of about three or four, when many children have their first intensive social encounters, techniques for controlling others by aggressive means are rapidly acquired.

The self as controller of others

The ways in which children's experience in interacting with others teaches them to use aggression have been traced in detail by Patterson, Littman, and Bricker (1967). Their observers spent thirty half-days during the fall and thirty half-days during the spring watching children at two nursery schools. The children's average age at the beginning of the school year was about three-and-a-half years. For every aggressive incident that occurred during the observation sessions, the aggressor, the victim, and the *consequences* for the aggressor were noted. Aggression included: (1) bodily attack, such as hitting, pushing, spitting, kicking, biting, jumping on, grabbing, or choking; (2) attack with an object; (3) verbal or symbolic attacks, such as spoken threats, threatening gestures, and derogations; and (4) infringement of

---

[1] Yarrow and Waxler (1976) have noted that among a group of children aged three to five, there was a group of boys who were highly aggressive and who seldom showed prosocial behavior (sharing, comforting). There are clearly certain children, then, who are specifically aggressive, not merely sociable. (The report does not tell us whether these children were among the older of the ones studied.)

property (taking others' toys) or invasion of territory (running through another child's sand or block construction). Consequences included: the victim giving up a toy to the aggressor, running away, crying or putting his or her arms up in self-defense. Such responses by a victim were classed as *positive reinforcers* of the aggressor's action. A second class of consequences was called *aversive* and included the victim hitting back, taking back the toy from the aggressor, or complaining to the teacher. If the aggressor's action was witnessed by the teacher and if the teacher intervened, this too was classified as an aversive consequence of the victim's action.

In all, 2,583 aggressive actions were recorded (about 17 per hour of observation), and well over three-quarters of these were followed by positive consequences for the aggressor—the victim yielded, cried, or withdrew. When an aggressor's action was followed by a positive consequence, the probability of the aggressor's repeating the attack on the same victim was increased. If the aggressor's action was followed by an aversive consequence, the probability of repetition was decreased. Certain children experienced a high rate of success in their aggressive encounters. Whether they were larger or stronger or somehow more dominant in manner we do not know. But some children clearly do experience more positive consequences for their aggressive actions than other children do.

Interesting behavioral changes were charted in the case of children who were relatively passive when they entered nursery school. Initially, these children seldom attacked others and seldom retaliated when they themselves were attacked. But as the school year progressed, these children, taken as a group, became more aggressive. Within the group of initially passive children, some interesting differences were observed. Some of the children, while nonaggressive, were nevertheless sociable. They liked to play with other children and therefore became involved in encounters with more aggressive children. At the outset they were often victims, but eventually some of the passive children turned on their attackers and began to retaliate. Having succeeded in stopping the attacks by the aggressive children, some of the passive children themselves became *initiators* of aggression; it was clear that they had become apt pupils in the "school for crime" provided by their peers. However, there were two groups of initially passive children who were not transformed into aggressors in this way. One group (small in number) liked to play with other children, were victimized, attempted to counterattack, but did not do so successfully. These passive children were not able to alter their victim status and did not increase their aggressive initiations toward other children. The other group was relatively unsociable, seldom interacted with peers, and became neither victims nor aggressors.

A very small number of children were successfully aggressive but nevertheless did not increase their rate of oppressive acts. For these children the sight of their victim's cringing, crying, or running evidently was not reinforcing. Or to put the matter another way: There may be differences among children in how susceptible they are to being reinforced for aggression.

The emergence of social structure

The work of Patterson, Littman, and Bricker clearly illustrates how children take the large step that permits them to become genuinely aggressive—how they discover that by causing distress or by threatening to do so they can get what they want from other children and ward off other children's intrusions. It should be noted, however, that fighting does not occur between any random pair of children who happen to get in each other's way. Instead, as a group of children continue to associate with each other they form a social system. At least a rudimentary hierarchy of dominance, or a pecking order, develops—and this remains fairly stable over time. Aggression occurs in the process of forming the hierarchy, and once it is established the hierarchy influences who will fight with whom.

Strayer and his colleagues (1977, 1978) have conducted extensive observations at several nursery schools by using video tapes to record *agonistic interactions* (exchanges involving attacks, threats, or struggles). In certain exchanges one child would aggress and the other would respond submissively—that is, seek help from an adult, cry, run away, cringe, flinch, or put up a hand to shield the face.[2] This behavior was identified by the researchers as *dominance* of one child by another.

Dominance, by definition, only works in one direction. In each nursery school there was a rank ordering of children. When a dominance issue arose between any given pair, one particular child almost always won while the other almost always submitted, the children seldom or never reversing positions. Furthermore, if A dominated B and B dominated C, A also dominated C—C never dominated A or B. D, however, dominated those lower on the scale.

Thus, while not all fights among children are dominance encounters, many are, and such encounters form part of an orderly pattern of social relationships. Most observers suggest that established dominance hierarchies serve to *reduce* the amount of fighting among children because children know in advance whom they may safely challenge and whom they had better leave alone.

It is difficult to decide what kind of evidence would be needed to support this contention. The best so far seems to come from six weeks of observations of a group of five- to seven-year-old children whose

[2] In one nursery school about a third of the agonistic interchanges between children involved the submission of one member of the pair.

social skills were so poorly developed that they were unable to attend regular school classes and had been referred for psychiatric treatment in a summer-preschool setting (Strayer et al., 1977). Among these children a dominance hierarchy did develop, but despite its existence, the children showed higher levels of agonistic behavior than did normal preschoolers (who, of course, were younger on the average). The problem appeared to be that the disturbed children did not respect the hierarchy—there were many more instances in which low-status children challenged children with high status or high-status children attacked those with low status (in normal preschools, children usually reserve their attacks for those close to them in the hierarchy). So although dominance hierarchies do normally function to regulate aggression within a group of children, there are children who do not know how to function within such a structure; when those children violate the group's consensus, they elevate the level of aggression within the group as a whole.

Alternate points of view

We have been discussing the development of aggression during the preschool years in largely cognitive terms. We have suggested that the changes that take place with age are a product of children's increasing ability to understand (1) the effects of their own actions and (2) how to use their actions to control others. A psychobiologist or an ethologist would interpret the evidence of developmental change quite differently, drawing close parallels between the developmental changes in human children and those in many species of animals and arguing for a developmental timetable that is a product of evolution and is under genetic control.

Suomi (1977) has given an account of the development of aggression in monkeys, placing the timing of its onset within a schedule of other developmental events. The timetable is as follows:

10–60 days old	Infants show curiosity to novel stimuli, but do not show fear.
60–80 days old	A fear grimace appears.
6–8 months old	An aggressive pattern appears.

Suomi labels these behaviors *unlearned* because the timing of their appearance seems to be quite independent of rearing conditions and their onset does not seem to require social experience. Sackett (1966) has shown, amazingly, that when a daily display of pictures of the social behavior of monkeys is projected onto the wall of cages housing monkeys reared in isolation, these monkeys do not react to pictured threat gestures until they have reached the proper age for the appearance of such reactions, and then they react in much the same way that normally reared monkeys do.[3] Suomi argues that the timetable has functional significance. When young monkeys begin to extend their explorations beyond the arms' reach of their mothers, a mechanism is needed that will bring them running back to the mothers' protection. Fear emerges at this time and acts as the needed mechanism, but its helpful effect depends on occurrence of prior events in the sequence. If a young monkey has been deprived of its mother or of a mother surrogate so that it has not had the opportunity to form an attachment, the onset of fear is simply disorganizing, and it cuts short the monkey's exploratory behavior.

Similarly, Suomi argues, the kind of social experience that precedes the onset of aggression is important in determining the form that aggression will take when it does emerge. Normally reared animals have several months of active social play, including a good deal of rough-and-tumble play, before aggression appears. But, as we saw in the case of dogs, the appearance of the aggressive pattern means the beginning of fighting, although the formation of dominance hierarchies soon regulates this behavior and serious injury is rare (at least among animals that are acquainted with one another). However, monkeys reared without access to age mates have not experienced active social play. As a result, they are excessively aggressive if, after the age of six to eight months, they are placed with other animals. Their encounters often involve serious injury, and these animals do not easily find a place in the dominance hierarchy. Thus, social experience does not determine the *onset* of aggression, but—so to speak—it determines how the animal copes with it.

Ethologists like to emphasize the fact that human beings are animals with an evolutionary history. They emphasize the considerable continuity in human biology with that of lower animals. They see no reason why this continuity should not exist for patterns of behavior as well; from this viewpoint the developmental history of aggression in normal human children bears a strong resemblance to what is seen in dogs and monkeys. For the first two or three years, children do not display the pattern of aggressive behavior that is characteristic of the human species—namely, fixations, frowning, directed hitting (or threat thereof). Then this pattern appears and is quite rapidly followed by the emergence of dominance hierarchies in groups of children who play together over an extended period. Ethologists might well say that there is no need to have recourse to such mentalistic concepts as *intention* in order to explain all this. Aggression, they would say, is simply unlearned behavior following its preprogrammed time schedule.

Let us consider first the question of whether aggression is learned or unlearned: It seems clear that it is a "natural" response in human

[3] Kenney, Mason, and Hill (1979) report that visual social experience will accelerate the onset of fear but that age remains a primary factor.

beings as well as in lower animals, and very likely, its onset does follow (at least roughly) a built-in timetable. To this extent, aggression is instinctive. However, as we have seen in the work by Patterson, Littman, and Bricker, aggression is also learned—in the sense that once it emerges its development is shaped by social consequences. There need be no contradiction in the view that both learning and instinct are involved in the development of aggression.

As far as intention is concerned, we are on more difficult ground. Human beings are intelligent creatures, and recent advances in the study of cognitive psychology have shown us that thought processes play an intricate role in regulating human behavior. Aggression is not a reflex, as a knee jerk is. It is a complex pattern of behavior that calls for considerable processing—interpretation—of information concerning the behavior of other people and the relation of the self to others. The spectacular growth of children's skills in processing information of all kinds could hardly fail to affect the kind of interpretations children make. Thus far we have emphasized (perhaps overemphasized) *intent* as a shorthand way of representing a range of cognitive activities that increasingly determine when and how aggression is expressed. The danger in emphasizing intent, however, is that it makes children's aggression seem more conscious, more deliberate, than it actually is. Children—and indeed humans of all ages—often aggress without knowing why. Or they act in ways that do not seem aggressive to themselves, while to objective observers their actions seem hurtful and motivated to hurt.

The idea of intent was introduced into the definition of aggression because it seemed unreasonable to include accidental hurting of another person. While accidental hurting is very rare in animals—at least after the very earliest period when they first experimentally chew one another's ears or climb recklessly over one another—humans frequently hurt other humans without meaning to. A child may swing a baseball bat without realizing that someone is standing close by, or misaim when throwing a ball, or ride a bicycle rapidly and fail to notice another rider's trajectory of movement. Human language provides the most subtle and widespread means of accidental injury. Consider the following episode:

> During a long ride in the car, a four-year-old boy lay down on the car seat with his head in his mother's lap. He gazed deeply into his mother's eyes. The mother felt pleased at this loving intimacy. Then the boy said, "Mom, your eyes are just like roadmaps!"

The mother was not pleased, of course, to have attention called to her bloodshot eyes. But she understood that the child did not intend to hurt her feelings. If her husband had said this, he would have had to have said it with just the right touch of humor so as not to be considered aggressive. The point is that the human use of tools, weapons, toys, and—above all—language has greatly magnified the opportunities for accidental injury. Thus, in studies of human aggression it becomes paramount to set aside accidents when analyzing the development of hurting as a means of control. Unconscious aggression poses an especially difficult problem since it is *not* accidental and yet the aggressor is not conscious of intent. We could ask whether there is such a thing as unconscious intent, but this would lead us down unproductive paths. At present the most we can say is that in emphasizing intentional acts of aggression, we have not meant to imply that children develop full insight into the reasons they lash out at others. Nor do we wish to say that all elements of the causal knowledge acquired by a child are brought into the forefront of consciousness when a child acts aggressively. We do mean to say that in order to carry out an act of aggression, unconscious or otherwise, a person must develop at least some of the kinds of understanding of self and others that have been traced so far in this chapter.

PARENTAL INFLUENCE

We have been following the cognitive and affective changes that make possible in young children the development of the capacity to express true aggression, and we have only lightly touched on the question of the parents' role in this development. Most parents are intimately and continuously involved with their young children, and their behavior can have a strong effect on whether their children will or will not use aggression in interactions with family members and playmates. In the following section, therefore, we take a more careful look at the ways in which parents—by deliberate teaching and by unthinking responding—influence their children's aggressive behavior.

Encouragement of aggression toward peers

During the third and fourth years of life, when children have begun active play with age mates and are in the first phases of developing techniques of social interaction, parents frequently participate in their children's relationships with other children. Preschool youngsters have many or most of their social encounters in their own neighborhoods and often in their own houses or yards where their mothers are within earshot. Mothers differ considerably in their readiness to take a hand in settling children's quarrels, and most mothers hesitate to create friction by disciplining other people's children. Frequently, however, they do encourage their own children to defend themselves against being victimized. In a Nottingham, England, interview study of 700 families with four-year-olds, John and Elizabeth Newson (1968) found that 61 percent of the mothers reported that they had (on at least one occasion) told their children to hit back at other children when attacked. For some of the parents, the issue was a painful one since they would have preferred to see the children settle their disputes without resorting to physical violence, but the parents felt unable to sustain this value when faced with the realities of the children's lives in the neighborhood play groups. One parent commented:

> Well, we've told him now—he's come in so many times crying—because he's never been one for fighting: I've always said to him "Now you *mustn't* fight, you *mustn't* hit." But now—he's had it so much done to him, one little girl dragged him down the steps by his hair, and they push him and hit him with sticks and that sort of thing—and now we just say to him "Well, you *must* go and stand up for yourself, you must go and do the same thing to them." (p. 121)

The mother of a daughter describes a similar sort of parental pressure: "I make her go and hit Susan back. I say 'Go and hit Susan back, else Mummy'll smack you,' and she knows. I do try to make her hit back, yes. I don't want to make her a bully, but I do try to make her defend herself" (p. 123).

Most mothers do set strict limits on what is regarded as allowable fighting. Children are frequently told not to hit with sticks, and some are instructed not to hit younger children even if they hit first. Returning the blows of certain other children, however, receives reluctant support. Some children, of course, do not require much encouragement when it comes to self-defense. When asked, "Do you ever tell her to hit another child back?" one mother replied, "Oh, I don't have to! Not Elaine!" (p. 123).

We see that in addition to learning from their personal experience in dealing with aggressive playmates, children learn from their parents' encouragement to focus their anger on specific targets and to attempt to control others' actions by producing pain or discomfort.

Reactions to aggression within the family

The role of the parent in the development of aggressive behavior toward family members can begin quite early. Goodenough (1931) cites a number of instances of parental behavior that easily can be interpreted as unintentional encouragement—even as reward—for displays of temper. The following is one example:

> A three-year-old girl . . . had been put to bed for her nap. After the mother left the room, the child moved her bed so that she could climb out of it into the bed of her sister, who slept in the same room. The mother heard her doing so, came in, and replaced the bed. The child

jumped up and down, screamed, and refused to go to sleep. The mother first threatened to spank her, then did so, then "appealed to her self-esteem," then ignored her for fifteen minutes, and finally allowed her to have her bed where she wanted it. (p. 227).

And in another family, "The child was trying unsuccessfully to climb onto the davenport. She asked for help repeatedly, but no attention was paid to her. Finally she began to kick and scream, whereupon she was lifted up" (p. 233). It is to be expected that with repeated experiences of this kind a child would learn to focus anger more and more on the parents and would do so as a means of inducing the parents to attend to the child's own wants and needs.

Of course, parents do not welcome being hit or being shouted at angrily; nevertheless, they themselves direct such behavior toward their children in the form of punishment. Children are expected to understand that this is the parent's right and that children are not permitted to retaliate. In other words, it is all right for children to be aggressive toward playmates (at least in self-defense), and it is all right for parents to be aggressive toward children. But it is *not* all right for children to be aggressive toward parents, for parents are agents of authority, and aggression toward agents of authority is not encouraged in any stable social system. The message from the parents, then, is a mixed one: Aggression is acceptable and works effectively sometimes, but it can also evoke penalties if misdirected.

Parents differ, of course, in the importance they attach to maintenance of their authority and in what they will do to prevent children from showing anger toward them. When Sears, Maccoby, and Levin (1957) asked several hundred mothers from an urban and suburban area of the Northeast how they felt about anger directed toward them by their children and how they reacted, the researchers received a wide range of responses. Their question was:

> Sometimes a child will get angry at his parents and hit them or kick them or shout angry things at them. How much of this sort of thing do you think parents ought to allow in a child of (his, her) age? How do you handle it when (child's name) acts like this? (p. 234)

Representative answers:

Mother A: "They never should allow him to hit them back. If he hits them, they should hit him right back. If you let him get away with it once he will always want to get away with it."

Mother B: "I don't think you should allow any of it. You should stop it. But they do it." (Can you give me an example of this with Ginny?) "Well, it might be when I want her to turn off the television and wash up for dinner and she will insist that she won't turn off the television. Well, I will just have to go over and turn the television set off, and she will scream and yell. I have to take her bodily out of the room and put her upstairs until she quiets down. And then let her come down after she stops the crying."

Mother C: "I'm afraid I couldn't go it too often. Once in a while he will, but he doesn't do it too often. He will say he doesn't love me any more at times but I can understand how he feels, besides what it is he wants. He is resentful, but that is only something you can expect of a child that old. As far as kicking, I wouldn't tolerate that. I just have given him to understand that they can't do that."

Mother D: "I think there's a certain amount that should be allowed. I think that it's something they have to get out of their system. If I saw that it was a habit, I'd certainly make provisions to prevent it, but in Susan's case every once in a while, she gets so furious with me that she does strike out, and I sort of overlook it a little bit, because I think it's very natural." (pp. 235–36)

The majority of parents expressed views that were *nonpermissive* (not tolerant of the legitimacy of this kind of behavior), a finding consistent with results of the interview study conducted in England by the Newsons (1968). Parents enforced their nonpermissiveness in very different ways, however. In these examples, both Mothers A and B were strongly nonpermissive, but Mother A was very *punitive* (reacted to aggression with counteraggression), while Mother B did not retaliate aggressively. The Sears group, through detailed questioning of mothers, was able to determine the frequency with which each child directed anger toward the parents. An analysis of these responses indicated that nonpermissiveness and punitiveness have different effects and that the highest rates of aggressive behavior occurred in children whose parents were relatively *permissive* but who were also relatively *punitive* in their reactions to the behavior when it occurred (see Figure 4-3). We will return later to the interpretation of these facts, when we discuss the interaction in the families of highly aggressive children.

Meanwhile, it is clear that parents provide abundant opportunities for children to develop conflicting feelings about the expression of aggression. Children discover that aggression is sometimes an effective way to get what they want, but they also run the risk of being punished for the very behavior that is effective in other respects.

Psychoanalytic writers have called attention to another aspect of the conflict children experience over aggression toward parents. The notion is that aggressive feelings create a serious conflict or inner mental struggle because the child loves the parent who is the object of anger and fears that the loved one may become angry in return and therefore less loving. As a result, the child's anger is not focused on the parent but is *repressed* or *displaced*. In psychoanalytic theory these are mental processes that are out of awareness and serve to provide

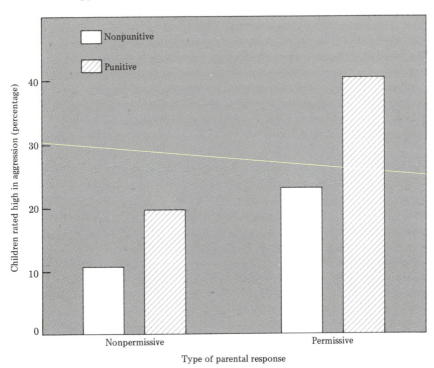

Figure 4-3.   Relationship between children's aggressiveness and parental patterns of response. Note that parents who are not accepting of children's aggression but who do not respond punitively to children's aggression have the least aggressive children. (Adapted from Sears, Maccoby, and Levin, 1957)

relief from conflict. *Repression* is the banishing of unacceptable ideas or feelings—keeping them out of awareness. *Displacement* is the transfer of unacceptable feelings from their original focus to some other object—in some instances toward the self. There is abundant clinical evidence that such processes occur in older children and in adults, but we do not know at what age young children become capable of these processes. It is clear, however, that many parents—often, no doubt, quite unwittingly—provide fuel for the conflict and motivate their children to repress or at least inhibit parent-directed aggression that might otherwise be displayed quite openly. In fact, some parents quite explicitly threaten to withdraw their affection for and support of—or even more extreme, to abandon—children who express anger toward them. An example from the Sears group's report:

(When you are scolding her, what else might you say?) "It's hard to think." (Do you warn her about what you might do if she doesn't behave?) "Yes, in fact I've used an awful threat with her at times, not recently, but when she'd say that she didn't like me, I wasn't a nice mommy, she wished she could live with Gertrude or something like that. I'd say 'Yes, you go ahead, I don't have to keep you either, Carol; I'm going to bring you back to Dr. Phillips and he can find another mommy for you.' She almost got hysterical then; she really believed that I was going to take her back to the hospital and she would be sent to some other mommy." (p. 343)

Two parallel instances come from the Newsons:

"I have said that if he makes me poorly when he's naughty I shall have to go away, and then he'll have no Mummy to look after him, and he'll have to live with someone else, I know that's all wrong, but I do. His Daddy'll say to him 'Pack his bags—get that bag out, and get his toys, he's going!' And he has one time put some of his clothes and toys *in* the bag; and it made him nearly demented—it upset me, but I didn't like to interfere, you see."

(What did you say?) "Well, she was having an argument with me, and she says to me 'You don't live here. Hop it.' So I says 'Oh, well, I can do that! Where's my coat? I'm moving!' So I got my coat from the back, and I was gone. I just stood outside the door, and she cried so bitter, she did. As soon as I came in, she got hold of my leg and wouldn't let go, sort of thing. I'll *never* say it no more." (reported in Bowlby, 1973, p. 228)

With interchanges of this sort, it is clear that considerable anxiety can be engendered in children over any hostile feelings they experience toward their parents. The parents, too, experience anxiety and conflict:

"Sometimes I do feel really remorseful: usually if I've said something to frighten them, like I'll leave them; and then I look at them lying in bed, all peaceful like, and I say to my husband 'Oh, dear, I'm a wicked woman, it's really wicked to talk like that to them.' But then the next day they're on again, and I get nasty all over again! I got *really* nasty tempered one time—I couldn't stay, I was afraid of myself, I just had to go and walk round the houses for a bit." (Newson and Newson, 1968, p. 503)

Cyclic buildup of family aggression

Although both parents and children experience anxiety (and often guilt) when they allow themselves to show anger toward other family members, the anger does continue to be expressed, and aggression among the members of some families reaches such levels that it disrupts many aspects of normal family functioning. Patterns of interaction between siblings and between parents and children in this kind of family have been analyzed in detail by Patterson (1976). Extensive home visits were made to families with boys between the ages of five and fourteen years (most were eight to eleven years old). The boys had been labeled "out of control" and had been referred to a therapeutic clinic; they were known to be unusually aggressive at school as well as at home. The interaction patterns of these families were compared with those in a group of families with boys of the same age who did not have such problems.

In this research observers, using a set of predetermined categories, recorded events in time sequence (so that the interrelationships among each family member's actions could be determined later). The following categories of behaviors were considered instances of coercion of one family member by another: disapprove, whine, noncomply, yell, destroy (objects or goods), physical negative (hit, push, slap, throw object at), ignore, humiliate, "high rate" (extremely vigorous movement), tease, command negative (for example, "Stop that!" "Shut up!"), cry. Some of these actions seem well within the usual meaning of *aggressive*. Others do not. Consider *ignore*, for example. Can A properly be said to be coercive toward B if B speaks to A (asks a question, perhaps, or makes a comment) and A acts as though the message had not been heard? Certainly not if A is somewhat deaf or is talking on the phone to someone else so that there is a good chance that she or he really did not hear B. But under other circumstances, deliberately ignoring another person's conversational overture is regarded as rude at the least and is sometimes considered to be insulting. The research findings confirmed that people do find these behaviors aversive. When interviewed, subjects said that they do, by and large, experience discomfort when they are the targets of any of these behaviors. In addition, when the subjects were observed, it was found that they were likely to discontinue whatever behavior preceded the coercive action. For example, if B was talking to A and A did any of the listed behaviors, the probability that B would talk to A in the ensuing time interval was greatly reduced. So for the moment let us accept the assumption that the coercive behaviors we listed are relevant to a discussion of the occurrence of aggression in family interaction. Interestingly, the rate of coercive behavior on the part of different family members was closely related. The parents and siblings of aggressive boys were considerably more coercive toward other family members than were people in the families of normal boys. Somehow a pattern of mutual coercion had developed in the problem families. How had this come about?

First, in problem families, coercive behavior often yields positive results—that is, the coercive individual gets his or her own way. However, even though the coercive individual is, in effect, positively reinforced for aggressive behavior, comparisons of different problem families show that variations among them in the rate of coercive behavior are *not* associated with the rate of reward for such behavior (Johnson et al., 1974; Taplin and Reid, 1977). Furthermore, when problem families are treated and instances of mutual coercion decline, family members do not receive less reward for their coerciveness on the occasions when it does occur (Taplin and Reid).

Patterson concludes that negative reinforcement is more important than positive reinforcement in maintaining coercive cycles of interaction. He suggests that family members become coercive not in order to get others to *do* certain things, but in order to get them to *stop* doing certain things. In other words, when one family member is making life unpleasant for another (by teasing or scolding, for example) the target often finds it possible to get the other person to stop by yelling or hitting. According to Patterson, the following is a typical sequence of events in families of aggressive children:

1. One child discovers that positive outcomes can result from coercion of siblings (usually younger ones). The signal to begin an attack is a sibling's having a desirable toy or even just being present when there is no adult nearby.

2. The siblings discover that they can stop these attacks by countercoercion. The signal for them to launch their attack is the first child's actual or threatened coercive attempt.

3. Assuming that adults do not intervene, the child who launched the original attack (for the sake of a positive reward) now must cope with the counterattack. The first child discovers that intensifying the response to the counterattack can be effective. The result is an increase in both rate and intensity for all the children involved.

4. The parents sooner or later must intervene, and they find themselves using coercive means to stop the children because the emotional level is too high for reasoning. Their countercoercion quite often works, at least in the short run.

5. The children then respond to their parents' coercive intervention by using countercoercion. They may understand that it is too risky to hit back at adults, but they discover that whining, crying, yelling, and other coersive behaviors will sometimes stop parental pressure.

6. There is considerable temptation for the parents—particularly the mother—to give in. Spending so much time in hour-by-hour interaction with the children, she often becomes weary of the fighting, and she is troubled by the picture of herself as an aggressive person who controls her children only by force. So she often settles for peace at any price. When she gives in to a child's coercive demands, the child's angry pressure on her ceases or at least temporarily diminishes. But she has bought a short-run gain at the expense of a long-run loss. She has increased the likelihood that the children will use aversive

techniques on her in the future, and when their behavior becomes too unbearable, she will turn back to countercoercion. So the situation seesaws back and forth between indulgence and punishment, the parents responding in remarkably inconsistent fashion to their children's behavior.

Children living in this kind of situation become resistant to punishment. In normal families, when parents really mean business and show it by punishment or some other form of clear power assertion, the children stop the undesired behavior. In families suffering from the kind of problems just described, the children are likely to *repeat* an action when they are punished for it.

Once a mutually coercive system of this kind becomes established, family life becomes unpleasant and difficult for everyone. Often the mother becomes everyone's favorite victim. The father blames her for not being effective in dealing with the children, and she blames herself, becoming depressed. In this atmosphere ordinary problem solving, even in small matters, becomes virtually impossible. The family cannot discuss what television program to watch or what to eat for dinner without someone blowing up. Family members begin to dislike each other and to avoid each other's company. They prefer eating alone to sitting down to a family meal. They seldom go on family outings. When they are together they are glumly silent or they are quarreling. The situation is intolerable for everyone. The father may begin stopping off for a few drinks after work to fortify himself against the unpleasantness he will face when he gets home. The mother responds angrily when he is late. And on and on.

Help for problem families

How can this mutually destructive cycle of attack and counterattack be interrupted? A therapeutic system has been worked out by the Patterson group. Treatment begins with a fairly extensive period of observation. The family's pattern of interaction is recorded so determination can be made of the ways in which family members are maintaining one another's coercive actions. The parents are then trained in a new set of child-management skills, which include the following elements:

1. The parents do not give in to coercion from the child.
2. The parents avoid countercoercion.
3. To stop the child's coercion, the parents initially use *time out*— that is, the child is confined in a safe place for a stated period of time until she or he calms down.

4. A point system is established whereby the child can earn desirable consequences for good behavior and lose them for bad behavior.

5. The parents are alert for occasions on which it is reasonable to show affection to and approval of the child, and they greatly increase the frequency of warmth and support shown to the child.

Initially the point system is applied to only a small set of the child's behaviors that have been chosen as targets for the family's change efforts. Also, the point system at first must be established by fiat, since the family's communication system for reaching agreement on anything is so weak. As the cycle of mutual coercion is dampened down, family members begin to be able to decide on appropriate penalties and rewards. The range of target behaviors is expanded, and parents are encouraged to accept point-system control for their own coercive behavior. When a father agrees that he will pay $2.50 if he hits a child, it sometimes has a remarkably salutary effect.

For a number of families, step 5 proves to be the most difficult. Family members are not accustomed to seeing anything good in each other's behavior, and they have been hurt too often to feel much affection for their tormentors. Hugging and smiling at a problem child at appropriate moments takes effort, and at first parents may feel that such gestures are artificial. But when genuine affection does begin to reappear, the family has reached a turning point.

Methods of this kind have succeeded in changing the interaction patterns of a number of problem families. For some families improvement is quite rapid. For others, treatment must continue for an extended period since it proves to be difficult for some parents to treat their children differently and for their children to respond differently. A minority of problem families have not responded to the treatment. The reasons some respond and others do not are not yet understood. The researchers are continuing their efforts to identify the processes at work in the "hard core" problem families who have thus far proved so difficult to help.

For purposes of understanding the development of aggressive behavior in children, a number of important points emerge from the reported research. Within the family setting children can learn aggression in a variety of ways. Parents can teach their children by instruction and by example how and when to be aggressive. They can also indirectly influence the amount of aggression the child displays by being unresponsive until the child is enraged or misbehaving intolerably and then (often inconsistently) giving in or meeting violence with violence. The family, as a small-scale social system, also teaches aggression when coercive behaviors become the principal means by which family members influence one another. In most families, however, such behavior plays a much smaller role in the system of mutual influence.

The influence of the school environment

The family is not the only social system that affects children's rate of aggression. A school is also a social system, and a class of pupils and their teacher constitute a social group. In their nursery-school studies, Patterson, Littman, and Bricker (1967) noted that the nature of the program of activities arranged by individual teachers and the way in which teachers exercised control over individual children had considerable bearing on the amount of aggression that occurred within a given group:

> It was our impression that the *group output* of assertive-aggressive behaviors was mainly a function of the differences in the program of activities characteristic of each school. For example, one of the teachers in School C was particularly effective in structuring the *kind* of interaction which took place. She frequently introduced play activities and games that provided discriminative stimuli for a wide variety of nonaggressive behaviors. She also seemed able to anticipate social settings in which aggressive behaviors were more likely to occur, and by removing one or more of the children or introducing a new activity she decreased the probability of aggressive behaviors. (p. 19)

A group of developmental psychologists visiting nursery schools in China in 1973 came to similar conclusions. The group included a number of people with considerable experience in observing the interactions of children in American nursery schools, and they were therefore familiar with what would be the "normal" rate of aggression in such settings. Even allowing for the presence of foreign observers, the incidence of aggression among the Chinese children was remarkably low. In three weeks of school visits, the observers noted only one incident: "One boy shoved another to the ground. The second boy cried. Quickly the teacher came over, sent the aggressor off, and comforted the crying child. In a moment the aggressor returned, apparently on the cue of another teacher, and helped brush the dust off the victim's clothes" (Kessen, 1975, p. 109).

It should be noted that the training regimen for Chinese children in 1973 was not completely pacifistic. In the fifth and sixth grade, children were taught to shoot rifles, and their classroom instruction was full of tales of aggressive-heroic action against "the enemies of society." Young adolescents certainly did not lack in assertiveness—or even in belligerence—in defending their ideology in discussion with foreign visitors. The visitors had the impression that children who were members of a school's leadership structure could be quite severe in their treatment of fellow students who did not conform to a stated rule of conduct. Thus prosocial aggression certainly occurred, but the children seemed to understand quite clearly what kind of aggression was socially approved and what was not.

Observations of aggression in cultures different from our own bring us to an important point: Aggression is intimately related to conceptions of rights and justice and the legitimacy of defending one's own interests or those of one's social group. Psychologists are accustomed to thinking of aggression as being under *stimulus control*—that is, under the influence of immediate environmental events, such as the presence of a particular victim or the occurrence of an uncomplimentary remark from another person. The relationship of aggression and *ideology*, or the society's system of values, is rarely considered; yet ideology affects children's interpretation of external events, as well as parents' response to children's actions. When we examine developmental changes in aggression during the years following preschool age, the increasing role of ideology becomes apparent.

CHANGES IN THE NATURE AND FUNCTION OF AGGRESSION

We have seen that very young children tend to display undirected rage. Gradually they learn that their angry behavior, when directed toward others, can cause distress and can produce certain desired results. A child can often attain a positive objective by hurting others, by threatening them, or simply by being a nuisance until the other person does what is wanted. Furthermore, these negative tactics can stop others from making unwelcome demands and from directing aggression toward the child. A considerable price must be paid, however, for adopting this mode of control. Physical fighting can hurt the aggressor almost as much as it can the victim, and verbal aggression almost always elicits unpleasant counterattacks. If aggressive behavior toward others occurs too frequently or continues too long, friendship and affection can be lost, and the child runs the risk of being avoided, lonely, and unpopular. Thus, children are motivated to search for alternative modes of conflict resolution. As they grow older they enter a bargaining mode in which they reach certain tacit agreements about what will be considered fair. When social groups reach such agreements, the occasions for fighting become progressively more rare.

The development of this process may be seen within families with children of different ages. Very young children do not understand the justification of a system of mutual rights and obligations. Demands from others are seen as impositions on autonomy and are resisted with angry outbursts. We saw in the early work of Goodenough that the frequency of such outbursts is approximately twice as great during the second year of life as it is among children of four or five years of age. Fawl (1963), observing children in a school setting, documented a further decrease in the incidence of emotional outbursts from preschool age to the early school years. Patterson (1976) enumerated the frequency of coercive behaviors in the younger and older siblings of normal boys (the comparison group in his family study). He reported the following rates of coercive behavior in children of different ages:

younger siblings	0.453 coercive responses per minute
subject (usually aged 8–11)	0.277 coercive responses per minute
older siblings	0.177 coercive responses per minute

We do not know the ages of the older and younger groups, but most of the younger siblings must have been preschoolers or first and second graders.

These rates are almost unbelievably high, but we should remember that the definition of coercion encompasses a wide range of distressing actions, including whining, crying, noncompliance with requests, and ignoring. These figures serve to remind us that young children do harass other members of their families frequently. For our present purposes, it is important to note the decline with age in these rates. And it is important to understand the changes in the child's life situation and mode of thinking, feeling, and interpreting situations, all of which lessen the frequency of both angry outbursts and coercive behaviors.

Frustration and aggression

We saw earlier that very young children respond with angry outbursts when parents attempt to impose routines and other forms of control on their behavior. In nursery school the interference by other children with a child's play can also be an occasion for aggression or counteraggression. A widely held theory about aggression suggests that it is a response to frustration (blocking of goal-directed behavior) (Dollard et al., 1939). Is the decline in angry outbursts and aggression related to age changes in the frequency, nature, or response to frustrating events?

1. Frequency of frustration. As children grow older, motor and problem-solving abilities mature, and children become less dependent on their caretakers and more easily able to cope with the world around them. The development of these skills, as well as the maturation of language (which makes possible the verbal mediation of difficult situations), ought to reduce the amount of frustration a child experiences. This reduction

may cause a decline in the occurrence of aggression by reducing the number of occasions for it.

2. Response to frustration. Children may continue to be frustrated fairly often but may have learned alternative, nonaggressive ways of coping with frustration and achieving objectives. At least in the early stages, part of what is learned is the control or inhibition of outward expressions of anger while alternative forms of problem solving take shape.

3. Nature of frustrating event. There may be changes with age in the *kind* of events that frustrate a child, and the frustrations experienced by older children may be less directly linked to an attackable target—that is, they may be self-induced rather than caused by someone else.

All three kinds of changes may be occurring, of course, and probably are. But the developmental changes are not quite so simple as they might appear to be. Consider, for example, the first possibility. It is difficult to be precise about how frequently a child is frustrated. A child's life could be considered highly frustrating, for example, if parents made many rules so that the child was not allowed to touch certain objects, put feet up on the furniture, jump on beds, or go beyond certain narrow spatial limits. A similar claim could be made if parents made many demands, so that the child was required, for example, to adhere to a strict standard of table manners, help with household chores and pick up toys and clothes, be polite to adults, and obey quickly when asked to do something. Does a child frustrated in these ways show frequent outbursts of anger? Not at all. When the extent of frustration is defined in terms of the quantity of restrictions and demands on the child, frustration levels turn out *not* to be related to the amount of aggression that the child displays at home (Sears, Maccoby, and Levin, 1957).[4] Frustration is apparently not so much a function of the objective level of demands and restrictions, but of these things in relation to what the child has come to expect. The usual routine, even if restrictive by the standards of other households, does not usually seem restrictive to the child who has grown up with it—what *is* is taken for granted.

Changes in parental requirements, however, can be acutely frustrating. The growing competencies of the child make it almost inevitable that parental requirements will be escalated to keep pace, and this probably builds an element of frustration into children's socialization. Indeed, increased competency probably results in some self-produced frustrations as newly learned skills enable the child to undertake more difficult enterprises. Thus, children probably do not experience a simple age-related decrease in frustration.

[4] Fawl (1963) also failed to find any relationship between children's aggressive acts or other signs of emotional disturbance and prior blockage of goal-directed behavior.

If frustration itself is not diminishing, perhaps children's ability to cope with frustration is increasing. Are children better able to inhibit and control their emotional reactions as they grow older so that these reactions are less likely to interfere with constructive problem solving? This issue is the subject of Chapter 5, and its discussion is therefore postponed. Let us simply note here that significant growth does take place in such controls and that these developmental changes in impulse control are undoubtedly involved in the decline in the frequency of aggression.

While frustration probably does not diminish as children grow older, the nature of situations that cause frustration does change radically. The child of thirteen months may be frustrated by not being able to walk more than a single step. The child of four years may be frustrated when the addition of one more block destroys a carefully constructed tower or when the tide comes in and ruins a sand castle. The child of ten can be frustrated by schoolwork, or by a social snub, or because a favorite blouse or shirt is not clean and ready to wear to school.

Perhaps the greatest change in the reasons for becoming angry and aggressive is the developing awareness of the concept of *fairness*. Growing children learn that they have certain rights, certain territory that they are allowed—even obligated—to defend. In other words, aggression can have its roots in moral thinking—a paradox, as Seymour Feshbach (1974) points out, but one that (at least after a certain age) seems true. Children learn rules that specify the conditions under which it is appropriate to inflict pain on others. A rule such as "an eye for an eye, a tooth for a tooth" not only justifies retaliatory action but may make the child feel such action is required. We will see later that being aggressive can bring with it a certain feeling of emotional release, but *only when the aggression is believed to be justified*. The relief may be a form of self-congratulation for having acted in an upright way.

A corollary to children's growing understanding that certain intrusions by others are unjustified and deserve aggressive response is the acceptance of certain other intrusions. Interference by a stranger may be experienced as frustrating, but interference from a friend or family member may be much less frustrating if the child is old enough to have entered into a system of mutually accepted rights and obligations with certain other persons. The eye-for-an-eye philosophy is only one stepping stone along a complex developmental path in which the ideology concerning what is right and what one's obligations to others are undergoes several rather basic reformulations. These changes will be examined in some detail in Chapter 8. For the present, the point of interest is that ideas about right and wrong start to become part of frustration and aggression in an important way at about the time children enter school.

From instrumental to hostile aggression

Hartup's study of schoolchildren in a relatively impoverished, urban setting in Minnesota (1974) provides some insight into the development of the ethic of self-defense and retaliation and its role in changing patterns of aggression. The researchers observed six classes of children in nursery school and first and second grade; the children were observed on the playgrounds and in the corridors as well as in the classrooms. Over a ten-week period, all instances of aggression were recorded—aggression being defined as "intentional physical and verbal responses that are directed toward an object or another person and that have the capacity to damage or injure." Narrative reports were prepared for each incident, giving as much detail as possible concerning the instigations and outcomes. For example:

> Marian (a seven-year-old) is complaining to all that David (who is also present) had squirted her on the pants she has to wear tonight. She says "I'm gonna do it to him to see how he likes it." She fills a can with water and David runs to the teacher and tells of her threat. The teacher takes the can from Marian. Marian attacks David and pulls his hair very hard. He cries and swings at Marian as the teacher tries to restrain him; then she takes him upstairs. . . . Later, Marian and Elaine go upstairs and into the room where David is seated with a teacher. He throws a book at Marian. The teacher asks Marian to leave. Marian kicks David, then leaves. David cries and screams, "Get out of here, they're just gonna tease me." (p. 339)

In analyzing incidents of this kind, the researchers distinguished between *instrumental* and *hostile* aggression. In instrumental aggression, distress is produced in another person in order to obtain something the aggressor wants, while in hostile aggression, hurting becomes an end in itself. Hartup, following Buss (1966), Feshbach (1970), and Rule (1974), adopts the assumption that hostile aggression has two prerequisites: The aggressor has been the recipient of an attack that is experienced as a threat to the person's essential self, or *ego*; and the aggressor has inferred that the ego threat was intentional on the part of the person who made it. As Hartup notes, the distinction between the two kinds of aggression is not conceptually clean and, in coding occurrences of aggression, not always easy to make. In the sequence between Marian and David, for example, was Marian showing hostile aggression? She clearly was, in the sense that she was attacking David's person, and her objective seemed to be to get even and restore the balance that presumably existed between the two before David squirted water on her. We cannot be certain that she interpreted David's action as intentional, but it does seem clear that she thought her ego (that is, her status vis-à-vis David) had been attacked. Her counterattack meant, "You can't do that to me"; in other words, she was telling David that she had rights he must not violate.

The decline in the frequency of aggressive incidents across age groups was almost entirely accounted for in Hartup's population by decreasing rates of instrumental aggression. Hostile aggression did not change greatly in frequency, but the way in which it was expressed did change. When insulted, for example, younger children fairly often responded by hitting; older children almost always responded by returning insult for insult. The older children seemed to be operating on the principle of letting the punishment fit the crime—assuming that retaliation should involve returning a given behavior with like behavior.

With development, then, aggression comes more and more to have the function of restoring a balance of power in the positions of two egos. The developmental requirement for this kind of aggression is that children must have a strong sense of self—they must understand their actual or desired positions in the power hierarchy, the rights of those positions, and the places and privileges of others. The power structure of a group of children of course has properties different from a structure that includes both adults and children. Children must come to understand that in interaction with adults, the adults have certain rights that the children do not share. This inequity in power is almost always accepted, and most children of age six or older seldom become angry about or aggressive because of the exercise of legitimate adult authority. For example a ten-year-old girl will not try to get even with her father because the father will not allow her to drive the family car. It is quite a different matter, however, if a playmate tries to forbid an action that the girl thinks other children have no right to question.

Power relationships among children change radically with time and circumstance. A great deal of the quarreling among siblings takes the form of arguments about who has the right to demand what of whom. Perhaps if parents clarified a reciprocal system of rights and obligations among siblings instead of reacting directly to acts of aggression, quarrels within the family might be more successfully moderated. One thing is clear: After the preschool years, aggression among children occurs primarily under circumstances in which existing networks of rights and obligations are either unclear or being challenged. The same probably holds true for conflicts between adolescents and their parents. Concepts of mutual rights and duties change profoundly during this period, and inevitable strain (and a probable increase in aggression) occurs if the views of parents and adolescent children do not change at the same rate.

Other aspects of age-related changes in children's cognitive and social competencies that have an impact on aggression are: (1) Children become more skilled at judging when the acts of other people are intentional and (2) group membership begins to influence aggressive output. When being a group member defines the child's sense of self, an attack on the group becomes equivalent to an attack on the child's own ego. A member of a juvenile gang takes personal affront when the gang or any of its symbols is derogated by members of another gang. An individual who closely identifies with a clan, a team, a lodge, a tribe, or a nation can feel the same way. We saw the rudimentary beginning of group identification and mutual group support when Marian recruited Elaine to go with her to retaliate against David. As children grow older, their groups become more cohesive, and pressure becomes strong to defend the group's interests with aggression where necessary.

THE DEVELOPMENT OF NONAGGRESSIVE MEANS OF ASSERTIVENESS

The development of aggression cannot be understood if one considers aggression to be an aspect of behavior that is isolated from other aspects of development occurring at the same time. We have seen that as early as the preschool years, children use aggression to protect their rights and their territory from incursions by other children. Aggression can be viewed, then, as a form of self-reliance and a more mature form of behavior than frightened withdrawal to adult protection or passive yielding to others' assertions. It is less mature, however, than nonaggressive forms of self-assertion and self-defense. Aggression carries a high cost; it is painful to the aggressor, and it jeopardizes continued social contact. It is common, therefore, for a child to adopt aggression as a means of self-assertion for a brief period and then discard it in favor of more mature techniques. The use of verbal skills—the ability to muster arguments in support of one's position and present them effectively—is of course a major alternative. Another useful alternative is bargaining: Children learn how to discover what each wants from the other and what each will concede in the interests of mutual satisfaction. But such skills are acquired only gradually. We must assume that children learn nonaggressive methods of conflict resolution at least partly in their own homes. It seems likely that the key to this learning is the development of the ability to share and understand the others' feelings.

The changing place of aggression in personality structure

We saw earlier that preschool children who often behaved aggressively tended to be the same children who frequently were seen playing happily with their age mates. Indeed, these children were usually quite well liked by other children and often took the lead in organizing activities that everyone enjoyed. By school age, however, this changes. Children who frequently get into fights are unpopular with other children. They either have very few friends or are avoided altogether and become social isolates. Their teachers complain that they do not cooperate with classroom routines or pay attention to instructions, and they usually do poorly in their academic work (Patterson, 1976). Furthermore, children (or most demonstrably, boys) who are clearly more aggressive than other children by the time they have reached school age tend to remain so as they grow older (Olweus, 1979). We can only surmise that children who remain highly aggressive at an age when other children's aggression is declining have all or some of the following problems. They may not have learned the rules about aggression that other children, as a social group, accept and enforce, so others tend to see their aggression as unjustified or inappropriate (e.g., these children may not have learned to fit into the dominance hierarchy). Their emotional reactions may still be at the impulsive, uncontrolled level that is common in younger children. Or, perhaps most important, they may have failed to learn prosocial feelings and alternative nonaggressive means of getting what they want. In most children, the development of affection and sympathy for others and the acquisition of skills in helping and cooperating with others serve to moderate aggressive impulses.

Empathy, altruism, and aggression

The ability to inhibit aggression, or to behave in nonaggressive ways, is not merely a matter of possessing alternative social skills. It is also a matter of feeling positive affection for others and having the desire not to hurt them. As we have noted, very young children only dimly understand that other people can experience distress comparable to their own. It has long been thought that *empathy*—the ability to appreciate other people's emotional states, to project one's self psychologically into another person's situation and experience vicariously part of what the other person experiences—is a central element in an individual's becoming socialized. More than three-quarters of a century ago, E. A. Ross wrote, "In every cluster there are predatory persons—moral idiots or moral lunatics, who can no more put themselves in the place of another than the beast can enter into the anguish of its prey or the parasite sympathize with his host" (1901, p. 51). Sympathizing with one's victim, Ross thought, must surely cause an attacker to inhibit, or at least moderate, an attack. In Ross's terms, young children must be "moral idiots" because of their inability to empathize with the distress of others. We have seen that children's readiness to hurt other people does decline as they grow older. We have reason to believe that their increasing ability to understand and sympathize with other people's feelings is a factor moderating their aggression.

The relationship between empathy and aggression has been studied by the Feshbachs (1969). They distinguish three components of empathy: (1) discriminating and labeling other people's emotional states, (2) being able to put one's self (mentally) in another person's place and understand how things would look from that person's point of view, and (3) sharing the other person's emotional response. The Feshbachs measure empathy by showing children pictures of other children experiencing different emotions (adults had previously agreed on and identified readily the emotional states the pictures displayed). The young subjects were asked how they felt after viewing a set of pictures that depicted a particular emotional state. A child's empathy score was based on the extent to which the child recognized and shared that emotion. Thus, the procedure focused on the first and third components of empathy.

The researchers report that in a group of children aged six to seven, the more empathic children were less aggressive toward their schoolmates (aggression being judged on the basis of teachers' reports), while with children aged four to five, high empathy scores were associated with high rates of aggression. Curiously, these results were obtained only for boys. Among girls, empathy and aggression were virtually unrelated.[5] These results suggest that (at least for boys) there may be a developmental change in the ability to inhibit aggression on the basis of feelings of sympathy for one's victim. The Feshbach procedure measures empathy in a rather abstract form. It is reasonable to suppose that children might be capable of inhibiting aggression at an age earlier than six or seven if they were dealing with people whom they knew intimately and with whom they had strong emotional ties.

The children in the Feshbach study differed considerably among themselves—even within groups in which the children were all the same age—in how empathically they responded to the emotional states displayed in the pictures. Clearly, if we wish to understand why some children are more aggressive than others, we need to know more about the conditions that would lead some children to be more empathic than others. Norma Feshbach has looked at the child-rearing attitudes and practices of the parents of children whose empathic abilities were assessed. She reports that certain characteristics are indeed associated with the high levels of empathy in the children. She found evidence that an accepting, nonpunitive parent who is not excessively restrictive has a more empathic child, on the average.

[5]Barnett, Matthews, and Howard (1979) found that among six- to seven-year-old boys (but not girls), the more empathic children were also less competitive.

The work on empathy serves to highlight a major point: There are modes of feeling and action that are incompatible with aggression. It is difficult to feel both sympathy for another's distress and hatred for that person at the same time. It is also difficult to engage in helpful, supportive behavior toward another and simultaneously show hostility. Some time ago, Bandura and Walters (1963) emphasized the importance of teaching children alternative—and incompatible—modes of behavior as a means of reducing the frequency of aggressive action. We now know that not only the development of empathic reactions but also the development of altruistic, or unselfish, behavior serve to reduce the likelihood that a child will behave aggressively. Even so simple a procedure as teaching children to say helpful words—like *nice, kind,* and *help*—rather than aggressive words—like *mean, hate,* and *hurt*—before they enter a social situation serves to reduce the level of aggression they show in that situation (Slaby, 1974). This finding suggests that a child's tendency to be aggressive does not depend entirely on the outcomes of the child's previous aggressive behaviors, even though such outcomes are important. Aggression is part of a network of behaviors, and in some cases aggression may be regarded as a residual—a kind of activity that occurs because other possible actions have failed to occur. Aggressiveness can be changed by increasing the likelihood that children will choose alternative forms of action as well as by training children directly with respect to aggression itself.

Is aggression ever helpful within the family?

We come to a final, difficult question concerning the role of aggression in family interactions. There is considerable evidence that feelings are reciprocated within families. When one family member smiles or shows other positive feelings, kindness and positive affect are likely to be returned, and when a family member is coercive, there is a strong tendency for the response to be countercoercive. Displays of anger tend to escalate to levels where rational problem-solving discussions between family members cannot occur. Is there any reason, then, why child-training efforts should not be directed single-mindedly toward stamping out children's aggression?

Our first reason for pulling back from such an extreme position is that, as we have seen, aggression is a form of self-assertion that may serve as a kind of half-way station to more effective and socially acceptable means of self-defense. Self-defense is not an isolated value, of course, and it needs to be placed in the context of developing respect for others' rights. But refusing to let oneself be unreasonably coerced by others is an important part of becoming socially competent. We are not saying that all children must go through a stage of using aggression as their primary means of self-defense, but many children do. To build up children's anxiety to the point of near-total inhibition of aggression may rob them of a necessary mode of action, at least temporarily, while alternative skills are being developed.

Another reason for permitting the expression of aggression is the commonly held belief that there are dangers in bottling up aggression. Much study has been devoted to the question of whether an aggressive blowup serves to permit the aggressor to "get it out of his or her system" and return to a calmer state of mind. Several things are now reasonably well demonstrated (for detailed evidence, see Geen and Quanty, 1977):

1. Being aggressive on one occasion does not reduce the probability of an individual's being aggressive on subsequent occasions. On the contrary, subsequent aggression is increased, even if only a short time has passed since the initial outburst.

2. Aggressive action does sometimes relieve the actor's inner tension (this statement holds if one is willing to accept blood pressure as an indicator of inner tension).

3. The release of tension occurs only if the actor feels justified in being aggressive and does not fear retaliation or feel guilt.

Horowitz and his associates (1978) have recently shown that adult patients in psychotherapy are able to move toward greater intimacy in a close relationship following a display of aggression, and in such situations, aggression does indeed clear the air. But children can hardly aggress against their parents without feeling some guilt, or at least fear of retaliation, which probably precludes the release of tension following such an episode. Parents can also feel nagging guilt after punishing their children, especially if their anger has been strong and the punishment possibly too severe. We doubt whether there is enough release of tension involved in an aggressive act by a child toward a parent, or by a parent toward a child, to counteract the additional aggressive buildup that ensues when the target counterattacks and the original agent must respond to a new source of tension.

Suppose that in order to avoid this buildup of tension, the aggrieved person simply inhibits aggression. This formula is recommended in much popular wisdom. "If you can't think of anything nice to say, don't say anything at all" is an admonition parents commonly deliver to children. Or, "Don't speak in anger—you'll say something you'll be sorry for later." Or, "I don't want to hear you talking like that to your mother. Go to your room and stay there till you can be pleasant." Sometimes a simple cooling-off period will serve to reduce the tension and restore a pleasant family atmosphere (especially if the family is one with many mutually rewarding activities going on). But often the problem that led to the original frustration has not disappeared, and when it recurs, the frustrated individual begins to brood and becomes silently preoccupied with grievances.

When the cumulative frustrations become too great and the individual finally does speak out, the heat of the outburst seems out of proportion to the incident that produced it. In fact, the individual is not reacting to one provocation, but to a long string of stored-up incidents that may have been considerably exaggerated in recollection: "You're *always* using my razor!" or, "You *never* knock when you come into my room!" or, "That's the *fifteenth* time you've interrupted me!" Family counselors have noted that a person's grievances against family members frequently are expressed in well-organized, detailed form, as though they had been rehearsed. Certainly, dwelling on grievances while inhibiting overt aggression can reduce communication among family members. When long-inhibited grievances do surface, they do so with an intensity that engenders counteraggression and interferes with any progress toward redress of the real interpersonal problems that exist.

Some practical suggestions from therapists

Clearly, then, there is a price to be paid for the inhibition of aggression. And a price is also paid for its expression. It appears to be a case of "damned if you do, damned if you don't." A solution for this cost-benefit problem has been offered by Thomas Gordon, a widely experienced practitioner who has worked with a large number of families in the interest of improving the quality of family life. In his book *Parent Effectiveness Training* (1970), he emphasizes the value of using "I-messages" rather than "you-messages" in conflict situations. That is, if a parent is irritated because a child is demanding attention over a trivial matter when the parent is tired, it is ineffective for the parent to either say nothing or comply with the child's wishes in order to avoid an argument. In the first case, the child will probably continue the annoying behavior, and the parent's irritation will mount. In the second case, the parent will feel resentful of an unwarranted intrusion and will either be tempted to retaliate in some way or will feel coerced and, possibly, depressed. The parent must speak out, but he or she has a choice as to what to say: "You are a pest" is the "you" possibility. "I am tired" is the "I" possibility.

According to Gordon, the "I" message is preferred because it helps the child understand the nature of the interpersonal problem and fosters the child's empathic feelings. The "you" message attacks the child's ego and escalates the interchange because it calls for counterattack in self-defense.

Haim Ginott (1965), another therapist with wide experience in dealing with distressed families, agrees with the Gordon position and makes an additional point. He believes that it is important to make a distinction between *angry feelings* and *aggressive actions.* Parents should not allow children to hurt other members of the family and should keep their own aggressive actions to a minimum, even when such an action can be justified as being a needed punishment. Angry feelings are inevitable, Ginott believes, and should be acknowledged. We have seen that an aggressor who feels justified in an aggression experiences a release of tension. However, Ginott believes that within families aggressive *actions* are inevitably accompanied by guilt feelings and are not therapeutic, and he suggests that release of tension cannot be expected from the *expression* of angry feelings, but only from the *acknowledgment* of those feelings. Contrast the two following sequences:

1. Child: Mommy, I *hate* Janet!

    Mother: Oh, no you don't honey. Janet is your sister and I *know* you love your sister.

2. Child: Mommy, I *hate* Janet!

    Mother: Yes, I can see you're really mad at her right now. Sometimes you love her, though.

According to Ginott, the second exchange will serve to release the child's tension, and the first will not. Although we know of no experimental evidence that bears on this hypothesis directly, the second exchange does seem less likely to result in high levels of anxiety over aggressive feelings, and it conveys the information that it is possible to feel both love and hate for the same person—knowledge that can contribute substantially to the development of emotional maturity.

Several themes have emerged from the research on family interaction (see the previously cited research by the Sears group and the Patterson group) and from the distilled wisdom of experienced clinicians—themes about which there is considerable agreement. Permitting aggression—letting the child display aggressive behavior toward other family members—does not work: The child only becomes more aggressive and generates countercoercion in other family members, with a destructive effect on the positive aspects of family functioning. Repressing the child's aggression through physical punishment, withdrawal of love, or denial of the child's angry feelings does not work either. What seems to be effective is fostering the normal developmental processes that allow children to abandon aggression in favor of more constructive ways of getting what they want. At present we have more information about what makes children aggressive than about what makes them nonaggressive. However, the work we have reviewed suggests that at least some of the following elements are involved in constructive parental treatment of children's aggression:

1. not yielding to children's attempts to control others by coercive means

2. arranging a cooling-off period if tempers are too aroused to permit constructive problem solving

3. focusing attention on the solution of the real interpersonal issues that are responsible for the initial frustration and anger

4. supporting empathic feelings by emphasizing how the child's behavior makes others feel and by building family loyalty

5. teaching nonaggressive social skills—undoubtedly an important aspect of this is providing opportunities for cooperative endeavors that have a positive outcome for all participants, so children will come to understand that social encounters do not always have to have a winner and a loser

We do not know whether children's expression of aggression is directly affected by parents' teaching of moral rules—the rights and obligations of the child in relation to others. But, the increasing role of the understanding of such rules in determining when and toward whom a child's aggression occurs suggests that this teaching does have an effect. Parents are not the only instructors in morality, however. We know that a great deal of what children learn about fairness and justice comes through play with other children. In fact, friends may be more important than parents in fostering this aspect of control of aggression.

SUMMARY AND COMMENTARY

Human beings share with other species certain behavioral traits when it comes to acting aggressively. Both animals and humans will attack others and, under certain conditions, fight to defend themselves. Both precede or accompany their attacks with certain facial expressions, bodily postures, and vocalizations that other members of the species understand to be threats. Aggression (in the sense of attack behavior and its accompanying gestures) is not present in human or animal infants and emerges at different ages according to species. Within a species, rearing conditions probably make some difference in timing—that is, when the aggressive pattern first appears—but emergence is also a matter of species-specific maturation. Thus, aggression clearly has an instinctive component; however, the frequency and intensity of an individual's aggression and the targets selected are influenced by the social environment and the individual's place in the social structure. Aggression, then, is learned as well as being instinctive.

Aggression is *intentional* in all species in the sense that the aggressor gives signals of an impending attack and focuses the attack on a specific target rather than striking out at random. However, intention takes much more complex forms in human beings; human cognition transforms human aggression (at least after early childhood) into a much more subtle and varied phenomenon than is found in lower animals.

In human children, the development of aggression occurs in the following steps:

1. In the first two years true aggression is not seen. Children have outbursts of anger, but these outbursts are seldom focused. A child who grabs a toy from another child is interested in getting the toy, not in hurting or dominating the other child.

2. By the age of about two-and-a-half or three, unmistakably aggressive behavior appears. Aggression becomes focused on specific targets, and threat gestures are made.

3. Between the ages of two-and-a-half and five, aggression occurs primarily during struggles over play materials and the control of space. During most of this period, aggression generally occurs during social play, and the more sociable and competent children are most frequently involved in fights.

4. There is development of dominance hierarchies, which help to define the rights to objects and space. These hierarchies probably function to reduce the incidence of overt fighting.

5. The frequency with which an individual child shows aggression is related to the child's success in using aggression in such struggles. However, some children seem to be readier than others to increase their level of aggression when their aggressive acts succeed.

6. We do not know precisely when the frequency of aggression begins to decline; no doubt the decline depends on whether the aggression is physical or verbal and whether the target is another child or members of the family. Available evidence suggests that aggression in normal children does decline fairly rapidly from the preschool years on.

7. After the preschool years, aggression changes qualitatively: It is less often a struggle over objects and more often a clash of egos. Insults (that is, ego attacks) become both a major means of hurting others and a major occasion for retaliation. Concepts of what is fair and understanding who has what rights

and obligations enter into the determination of what issues will be fought over and when individuals will defend themselves.

8. Children become much more sophisticated in judging when others have intended to hurt (and hence, when retaliation is justified) and how to hurt their chosen victims. However, their positive social skills, particularly their ability to communicate with others and cooperate with them in achieving joint goals, also expand. Thus, while children's aggressive capacities are becoming more refined, so are their alternatives. The behavioral outcome represents a balance between the two.

9. In most children, after about the age of six or seven, the ability to *empathize* with others begins to be a force that moderates aggression.

From the outset, parents play a role in the development of children's aggression. The frequency of the child's outbursts of anger increases during the second year, when parents respond less readily to the child's expressions of needs and begin to impose demands of their own for conformity to household routines and rules of behavior. When children begin to focus their anger and to hurt others intentionally, parents begin to regulate the timing and direction of expression of the anger. Most parents allow or even encourage their children to defend themselves when attacked by other children but strictly limit aggression within the family.

There are certain children who display abnormally high levels of aggression both within and outside the home, compared with other children of the same age. The patterns of family interaction in the homes of such children have been examined. In these families:

10. All members tend to use coercive tactics when trying to influence one another, and all respond aggressively to influence attempts. Thus, cycles of mutual aggression escalate rapidly.

11. Coercive cycles interfere with more constructive problem solving by making dispassionate discussion nearly impossible and interaction so unpleasant that family members avoid one another.

Therapeutic work with these families has indicated:

12. Coercive cycles can be reduced if parents do not yield to their children's aggressive pressure and if they respond nonpunitively.

This finding is consistent with the work with more normal families, where it has been shown that the lowest levels of aggression are found in children whose parents firmly refuse to allow aggression toward other family members and enforce their rules with a minimum of punishment. Equally important (though less well documented):

13. Children's developmental transition from aggressive to non-aggressive means of resolving social disputes is fostered when parents teach a variety of positive social skills, including sensitivity to the feelings of others.

CHAPTER 5

Impulse Control

Young children are impulsive. They act without thinking. They respond to immediate stimuli without remembering the lessons of the past or considering future consequences. Children's impulsiveness reflects a larger fact about their behavior: They do not impose much organization on their actions. The sequence of their activity often seems almost random. Unlike adults, they do not integrate their pursuit of larger goals with movement toward smaller subgoals. They often simply repeat previous activities, or they move quickly from one unrelated activity to another. What makes their behavior different from adults' behavior is the absence of organization in the progression of action.

In order to understand impulsiveness, we must first consider its opposite. What is nonimpulsive—organized—behavior? How do people organize their actions? What internal mechanisms do they mobilize in the interests of self-control? How do these abilities develop? To answer these questions, we begin by looking at the infant's mastery of self-control as she or he learns to delay simple motor movements. We then move on to a discussion of control and the lack of control of complex actions and higher-level mental activities, and we also look at the development of the child's ability to delay emotional satisfaction. The chapter ends with a discussion of the implications these issues have for the parent-child interaction, considering (1) how parents carry out the regulating functions that children cannot manage for themselves and (2) how parental techniques contribute to the development of the child's self-regulatory functions.

THE ORGANIZATION OF BEHAVIOR

In order to clarify what we mean by *organization* in behavior, let us consider a series of actions carried out by an adult who is behaving in an unorganized way. Imagine that a man is working at his desk and breaks the point of his pencil. The pencil sharpener is in the kitchen. He goes to the kitchen to sharpen the pencil and on the way passes the refrigerator. He decides to have a snack. While making a sandwich, he realizes he will want something to drink, and he decides to mix a pitcher of juice. While getting water for the mixture, he notices a plant that needs water. While watering the plant, he remembers that several plants in the living room probably also need water. He goes into the living room to water them, sees the morning newspaper, and remembers he hadn't finished the comic page. He settles down to read, forgetting the half-made sandwich on the kitchen table.

While all of us act in a like way occasionally, this vignette does not describe typical adult behavior. Usually we can postpone a snack until we have finished a specified portion of our work. We would most likely take the newspaper into the kitchen, finish making the sandwich, and read while eating. In other words, we know which of a set of actions can successfully be performed simultaneously and which cannot. We normally organize our behavior to take advantage of these possibilities and increase the number of items on our agenda that we can carry out. We have nested sets of plans: large, overarching ones that may take years to complete (such as going through college); smaller plans that nevertheless cover considerable spans of time (such as registering for a specific course, going to class regularly, doing the required work, taking the exam); plans that organize the activities of a single day and that specify when we work, eat, or meet our friends; and finally, moment-to-moment organizational structures that govern the order in which specific actions will be carried out. (For a discussion of the hierarchical organization of plans, see Miller, Galanter, and Pribram, *Plans and the Structure of Behavior*, 1960, and Schank and Abelson, *Scripts, Plans, Goals, and Understanding*, 1977.) Sometimes a degree of organization is imposed by intrinsic characteristics of actions and their outcomes. We cannot eat dinner until we have prepared it, nor dry the dishes until we have washed them. Quite often, however, we must choose among alternative sequences. With maturity we learn not to waste time agonizing over minor alternatives that have insignificant consequences, but to spend the necessary time and effort on choices that matter.

Early childhood may seem like a time when the individual does no choosing at all—when the person is entirely under the control of external circumstances and flits from one thing to another depending on the demands of the immediate situation. But we must be careful about this kind of glib generalization. The work of Piaget and his followers has taught us that even in infancy, children are quite selective about the elements of a situation they notice and use. At about the beginning of the second year of life, Piaget tells us, children become "little scientists," engaging in fairly sustained bouts of rather systematic play—for example, varying the force they impose on an object and watching changes in the object's motion. This amounts to the imposition of a plan on a sequence of actions, reminding us that behavior is probably always organized to some degree, from the earliest time of life.

Like so many other kinds of behavior, the ability to organize and regulate actions changes as children grow and develop:

1. The child begins to be able to delay certain actions until a time when they will fit in more appropriately with concurrent actions or will have more acceptable consequences.

2. Future consequences are weighted more heavily in the choice of present actions.

3. If the pursuit of a goal is temporarily blocked by an externally imposed barrier, the child is able to put the blocked activity on hold while attempting to find a way around the barrier.

4. When goal activity is blocked, the child does not become so emotionally aroused that his or her behavior becomes disorganized in a tantrum episode.

5. The child becomes capable of doing more than one thing at a time—integrating those enterprises that are compatible.

6. The child becomes more able to *concentrate*—to block out extraneous, irrelevant stimulation and maximize the input of information (from the external environment and from memory) needed for the execution of the current plan.

Underlying this growth in control is the development of several self-regulating mechanisms. Children must learn *inhibition*. They must learn not to carry out immediately every action that is ready for execution and that the environment is stimulating them to perform. Choosing from among alternatives means deciding to do some things and deciding *not* to do others. Children must also develop a *future-time orientation*. They must learn to think ahead and consider the total balance of desired outcomes, inhibiting certain actions that might yield a small immediate gain at the price of a long-term loss. The process of looking ahead also implies looking backward. That is, previous experience must be used to assess probable immediate and long-range outcomes. Memory is the basis of anticipation. So in a sense, the time frame for children's behavior expands in both directions—events in future time are given more weight through use of information from the past. Finally, children must learn *emotional control*. Inhibition, delay, detour, and the sacrifice of short-term gains—all are frustrating and produce emotional reactions. Emotions can be channeled into constructive problem solving or can take the form of disorganizing emotional storms. The management of emotional states occupies a central place in the development of children's capacity to maintain and improve the level of organization of their behavior.

The ability to organize behavior affects every aspect of children's lives. The quality of their solitary activities—the depth of solitary play, the complexity of problems that can be solved, even the capacity to anticipate dangers and thus guard their own safety—depends on the extent to which self-controlling mechanisms are available. Social interactions are affected too. We saw in Chapter 2 that the quality of attachment changes when children become able to wait at least briefly for their parents' attention, thus coordinating their ongoing stream of action with an adult's. Sustaining cooperative play with another child also involves enduring the momentary frustration of taking turns. Clearly, a child who has not yet established at least a moderate level of impulse control requires a different kind of parenting than a child who has developed some control. The study of impulse control, then, must consider both the development of the child's self-controlling mechanisms and the way the parent-child relationship is related to this development.

THE INHIBITION OF ACTION

The first step in the development of self-control is learning to stop a motor movement. Before most children can walk, they (fortunately) begin to be able *not* to touch, not to act. When they do become mobile, they may seem extremely active—in the sense that they do a great deal of running, jumping, and climbing—but their activity is not normally a matter of blind rushing about. Some children, however, are handicapped in their ability to impose restraints on their physical activity. Their poorly regulated and often inappropriate behavior can create serious problems for them and for their families. Difficulty inhibiting action can also take the form of premature judgments. The child who can reflect and plan before acting has a skill that is particularly useful in gaining mastery of the environment.

Inhibiting motor movements

Suppose an infant in a highchair has been happily reaching for and manipulating familiar toys and then an entirely unfamiliar object is placed in front of the child. The infant will react to the strangeness of the object—there will be a sudden sobering of the child's facial expression. But an infant younger than eight months will reach out and pick up the object. A month later, the infant's expression continues to show surprise and wariness, but the object is not picked up. In fact, the child will now pull back and remain quite still, watching the object (Schaffer, 1974). We see here the beginning of the ability to *inhibit* a movement.

Years pass before this ability is fully mature. Anyone who has ever supervised children's outdoor sports activities—potato-sack races, three-legged races, and the like—knows about children's problems with "ready, set, go" signals. Children younger than five will quite frequently jump the gun. A. R. Luria (1961) traced the development, between the ages of two and four, of children's ability to respond motorically to stop and go signals. Luria gave each child a small rubber bulb to hold and instructed the child to press the bulb when a green light went on and not to press the bulb when a red light went on. The younger children tended to press the bulb for the red as well as for the green light, even though other tests showed they could easily discriminate between the two lights. Luria believed that the younger children's difficulty with the don't-press situation stemmed from their inability to use verbal self-instruction in an inhibitory way. Miller, Shelton, and Flavell (1970), repeating these experiments, concluded that the child's difficulty with don't-press instructions had little to do with the use of specifically verbal self-instructions. They did find that the difficulty with inhibition was quite real, however. Their young subjects could easily press when signaled to do so, but they could not easily refrain from pressing. They documented a clear improvement between the ages of three years two months and four years eleven months in children's ability to inhibit a given action on demand.

A young child's difficulty with motor inhibition applies not only to performing or not performing an action, but also to regulating the pace of movement. Children who are able to carry out a task at a moderate or fast pace may be unable to do the same thing slowly. Kagan noted this problem in some of his early studies of impulsiveness, when he asked preschool children to draw a line as slowly as possible. He found that many children would begin the line slowly and then complete the line with a sudden jerky movement; apparently they could inhibit the pace of movement only briefly.

Subsequent studies of response inhibition have added other procedures to the draw-a-line-slowly task (Maccoby et al., 1965; Ward, 1973). For example, a narrow path on the floor is laid out with two strips of masking tape, and children are asked to walk between the strips without stepping on them. A large-scale longitudinal study of children from low-income neighborhoods in several different parts of the United States revealed that between the ages of three-and-a-half and five years, considerable change took place in children's ability to slow the pace of their movement in both the walking task and when drawing a line slowly. When working at their normal pace, the rate of movement increased as the children grew older, indicating that motor coordination had improved. At the younger ages the children had considerable difficulty in executing the slow movements; however, they were able to move more slowly at age five than at age four, and more slowly still at age six (Ward, 1973).

If infants of nine months can stop themselves from reaching for an unfamiliar object, why should older children have difficulty inhibiting a movement of their hands when asked not to press or have difficulty slowing down their walking or drawing? Clearly the development of the ability to inhibit movement occurs gradually and varies according to situation and type of movement. We know very little about which aspects of inhibition are especially easy or difficult for young children. At present we can only say that at a certain point in the development of these skills, go signals are easier to follow than are stop or slow signals, whether the signals come from outside or are self-administered.

Activity level

If an adult tried to imitate the movements of a child of two-and-a-half, the adult would be exhausted very soon. A young child's expenditure of energy in running, jumping, climbing, pouncing, and wiggling can amaze an adult who is not accustomed to the company of preschoolers. A discussion of activity is included in this chapter because the kind and amount of children's physical activity and their ability to regulate their own behavior are related to their ability to sustain attention to a chosen task and resist disorganizing distractions. Regulation of motoric activity goes beyond the simple process of inhibition, although inhibition is of course involved.

During the first two years of life, children learn to crawl, then to walk, and then to run. With each new locomotor skill, faster and farther movement is possible, and activity level, at least as measured by the amount of ground traversed in a given time, increases (Kagan, 1971). Does children's general activity level increase or decrease after the age of two? This may not be a very meaningful question. Whether children are sitting still, walking, climbing, or running, depends on whether they are indoors or outdoors, playing with blocks or a jungle gym, and alone or with other young children. In fairly regular cycles during a twenty-four-hour period, children move from sleep to quiet wakefulness to periods of high activity.

The effect of context on activities is illustrated by the work of Routh, Shroeder, and O'Tuama (1974). They gave toys to a group of children between the ages of three and nine years, and they found a decrease with age in the children's movement around the playroom.

At least this was true when the children were alone in the room. The presence of another person changes the possibilities for active play, however, so the age changes in activity that are seen when the children are alone are not duplicated when the children are with others (Routh, Walton, and Pedan-Belkin, 1978). Nevertheless, interesting questions can be asked about the nature of young children's locomotor activity and how it changes with age.

Do young children need more physical activity than older people? On a long car trip many parents feel that they must stop periodically to let their two- or three-year-old child run about. For the same reason, schools provide recesses for young children. There seem to be two theories about why such activity breaks are desirable:

1. There is a buildup of energy that occurs during periods of inactivity, and the energy will produce intolerable restlessness unless it is expended. Only after children have gotten rid of extra energy can they settle down to more quiet activity. The assumption is that young children have a higher level of energy and that the buildup is faster than in older people.

2. Energy expenditure promotes alertness. The idea here is that people become lethargic during periods of inactivity. If they do not fall asleep, they become bored and have difficulty concentrating or taking an interest in their surroundings. A period of physical activity recharges energy levels and improves subsequent concentration and behavioral organization. Young children probably become bored or distracted more easily than older people, and they therefore may be said to have more need for the arousing activity that will sustain organized behavior.

Both positions may be true in certain ways. Exercise physiologists have found that both too much or too little arousal can interfere with organized activity. There is an optimum level of arousal, and physical activity is probably implicated in the maintenance of this level. In general, however, the physiologists lean toward the idea that exercise increases rather than decreases arousal. Physical activity readies the body for quick use of its energy store. During exercise, glucose and then fatty acids become more available for use as energy. Whether young children need such recharging especially often is something we simply do not know.

Do young children literally have more energy than older people? We know that between the ages of two and four, the speed at which the body burns its fuel (the *basal metabolism rate*) is at its highest level. In fact, during this preschool period the rate is *much* higher than it is in adults and thereafter regularly declines with age throughout the life cycle (Eichorn, 1970). It is worth noting that throughout childhood boys have a higher basal metabolism rate than girls. A high basal metabolism rate does not necessarily mean that young children have more energy to expend in activity, however. They may just use up more energy in the process of maintaining basic bodily functions. Or it is even possible that their high levels of physical activity lead to a high basal metabolism rate, rather than the reverse. We do not know what the relationship is between the physiology of energy exchange and the amount of overt physical activity people of different ages or sexes engage in.

While the total amount of bodily activity probably does decline with age, this is difficult to prove. The problem is that younger children engage in different physical activities than older children. Young children seem to move for the sake of moving. They like to jump on beds and furniture. They will go round and round the house on a wheeled toy or chase one another from room to room until the noise becomes so irritating that adults insist they stop. In contrast, older children spend more time in indoor situations (such as classrooms), which call for quiet sitting rather than active moving. Outdoor activities become more organized and more constrained by rules as children become older. Activity level at a given moment often depends on the part being taken in group activity; for example, whether the child is the pitcher or a fielder in a baseball game.

Activity level, then, is greatly affected by age-related changes in the situations in which children spend their time. In addition, changes take place in the way children use toys. In situations with minimal constraints, young children spend relatively brief periods in sustained play with a single toy and shift quickly from one activity to another. Such changes in focus usually mean that the child is moving around a room between bouts of quieter play. Older children, playing in the same situation, concentrate for a longer period on a single enterprise, with a resulting reduction in overall activity level. Kagan (1971) refers to these attentional shifts as the *tempo* of a child's play and shows that younger children have more of these shifts. Maccoby and Feldman (1972) documented a similar trend. They observed children in their laboratory playroom and recorded the longest period of uninterrupted play with a single toy. They found that at age two the average longest period of sustained play was thirty seconds, while at age two-and-a-half it was forty-two seconds, and at age three, fifty-five seconds. These findings suggest that one reason older children are less active in indoor situations is that their play has increasing depth or focus.

The problem of overactivity

We have been discussing normal developmental change in levels of activity. But at any given age, children differ in their activity levels. Are certain children consistently more active than others? Are they more active over long periods of time? If we are talking about children within the normal range—children who have no neurological damage—the answer seems to be "no," at least for the first few years of life. Certain infants are very active. Compared with other children they are more likely to squirm during bathing and dressing, move while asleep, roll over at an early age, and move quickly around the room once they have learned to crawl. The activity level of individual children is moderately predictable from the age of nine months to about two years, but present evidence indicates that children who are especially active during their first two years are no more active than average by the time they reach the age of three or four (Buss and Plomin, 1975). Once children have grown older, however, individual activity levels remain more stable over time. If children's activity is rated on the basis of such things as whether time is spent in active outdoor sports and games or in quiet games and reading, children who are highly active in the third and fourth grades tend to receive similar ratings in the fifth and sixth grades (Walker, 1967). And covering a wider age span, Battle and Lacey (1972) report moderate relationships between activity level at preschool age and during the grade school years and early adolescence. Sometime before children start school, their activity level probably becomes moderately stabilized, and it becomes possible to predict future activity level from present functioning.

Studies of twins suggest that higher activity levels may be, to some extent, built in—that is, there may be a genetic predisposition toward being active or inactive. Identical twins are more alike than same-sex fraternal twins in their activity level, and there may be some parent-child resemblance as well (reported in Ross and Ross, 1976). Of course, the tendency to be highly active, like any inherited predisposition, can be greatly modified by experience.

Especially consistent in their activity level are *hyperactive* children. Hyperactive children are not merely highly active. They exhibit a clinically identifiable set of behaviors, which Ross and Ross (1976) define as follows:

> The term hyperactive refers to a child who consistently exhibits a high level of activity in situations where it is clearly inappropriate, is unable to inhibit his activity on command, often appears capable of only one speed of response, and is often characterized by other physiological, learning, and behavioral symptoms and problems. (pp. 11–12)

A child who is merely highly active may or may not be impulsive; that is, such a child may manifest some or none of the behaviors discussed elsewhere in this chapter. Such children will usually be able to inhibit their activity, at least for considerable periods, in situations that call for being quietly attentive. Hyperactive children have great difficulty with such inhibition. They become uncontrollably restless in situations where moving about is inappropriate.

Ross and Ross (1976) present detailed descriptions of hyperactive children at different ages. Here they describe a four-year-old boy:

> His activity was characterized by a high speed coupled with an erratic quality. He rarely stood still: when he was not running, jumping, or climbing, he jiggled up and down in place much as a boxer does while waiting for his opponent's next move. He lacked fine motor skills and some of his gross motor behavior was characterized by clumsiness and awkwardness. He spent a major part of each morning running, climbing and swinging. If an adult offered to push him or help him with any project he sometimes accepted the help, but at other times he burst into screams of rage and often pounded the adult with his fists. When he went to the toy corner, he would throw all the toys off the shelves until he found the one he wanted. If another child had the toy he wanted, he took it by force; then, when an adult intervened, he had a tantrum. He had a short attention span and was unable to sit in a group and listen to a short story. (p. 34)

In a sense, the term *hyperactive* may be a misleading label because these children are not more active than other children in all respects. If their running is measured by a pedometer, it turns out that they do not run more than the average child of the same age. Nor do they move about more from one place to another in a room. They do show more of certain kinds of movement, however: They wiggle, squirm, sway, rock their bodies while sitting or standing, and play nervously or absently with objects (Collins, Whalen, and Henker, in press). *Restless* movement, then, distinguishes them most clearly from other children. Surprisingly, hyperactive children often cannot run as fast as other children, nor can they slow down their rate of movement on demand. What is different about them—the thing that makes other people see them as excessively active—is that their activity is disorganized and not modulated or regulated to meet the demands of a given situation.

Hyperactive children, like active children, become more able to control and inhibit their movements as they grow older (Bradley, 1957; Werry, 1968), although other symptoms frequently remain. Hyperactivity is very much more common in boys than in girls—clinicians' estimates range from as high as ten hyperactive boys for every hyperactive girl to a more commonly given ratio of six to one.

Clearly, hyperactive children and their families are faced with a serious problem. Few observers agree on frequency, causes, and treatment of the condition. Some estimates suggest that 10 percent or more of American children suffer from some degree of hyperactivity; others suggest the frequency rate is much lower. In a fairly substantial number of cases, neurological damage is probably partly responsible for the child's problems. Such damage can occur prenatally, as when a mother contracts rubella during the first trimester of pregnancy. The damage can also occur at birth when labor is prolonged and the baby gets too little oxygen, or it can occur at a later time when environmental pollutants—such as lead—are ingested. Drug therapy clearly has proved effective for some—certainly not all—hyperactive children. But these medications may cause serious side effects, and many experts now believe that drugs have been relied on too heavily.

Let us return to the larger issue of activity level: Is there any connection between activity level in normal children and the impulsive behavior pattern of early childhood? Normal children are often very active. They enjoy physical movement for its own sake and engage in a great deal of it. Does their activity restrict their ability to stop and think? Judging from what we have discovered about hyperactive children, the answer is probably "no." Hyperactive children are impulsive, and they do have great difficulty in modulating their activity when they need to do so in order to focus attention on quiet tasks. But since they do not do more running and moving from place to place than other children, we can only suspect that this kind of activity is not causal in problems of impulse control. More likely it is the other way around: Lack of behavioral organization probably expresses itself in restless movement, so the kind of excess bodily activity that one sees in hyperactive children is more a symptom than a cause of impulsiveness.

Impulsive versus reflective problem solving

Impulsiveness can be involved in mental as well as physical activities and sometimes takes the form of making premature decisions. Choosing among alternatives takes time and effort. The course of action that will lead to the greatest ultimate advantage is not always immediately apparent, and often consequences must be carefully considered. Certain kinds of problem-solving tasks have several possible solutions, and more than one of these may come very close to being right or the best. In such a situation, settling for a reasonable answer is easy; continuing to look for one best answer takes patience. Young children tend to lose patience and jump to quick conclusions without troubling to find out whether any better answer is available. This kind of problem solving has been called *impulsive* responding. Adopting a careful strategy of searching until the best answer has been found is called the *reflective* style of problem solving.

Psychologists have looked at the problem-solving styles of chil-

Figure 5-1.   Sample items from the Matching Familiar Figures task. The child must find the figure that matches the one at the top. Note that the exact copies are the upper left for the teddy bear and the upper center for the tree. (Kagan et al., 1964)

dren over a range of ages. Figure 5-1 shows the kind of problem that tests whether subjects are impulsive or reflective in their approach to problem solving (Kagan et al., 1964).

The child is shown a picture of a familiar animal or object and asked to choose from a set of similar pictures the one that *exactly* matches. The task is repeated for a series of pictures. In most psychological tests, those people who work quickly also make few errors. The Matching Familiar Figures (MFF) task is unusual in that many people who work quickly make many errors (the impulsive subjects), and many who respond slowly make few errors (the reflective subjects). In addition, there is a smaller group made up of those who respond quickly and make few errors, and another group who are slow and also inaccurate. These last two groups are difficult to classify along the impulsive-reflective dimension, but most children fit one or the other of the two major patterns, at least by the time they are five or six years old. Children younger than this frequently take quite a long time making their choices, but they still make many errors. Their long response times do not usually reflect a careful strategy of search. In fact, the children do not seem to realize that a prolonged search would help them find the right answer. They often spend their extra time trying to socialize with the experimenter or in talking or thinking about things irrelevant to the task. After the preschool years, however, a clear relationship emerges between time taken to do the task and the number of errors made.

Figure 5-2 shows that as children grow older they take more time and make fewer errors on the MFF task. That is, they become more reflective. Children differ, however, in how rapidly these changes take place. At any given age some children are relatively reflective and

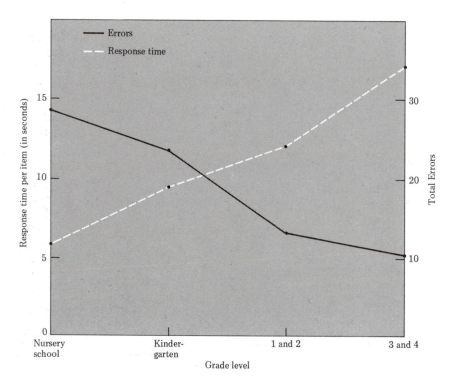

Figure 5-2.   Age changes in speed and accuracy of judgments. The scores are based on group averages on the Matching Familiar Figures task. Note that responses are slower and errors are fewer as age increases. (Adapted from Messer, 1976)

others are relatively impulsive. It is important to know whether differences among children are stable and whether the findings generalize to other tasks. Does a child who responds impulsively on one occasion do so on other occasions? Is a reflective or impulsive style in a given child something that lasts for a long time? And does a child who is impulsive on this test tend to make quick but inaccurate choices in other problem-solving situations where taking more time would mean greater accuracy? As far as stability is concerned, a child who on one occasion is more impulsive than other children is likely to be so when assessed again a week later. Over longer intervals, however, it is more difficult to predict which children will be more impulsive. Although the evidence is not consistent, the indications are that as children grow older they become somewhat more consistent. That is, it becomes possible to predict over several years' time that certain children will probably remain more impulsive and that others of the same age will remain more reflective, although the predictions are by no means perfect.

How about the generality of reflectiveness—is it a characteristic that affects performance in a variety of tasks? The answer is "yes," to some degree (Messer, 1976). When tasks other than the MFF are used to measure a child's problem-solving style, moderate relationships are found among the reflectiveness of individual children's approaches to different games and to the MFF Task. It is reasonable to say, then, that by about age six certain children have become fairly consistent in their use of a reflective approach to the solving of problems that require careful consideration of alternatives, while other children of this age are more consistently impulsive. Remember, of course, that a normally reflective child is quite capable of responding impulsively, and vice versa, depending on mood and a variety of aspects of the immediate situation.

Kagan (1971) has looked for analogues to reflectivity or impulsiveness in the behavior of very young children. He found differences in the responses of children at the age of one year or younger. When offered a novel object to look at, some of Kagan's young subjects seemed to dwell on it for a long, sustained period before looking away, while others examined it only briefly before losing interest. When crawling or walking around an unfamiliar room in which there were a variety of objects, some infants spent a long time exploring a new object before turning to another, while others became bored quickly and changed their focus of attention frequently. Kagan suggests several possible reasons why a child may lose interest in an object and rapidly shift interest to a new one:

1. The child processes all the information about the first object rapidly; that is, the child quickly uses up the interesting potential of an object.

2. The child processes only part of an object's potential; that is, the object is contacted superficially, not explored fully.

3. The child processes the information in an object quite fully but has only a limited repertoire of actions to be applied to the object.

Kagan observed a group of children at the ages of four, eight, thirteen, and twenty-seven months. He monitored the extent to which they were able to keep their attention on novel visual displays. When the children were old enough to be mobile, Kagan watched their movement as they explored a room and counted the changes in the focus of attention. He was able to measure impulsiveness-reflectivity in the twenty-seven-month-old children by having them find a hidden picture embedded in a larger picture. The hidden pictures, of course, were familiar (for example, a cat) and were not very fully hidden. Nevertheless, to find the hidden element a child usually had to persist in searching for the hidden element in the picture. The reflective children (those who responded slowly and accurately) were identified, and their earlier histories were compared with those of the children who responded quickly and inaccurately. The children who were impulsive at twenty-seven months generally showed the following characteristics in infancy: (1) only brief attention to visual displays, (2) much restless twisting of the body during testing (boys only), (3) many quick shifts of attention from one object to another during play and few sustained bouts of play with single objects. The relationships were not strong. They suggest, Kagan says, that "the infant's attributes obviously do not determine the reflection-impulsivity dimension, but they do exert a subtle influence on it" (1971, p. 150).

Kagan's findings indicate that impulsive children get bored easily. The loss of interest does not result from rapid processing of all available information, but from superficial processing and failure to impose a plan of action. To illustrate, Kagan compares the play of two children. One child breaks up a ball of clay into fifteen small pieces and feeds them one by one to a doll, pretending they are cookies. The other child breaks the ball into three pieces, drops them on the floor, and then grabs some blocks. The first child has a plan of action, and we assume that the child has, somewhere in her or his thoughts, a representation of the activity's goal. We do not know whether the child is attempting to use up all the cookies or make sure that the doll is fully fed, but there appears to be some end that is not achieved until the whole sequence of actions has been completed. Kagan believes that the reflective child is one who more completely "refers events to existing structures." We can see variations among children barely two years old in the extent to which their actions are planned, and this organization, Kagan believes, may be the essence of a reflective approach to problem solving.

A reflective style may be observed when children are solving problems imposed by adults and during play and other forms of self-imposed, self-initiated activities. Certain forms of solitary play and social games like chess or checkers call for mental exploration of alternatives and the withholding of action until the most suitable alternative has been found. Even listening to music can be done with various degrees of reflection. The skilled classical musician or educated listener hears a complex structure of themes stated and restated with subtle variations—a structure that must be searched for and is completely missed by the inexperienced listener. The growth of reflectivity in childhood may be seen as one outcome of the development of mental structures permitting an increasingly complex use of materials available in the environment. These developments can be seen in the rapid changes during the preschool years in the way children play with certain toys. A child of eighteen months or two years who is given a toy telephone will hold the receiver and drag the box around the room by the cord, as though it were a pull toy. A child of three or four will dial and pretend to hold a conversation with someone, pausing for the imagined other person to speak, and then replying. Thus the child shows an awareness of a conversation's structure and the ability to impose this structure on play activities.

Young children who have difficulty sustaining planned activity were once thought to have a short attention span. Yet children who cannot focus on an object for more than a few moments in a free-play situation can watch television for half an hour without losing interest. Clearly, time is not the issue when considering attention. "Attention span" depends on whether an activity is structured from the outside, perhaps through a rapid sequence of attention-getting events (as in a television program) or whether the activity requires the child to develop and impose the structure. Young children and impulsive older children are limited in their ability to impose structure on their own activities.

Considering the relationship between reflectivity and other aspects of self-imposed organization of behavior, it is not surprising that children who are reflective in games and problem-solving tests show better than average impulse control of other kinds as well. They can slow down their rate of movement in a test of inhibition of motor movement and can sustain attention to a task for longer periods than impulsive children. (See Messer, 1976, for a review of studies.)

THE CONTROL OF EMOTIONS

Young children are frequently flooded by emotional states that dominate both mind and body. Infants are often highly aroused—they turn red, cry vigorously, and thrash their arms and legs. In such a state, babies have little interest in food, toys, or events that would normally capture their attention. They must be soothed before they can continue in more normal interchanges with their environment. In the second year of life, emotional outbursts continue to be frequent. Children of eighteen to twenty-four months seem to cry or lose their tempers on slight provocation.

As children grow older the frequency of emotional storms diminishes. Somehow they are learning to control intense emotions. In the course of this development, children must learn to inhibit the strong feelings that previously disorganized their behavior, and they must learn to cope with circumstances that interfere with immediate or complete satisfaction of their needs and wishes.

Tolerating frustration

We saw in Chapter 4 that episodes of crying and loss of temper in frustrating situations seem to decrease substantially during the pre- and early school years. In Chapter 2 we noted the considerable decline between the ages of two and three in the likelihood of children crying if left alone briefly in a strange room. At this age, children control their tears, even though they show other signs of discomfort, such as lessening their play. Thus, there is reason to believe that children begin to impose some degree of control over their frustration at a fairly early age. A study by Van Leishout (1975) illustrates this. He studied children's reactions to a frustrating situation. The children were observed at eighteen months and again at two years. They were allowed to begin playing with an attractive toy. Their mothers would then take the toy and put it into a clear plastic box which had a catch the children could not open. Some of the children quite patiently set about trying to open the box to get at the toy. Others became angry with the box or with their mothers. The point of interest is the way they changed in the amount and direction of emotional upset during the interval between tests. The frequency of temper reactions was high for both sexes at eighteen months. By two years the incidence of this kind of reaction had declined markedly for the girls. Among the boys frequency of anger toward their mothers remained high. Unfortunately we do not have systematic data on developmental change in the two sexes in subsequent years. All we can say at present is that the Van Leishout findings (and those of Goodenough, discussed in Chapter 4) suggest that girls make faster progress than boys in learning to tolerate frustration without having an emotional outburst.

During the preschool years children somehow learn to endure frustration without becoming so emotionally aroused that their behavior is disorganized. It seems obvious that some inhibitory process must be developing, but the nature of the change is difficult to describe. This topic has inspired little developmental research, and we do not know precisely how children control their emotional upsets nor how they learn this control. Perhaps children learn to inhibit the arousal itself, so they do not become so emotionally upset over frustration. Or perhaps they are just as upset, but learn to become less disorganized and to cover up the way they feel. When we say that an adult is cool or unflappable, we may mean that the person shows either kind of response. With children it is likely that both kinds of inhibitory processes must be acquired. A buildup of feelings takes place during states of acute frustration, and probably this increase is due at least in part to the feedback from the individual's own upset state. Perhaps adults have learned ways to interrupt the buildup process, by deliberately thinking about something else or engaging in an activity incompatible with continued arousal. These processes will be considered in more detail in the next section. Whatever the process, one of the tasks of children's preschool years is the establishment of some degree of voluntary control over intense emotional states.

Parents during this period frequently become aware of willful elements in children's intense crying, and they recognize that children are capable of turning their tears on and off. When she noticed a cut on her four-year-old son's hand, one mother said, "Why, honey, you've hurt yourself! I didn't hear you crying." Said the boy, "I didn't know you were home!"

Acquiring the ability to cry deliberately is not the major achievement in the child's increasing ability to control emotions. More important is the ability *not* to have an emotional storm when genuinely upset or, even more important, not to become strongly upset in the first place over frustrating events. To highlight the nature of the normal child's achievement in acquiring control of emotional outbursts, it will be useful to consider the behavior of children who are deviant in that they have *not* achieved the usual controls. For this purpose, we will draw on Fritz Redl and David Wineman's detailed description of the behavior of a group of hyperaggressive preadolescent boys (1951, 1952). Redl and Wineman established a residential treatment center, called Pioneer House, in the late 1940s. The center housed six to eight boys, most between the ages of eight and ten years, who had been referred by public agencies for being "out of control." The boys' parents were missing or had stopped trying to supervise or care for them. Most of the boys had lived in a series of foster homes, where they had proved to be too aggressive and too impulsive for a family-living situation. Their schooling had been fragmentary, not only because they had moved and changed schools, but also because their behavior was so disruptive that schools could not cope with them. According to Redl and Wineman's diagnosis, their core problem was a profound deficiency in every aspect of impulse control. Two examples of the boys' behavior at the beginning of treatment vividly demonstrate the problems created by low levels of frustration tolerance:

> The kids burst out of the station wagon in their usual exuberant mood and barged madly up the steps into the house. Luckily, this time the door was open so the usual pounding, kicking of door, etc., wasn't necessary. I was in my office tied up in a phone call and the door was closed. Mike yelled for me, shouting something about his jack knife which I was keeping in the drawer for him. I put my hand over the receiver and said "O.K., come on in." But the lock had slipped on the door and he could not open it. Before I even had a chance to excuse myself from my phone conversation, and say "Just a minute, I'll be back" he was pounding on the door, kicking it, calling me a "sonofabitch" repetitively. I opened the door and gave him his knife. Even this failed to quiet his furor, and when I commented on the obvious fact that I hadn't even meant to make him wait, that the lock had slipped, all I got was a snarling, contemptuous "shit." (1951, p. 92)
>
> One of the most regularly occurring frustration reactions, during the early phase of treatment, would be produced when, on our numerous station wagon trips, we had to stop and wait for traffic signal lights. This was intolerable to the children. Even though they knew this delay would be automatically terminated in thirty to forty-five seconds, though they could so to speak *see* it right out there in front of their noses, still they were unable to handle their tension. Aggressive behavior would break out: throwing things at the counselor who was driving, cursing and hitting each other, etc. Shouts of "Goddamit, let's go, hit the bastard up there, what the hell are we waiting for," would fill the air. (p. 92)

Such a low level of frustration tolerance is of course quite abnormal for children as old as eight or ten. At that age most children can wait quite patiently if an enterprise is interrupted. Needless to say, the Pioneer House boys found it impossible to wait in line for anything— meals, movie tickets, packages at the post office—and the organizers of the Pioneer House activities carefully kept the children out of situations in which waiting would be required, at least until the treatment program had begun to take effect.

We saw earlier that one of the normal achievements of early childhood is the progression toward a more reflective use of play materials. Children use these materials in more mature ways, imposing a structure or plan on their activities with the materials. Both the depth and duration of involvement in a given enterprise increase, and there is less flitting from one activity to another. In the early phases of treatment, the boys of Pioneer House had notable difficulty maintaining their focus on quiet activities or using play materials resourcefully. When given modeling clay, they would throw it around the room or incorporate it symbolically into wild anal or sexual horseplay. This example of their use of an old mahogany wind-up phonograph is typical of the primitive quality of their play:

Tiring within minutes of its entertainment value as a record player, they would climb up and perch on its top and then jump off onto an adjoining piece of furniture. Or they would sail records at each other or against the wall. In view of the fact that, later on, record playing became one of their most popular activities, this initial, unsublimated handling of the phonograph is especially impressive. (p. 111)

Is there any relationship between these children's impoverished use of play materials and their explosive emotional reactions to even mild frustrations? Is the ability to tolerate frustration a necessary prerequisite to the kind of planning that is required to construct something out of clay? Or is the ability to plan a sustained sequence of actions a prerequisite to frustration tolerance? The nature of the linkage is unknown, but the therapists at Pioneer House argue strongly that both kinds of achievements stem from a central process: the development of *ego controls*. From their psychodynamic point of view, the ego is a person's central controlling agency, mediating between inner needs and the demands of reality. The ego's control can be weak or strong; in normal children, it gains strength as the child matures. Whatever the inner dynamics of the Pioneer House boys' behavior, it is clear that their frustration reactions were initially quite out of control. The boys seemed to be incapable of moderating or preventing the buildup of temper tantrums. They were also impulsive in many other respects. The existence of this form of deviancy reminds us forcibly that the acquisition of controls is not automatic and is a central part of the socialization process.

Delaying gratification

People of all ages face frequent choices between immediately acquiring a moderately gratifying reward and waiting for or working toward a more desirable reward, which can only be obtained at a later time. The child who gets a twenty-five-cent-a-week allowance can immediately buy a relatively cheap item or can save and combine several allowances to get something more valuable. The adult who has accumulated three days of vacation time can immediately go on a three-day ski trip or can accumulate more time for a longer vacation. By choosing to wait, the individual deliberately incurs some degree of frustration, and therefore the ability to postpone gratification is surely part of (or perhaps a *consequence* of) the development of frustration tolerance—and so this could reasonably have been discussed in the preceding section. However, the topic is highlighted separately because it has been researched quite thoroughly, and the research has generated findings of considerable importance.

In a typical experimental situation, experimenters offer a child a choice between a highly desirable prize, which can only be obtained if the child is willing to wait for it, and a less desirable prize, which can be had immediately (Mischel, 1958; Mischel and Staub, 1965). In one version of the situation, a preschool child is shown two marshmallows and a pretzel (pilot work has shown that almost all preschool-age children prefer marshmallows to pretzels). The experimenter explains that he will leave the room, taking the marshmallows and the pretzel with him. If the child waits until the experimenter decides to come back, the child will get the marshmallows. The child can call the experimenter back at any time by pressing a button, but then the child will only get the pretzel.

Does the ability to tolerate (and to choose) the frustration of waiting for a larger reward increase as children grow older? When comparing the behavior of children in different age groups, experimenters must provide choices that do not become less or more valuable with age. If a choice is offered, for example, between a teddy bear now or a chess set in a few days, younger children's choice of the teddy bear would not necessarily mean that they are impulsive or unable to tolerate frustration. In one study, Mischel and Metzner (1962) offered children of various ages a choice between two candy bars that differed only in size. Preliminary work showed not surprisingly that children of all ages preferred the larger candy bar. The children were told that they could have the small one immediately or wait and have the larger one. (The waiting period was varied: Sometimes it was a day, sometimes longer.) In this study, a clear developmental progression was evident in the ability to wait for the larger reward. The proportion of children at each age level choosing the smaller, immediate reward was kindergarten, 72 percent; first and second grades, 67 percent; third and fourth grades, 49 percent; fifth and sixth grades, 38 percent. A similar decline in impulsive choices between the ages of five and ten has been found recently by Weisz (1978). It is possible, of course, that older children simply do not like candy as much as younger children do, so that the lure of the immediately present candy is not as great. A more likely explanation, however, is that between the ages of five and twelve, children are somehow increasingly able to *wait* while holding in check their impulses to grab the immediately available lure.

As might be expected, children find waiting easier if they do not have to wait too long (Mischel and Grusec, 1967; Mischel and Metzner, 1962). Whether they wait or not also depends on their belief in the reality of the promised larger reward. Mischel and Grusec offered fourth and fifth graders choices between each of three different pairs of rewards (each pair having one highly desirable object and one less desirable object). When the children were told that the experimenter would "definitely be back" to deliver the larger rewards, they usually chose to wait for two out of the three larger rewards. When told that there was only a fifty-fifty chance that the experimenter would return, the larger rewards were chosen about one time out of three. When the probability of the experimenter's return was even smaller, fewer children took the risk of choosing even one larger reward.

The implications are clear: Children can more easily deal with the frustration of waiting if they trust the adult who has made the promise—that is, they trust that the promise will be kept. For ethical reasons experimenters have never deliberately broken a promise to return with a larger reward in order to see how this would affect a child's subsequent choices, but it is likely that a child who has frequently experienced broken promises would develop a bird-in-the-hand philosophy and would not be willing to risk waiting for delayed rewards that depend on someone else's good faith. Does a younger child's choice of immediate rewards imply that the child is more skeptical than an older child about the good faith of adult experimenters? Probably not. The issue for most young children is not trust, but rather inability to keep future events in mind. Young children do not give much thought to the future—their attention is on the here and now.

Obtaining a larger reward sometimes requires not just waiting, but a considerable amount of effort. In some versions of Mischel's experiment, the young subjects had to persist in a boring or difficult task in order to get the more desirable prize. With age, children are increasingly more willing to put forth effort, reflecting the development of a form of self-discipline that goes beyond mere waiting. What lies behind children's willingness to choose a delayed reward that depends on their own efforts? Not surprisingly, this kind of delay of gratification depends in part on children's confidence that they can do well enough on the task to earn the larger reward. Mischel and Staub (1965) gave coding and fairly difficult design tasks to groups of eighth-grade boys. Conditions were arranged so that the boys in one group would think they had done the task poorly. The others were given the impression that their performance was highly successful. Both groups were then given opportunities to choose (1) between a small reward that did not require work, and a more desirable reward requiring the performance of a task and (2) between a small reward that they would receive immediately and a more desirable reward requiring waiting. In addition, before they actually tried the tasks, the boys were asked whether they were usually good or not so good at doing that sort of task (compared with others of their age). The following findings were reported:

1. Under the *work* condition, the boys were more likely to choose to work for the larger reward if they had just succeeded at a similar task. Success at an unrelated task did not significantly influence their willingness to work. However, if they had a *generalized expectation of success*—that is, if they were confident that they could do better than other boys their age on a

range of performance tests—they were more likely to want to work for the larger reward.

2. Under the *wait* condition, the boys were more likely to choose the larger, delayed reward if they had a high level of self-confidence in their ability to succeed at tasks of the kind required. Immediately preceding success or failure had little effect.

A child's willingness to forego an immediate small reward and work for a larger one does seem to depend on the confidence that is generated by prior experiences with success. This confidence may be quite specific—confined to a narrow range of tasks and based on a single, recent success with a similar task. Or it may be quite broad—reflecting an optimistic attitude toward a wide range of tasks and presumably based on prior successes with a variety of tasks. Before accepting this interpretation of the Mischel and Staub results, however, we must consider another possibility. Perhaps failing at a task generates an unhappy or depressed mood, and unhappy subjects choose immediate gratification to cheer themselves up. This reasoning probably does not explain the results. First, prior failure had little effect on the boys' choices of rewards when the alternative was *waiting* rather than working. Furthermore, it has been shown in the other work (Mischel, Coates, and Raskoff, 1968) that when children who have just succeeded at a task turn to a new task, they are more likely to gratify themselves (by dipping into a freely available bowl of goodies) than are children who have previously failed. Thus, the explanation of the effects of prior failure on willingness to work for delayed reward appears clear-cut: Failure affects children's confidence in actually being able to earn the more desirable item, and lacking this confidence, they settle for second best—a reward they can obtain immediately without working.

In view of these results, it is not surprising that children's performance on delay-of-gratification tests is related to their sense of mastery over events that do occur. So-called *locus of control* measures can determine whether children see themselves as masters of their fate or think that good and bad outcomes are a matter of luck. Some children believe that they control their successes but that their failures are not their fault. In contrast, other children believe that they fail because of their own stupidity or carelessness but that they succeed because they are lucky. Quite often, however, the feelings of control or lack of control are the same for both success and failure. Mischel, Zeiss, and Zeiss (1974) found that children who believed they could determine their own successes through their own efforts were more willing to work for a delayed reward.

So far we have seen that children's willingness to wait or work for a delayed reward is increased if they have reason to believe that the delayed reward will be forthcoming. Willingness is also related to children's belief that they have the capacity and power to do whatever needs to be done to bridge the period of delay. If it is a matter of working for the larger reward, children must have confidence that they know how to do the required work, and they must believe that their own good work will produce desired outcomes. But why should younger children be so much more likely to choose immediate rewards? There is no reason for younger children to be less confident than older children that promised rewards will be forthcoming. Perhaps they have less confidence in their ability to perform the tasks required in order to obtain the larger reward. However, when young children are required to work for a reward, the difficulty of the task is usually scaled to their capacity to perform it. Thus there is no reason to believe that they have more general expectations of failure than older children do. We do not know for sure whether internal locus of control increases with age. If it does, this may help to explain why young children have difficulty accepting delay.

But there is another reason why children have problems with delay. They do not know what they can do during the delay interval to minimize frustration. Waiting is a skill that must be acquired. Children have to learn how to fill time during a delay without distracting themselves so completely that they lose sight of the ultimate goal. The recent work of Mischel and his colleagues (Mischel and Underwood, 1974) has provided some clear and important answers to the question of precisely what children are learning to do when they learn to delay. Their studies suggest that children are learning to control *what they think about* during the waiting period. Freud thought that impulses come under control in part because children begin to substitute imagined *wish fulfillment* for real gratification. That is, his theory assumes that partial gratification is obtained from an imaginary image of the desired object and that this makes it possible to forego real gratification at least for a brief time. In the Freudian interpretation of Michel's choice situations, waiting is possible because the child holds in mind the image of the more desirable prize.

To test this theory, Mischel and his colleagues had to find a way to influence the content of their young subjects' thoughts. As a first step, they simply allowed two marshmallows and a pretzel to be visible but out of reach during a waiting period. Preschoolers were offered choices between the marshmallows later or a pretzel immediately when: (1) only the marshmallows were visible, (2) only the pretzel was visible, and (3) neither was visible. The results were surprising: Children waited more successfully for the more desirable reward when *neither one* was visible. When both were present, they could hardly wait at all and signaled for the pretzel immediately. Neither seeing the marshmallows nor seeing the pretzel helped the children to wait.

The researchers wondered whether a real reward affects children differently from its image. Perhaps the real reward arouses intense desires and tempts the child beyond bearing. To directly investigate *imagery*, Mischel's group asked some preschoolers to think about the rewards during the waiting period and others to think about irrelevant but pleasant things (for example, "things that are fun to do"). The results were very clear: The children who thought about the promised rewards were capable of only very short delays. The children who thought about irrelevant, distracting events—or who deliberately tried to keep their mind blank and think about nothing at all—were better able to wait. These results fitted nicely with the investigators' informal observations (through a one-way mirror) of the behavior of children who waited without having had any instructions. The children in this group who waited most successfully seemed to have worked out ingenious methods for distracting themselves—singing songs, talking to themselves, inventing little games, or occasionally taking a nap. The successful waiters seemed to be trying to fill the waiting time with activities that were incompatible with simply sitting and thinking about the desired objects. Mischel's findings suggest that Freud was wrong. Children do not learn to control their impulsive insistence on immediate gratification by conjuring up an image of the desired object and obtaining a substitute, immediate gratification therefrom. Images only intensify desire for the real thing.

Is there *no* sense in which imagining will help children endure delay? In their most recent work, the Mischel group have begun to distinguish between hot and cold kinds of thinking. Thoughts about how marshmallows are sweet and chewy and how pretzels are salty and crunchy are consummatory, or hot, cognitions. Thoughts about a marshmallow's resemblance to a white puffy cloud and a pretzel stick's resemblance to a log are cold, or nonconsummatory, cognitions. Their findings suggest that cold cognitions help children to wait for more desirable rewards, while hot cognitions dramatically reduce the amount of waiting that children can sustain. In this situation also we see that Freud's idea about controlling impulse through substitute mental gratification is not valid. However, during a waiting or working period, reminders of the promised reward probably are useful, as long as the thoughts do not arouse appetites unduly.

Young children are only dimly aware of the strategies that would enable them to tolerate a delay period. If asked, a five-year-old may say that covering up the reward is better than watching it during the delay, while a four-year-old seldom knows the value of the cover-up. But even the knowledgeable five-year-old may be unable to call up spontaneously the right strategy in real-life situations. At that age young children often make poor judgments about what kinds of thoughts will make waiting easier or harder. They may believe, for example, that thinking about the sweet taste of the marshmallow is better than thinking about its nonedible qualities, although this strategy will interfere with their ability to wait. Sometime between the ages of seven and nine, however, children improve considerably in their understanding of the superiority of cool cognition (Mischel and Underwood, 1974).

Clearly, impulse control requires more than merely inhibiting motor actions. To control their behavior, individuals must make use of their thought processes—using thinking for self-distraction and to cool intense feelings of frustration. This kind of thinking is as much an acquired skill as is the ability to throw a ball accurately or count from one to ten.

Controlling excitement

We have been tracing the changes that take place during childhood. From impulsive activity geared to the here and now, children move toward more planned, controlled modulation of action, in which behavior is governed by the child's own goals and the demands of both present and future events. We have seen that acquiring the ability to plan requires that children establish some control over their own emotional states. We discussed specifically the inhibition or avoidance of angry outbursts following frustration, noting that anger is likely to interfere with waiting, working, and reflective thought. Wild excitement is another emotional state that is incompatible with reflection. It is an uncontrolled state and can spread quickly among a group of children and contribute to recklessness, which would not be seen in a group of children who were in a calmer mood. The group-contagion process is well illustrated by the following episode at Pioneer House:

> Before dinner tonight, the group was scattered around the living room floor playing with various quiet games—checkers, parchisi, cards. All was quiet and peaceful until Mike, who was playing cards with Andy, picked up one of the cards and idly sailed it across the room. Then he sailed another one, and this time called attention to it. Andy then whooped gaily and heaved several cards around. Danny, clear on the other side of the room, began to throw checkers. When the executive director started to interfere, it had no effect on the situation whatever, and Bill picked up the checker board saying "Watch this one!" and heaved it. Larry elatedly grabbed a small wooden bowling pin and raucously threw it in the fireplace. The others were also throwing whatever was around and within reach—the air was thick with checkers, cards, pieces of candy, all in motion. Andy especially was exploiting the whole episode and Dave finally removed him from the room, taking him into the office where he had, to finish the whole show, a screaming tantrum which lasted about twenty minutes. (Redl and Wineman, 1951, p. 104)

Children vary a great deal from time to time and situation to situation in how impulsive they are. Even the most reflective child will lose his or her cool under certain circumstances. Still, there is reason to believe that some children are more ready than others to be aroused to states of high excitement. Redl and Wineman pointed out that their Pioneers had a very low boiling point and were especially subject to contagion from other children. They had an opportunity to compare their impulsive, hyperaggressive boys with normal boys when the Pioneer House children went to summer camp. When one of the impulsive children began to act in a wild, uncontrolled way, other Pioneer House cabin mates would immediately join in, while children with calmer temperaments would simply look on or return to reading a comic book. In certain children impulsiveness is a long-lasting and fairly pervasive characteristic that may be at least partly biological in origin (see the discussion of hyperactivity earlier in this chapter). Undoubtedly parents' methods of dealing with their children's impulsiveness also have some bearing on its developmental course.

As noted above, psychoanalytic writers group the inhibitory, planning, and modulating processes under a single term—ego controls. In normal young children, these writers argue, the ego is weak and gains strength in a number of ways, a major one being identification with the parents. Redl and Wineman designed their therapeutic regime from the standpoint of ego theory. Their aim was to strengthen the weak, damaged egos of children who had missed the normal experiences that would have enabled them to develop ego controls.

Whether the concept of ego strength adds materially to our understanding of the development of impulse control in early childhood is a matter of controversy. Whatever position one takes, most observers agree that control processes do develop and that daily interaction with parents affects the child's success in achieving these controls. We turn now to an exploration of the role parents play in their children's acquisition of impulse controls.

IMPLICATIONS FOR CHILD REARING: THE PARENTS' ROLE IN CHILDREN'S IMPULSIVENESS

Surprisingly little direct research has been done on the outcomes of different parental strategies for dealing with impulsiveness in normal young children. In this section, therefore, we will attempt to analyze the demands placed on parents by childhood impulsiveness. Then we will look at the work of researchers who have studied abnormally impulsive children, and we will see whether this work provides clues to possible parental strategies and their effects.

As we have seen, young children are more impulsive than older children. While there are great differences among children in the extent to which they can control their bodily movements, tolerate frustration, or delay immediate action in the interests of reflective thought and later rewards, *all* young children are impulsive in their early years in comparison with their own behavior later on. This fact of early childhood imposes certain demands on the people who are responsible for the care of children: They must (1) create an environment in which young children can safely act on impulse, (2) assume regulating functions until the children can regulate themselves, and (3) foster, in a variety of ways, the development of self-control. These tasks imply a large number of varied responsibilities. Parents must organize children's physical environment and supervise their activities and interpersonal relationships. They must do their children's planning and remembering. They must try to avoid being impulsive themselves, so as to provide their children with models of organized and well-controlled behavior. Finally, parents must provide children with opportunities to make thoughtful choices and to experience the consequences of their decisions.

Situational management

That young children cannot anticipate the consequences of their actions and cannot organize their lives in relation to the flow of events around them has enormous implications for the kinds of situations in which they can function safely. Children cannot be left unattended, and parents must make sure that a responsible person—someone who is specifically willing and competent to assume caretaking functions—is with the child at all times. But far more than this goes into the management of a child's day.

A regular, predictable schedule—established routines of eating, sleeping, and play—has great importance in the management of impulsive behavior. In a certain sense, external structure is substituting for internal structure. As we have seen, children of two-and-a-half have made considerable progress in concentration and can play with a toy without flitting from one focus of attention to another. But their concentration is easily disturbed by the occurrence of unexpected events: the arrival of a stranger, the unexplained departure of the mother, the appearance of unfamiliar objects. A two-year-old is upset by seemingly minor deviations from the familiar routine, such as family members changing their accustomed places at the dinner table or a parent omitting one element from the familiar bedtime routine. Children of this age seem to want most aspects of their environment to stay put—remain predictable—so they can focus more easily on the mastery of only a restricted number of elements. The implication of these observations is that parents of young children will do well to ration judiciously the amount of novelty that impinges on the children.

Keeping absolutely everything the same would limit growth. But too much change interferes with children's ability to cope with novelty.

While regular routines have an important stabilizing effect in the lives of normal young children, routines are especially important with excessively impulsive children. People working with such children stress the value of rather rigid repetitiveness. The boys of Pioneer House responded well to routine:

> We found . . . that the mere existence or evolvement of a time schedule for certain life tasks, the mere repetitiveness of the same or similar situations to be gone through in the morning, in the evening, at bedtime, the mere development of a clear expectation pattern of just what the sequence of evening treat, story telling, lights out, etc., would be, would in themselves, after the first resistance was overcome, have a relaxing, quieting and soothing effect on the personality of our children and actually, therefore, become an ego-strengthening factor. (Redl and Wineman, 1951, pp. 292–93)

Professionals working with hyperactive children commonly recommend that the environment be made as *structured* as possible. It is difficult to say exactly what they mean by structure—in part they undoubtedly mean providing the kind of predictability that we have been discussing. But there is another implication; that is, that children be given an organized program of activities—that they be told what to do next. Young children frequently complain that they have nothing to do. An adult who likes to read or watch television may expect young children to amuse themselves, not understanding that they cannot "go off and play" when asked to do so unless opportunities are provided for activities that are at the right level to evoke sustained interest. Toys provide useful opportunities for children to have fun and to develop mastery of their environment. But they can quickly lose their entertainment value and often adults will have to structure their use. Building with erector sets or blocks calls for at least a rudimentary plan of action. Such toys are often given to children who are too young to go beyond the brief fascination of discovering how the blocks can be joined together and pulled apart. The child may then find nothing more in the toys to claim her or his attention. An adult could show how hitting one piece with another can make it spin or jump, and the child might then spend five or ten minutes exploring that possibility. But the building materials will not hold the child's prolonged attention until the child can put the materials to their intended use—using them to build. This activity calls for imagining what is to be built—a house, a boat or a person—and employing a strategy for matching the construction with this image. In the initial stages of developing such a strategy, the child can benefit greatly from playing with an adult or older child who can demonstrate strategic elements. Without occasional help, even the child who is mature enough to use the toy is likely to lose interest. Parents frequently complain "How can she possibly be bored? She's got a whole room full of toys!" But the child *is* bored, because all the familiar strategies for playing with these toys have been exhausted, and the child is not being helped to develop new strategies. No wonder children respond so enthusiastically to the suggestion "Why don't you watch television for a while?" This activity is largely structured for them, although even here their understanding of what they see is determined by the mental structures they bring to their viewing.

The job of managing the child's day, then, involves setting up a series of appropriate activity opportunities, interspersed with the routines involved in eating, sleeping, washing, and dressing. Providing opportunity for activity often means finding a playmate of the same age. Or it can mean simply allowing the child to share in any adult activities that the child can comprehend and manage. A child of two or three will quite happily "help" make beds, do dishes, prepare dinner, wash clothes, roll pastry, or care for a baby. Perhaps child care seems burdensome to many modern parents because adults now spend only a small portion of their day in activities that can be easily shared with children. Smaller family size and increased use of labor-saving devices have changed the pattern of household activities. A number of people of different ages, engaged in a variety of tasks, are no longer present in the household. Thus, the range of activities that a young child might share is narrower, and the child's involvement becomes a nuisance that falls heavily on the small number of people who make up the immediate family.

Joint activity with adults provides a specific cognitive benefit: Children have an opportunity to participate in complex sequences of activity. As we have seen, young children left to their own devices have difficulty sustaining an organized chain of action over time. They tend to focus their attention in fairly short bursts. A study by Holmberg (1977) illustrates the effect of shared activities on children's behavior. Holmberg counted connected chains of four or more action-reaction elements, looking at differences in the number of these chains when children were interacting with adults or with children their own age. The young subjects ranged in age from twelve to forty-two months, and among the younger ones, the number of extended or *elaborated* sequences was increased by interaction with an adult. In other words, a competent partner enabled them to maintain a longer connected sequence of behavior. We can only assume that such experiences help to move the child along the developmental path toward increasing duration of focused activity and away from the less mature tendency to shift quickly from one activity to another.

Successful management of the sequence of young children's activities includes making sure that they will not have to wait too long for events to begin. We have seen that children do not have well-developed strategies for filling waiting time, and they therefore have difficulty maintaining control when standing in line, waiting in the car while adults shop, and in similar situations. Sitting in church through a long sermon is equivalent to simply sitting and waiting, since the young child cannot join in the activity which is (at least sometimes!) absorbing the attention of the adults: listening to, and thinking about, the sermon's message. The staff of Pioneer House found that there were more frequent outbursts of wild, impulsive behavior during the periods between the end of one activity and the beginning of another, when no activity structure was provided and the children had to wait.

Child-proofing the environment—removing potential hazards—is another aspect of situational management that allows adults to live in relative peace with impulsive young children. Attractive but breakable or dangerous objects can be put out of reach. Certain areas of the house—a tool closet, the study—can be firmly established as off limits. Doors that lead to a dangerous street or body of water can be fitted with an out-of-reach latch. The ways in which a child's environment can be safeguarded are too numerous to list here, but the major point is that the rate at which children are exposed to hazards and taught to deal with them can be paced to match the development of their impulse controls.

Performing the child's ego functions

The young child has a limited capacity to plan. Children have to learn how to organize sequences of actions, integrate them with the actions and time schedules of other people, and anticipate the requirements of forthcoming situations. As a result, adults must function as the child's memory and anticipation center. If the family is going on a day-long excursion to the beach, the child simply hops into the car and is ready to go. Children do not know what might happen later in the day. They do not know that they might get cold, hungry, or bored. Or even if they "know" in an abstract sense, they are unlikely to think about any of these possibilities at the moment they leave the house. The adults, therefore, must do the necessary anticipating for the children. In planning an outing, they must check off mental lists involving everyone's needs.

When responsible for several children of different ages who engage in quite different activities, adults have a great variety of reminding functions to perform. Young children must be reminded about the routines of physical care—brushing their teeth, using the toilet, washing their hands before coming to the table, getting ready for bed. Older children need fewer reminders about routine things, but they need help with activities that do not occur every day or for which a routine is just being established—feeding a new pet, setting the alarm clock on days they have to get up early, looking over the clothes that will be needed for a special occasion to make sure they are clean. For efficient reminding the adult must know the details of each child's needs and activities—a highly complex task when the adult is planning for four or five lives.

We have seen that children do not systematically consider all available options before making a choice. They lack knowledge of the possible outcomes of various choices and are unwilling to weigh possible future unpleasant consequences against present pleasures. These limitations mean that many choices should be made for them. Adult caretakers sometimes do not consider children's level of maturity, allow them to make inappropriate choices, and then blame them for the unpleasant consequences. A child of six or seven may beg to keep a puppy or kitten, having in mind only the pleasures of cuddling it and not thinking of the work of feeding it and cleaning up after it. The child is reminded of these chores and then permitted to make an impulsive decision to keep the pet anyway. The child promises to do all the work needed to care for it, but the promise is unrealistic, of course. The child often will be in school or in a hurry to do something else when the animal needs feeding or exercise, and the child may be frightened or helpless when the animal is sick. The child does not fully realize, if the puppy is a large-sized breed, that a fence may have to be built to keep the animal from wandering. All this means that the adults must make this decision—they are the only ones who have the relevant knowledge and are in a position to take responsibility for the consequences of the decision. If they persuade themselves that the child made the decision, they will find themselves saying later: "You *promised* to do it, and now you're making me do it!" or "I *told* you you'd forget to feed it!" or even, "You lied to me."

Many decisions can be shared with children. In buying clothing, for example, parents can decide in advance what fabrics or colors are acceptable. The nonwashable party dress is ruled out. But if any one of the three or four garments on display would be acceptable to the parent, the child can be allowed to choose among these alternatives. In regard to food for the family meals, children know what *they* like and dislike, but they probably do not understand the preferences of other family members or the work required to prepare special foods for special tastes. Food choices can be offered that are within the realistic limits set by these factors. Increasingly, as their capacity for anticipating and handling consequences develops and their impulsiveness declines, children will be able to make choices on their own and to participate in decisions affecting the family. But until these capacities are well developed, the parent must fill in as chooser and decider.

Parental self-control

Young children's frequent emotional outbursts strain the parent's own capacity for control. Emotional reactions are usually reciprocal. When A becomes angry at B, B is likely to react by becoming angry at A. Likewise, a pleasant act will beget a pleasant reaction. When a young child gets angry, the parent must inhibit the tendency to respond in kind. A mother caring for boys aged two, three, and four once said: "The hardest part is controlling the tempers of four people! The boys seem to get upset over small things. They are so unreasonable, it's hard not to get mad at them. Sometimes I wish I could just stamp my foot and scream the way they do!" Instead, the well-functioning parent must try to respond objectively to the child's display of feelings, attempting to soothe and help solve the child's problem.

Adults have not completely outgrown impulsiveness, of course. Sometimes they yield to the temptation to spend money for a luxury when they know they will need it later for a necessity. Sometimes they eat something they know is bad for them. Adults are likely to act impulsively when tired, depressed, or when they have been drinking. Effort and a good state of morale are needed for adults to keep functioning at a mature level. And even greater maturity is required to carry out the reflective, inhibitory functions for several other people, especially when the beneficiaries may resent the actions the adult must carry out. Forcing a child to take an unwanted medicine or to forego a tasty but harmful food is done at considerable personal cost. When the child shows resentment, parents are tempted to say: "Well, go ahead and *get* sick, then," although they know the decision really must not be left to the child. In view of the requirements for maturity that parenthood entails, it is not surprising that very young parents have difficulty taking on the parenting role. These parents find it difficult to control their own tempers and to exercise foresight needed for making decisions.

Teaching impulse control

So far we have been implying that parents must assume substitute controlling functions, while *waiting* for children to become old enough to have their own controls. However, different children acquire controls at varying rates, and the process is by no means simply one of waiting for a child to grow older. It is primarily a learning process, which the parents can help or hinder.

We saw that children can more easily forego an immediate treat for a better one later on if they have confidence that the promised reward will actually be forthcoming. It matters, then, whether the parent is trustworthy. No parent can keep every promise on absolutely every occasion, but a parent who comes close will help the child to acquire inner controls. Trustworthiness entails more than keeping promises. Parents must also respect decisions the child has been allowed to make and adhere to rules or routines previously established for the child. If rules are capriciously set aside for the parent's temporary convenience (for example, the child is allowed to be late for school because the parent is tired, wants to sleep an extra half hour, and does not get up to help the child), the child will find it harder to learn to organize time because of the parent's unpredictability.

In gradually transferring planning functions to the child, the parent can help to provide strategies for self-reminding. For example, the parent can suggest that if the child wants to remember to take something to school the following day, the "something" should be placed next to the front door. In a similar vein, it is possible for the parent to help the child develop strategies for postponing gratification. The Mischel work showed that waiting is made easier by not thinking about the reward during the waiting period—or at least, by not thinking about its consummatory qualities. The parent can help, if the child's excitement mounts too high during a waiting period, by suggesting an intervening activity or another subject for thought.

Parents can have a considerable influence on their children's self-restraint without direct teaching, merely through the example they set. Some years ago, research by Bandura and Mischel (1965) demonstrated that children are more likely to choose a delayed reward over an immediate smaller one if they have just seen someone they respect make delayed choices. Since that time, dozens of studies have demonstrated the effect of models on various aspects of self-control. Stumphauzer (1972) carried out an especially interesting study. Working at a correctional institution for youthful offenders, he selected a group of highly impulsive inmates, as judged by their choices on a delay-of-gratification test. He allowed half of the group to observe the behavior of a somewhat older inmate who was to be discharged shortly and who had a high-prestige job within the institution. The model mainly made delayed choices and made remarks during the testing session such as "I can wait for that." The impulsive inmates who were exposed to this model subsequently changed their choice behavior and made many more delayed choices than similar inmates who did not have the opportunity to learn from a model. Thus, even young adults who have long-lasting impulsive habits can be influenced by the example of others.

Parents, of course, have opportunities to serve as models of self-restraint throughout the child-rearing years, though for very young children, and for exceptionally impulsive children, they must make the modeling quite explicit for it to be understood (Ross and Ross,

1976). For example, the Rosses suggest the following role for the parents in a treatment program for a hyperactive, impulsive six-year-old boy:

> The child's problem was not attentional, he was able to maintain attention; rather, it was that his responses in school, games, and choice situations were consistently hasty, impetuous, and lacking in forethought . . . Because he was so quick to respond, he frequently accepted the first alternative without even waiting to hear the second. His parents were instructed to offer him a reasonably attractive opportunity, for example "Would you like a Coke, or . . . and when he accepted without waiting to hear the alternative, to give him what was offered. When he was actively engaged with the chosen alternative, they offered the same choice to one of his siblings, all of whom were highly reflective by comparison. The second alternative was always more attractive, and consequently was chosen. When the child saw his siblings enjoying the more attractive choice he was invariably indignant and disappointed. At this point one of his parents explained that he had accepted without stopping to think, and the consequence was disappointing. His parents were also instructed to use modeling procedures to enhance these demonstrations on the folly of impulsivity. At intervals one parent would make a hasty choice, and complain about the consequences, chastising himself all the while for not stopping to think. Occasionally, the child did spontaneously stop and think, and he received strong positive reinforcement for such action. Sometimes his parents urged him to think, helped him weigh the alternatives, and arranged situations so when he did act reflectively he received both social and situational reinforcement. (pp. 158–59)

Children who are in the normal range of impulsiveness do not need such a concentrated, contrived program—they usually seem to learn about the benefits of reflective choices without this kind of emphasis. Nevertheless, the procedures described here do point to some of the behaviors in the parent-child interaction that can foster the child's acquisition of a reflective mode of responding. When parents exercise forethought or self-restraint, it is often not obvious to the child that they are doing so. The child only sees the behavioral outcome, not the conflict that preceded it. If parents, in making their own decisions, talk about the alternative choices and the probable outcomes, the child will be provided with valuable learning opportunities.

A theme that recurs in the writings of professionals dealing with hyperactive or aggressively impulsive children is that the adults dealing with such children must set clear limits and maintain firm controls. Children know that highly impulsive behavior can be destructive to themselves and others. They find it comforting to know that someone can be counted on to stop them before they go too far. Part of the parent's effort, then, must be focused on the impulsive behavior itself: on stopping it and on teaching the child inhibitory strategies (as was being done in the case of the hyperactive child described above). But children can also be helped to control their impulsive behavior through indirect means. Impulsive behavior can be seen as a kind of default option. It is a way for children to respond when they do not know what else to do to achieve a better outcome. Training in alternative modes of coping with problem situations is one of the major means whereby children can learn to outgrow their impulsiveness and to impose organization on their own behavior.

We saw in the Mischel work that children are much more willing to work for a delayed reward if they have confidence that their performance will enable them to earn the reward. Furthermore, if children are helped to acquire performance skills so that they can rely on their own efforts, they can avoid some of the frustrations that are inherent in incompetency. The point is nicely illustrated by a study done many years ago with a group of impulsive children (Keister and Updegraff, 1937). When given a frustrating task, such as fitting small toys into the top layer of a box so that the lid would go on, these children were more likely than others of their ages to become angry or sulk or whine and to ask for help without seriously attempting to do the task independently. They gave up very quickly. These children were given training designed to improve their frustration tolerance. They were introduced first to easy tasks on which it was almost certain they could succeed. Then the investigators introduced new tasks, which increased in difficulty but were still within the range of the children's competency if they tried a little harder. A series of success experiences were thus provided. Following a fairly extended period of such training, the children were retested on the original frustrating task. They now attacked the task with eagerness and interest; they were now *more* able than the other children in their class to persist in the task without crying, whining, sulking, or showing anger; they seldom asked for help.

The early histories of undercontrolled adolescents

We have been examining some of the parenting skills that are needed if parents are to deal adequately with the impulsiveness of their children and help them to outgrow it. Some parents perform these functions more skillfully than others. What are the long-term consequences for children of different approaches to parenting? Block, in collaboration with Haan (1971), examined the records of individuals who were studied from early childhood into adulthood. Some of these individuals were in junior and senior high school during the depression years of the 1930s, while others were adolescents during World War II. Some members of both groups could be clearly identified as undercontrolled during adolescence, and many of these individuals continued to show symptoms of undercontrol when they became adults. By *undercontrolled* Block means that the individuals were impulsive. Compared to age mates, they were less able to wait for things they wanted and demanded immediate gratification and gave little attention to consequences. Their expression of emotions was often explosive and unregulated. They had poor ability to maintain attention and commitment to tasks they undertook. Their behavior had a superficial, unorganized, flitting quality, and they changed their minds and their enthusiasms frequently. Of course, in adolescence their impulsiveness was expressed differently than if they had been preschoolers. But the parallels are clear. The parents of the children in the longitudinal study had been interviewed at several points while the children were growing up so that the researchers were able to assess certain aspects of their reactions to their children and their attitudes toward child rearing. The parents of undercontrolled children differed from other parents in the following respects:

1. There was considerable conflict between the parents.
2. The parents tended to disagree with each other about child-rearing values.
3. The parents neglected their teaching functions: They did not take the time or trouble to transmit age-appropriate skills to the children.
4. The parents seldom assigned chores or required the children to assume responsibility for fulfilling their personal needs or those of other family members.
5. The parents placed few demands for achievement on the children.

The implications of these findings will be discussed more fully in Chapter 10. For the present, it is difficult to improve on the words of Jack Block, as he discusses the parenting activities that are needed if children are to develop self-controls.

> In order for a child to become appropriately controlled, someone has to invest time and trouble. . . . Sustained parental attention is required to maintain a predictively consequential environment. It is troublesome, interrupting and onorous to have to discipline a child; it is far easier—immediately—to ignore the occasion for instruction or punishment. The parents of the undercontrollers, by virtue of their own impulsivity and self-absorption, simply did not invest the time nor exhibit the constancy needed to deliver the precepts of self-regulation to their child. Controlling the world of their child for the good of their child was not felt or acted on as a responsibility. . . . they did not provide to their children motivating illustrations that at times one must not do what one really wants to do, simply for the sake of another person. (1971, pp. 263–64)

Block notes further that the parents of undercontrollers had used discipline primarily when they themselves were extremely angry. Their children, he says, usually became panicky and passive under the attack of an out-of-control, infuriated parent—a state that prevented them from understanding the disciplinary lesson.

Too much impulse control?

Implicit in our discussion so far has been the assumption that impulsivity interferes with social and intellectual development. The evidence has supported this view, at least for children who remain highly impulsive beyond the usual age. We must now ask about the other end of the scale: Can there be too much control? We all know people who inhibit nearly all expression of emotion, who plan so much for the future that they seem unable to enjoy the present, and who cannot take quick action even when it is realistically called for. Strangely, in Block's longitudinal samples, such individuals could be found among the males, but very few females fitted the pattern. Block discussed a group of boys who were overcontrolled in adolescence and who continued to be so into adulthood. He reported that family life had been authoritarian and joyless as they grew up. The parents were conservative and inhibited; most especially, they were constrained in regard to sexual impulses in themselves and in their children. While Block did not say so, we may suspect that these parents were also repressive toward their children's displays of anger. The boys were given household responsibilities, and there was strong pressure for compliance with parental demands. The mother enforced her demands by making the boy feel guilty if he did not comply—drawing his attention to how much he was hurting her by disobedience. As we have seen earlier, in such maternal reactions there is a strong element of threat, the implication being that the child runs the risk of losing the mother's affection if he continues to hurt her feelings by his noncompliance.

When it comes to impulse control, then, there is a happy medium. Sometimes open expression of feelings, quick action, and risk taking are appropriate; sometimes they are not. The child's task is to learn impulse modulation and regulation, not total inhibition. And as we have seen, styles of parenting affect this learning: Parents can either teach or fail to teach adequate controls, or parents can instill too much control. We will return to the matter of parental styles and their effects in Chapter 10.

SUMMARY AND COMMENTARY

In this chapter we have considered how children learn to organize and control their own behavior. Mature behavioral organization requires the individual to develop plans of action, to keep several plans of action in mind simultaneously, and to coordinate the actions relevant to different plans in such a way that several objectives can be achieved efficiently. *Inhibition* plays a large role in behavioral organization. Children must learn to:

1. Inhibit movements. In the first few years of life, stopping actions or slowing down the pace of movement seems to be harder for children than starting actions.

2. Inhibit emotional outbursts. Young children become emotional when they encounter barriers or waiting periods. Their emotional outbursts disorganize their problem solving and efforts to delay action. Normal children's ability to tolerate frustration without being emotionally upset increases markedly during the preschool years and continues to improve (although more slowly) in later childhood and even adulthood.

3. Inhibit premature judgments. As they grow older, children become more *reflective*. That is, when they encounter a problem that has more than one possible solution, they develop the patience to continue searching for the best solution rather than settling for a less adequate solution that can be arrived at quickly.

4. Inhibit premature choices. In many situations a choice exists between accepting an immediate gratification, even if it means sacrificing longer-term goals, and waiting or working for goals that will be more satisfying in the long run. Young children usually choose the immediate reward, but as they grow older they weigh long-term goals more heavily.

Inhibition is also involved in the development of attention. Young children allow their attention to be captured by the most immediate, most salient stimulus, while older children learn to concentrate—that is, to focus attention on task-relevant information and ignore inputs that are not germane to what they have set out to do.

We have little information on how these developmental changes come about. No doubt they are linked to general cognitive development and to the accumulation of experiences that enable the child to predict the outcome of various courses of action. As children develop more skills, they begin to have confidence in their ability to do the work or the problem solving needed to achieve delayed goals. And indeed:

5. Children who believe that they themselves can control what happens to them, who do not feel that they are the pawns of luck or fate, are more able to inhibit impulsive choices.

Parents have a complex role in dealing with impulsive young children and assisting them to achieve impulse control. While children are still young enough to have little control, parents must:

6. Manage the situations in which children spend their time to protect them from the consequences of their own impulsivity. They must restrict children to safe places, provide age-appropriate activities, and minimize temptations and waiting times.

7. Carry out for children the ego functions that they cannot carry out for themselves. In this role the parents must impose controls on children's emotional outbursts, provide structure in the form of routines, make choices for the children, and anticipate consequences of the children's actions.

Carrying out these functions calls for a high level of control by the parents over their own impulses. Gradually, they transfer controlling functions to the children by:

8. Teaching coping skills. Parents can help children be less impulsive if they show the children how to fill waiting time and give them tasks that are challenging but within their capacity, so that they can have success experiences in problem solving.

9. Helping children to anticipate consequences. To some extent this objective can be accomplished by discussing possible outcomes of various actions with children and reminding them of relevant past experiences. But more important the parents can provide a predictable interpersonal environment. In other words, parents can foster impulse control by being consistent in their discipline and clear in their values.

10. Setting an example of controlled, planned behavior. Experiments show that children show better impulse control after they have been exposed to a self-controlled model.

Studies of undercontrolled adolescents have shown that their parents have neglected both disciplinary and teaching functions and that the parents were conflicted about their own values.

One of the major accomplishments of normal childhood is the acquisition of controls over impulsive behavior. However, children can become overcontrolled. Studies have shown that:

11. Overcontrolled adolescents come from families where the parents are authoritarian and are inhibited about displaying

their own emotions. These parents also frequently control the children by playing upon their guilt feelings.

We have stressed the importance of finding an intermediate path whereby children can be guided toward modulating their impulses without totally inhibiting their expression.

CHAPTER **6**

Sex Differences

and Sex Typing

A CHILD'S SEX is a biological fact. It is also a social fact. When an infant is born, most people immediately ask, "Is it a boy or a girl?" The presence of an infant or young child whose sex is not immediately obvious makes some adults quite uncomfortable. Partly, of course, their discomfort results from limitations in the English language: We cannot talk about a child without using a sex-specific personal pronoun, and referring to a child as "it" seems unfriendly. But the discomfort probably goes deeper: We are prepared to

A number of writers have recommended using the word *gender* in place of *sex* in discussing subject matter similar to the material in this chapter. Thus, these writers use the terms *gender identity, gender differences,* and *gender role* in an attempt to avoid the implication that sex-typed behavior is a function of biological sex. Some use the word *sex* for behavior that has its origins in biology and *gender* for behavior that grows out of social shaping. This terminology has not been adopted here for several reasons. The term *gender* seems to prejudge important questions about the origins of sex-linked behavior. In point of fact, we cannot yet be sure about the mix of social and biological factors which underlie a number of the behavioral differences between males and females. The nature of the causal factors should be investigated rather than implied at the outset through the choice of terminology. Furthermore, when we study these differences, we classify children on the basis of their biological sex and then compare the behavior of the two classes. And when societies develop the sets of behavioral expectations we know as sex roles, they use biological sex as the means of selecting targets. Thus, sex is the major independent variable (see also Barrett, 1979). The term *sex* will therefore be used in this chapter. But no implication of biological causality for sex-related differences is intended.

203

react in certain ways that depend on a child's sex, and our social equilibrium is disturbed if we cannot make use of our prepared behavior. Luria and Rubin have shown that stereotypes even influence adults' perception of newborn infants. When viewed for the first time behind the window of the hospital nursery, infants known to be boys (or merely believed to be boys) are seen as robust, strong, and large-featured, while girls are seen as delicate, fine-featured, and "soft," even when there is little basis in fact for such attributions (Luria and Rubin; in press; Rubin, Provenzano, and Luria, 1974).

Social beliefs about the characteristics of the two sexes vary considerably in accuracy and in the firmness with which they are rooted in the biology of sex. It is widely believed, for example, that men have more arm and shoulder strength than women. This belief reflects reality: Men are, on the average, stronger than women, although, of course, many women are stronger than many men. The difference is an outcome of sex-linked biological processes and can be influenced to only a limited extent by exercise and work patterns. The belief that women are more likely than men to wear skirts also accurately reflects social reality in Western societies, but this difference is much less clearly related to biology and consequently is something that cultures are free to change. Other cultural beliefs may not accurately reflect social reality at all. For example, little support can be found for the belief that in early childhood girls are more intensely attached to their parents than boys. Many beliefs about the psychological characteristics of the two sexes undoubtedly represent cultural inventions that are woven around a core of social or biological fact. Differentiating between truth and cultural myth is extraordinarily difficult, especially since people's beliefs sometimes become self-fulfilling prophecies.

In the sections that follow we will first emphasize biology—discussing the differentiation of the sexes that takes place before birth and the physical and behavioral differences that may affect social development. Then we will discuss the development of concepts of sex identity and sex roles and consider how these ideas influence the way the two sexes behave. And finally we will consider the interweaving of biological factors with socialization pressures in determining the course that development takes. But first cautions are in order:

1. When sex differences are found, they are only averages. A great deal of variation exists within each sex, and the characteristics of the two sexes overlap greatly. Certain bodily features, of course, are distinctly male or female, and except for occasional ambiguous cases, qualitative sex differences in physical characteristics do exist. In terms of psychological characteristics, however, the sexes are more alike than different, and any average sex difference must be seen from the perspective of overall similarity.

2. The existing research on sex differences has primarily used white, middle-class American children as subjects. In most cases we know very little about how widely the comparisons would generalize to other cultures and other times.

3. A sex difference has news value. A finding of *no* sex difference does not. Thus, there is a bias in reporting: Studies that show the sexes to be similar are not likely to be included in published papers, nor to be found in reviews, summaries, and textbooks based on published research. This bias makes it difficult to balance what is known about differences against what is known about similarities.

4. When a sex difference is found consistently in a number of studies, many people assume that the difference must be "natural"—that is, primarily biological. In fact, establishing a difference usually tells nothing about its origin. The relative contributions of biology and cultural shaping must be established to understand causes, which is a separate and much more difficult research issue.

5. In observational studies done after infancy or early childhood, concealing the sex of the subject is usually impossible. It has been shown that an observer's report can be influenced by subjective judgments about the subject's sex. Condry and Condry (1976) prepared a videotape of a nine-month-old infant's reaction to a variety of situations, and they showed the film to college-age viewers. Some students were led to believe the infant was a boy, and others that the infant was a girl (the child's name was varied appropriately). When the infant showed a strong reaction to a jack-in-the-box, the reaction was more often labeled *anger* if the child was thought to be a boy, and it was labeled *fear* when the infant was thought to be a girl.

6. Matters related to differences between the sexes have strong personal and political implications. People disagree about definitions, causes, and the possibility of changing behavior and attitudes. Every writer and reader brings some bias to the consideration of these issues; it is extraordinarily difficult to remain objective.

SEX DIFFERENCES

Physiological sex differentiation

The basic pattern of fetal development is female. Beginning at about the sixth week of gestation, the male fetus's testes begin to produce the hormone *testosterone*, which acts upon the otherwise female pattern to produce a child with male genitals. If for some reason the testes do not produce the requisite amounts of testosterone, the genetically male child will develop as a female. But the presence of testosterone is not enough. If the "female" fetus is to change into a male, the target organs must recognize and respond to the hormone. Infants who have a genetic defect in which the target sites are insensitive to testosterone develop in the uterus as females, even though they are genetically male and their testes are actively producing normal amounts of male hormone (see Luria and Rose, 1979, for a fuller account of the prenatal physiological events and timing).

The effects of prenatal testosterone are not confined to the development of male genital structures. This hormone also predisposes the developing organism to react in sex-linked ways to events that will take place long after birth. In animals the appearance of male patterns of sexual behavior following puberty depends on the appropriate hormonal events having taken place prenatally. Of course, the hormonal changes of puberty are also important in bringing about sex-appropriate reproductive behavior, but these effects also depend on prior hormonal sensitization during the prenatal period.

Male infants are born with higher levels of testerone than girls, although girls also have appreciable amounts of the hormone. Some testosterone is produced by the fetal adrenals, and some derives from hormonal conversion by the placenta. These sources are active in both sexes, but in boys an additional amount is contributed by the testes. The potential effects of a hormone on target sites in the body depend on the proportion of the hormone that is *unbound*. Certain proteins in the blood take up and neutralize, or *bind*, hormones. The proportion of unbound testosterone is especially great at birth. Male infants experience a further surge of unbound testosterone at the age of one to two months (see Figure 6-1). The amount of unbound testosterone is thereafter very low in both sexes until puberty. However, the hormones present before or just after birth may sensitize brain structures, and thereby affect behavioral development occurring at a later time in childhood when the hormones are no longer present.

Male fetuses are more vulnerable to mishaps of pregnancy and childbirth. A higher proportion of males than females are spontaneously aborted; the approximately equal sex ratio at birth exists only because more males than females are conceived. The incidence of various congenital defects is greater among male infants, as is the incidence of *anoxia* (lack of oxygen due to the infant's being slow to begin breathing). Let us hasten to say that the large majority of male fetuses develop normally and undergo the birth process without damage. Nevertheless, greater male vulnerability remains a fact, and a puzzling one. Two explanations have been offered: (1) males must undergo an additional process during fetal growth, and this change from

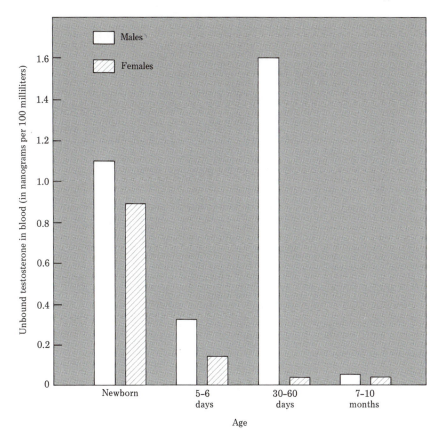

Figure 6-1. Age and sex differences in unbound testosterone. Blood was obtained from the umbilical cord of newborns and from the peripheral blood supply of older infants. Note the increased amount of the hormone in the blood of one- to two-month-old male infants. (Adapted from Forest et al., 1974)

a female to a male pattern of differentiation increases the chance of some process going wrong; (2) females have extra genetic protection with respect to any aspect of development affected by a gene on the X chromosome because they have two of these chromosomes (males only have one). In the female body both X chromosomes are active, but only one is dominant in each cell. Thus, the female has a mosaic of cells, some expressing the characteristics of one X chromosome and the rest expressing the other. A defective or weakening characteristic carried by one X chromosome is therefore counteracted by the action of the healthier genes carried on the second X chromosome. Males do not have this protection.

How do normal male and female infants differ at birth? In most samples that have been studied males are slightly longer and heavier.

Males may also be stronger, although of course strength is difficult to measure in newborns. One measure of strength is the *prone head reaction* (in which an infant is placed face-down on a flat surface; if the child is able to lift his or her chin from the table top, this distance is measured). In two samples out of three assessed by this procedure (Bell, Weller, and Waldrop, 1971; Jacklin, Snow and Maccoby, 1980) male infants lifted their chins higher on the average. Another measure of strength is the *grasp reflex* (the tendency of newborns to grip quite firmly a rod or ring that is placed in the hand). When a ring is attached to a spring scale and placed in the infant's grasp, the strength of the infant's pull can be measured. In two samples of newborns, male infants pulled harder—however, the sex difference was significant in only one of these samples (Jacklin, Snow, and Maccoby, 1980).

One early study (Bell, Weller, and Waldrop, 1971) reported that female newborns were more sensitive to touch. A newborn's sensitivity can be tested by stimulating the foot lightly with a series of nylon bristles and increasing the stiffness of the bristles until the infants pull up their feet. Infants differ in sensitivity, and some require a fairly strong pressure before they react. In three samples of newborn infants recently tested in this way (Jacklin, Snow, and Maccoby, 1980), no sex differences in tactile sensitivity have been found. In view of these findings and the inconsistent results of previous research, it seems likely that Bell's observations represented a sampling aberration and that the sexes do not differ in tactile sensitivity to any meaningful degree at the time they are born.

Maturity and maturation rate

We have already commented in Chapter 2 on the variations among species in maturity at birth—that is, in how far the newborn has developed along the path leading to adult functioning. Some observers have suggested that human female infants are more mature at birth than males. One basis for this assertion is the finding that girls' bones are somewhat farther along in the hardening process at birth (Flory, 1936). Researchers have also looked for sex differences in the maturity of the nervous system at birth and during subsequent maturation. Studies of the brains of infants who died at birth or at subsequent ages (Conel, 1952, 1959) reveal that human brains are fairly immature at birth, at least with respect to the *myelinization* of the nervous tissue (the growth of the sheath surrounding certain nerve fibers). The progress of myelinization during the first several years of life has been traced. There is some hint in the data that female brains may myelinize faster, but too few male and female brains have been available at each age level to permit any clear conclusions about sex differences. Witelson and Pallie (1973) examined the brains of ten infants who died at birth; they were particularly interested in the size of the temporal lobes—the area of the brain that is especially important in language functions. In adults the area known as the temporal planum is considerably larger in the left cerebral hemisphere than the right, reflecting the specialization of the left side of the brain for linguistic functions. The researchers found that this size discrepancy also exists in newborns, in about the same degree in the two sexes. The evidence is thin, of course, considering the very small number of brains studied, but it suggests that no marked sex difference exists in the readiness of the newborn's brain for language acquisition.

Are there sex differences in rate of maturation following birth? The evidence is contradictory. We know that girls' bones continue to solidify faster than boys' bones (Roche, 1979) and that girls reach puberty sooner. Furthermore, boys are most likely to experience a lag in early neurological development—that is, among the few infants who have mild, brief convulsions, which may reflect the immaturity of certain neural structures, the majority are boys. In addition, the onset of such symptoms, if it occurs at all in girls, occurs at an earlier age, suggesting that there are more boys who continue in a neurologically immature state during a longer period of their infancy (Taylor and Ounsted, 1972). Despite this evidence, girls and boys are probably more similar than different in respect to maturation. Many of their physiological and psychological systems develop at the same rate. For example, no sex differences have been found in the average age of onset of standard developmental milestones—sitting up, eruption of teeth, refined thumb-and-forefinger grasping, walking—even though individual children develop at different rates (Bayley, 1965). Similarly, although children's sleep patterns undergo considerable maturation during the early years of life—the periods of longest sleep and longest wakefulness stretch out and the number of transitions from sleeping to waking declines—the differences among children in maturing of sleep patterns are not related to children's sex (Jacklin el al., 1979).

If the maturing of sleep patterns and the passing of a series of sensory-motor milestones indicate something about the rate at which the brain is maturing, then the two sexes would appear to be on highly similar timetables for brain maturation. However, differences may exist in the rate at which different parts of the brain become specialized for different functions. The brain becomes progressively *lateralized* (that is, the two sides of the brain begin to control somewhat different functions), although, of course, the two sides of the brain do cooperate and their functions do overlap greatly. Among most adults the left hemisphere dominates speech and other language functions, while the right hemisphere is more active in processing various kinds of spatial information, including recognizing shapes by touch. And since the right side of the brain controls the left side of the body, shapes felt with the left hand are normally recognized more quickly and accurately than shapes felt with the right hand. Witelson (1976) has reported that by the age of six boys show a clear left-hand superiority for perception of shapes by touch, suggesting early lateralization of this function. Girls, she finds, do not begin to show hemispheric differentiation until about the age of ten. If this finding were true, it would provide evidence that in this respect at least, boys' brains mature faster than girls'. However, a more recent study has found both sexes to be lateralized for touch at age seven (Cioffi and Kandel, 1979). And researchers agree that both sexes are lateralized for language functions by the same age. So, although the evidence is not all in, it seems likely that brain lateralization is well established for most children of both sexes by the time they enter school.

Witelson has suggested that lateralization may be more important for boys than for girls. She finds that a very high proportion of boys with reading problems (but of normal intelligence) fail to show a left-hand advantage in recognizing shapes by touch. In contrast, girls' success in reading seems unrelated to lateralization of touch perception. Perhaps boys' language functions are more vulnerable, so that the left hemisphere of boys' brains must be freer from other functions if language processes are to develop normally. Girls may be able to develop normal language processes even when other functions are being controlled by the same hemisphere. For the present, this hypothesis remains an intriguing possibility for which further evidence is needed.

The question of sex differences in maturation rates is controversial and has implications for educational policy. It is widely believed that girls mature faster during the preschool years. Some educators have recommended that girls start school at six and boys at seven, on the grounds that boys are not maturationally ready for school at the earlier age. It is true that there are more boys who have difficulty learning to read—for example, boys outnumber girls in remedial reading classes by a ratio of at least four to one. This problem does not necessarily imply any delay in the overall maturation of their central nervous systems, however. Boys may simply be slower to develop the necessary competencies in using and understanding language, although the evidence on this issue is contradictory. Sex differences are not usually found in five- and six-year-olds' performance on tests of vocabulary size, length of utterances, grammatical complexity, and other aspects of language development (except perhaps when the children are from very low-income families). Yet studies of language development suggest that on the average girls take the first steps in language acquisition a little earlier than boys (Nelson, 1973; Schachter et al., 1978). Kagan (personal communication) reports that most boys and girls in his studies of Chinese and Caucasian toddlers developed language at about the same rate but that the very slow-developers were almost always boys.

We cannot delve deeply here into the reasons why a minority of children have difficulty in learning to read—and why this minority includes more boys than girls. This sex difference may be a product of differences in willingness to learn, rather than neurological development. We merely stress here that the difference in the incidence of reading difficulties should not be attributed to an overall difference in girls' and boys' maturation rates because: (1) there is no such thing as an overall maturation rate—different functions mature at different rates and (2) rates of growth of different functions may be quite unrelated. Many years ago Bayley (1956) showed that the rate of intellectual development is unrelated to the rate of growth in stature. In other words, the fact that girls' wrist bones ossify faster than boys' tells us nothing about neurological maturity or readiness for school at the age of six.

Energy and activity

As we noted in Chapter 5, boys have a higher basal metabolism rate than girls. Boys do not necessarily have more surplus energy to expend, however; they may simply need more food to sustain a given level of activity. The implications of a high metabolism rate for behavior are simply not known.

During the first two years of life, when children spend time primarily in their own homes in the company of their adult caretakers and older siblings, boys and girls appear to be about equally active. Groups of children have been observed in their homes or laboratory playrooms, and records have been made of the amount of squirming they do while being dressed, the amount of splashing and movement while being bathed, and the distance they cover in the course of their play. Mothers have also been asked to describe their young children's activity levels. These studies show rather consistent differences in activity level for individual infants and toddlers, but the differences are seldom significantly related to the children's sex (Jacklin and Maccoby, 1978). Many observers find no sex difference in the activity level of groups of three-year-olds, but when a difference is found, boys are almost always the more active sex.

The amount of activity a child displays is determined in large part, of course, by the amount of space available for play and the nature of the play materials provided. Children of both sexes are more active when playing on swings, jungle gyms, and trampolines than when playing with blocks or crayons. The effect of a play situation is not always what might be expected, however. Halverson (1978) found that preschool children burst into especially vigorous activity when asked to "rest" in a softly carpeted room equipped only with pillows. Anyone who has lived through the pillow fights at "slumber" parties will recognize that certain situations seem to be an invitation to rough-housing. As we shall see below, preschool boys seem readier than girls to respond to such an invitation.

Social play

Do boys and girls play in different ways? During the first two years of life, when children usually play by themselves or with an older person, the play patterns of girls and boys are similar. When brought into a strange room that is equipped with toys, girls and boys are about equally likely to explore the room. The length of time that a child continues to focus attention on a toy before shifting to something new is not a function of the child's sex. However, when a variety of toys are offered, boys and girls may demonstrate different preferences. Smith and Daglish (1977) observed children of fourteen or twenty-two months in their own homes and found that boys were more likely to play with trucks and cars, and girls with dolls and soft toys. Other workers have reported a similar trend (Fagot, 1974; Fein et al., 1975). Of course, children may simply be playing with the sex-typed toys that their parents have provided, rather than actively expressing a preference. However, Smith and Daglish's young subjects spent more time playing with sex-appropriate toys than with other equally available toys. This finding does suggest that children as young as two years old have begun to develop sex-typed toy preferences. Certainly by nursery-school age such preferences are abundantly clear. In a situation in which many toys and activities are available, boys will choose to play with toy trucks, cars, and airplanes, while girls choose dolls, cooking equipment, and painting or crayoning (Conner and Serbin, 1977). Of course, many activities, including books, play-dough, puzzles, and number and letter games, are equally attractive.

Boys and girls of preschool age frequently segregate themselves into male and female play groups. The tendency of children to choose same-sex playmates is illustrated in Strayer's (1977) extensive observations of the social interaction of a group of Canadian nursery-school children. His observations of each child's most frequent "nearest neighbor" revealed four distinct social groups. Each group had a focal pair who related reciprocally to one another, and several other members who related to one or another member of the focal pair. The pattern of interaction is illustrated in Figure 6-2. Group A is made up of four boys and one girl who stayed near one of the focal boys. Group D shows the reverse pattern: a group of four girls and one boy who stayed near a focal girl. Every focal pair consisted of same-sex children.

Strayer obtained similar results with two additional groups of children. Stable social groups could be identified, and the members were

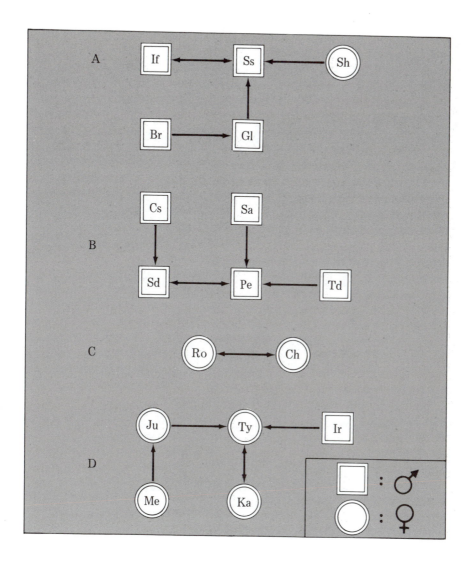

Figure 6-2.   Four stable social groups in a preschool class. The double-headed
arrows represent the focal pair in each group. Note that the groups consist
mainly of children of the same sex and that all focal pairs are the same sex.
(From Strayer, 1977)

generally of the same sex. A girl who preferred to play with boys was always a kind of hanger-on, attached to the periphery of the play group through association with one of its members. Similarly, a boy in a girl's play group was never a central figure.

Preschool teachers sometimes try to shift children's play-group patterns in the direction of more mixed-sex play. In a study by Serbin, Tonick, Sternglanz (1977) children were first observed in their spontaneously occurring play groups to determine a base line for same-sex versus mixed-sex play. Then, for a ten-day period they were given extra attention and approval by the teachers whenever they played with an opposite-sex child. During the training period substantial increases occurred in the amount of cross-sex play, and such play continued to increase steadily during the ten-day experiment. But when the reinforcement was discontinued, the children returned very rapidly to their earlier sex-segregated choices.

As children grow older and enter elementary school, a further development takes place: The girls' play groups become smaller and each girl usually has one or two best friends, while boys continue to play in larger groups (Bernat, 1979; Omark and Edelman, 1973; Waldrop, 1975). But sex segregation continues, and fewer children have cross-sex playmates.

How early can a preference for same-sex playmates be detected? A study of thirty-three-month-olds shows that even at this age, children respond differently—and more positively—to children of their own sex (Jacklin and Maccoby, 1978). Pairs of previously unacquainted children were brought into a laboratory playroom—some were same-sex pairs, others were mixed-sex pairs. Mothers were asked to dress their children in pants and a T-shirt and to remove sex-typed decorative items such as hair ribbons or holsters, so that the child's sex would not be strongly signaled. The adult observers said they were sure of the sex of about half the children (sometimes, though confident, they were wrong!). In order to increase the children's interaction and encourage sharing, competition, and dominance, the children were given a series of toys and in several cases were required to share one attractive toy. An observer dictated a running account of the children's actions, and this record was used to determine frequency of solitary play versus socially directed play. Directed play included taking a toy (or attempting to take it) from the other child, resisting or yielding to the other child's attempt to take a toy, offering a toy, accepting an offer, smiling at partner, issuing a vocal command or prohibition, patting or hugging, pushing or hitting. Figure 6-3 shows that both boys and girls directed more social behavior toward partners of their own sex. Much of this behavior was friendly, but sometimes one child grabbed the other's toy. Boy-boy pairs were more likely to engage in a tug of war over a toy than girl-girl or boy-girl pairs. While both boys and girls were somewhat more likely to cry or retreat to-

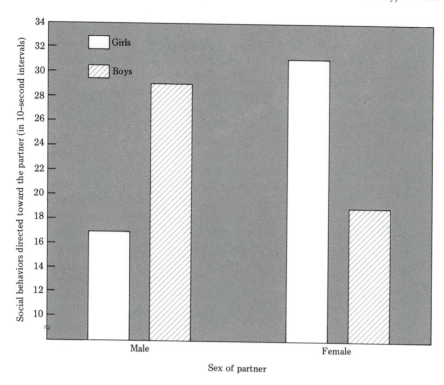

Figure 6-3. Sex preferences in play at age thirty-three months. Note that both boys and girls direct more social behavior toward playmates of the same sex. (Adapted from Jacklin and Maccoby, 1978)

ward their mothers (who were quietly seated in the room) when playing with a boy partner, girls were particularly affected by a male partner and tended to retreat or stand quietly watching the boy play with the toys. Girls with female partners rarely exhibited such behavior.

Apparently, very young boys do something that makes their partners wary. Male partners also find this "something" exciting and interesting—their tendency to withdraw is counterbalanced by the positive attraction—while girls are less interested. We do not know what the "something" is. But it seems that even at this early age children are already developing somewhat distinctive styles of play and that play style makes a same-sex partner more compatible. Precisely what signals the children send and receive remains a mystery. The children in these studies were less than three years old, and most of them had not been to preschool or participated regularly in play groups. Yet clearly, the groundwork had already been laid for the formation of the same-sex play groups that Strayer observed and also perhaps for qualitatively different patterns of play.

A study by DiPietro (1979) illustrates the kind of qualitative differences that typify group play at nursery-school age. Four-and-a-half-year-olds were brought, in same-sex groups of three, into a mobile home that was stripped of furnishings and deeply carpeted. The only play equipment consisted of a small trampoline (large inner tube with a canvas webbing), a beach ball, and later in the session, a Bobo doll (a child-size inflated toy with weighted feet, which springs back to an upright position when pushed or struck down). When allowed to play freely in this environment, some of the girls' groups developed a distinctive pattern of interaction that was almost never shown by boys: They organized their play by making rules. If one girl insisted on going first or taking a longer turn than the others, her partners would react by invoking the rules and arguing, rather than by using physical coercion. A distinctive male pattern of play also emerged. The boys engaged in a good deal of playful rough-housing and wrestling, which was very seldom aggressive in the sense discussed in Chapter 4—that is, there was seldom evidence of anger or intent to injure.

DiPietro recorded her young subjects' physical activity—the amount of jumping and running or standing and sitting quietly. She found only a small sex difference in level of physical activity. The girls were nearly as active as the boys. They jumped on the trampoline and moved quickly with the beach ball, but they seldom engaged in rough-housing. The girls seldom tried to hit each other with the beach ball or push or play tug of war—things the boys did quite frequently (usually accompanying the activity with shouts of glee or excited laughter).

The friendly rough-and-tumble of boys' play is sometimes hard to distinguish from more serious encounters with mutual intent to hurt, and rough-housing can turn into aggression quite quickly. Both types of interaction are more typical of boys' than girls' groups. In fact, the tendency of males to be more aggressive than females is perhaps the most firmly established sex difference and is a characteristic that transcends culture (Whiting and Edwards, 1973; Whiting and Whiting, 1975). Boys are not more aggressive in all situations, and the sex difference has not emerged in a number of studies where it might have been expected. Nevertheless, males do predominate as both the agents and the victims of aggression in a wide variety of situations (circumstances in which females are more aggressive are rare), and they are both physically and verbally more aggressive than females (Barrett, 1979; Frodi, MacCaulay, and Thome, 1977; Maccoby and Jacklin, 1974). The sex difference in the incidence of aggressive behavior has been found in a number of different cultures, ranging from tribal villages to highly industrialized societies (Whiting and Whiting, 1975), and while the frequency of aggression declines with age (see Chapter 4), the sex difference persists into adulthood.

The fights that erupt in boys' groups are often related to forming and maintaining dominance hierarchies. As we saw from the work of

Strayer (Chapter 4), fights occur most often between two children who have not yet settled the issue of who is dominant. Struggles for dominance occur much more frequently in boys' than in girls' play groups (Strayer, 1977). In the Whitings' cross-cultural studies the term *egoistic dominance* was used to describe dominance interactions in which pressure is exerted on another person for the actor's own benefit rather than for the benefit of the target. In five out of six societies in different parts of the world, boys showed more egoistic dominance than girls (Whiting and Whiting, 1973, 1975). Edwards and Whiting (1977) also report higher male rates of these kinds of egoistic behaviors in five out of six African villages. The African children of both sexes made more same-sex social overtures and were more likely to insult or disparage children of the opposite sex. Sex differences in the quality of the African children's social interactions are reminiscent of DiPietro's young American subjects: Boys more often competed, assaulted, teased in a friendly way, or showed off to one another; girls more often offered help or affection to one another and more often used social commands (for example, "let's do . . ." or "you do this, I'll do that"). In other words, girls appeared to be setting up an agreed-upon procedure for social activity—what DiPietro saw as setting up and using rules.

In another cross-cultural study comparing Anglo-American and Mexican-American children, five- through nine-year-olds were offered opportunities to make choices that would give them more rewards than their partners, equal rewards with their partners, or smaller rewards than their partners. Girls in both cultures and at all ages studied were more likely to try to equalize the rewards. Boys not only chose more for themselves but also made choices that reduced the partner's reward—even when this action did not get more for the child himself (Knight and Kagan, 1977).

We see, then, that sex segregation of play groups and sex differences in patterns of play are not limited to technologically advanced societies or to middle-class children.

Nurturance toward infants and young children

In all the cultures of the world women are the primary caretakers of infants and young children. Even in societies where women's labor outside the home is needed or encouraged by egalitarian ideologies (for example, Sweden, China, the Israeli kibbutzim, the Soviet Union), child care is provided in facilities staffed almost exclusively by women. Within this universal female dominance of the child-care functions, however, great variations exist in the role that men play in the rearing of children and the nature of their responsibilities toward them.

Of course, the role of women in child care has biological roots.

When a woman bears and breast-feeds many children, this means that she is occupied with youngsters for the major portion of her adult life. Traditionally it has been efficient for societies to assign women child-care duties in addition to feeding since they have had to stay near the children in any case. Furthermore, women's role as primary caretakers in the years when the child is being breast-fed leads to the formation of a strong attachment between mother and child so that the mother becomes the "natural" socialization agent in the child's early years (see Chapters 2 and 3).

In recent years profound changes have been occurring in these conditions. Women have smaller families; they may breast-feed for only a few months or not at all. Many women spend much of their adult lives working away from the home in occupations that are incompatible with simultaneous child care. These changes have led to insistent questions about the possibility (or desirability) of more equal sharing of child-care functions by men and women. A discussion of changes that *might* take place in role sharing is beyond the purposes of the present chapter. We can, however, describe what is known about the responsiveness of males and females to infants and young children. This description may help to provide perspective for any discussion of changing roles. We begin by describing what is known about the reactions of the two sexes to infants and young children. Later in the chapter the possible origins of these differences will be addressed.

In the mammalian animal kingdom there can be no doubt that females are the more nurturant sex. In females of all species hormones associated with birth and lactation serve to elevate responsiveness to infants. But among monkeys and apes, it is not only the mature lactating females who show special interest in infants; prepubescent females also seek to *nurture* them (that is, groom them, hold them, and so forth). The male behavioral repertoire includes many of the necessary caretaking responses, but such behavior is fairly difficult to elicit. In some species male aggressiveness interferes with caretaking. The male may attack a young animal on first contact, with caretaking behavior appearing only after fairly prolonged contact. As we saw in Chapter 2, the role that wild male subhuman primates play in the care and protection of infants varies considerably among subspecies.

When monkeys are raised in artificially created nuclear families, the males and females have quite different relationships with the young. Suomi (1977b) describes the social behavior of wild-born rhesus monkeys who had been living for some time in cages at the onset of the study and who were observed frequently over a three-year period. Each cage contained an adult male and female and their offspring; the infants could get out of the cage—and into other cages—through a small passage that was not large enough for the adults. In the course of daily life the adult males exhibited more social play with infants than did the adult females; the adult females showed more clasping, cradling, and protectiveness—behaviors that were hardly ever seen in the adult males. When an infant of either sex initiated grooming or nestled close to an adult male, he was more likely than the adult female to ignore such an overture. The adult males initiated approximately equal amounts of social play with their offspring of both sexes, but when other infants visited the cage, the adult male showed playful interest only in the visiting males. The adult males also frequently exhibited hostility toward the young male visitors—something the adult females did not do. The adult male's pattern of social behavior was largely unaffected by the birth of a new infant. The adult female's social behavior toward her mate and offspring was greatly affected by this birth.

Before considering whether the reactions of male and female adult subhuman primates have implications for the human species, let us review what is known about the responsiveness to infants of humans of various ages in various environments. We begin with cross-cultural evidence. In the several cultures described by Edwards and Whiting (1977) girls as young as three to six years old were more likely than boys to show friendly interest in infants and offer them help and affection. Boys in this age group less often made a social approach to an infant or toddler. If boys did make such an approach, they often tried to dominate the younger child—to take away a toy or food or to get the younger child to do something for them. In eight different societies in Africa and other parts of the world, Edwards and Whiting found that girls in middle childhood (six to ten years old) are more likely than boys to offer food, help, or attention to a younger child. This finding is not surprising since girls in these societies have many child-care responsibilities. However, the girls were also more nurturant in situations in which they were not officially baby-sitting.

Some studies with American children have similar results. For example, O'Bryant and Brophy (1976) asked pairs of fifth-graders and kindergarten children to count tickets and clip them into stacks of five. The younger child in each pair was given a much larger pile of tickets. In this situation about half the fifth-grade girls helped the younger child, while only about a fifth of the boys did so.

There are several studies in which people of different ages have been observed in a waiting room in which an unfamiliar infant was also present. Feldman and Nash (1977) observed a group of eight- to nine-year-olds and a group of adolescents in such a situation and recorded responses to the infant: frequency of looking, smiling, talking, showing objects, making funny faces, and approaching and touching or holding the baby. They also recorded the number of times their subjects *ignored* the infant's signals for attention. Girls were more responsive to the infants than boys (see Table 6-1) in the sense that they less often ignored the infant's signals. Frodi and Lamb (1978) used the same observation situation and also found that girls are more

TABLE 6-1   Percent of infant bids for attention that are ignored

AGE	BOYS	GIRLS
8–9	0.19	0.10
14–15	0.25	0.20

SOURCE: Feldman and Nash, unpublished data.

responsive than boys. It is worth noting that the girls became less rather than more responsive to infants during adolescence, a time when relationships with the opposite sex become important. This finding is one among many illustrations of the fact that sexual impulses and maternal impulses are by no means identical!

Is there a sex difference in the responsiveness of adult men and women to young infants? Feldman and Nash (1978) have used their waiting-room situation to study young adults in several phases of the life cycle. Some were young couples cohabiting but not married; some were married but not involved in child bearing; some were married and expecting a baby; some were parents of a first infant. Females without children were only slightly more responsive to the baby than men. The new mothers behaved differently: These women were more responsive—exceeding the other females and all men by about ten percent. In other words, the woman's interest in an unfamiliar infant was considerably affected by her own life-cycle stage, the man's was not.

Is there a sex difference in the responsiveness of men and women to their own children? Parke and Sawin (1976) observed mothers and fathers (separately and together) with their newborn infants in the hospital. Fathers were at least as likely as mothers to hold their infants close, rock them, smile or talk to them, and look directly into their child's face. Furthermore, new fathers were as skillful and gentle as new mothers in their handling of the babies. When the infants were older and could be observed at home, no difference was found in parents' interest in their infant or responsiveness to the child's signals. Mothers and fathers did differ in the way in which they interacted with the child: Mothers tended to do more routine caretaking, and fathers tended to offer more playful stimulation. Parke and Sawin also found that fathers may take somewhat more interest in their sons than in their daughters. By the end of the first year fathers and mothers had developed fairly distinctive styles of play with the infant. Fathers were rougher; they did more tossing and playful wrestling.

Mothers were more likely to use toys when playing with the child (see, for example, studies by Frodi and Lamb, 1978).

In summary, there is considerable evidence that girls and women are more interested in infants and more responsive to them than men and boys, but a female's interest varies over her life cycle—during certain periods she may be especially responsive. There is also evidence that girls are more nurturant toward younger children who have grown out of babyhood but still need help and care. In both human beings and subhuman primates, fathers can play a very active role in interaction with their infants and young children if their life situation brings them into frequent contact with their young. The nature of a father's interaction differs somewhat from that of a mother's: It is more oriented around play.

How much of the sex difference in responsiveness to infants and young children is an outcome of the social assignment of child-care responsibilities to women and girls? Probably a great deal, but the question is still open. We do not know whether there is any biological contribution to these differences, nor whether the more playful male style of interaction or the more cuddly female style is better for children in the long run. We do know, however, that most adults of both sexes possess the competencies needed to take care of children. Furthermore, children undoubtedly benefit from the styles of interaction of both their parents.

Relationships with parents

Observations of different age children in various settings suggest that some differences exist in the quality of girls' and boys' interaction with their parents. Boys are more resistive than girls to the teaching and training efforts of their parents and more likely to make counterdemands. Martin (1980) found that as early as ten months of age boys are more insistent in their demands for their mothers' attention. He set up a laboratory situation in which each mother filled out a questionnaire while her infant either played with toys on the floor or sat in a highchair. The infants signaled the mother in various ways, and the mothers usually responded with a look, smile, or word, and then returned to work. Boys were less willing to accept the withdrawal of attention: They would increase the intensity of their demands if the mother had not responded fully before returning to work, while girls were more willing to accept a low-level response.

Twelve-month-old boys, observed in a waiting room with their fathers, were more likely than girls to get into mischief—handle ash trays, vases, and other forbidden objects (Maccoby and Jacklin, 1979). Observations of children in their own homes suggest that one- or two-year-old boys are more likely to engage in activities forbidden by parents: touching fragile or dangerous objects, climbing on furniture, pulling at curtains (Minton, Kagan, and Levine 1971; Smith and Daglish, 1977). Moreover, four- or five-year-old boys are less likely to comply with a parental request, whether the father or the mother makes the request (Hetherington, Cox, and Cox, 1976). Thus, evidence is beginning to accumulate that girls are somewhat more likely to cooperate with parental requirements, and, by implication, that it takes stronger parental pressure—stronger signaling that the parent really means business—to get a son to comply.

Girls seem more ready and more willing than boys to enter into reciprocal interactions with their parents—especially with their mothers. Gunnar and Donahu (1980) observed pairs of mothers and twelve-month-old infants playing together in their laboratory and found that girls were more likely to respond to the mother's initiative with a reciprocating playful move. Boys were more likely to ignore the mother's overture, even though the mothers showed no sex bias in their responses to their child's initiation.

The cross-cultural evidence also points to some sex differences in children's orientation toward their adult caretakers. In the societies Edwards and Whiting studied, girls were more likely to approach their mothers sociably, wanting to play or offering to share in the mother's activities. Boys—even when quite young—approached their mothers with egoistic demands, asking for some form of service or attempting to control or dominate. Thus, the relationship between mothers and sons was more likely to focus on disciplinary issues, while the interaction with daughters more often took the form of shared activities.

And finally, the coercive cycles of interaction described by Patterson (see Chapter 4) are much more likely to develop between parents and a son than between parents and a daughter, judging from the high proportion of boys who appear in his studies of problem children in distressed families. All these findings seem to suggest that boys are at greater risk for getting into a battle of wills with their parents. Whether these battles are more likely to develop with a boy's mother or his father is not yet known.

A number of workers have found that boys' relationships with their parents deteriorate more rapidly when the family is under unusual stress—perhaps because the relationships are initially more fragile (Hetherington, Cox, and Cox, 1979; Rutter, 1970). This stress seems to affect girls and boys differently. Boys are more likely to become rebellious at home and to develop problems at school (including a deterioration in academic performance). Girls, of course, are affected too and show delayed effects during their adolescence (Hetherington, 1972). But in early childhood it is the boys who more often become hard to control under the stress of divorce and develop coercive cycles with their parents. In general, boys' behavior disorders are more strongly correlated with family discord than girls' (Rutter, 1970; Wolkind and Rutter, 1973)—further evidence that a boy's development is more vulnerable to disruption from disordered parenting. Perhaps there is some truth to the old wives' tale that boys are harder to raise than girls.

We have been discussing what children of the two sexes *do*—how their behavior differs. Of course, our chronicle has not been complete. We have said little about the many ways in which the activities and interests of the two sexes differ. From a fairly early age, the two sexes prefer somewhat different toys; boys soon become more interested in sports, and this difference persists into adulthood; choices of favorite television programs and books also differ by sex, and so do dreams and fantasies. These differences will not be listed here—we will return to them when individual differences in sex typing are discussed below.

Sex similarities

In our focus on the differences between the sexes we must not overlook the fact that (1) many aspects of the social behavior of the two sexes are much alike and (2) when discrepancies are found, they are usually small and based on average group behavior. Both girls and boys form strong attachments to their parents and derive a sense of security from their parents' presence. Personality characteristics such as shyness or sociability are not related to children's sex in any consistent way; neither sex is more generous or helpful than the other, except in nurturance toward infants and younger children. Studies of people's willingness to help another person in distress or share valued possessions with others have shown that altruistic behavior depends on whether the other person is the same sex or age as the subject and what kind of help is needed; neither sex shows an especially strong tendency to be helpful to others across all situations. There is some evidence, however, that girls are more likely to share in the emotions of others—to feel happy when others are happy, distressed when they are distressed (see Hoffman, 1977).

When the behavior of individuals is examined, it becomes clear how misleading sex differences in average scores can be. Many individual girls delight in rough-and-tumble games, and many individual boys prefer more tranquil and rule-governed pursuits. Similarly, many individual girls are negativistic and difficult to control, while many individual boys are easy-going and tolerant of frustration. So, even if group sex differences are found in a given behavioral domain—physical, cognitive, emotional, or social—the behavior of individual members of the two sexes is often very similar. Men and women, boys and girls are more alike than they are different.

SEX IDENTITY

During the first few years of life, when sex differences in behavior appear, children are beginning to form concepts about their own identity. The major discussion of self-recognition and self-definition is presented in Chapter 7. For the present we consider a key aspect of the self-concept: the sense of being a person of a given sex and the understanding of the implications of that fact. Full comprehension of what it means to be male or female comes only gradually. The first step is self-labeling. But a child can say "I am a boy" or "I am a girl" without understanding that (1) the label implies membership in a group who share the classification and (2) sex identity is a permanent, life-long attribute. These facts are learned slowly, as is the acquisition of beliefs about the kind of behavior that is appropriate for people of each sex.

Knowing the sex of self and others

A little girl of three is likely to stamp her foot and reach the point of tears if you insist that she is a boy. A little boy will be equally upset if you mistake his sex. But this reaction does not mean that children understand their own sex identity. A three-year-old named Jane might also respond angrily if you insisted on calling her Mary. Young children seem to think of their sex as a label, without any implication of class membership. The acquisition of understanding about what these labels mean is a gradual process.

In a set of ingenious experiments with children aged two, two-and-a-half, and three, Thompson (1975) explored the issue of children's understanding of gender words. He used the following procedure:

> The child was seated in the mother's lap, facing two small rear-projection screens placed side by side and within the child's reach. Above each screen was a bunny face with eyes and mouth that would light up when the experimenter pressed a button. Two pictures would appear on the screen—for example, a ball and a spoon. The experimenter would ask: "Where is the ball?" and if the child pointed to, or touched, the correct picture, the bunny face above that picture would light up. After some practice with pictures of familiar objects (to which the child was responding correctly), pictures of male-female or boy-girl pairs dressed in typically sex-typed clothing and with sex-appropriate haircuts would be shown, and the child would be asked: "Where is the man?" or "lady" or "boy" or "mommy."

In another task the children were given sex-stereotyped boy and girl paper dolls and magazine pictures and were asked to sort the pictures by sex. The children were also asked questions about their own sex and their similarity to the various pictures. A Polaroid photograph was taken of each child, and the children were asked to add the snapshot to the previously sorted pictures. Finally, two neutral pictures (for example, two apples) were labeled "good" or "bad," or "for boys" or "for girls," and the children were asked to choose one of these to take home. Table 6-2 shows age differences in response to these tasks. Since the children had a 50 percent chance of guessing correctly (sex-appropriately), Thompson regarded this level of performance as indicative of an absence of sex-typed choosing. A rate of 75 percent correct may mean one of two things: (1) that some of the children understand and use sex labels while others do not; or (2) that most of the children are using sex labels correctly part of the time but not consistently. The table uses the terms "occasionally," "sometimes," or "often" to indicate how fully developed the children's understanding was in each task. We see that two-year-olds understand very little about sex identity. They can identify their own pictures, but they do not know that their own picture belongs in a box of pictures "for boys" or "for girls." They have begun to understand the meaning of gender words such as "man" and "woman"—that is, they know some of the defining characteristics of the classes that these words refer to. They are even beginning to know that certain activities and objects are associated with each sex (for example, they know that a necktie should be put with "things for daddies" and a lipstick with "things for mommies"). But they do not yet know that they themselves share a gender category with certain other people. By the age of two-and-a-half years children have begun to understand some of these issues; they are beginning to be able to answer questions correctly about their own sex and to identify the sex of people shown in pictures; they are beginning to know that they are more similar to a pictured person who is of their own sex. By age three, these understandings are well advanced, but children are still not reacting to sex-typed labels as a basis for choosing objects appropriate to their own sex. That is, things labeled "for boys" are not automatically selected as preferable by a boy. Thompson found practically no difference between boys and girls in the rate at which understanding of these aspects of sex identity was acquired.

What cues do young children use to identify the sex of other people? To investigate this question Thompson and Bentler (1971) showed a doll with anomalous sex characteristics to children aged four, five, or six and to a group of adults. The doll had either male or female genitals, male or female secondary sex characteristics (breasts versus a muscular torso), and long or short (and masculine-looking) hair. These three characteristics could be shown in all combinations—for example, a doll might have a feminine body build and a feminine hairstyle but male genitals. Each subject saw only one doll, and all sides of the nude

TABLE 6-2 Children's understanding of gender labels for themselves and others [1]

	AGE		
	Two	Two and a half	Three
CAN THE CHILD CORRECTLY (better than chance):			
Answer "Which one is you?" in a set of pictures including own and several opposite-sex	yes (82) [2]	yes (100)	yes (100)
Point to appropriate picture when asked "which is the 'man' 'woman' 'boy' 'girl' 'he' 'she' 'brother' 'sister'	occasionally (62)	often (79)	yes (89)
Answer: "Are you a boy (girl)?"	no (45)	yes (83)	yes (88)
Answer: "Are you like this doll (boy) or this doll (girl)?"	no (50)	sometimes (68)	yes (82)
Place stranger's picture in box "for some girls (boys)"	no (50)	yes (95)	yes (95)
Place own picture in box "for some girls (boys)"	no (57)	often (75)	yes (95)
Place "things for mommys" and "things for daddys" in appropriate box	occasionally (61)	often (78)	yes (86)
Answer: "Are you going to be a mommy (daddy)?"	no (35)	no (55)	occasionally (61)
Prefer an object labeled "good"	no (58)	sometimes (70)	often (79)
Prefer an object labeled sex appropriately ("for boys" or "for girls")	no (52)	no (57)	often (78)

[1] A 50 percent score represents chance responding; a 75 percent score is halfway between a chance level and consistently correct responding.

[2] All numbers in parentheses represent the percentage of all responses that were correct—that is, appropriately sex typed.

SOURCE: From Thompson (1975)

doll were shown. The subjects were given two piles of clothing—one masculine and one feminine—and were asked to choose the clothes that would be appropriate for the doll to wear to a party and to the beach. They were also asked to suggest a name for the doll, to say whether they thought the doll would be a "mommy" or a "daddy," and to explain why.

The researchers found that the children were using the doll's hair length as their primary cue to its sex. Biological sex characteristics were a much less influential cue. Only 14 of the 144 children mentioned upper-body characteristics in explaining their label for the doll, and only 24 mentioned genitals. Adults used both primary and secondary sex characteristics as primary cues, and the mommy-or-daddy question increased their reliance on these characteristics. In contrast, the children also used hair length for this question. Surprisingly, little improvement in the children's understanding of the biological basis for sex identity was found between the ages of four and six. Other studies have shown that young children rely heavily on clothing for cues to the sex of the people around them. One might have thought that they (and adults too) do this out of necessity because the more reliable biological signs are normally concealed, but Thompson and Bentler's study suggests that children do not make good use of biological information even when it is available.

Sex constancy

Kohlberg (1966) has emphasized the importance of *sex constancy* in the development of the child's understanding of sex identity. Sex constancy is Kohlberg's term for the concept that an individual's sex is a permanent attribute of the person, regardless of changes in the person's hair, clothing, and activities. Emmerich and his colleagues (1976) gave a sex-constancy test to several thousand economically disadvantaged children, ranging in age from four to seven. The researchers used drawings of boys and girls (see Figure 6-4), which were fastened into a ring notebook and cut at the neck, so the subjects could be shown all-girl and all-boy pictures as well as a figure with a masculine head dressed in girls' clothing and vice versa. Starting with an all-girl doll, the experimenter would say, "This is Janie," and, flipping the pages when appropriate, would continue with the following questions:

1. If Janie really wants to be a boy, can she be?
2. If Janie played with trucks and did boy things, what would she be? Would she be a girl or a boy?
3. If Janie puts on boys' clothes (like this), what would she be? Would she be a girl or would she be a boy?

Figure 6-4.   Two sample items from Emmerich's sex-constancy test. The actual figures are approximately eight inches high and cut at the neck. (Adapted from Emmerich et al., 1976)

4. If Janie has her hair cut short (like this), what would she be? Would she be a girl or would she be a boy?

5. If Janie has her hair cut short (like this), and wears boys' clothes (like this), what would she be? Would she be a girl or would she be a boy. (p. 4).

The same procedure was then followed a second time, starting with a boy's picture and boy's name (the order of the two series was reversed for some subjects). At each step the children were asked to explain why they thought the figure was or wasn't still a girl or boy. The experimenters deliberately biased the procedure in the direction of sex-constant answers by keeping a sex-typed name and using constant pronouns (she, he) throughout. Nevertheless, surprisingly few children thought that Janie remained a girl when her activities, clothing, and haircut had been changed. Only about 24 percent of the answers showed constancy, and little improvement was shown with age.

Research with other populations indicates that many children achieve sex constancy at a considerably earlier age than seven. And in fact, a number of children in Emmerich's sample may have understood more than they were able to reveal in an interview situation in which the score depended heavily on articulateness. Emmerich's cognitively advanced subjects showed more constancy in their answers and gave more adequate explanations. The brighter children would say such things as "She was born a girl" or "Cause she ain't got no magic; can't change without an operation" (p. 75). The children who showed little constancy tended to give inadequate justifications even on the few occasions when they said the doll's sex had remained the *same*. Typical responses included: "I want her to be a girl; I won't let her be a boy"; "I'll hit him if he tries to be a girl"; "She doesn't want to be a boy and play trucks"; (in the case of an initially male doll) "My daddy would yell and tell him to get off those girl clothes"; (with the boy doll) "He supposed to stay a boy. He's a good boy, [he] has to" (pp. 72–74).

The children seemed to think that a child changing sex was somehow weird or naughty, but most did not doubt that the sex would change if the hair, clothes, and activities were transformed. Emmerich draws an analogy between sex constancy and the *conservation* of size, quantity, weight, and so forth. (Conservation is Piaget's term for the concept that properties of objects remain the same through changes in appearance.) Emmerich interprets the relationship between sex constancy and other aspects of cognitive growth to mean that sex constancy is achieved along with other kinds of conservation as part of the shift from Piaget's preoperational to the operational stage of thinking. We do not know how closely a child's achievement of sex constancy is tied to other specific aspects of operational thinking. Clearly, however, general cognitive development has a great deal to do with the increasing ability of the child to understand that an individual's sex stays the same despite transformation in external trappings.

Does children's understanding that sex is unchangeable influence their behavior? We have seen that young children prefer same-sex playmates long before they understand the constancy of sex. But Kohlberg (1966) suggests that children's interest in same-sex persons may take on a new quality when constancy is present: They may begin to observe such persons closely to discover generalities about the behavior, values, and attitudes of people of their own sex. Slaby and Frey (1975) provide support for Kohlberg's hypothesis. These researchers offered young children an opportunity to look at a screen. On half the screen there was a picture of a man and on the other half there was a picture of a woman—both were engaged in the same activity. The child was able to look at one side of the screen or the other, but not both at once. Boys who understood sex constancy quite consistently chose to look at the person of their own sex; boys who had not yet achieved sex constancy were indiscriminate in their viewing. The relationship of model selection to sex constancy was not found for girls, and subsequent research (Bryan and Luria, 1978) found no evidence of selective attention to same-sex models among children of either sex who were clearly old enough to understand sex constancy. However, the Slaby and Frey results have now been replicated by Ruble (1979), for four- to six-year-olds of both sexes. Thus, evidence is accumulating that understanding sex constancy plays a role in motivating children to acquire sex-appropriate information.

The origins of sex identity

How do boys and girls come to understand and accept their sex identity? In discussing this question, we must stress the distinction between *sex identity* and *sex typing*. A girl can know that she is a girl, expect to grow up as a woman, never seriously want to be a boy, and nevertheless be a tomboy—enjoying boys' games and toys and preferring to play with boys. She has a firm, fully accepted female *identity*, but she does not adopt all the *sex-typed* behaviors that her culture labels feminine nor avoid those labeled masculine. Similarly, a boy can remain outside the rough-and-tumble of the usual boys' play group and still be quite clearly a boy, in the sense that he does not want to be a girl and others think of him and treat him as a boy.

A child's sex identity is almost always well established by the age of three. While children of this age do not understand the biological criteria that determine sex, they nevertheless understand that they are male or female. How do they know what sex they are? Quite simply, because other people tell them. Consider, for example, the rare cases of children whose sex at birth is ambiguous and must be arbitrarily assigned. These cases include genetic females who have masculinized genital structures because they received too much testosterone during the critical phases of prenatal growth and genetic males whose target genital tissues do not develop because of insensitivity to testosterone. In recent years the development of techniques for analyzing the chromosomal composition of body cells has made it possible to determine the genetic sex of ambiguous newborns. In the past, the parents or attending physician would make a decision about the child's probable sex and the child would be raised accordingly. John Money and his colleagues (Money, Hampson and Hampson, 1957) studied 100 children whose physiological sex was ambiguous and whose sex was arbitrarily assigned at birth. They concluded:

1. A child will almost always comfortably accept whatever sex identity is assigned, whether or not the assignment is consistent with the child's genetic sex.

2. Before the age of about two-and-a-half years a child's sex identity can be changed without creating any great psychological trauma. Parents need only give the child a new name, hairstyle, and clothes that are appropriate to the new sex, and begin to think of their child in terms of the reassigned sex. Appropriate treatment on their part and appropriate reactions by the child will follow naturally.

3. After the age of three a child's sex identity is quite fully established. Case studies of five children for whom sex reassignment was attempted after this age indicate that the change was psychologically damaging to several of the children.

We do not know, of course, whether the difficulties in reassignment after the age of three were related to the child's own sense of identity or to other people's confused treatment. By this age the child's acquaintances would be aware of the child's original sex and their social expectations might prevent the child from breaking out into another identity.

As further evidence of the power of social assignment of a sex identity, Money (1975) cites the astonishing case of a pair of identical twins, one of whom lost his penis in a circumcision accident at the age of seven months. With medical advice the parents decided to raise this child as a girl. First, only the child's name, clothing, hairstyle, and toys were changed. Toward the end of the second year, surgical steps were taken to continue the transition to female structures. Plans were made for hormonal treatment at puberty, so that feminine secondary sex characteristics would develop. When the sex reassignment was made, the parents began thinking of the child as a girl and treating her as such. For example, the mother thought it was amusing when the boy twin urinated outdoors but took a much different attitude about her daughter, insisting that she should come indoors and be more modest. By the age of four the little girl was taking pride in her long hair. She had become neat and concerned about her appearance—characteristics not shared by her brother, who did not mind getting dirty. On the other hand, the little girl liked boys' games and didn't particularly like to play with dolls. She was also described as bossy. At the time of this writing, the children have reached school age. We do not know what the future holds for this child but clearly she thinks of herself as a girl and expects to grow up to be a woman. This outcome is consistent with the reaction of other children whose sex has been arbitrarily assigned before the age of three.

Money and his colleagues note that such children seldom become homosexuals—that is, they do not develop sexual interest in persons of the same sex as their assigned sex. We know very little about the origins of homosexuality, but we do know that it is usually not an inversion of sex identity. Male homosexuals know that they are men, and female homosexuals know that they are women, and most accept their identity, even though they are sexually attracted to individuals of the same sex. The main point Money and his associates wish to make is that social assignment plays a powerful role in a child's sexual identity. The researchers do not wish to deny the importance of biology, of course. Children's biological sex is the primary cue that leads to the assignment of their social sex, and so the two are almost always consonant. Furthermore as soon as the child understands the meaning of genital organs as sex-identifiers, this biological information reinforces the identity already created by the sex-appropriate name, clothing, toys, and the personal pronouns used by others. A major discrepancy between the newly understood biological information and the previously established social identity might create problems for the child. But in the vast majority of cases no discrepancy exists, and the child grows up content with the sexual identity that society—and biology—assigned at birth.

The Money account is highly persuasive. However, two kinds of occurrences require us to maintain some reservations. First, his explanation does not account for the existence of transsexuals. These—very few in number—are people whose genetic sex has been properly identified at birth, who have been given appropriate names and raised by their parents and treated by others in accordance with this identity. They have refused to accept their identity, however, and attempt to change it when they are old enough to take charge of their own lives. One such person speaks of being a female "entombed" in a man's body (Morris, 1974). Transsexuals have usually spent an unhappy childhood, being ridiculed by other children and shamed by their parents for their cross-sex tendencies. We can only wonder how they have managed to resist the combined weight of social pressure and their own cognitive understanding of their biological and socially assigned sex. We know very little about the internal dynamics or external events that are responsible for their resistance to social pressure, but their existence demonstrates that not all children will accept the sex identity assigned to them at birth.

A second bit of evidence calls into question the idea that once sex identity is formed, it is difficult and dangerous to attempt to change it. A group of children were found in an isolated village in the Dominican Republic who were born looking like girls and only at puberty were discovered to be genetic boys (Imperato-McGinley, 1974). These children suffered from a rare genetic defect: Their genital structures were unresponsive to testosterone during the prenatal period, but during puberty they developed male genitals, beards, deep voices, and muscular torsos. Although they were raised as girls, when the masculine characteristics appeared, they were simply given masculine names and treated as young men thereafter. Imperato-McGinley reported that these adolescents uneventfully took on their new identity—began to date girls, developed masculine occupational aspirations, and so forth. A follow-up of seven adult men with this sex-change history found that one was a withdrawn man living alone, while the others seemed to be leading normal lives as married men. Some of them were fathers of children, and one had not only a wife but a mistress!

These cases are currently being followed up with more detailed assessments. More will be known soon about the effect on them of this major change in identity. Meanwhile, their existence does not deny the power of social ascription. It merely suggests that if society can assign a sex identity to a child, it can also *reassign* that identity. We should note that the change was supported in two ways: (1) the boys had unmistakable biological evidence of their new status and (2) enough cases had occurred so that a label had been adopted (a word meaning "penis at 12"), and the community recognized that the afflicted individuals needed a changed identity and fostered the transition with a change in social treatment.

SEX ROLES

Learning what sex one is and that one's sex will remain the same throughout life is a fairly simple matter for almost all children. Furthermore, as we have seen, *accepting* one's sex identity is also not problematic for the vast majority of children. However, learning how people of their sex are supposed to behave may be more difficult, and not all children accept these sex-typed prescriptions with enthusiasm. Every society makes certain distinctions in the *roles* that are assigned to men and women. And children in their play often act out the sex-related roles they expect to assume when they are older.

What sex roles are

A *role* is a set of duties, rights, obligations, and expected behaviors that go with being in a certain position in a social structure. The content of a role is determined by other people's expectations (that is, what they consider role-appropriate behavior) and by the intersection of the role with other roles (that is, by the way in which functions, responsibilities, and powers are divided among related roles such as doctor and nurse or foreman and worker). Knowing someone's role tells us a good deal about how that person probably *will* behave and how others believe the person *ought* to behave. In the latter sense, roles are prescriptive.

Is a person's sex a role in the sense discussed above? Yes and no. Not all behavioral differences between the sexes are part of sex roles.

For example, the fact that males urinate standing up and females do not is dictated by biology not by social expectations. Different social expectations may be based on the physical differences between the two sexes, so that role prescriptions are added to a biological base. In other cases, role-prescribed activities may be completely independent of biological sex (for example, which member of a couple goes through a door first).

Sex is not a role in the sense that *truck driver* or *lawyer* are roles. Sex is much more diffuse and permeates other roles. Thus, many occupations are sex-linked, in that only men or only women are expected to take them on. At present, for example, the roles of nurse, secretary, truck driver, and soldier are strongly sex-linked. (The sex linkage of occupational roles is something that can change. When the typewriter was first invented, almost all secretaries were men.) In addition, other aspects of people's lives are greatly influenced by sex-linked social expectations. For example, when a couple is just beginning to date, the man, not the woman, is usually expected to suggest the date, drive the car, and pay the check while the woman has the greater right to refuse a sexual encounter. If someone insults the woman, the man is expected to make a counterthreat. In the dating situation, then, sex becomes a role in the fullest sense.

The relations between the sexes have varied considerably at different times and in different places in the inclusiveness and restrictiveness of sex-role prescriptions. For example, almost every aspect of the life of the traditional Moslem woman is determined by her sex, including the kind and amount of education she will receive, the places inside and outside the house where she is allowed to go, and the tasks with which she occupies her time. In modern Western society much of our behavior is sex-role-free. Nevertheless, many sex-linked behavioral prescriptions exist, and numerous books have been written that describe in detail how subtle and how pervasive such prescriptions can be, even in social groups that seem quite emancipated from traditional sex-role concepts.

As children grow, they learn more about how females and males are expected to behave. And they use this information to guide and monitor their own behavior and to adapt that behavior to take account of the sex of the people with whom they are interacting.

Concepts of the "rightness" of sex-appropriate behavior

As children begin to understand the social expectations associated with being female or male, do they feel bound to conform to these expectations? Do they see sex roles as mere conventions, like table manners or styles of dress, that people are free to change as they wish? Or do they think that sex-role attributes have the status of "musts" or "oughts"?

William Damon (1977) has studied children aged four through nine in order to answer these questions. In his procedure children are told a story about a little boy, George, who likes to play with dolls. His parents tell him that little boys shouldn't play with dolls, that only girls should, and they buy him a lot of toys appropriate for boys. But George still would rather play with dolls. The young subjects are asked for their views on whether George is right or wrong. The examiners vary the wording of their questions as they ask for opinions on the following issues:

1. Why do people tell George not to play with dolls? Are they right?
2. Is there a rule that boys shouldn't play with dolls? Where does it come from?
3. What should George do?
4. What will happen to George if he keeps playing with dolls? What if no one ever sees him? Does George have a right to play with dolls?
5. Is it fair for George's parents to punish him for playing with dolls?
6. What if George says that his sister, Michele, gets to play with dolls all she wants, so why can't he? Is that fair to George?
7. What if George wanted to wear a dress to school? Can he do that? What's wrong with that? Does he have a right to do that? (p. 242)

These questions are followed by an expansion of the story: George goes to Scotland and discovers that Scottish men wear kilts—a kind of skirt—when they want to dress up. The subjects are then told that this has been customary in Scotland for hundreds of years and are asked whether it is all right for a boy to wear a skirt in Scotland but not in an American school or home, and why. Further issues are brought up: Is it all right for a boy to become a nurse or a girl to become a truck driver?

Obviously, children as young as four have difficulty talking about these complex matters. The youngest children's answers tend to be brief and repetitive. Sometimes the whole series of questions cannot be completed. Nevertheless, the answers are enlightening. Consider the responses of Jack, age four:

(Is it O.K. for boys to play with the dolls?) Yes. (Why?) Because they wanted to. (Is there a rule against it?) No. (So what should George do?) Play with dolls. (Why?) Because it's up to him. (Do you think little boys should play with dolls?) I think. (I see.) I do play with my Teddy Bear. (Would it be fair if his parents punished him for it?) I don't know. (Do you think it would be fair?) No! (Why?) Because then it wouldn't be fair, because then he wouldn't have any fun. (What if George says that his sister gets to play with dolls all she wants, so why can't he?) Yes, because him and she want to play with dolls. (But George is a little boy. Does that make a difference?) No. (What if George wanted to wear a dress to school?) What kind? A girl's dress? No way! (What's wrong with it?) Because it's not his. (What if it was his?) I don't know. (Can boys have dresses?) They have clothes. (Can they have dresses?) No. (Why not?) Because boys don't wear them. (Does George have the right to wear a dress to school if he wants to?) Yes, but he didn't want to. (What if he wanted to?) It's up to him. (Why?) Because it's his mind. (Is it O.K. that boys wear skirts?) If they want to. We don't like to here. (Why don't you like to?) Me and Teddy always wear pants, cause we're boys. (p. 249)

By the age of about six, however, most children have come to believe that it is *wrong* for George to play or dress in girlish ways. Michael, aged five years eleven months, says:

(Why do you think people tell George not to play with dolls?) Well, he should only play with things that boys play with. The things that he's playing with now is girls' stuff. . . . (Can George play with Barbie dolls if he wants to?) No sir! (How come?) If he doesn't want to play with dolls, then he's right, but if he does want to play with dolls, he's double wrong. (Why is he double wrong?) All the time he's playing with girls' stuff. (Do you think people are right when they tell George not to play with girls' dolls?) Yes. (What should George do?) He should stop playing with the girls' dolls and start playing with the G.I. Joe. (Why can a boy play with a G.I. Joe and not a Barbie doll?) Because if a boy is playing with something, like if a boy plays with a Barbie doll, then he's just going to get people teasing him, and if he tries to play more, to get girls to like him, then the girls won't like him either. (p. 255)

Another boy of similar age says that it is right for parents to punish George for playing with dolls but that it would be all right for George to play in this way in private if no one ever saw him. In other words, the children's views of what was "right" and "wrong" in this connection were mainly determined by how they thought other people would react.

Some changes begin to occur in these attitudes by the time the children are nine years old. James, eight years ten months, says:

(What do you think his parents should do?) They should try to get him trucks and stuff, and see if he will play with those. (What if, you know, he kept on playing with dolls, what do you think would happen? Do you think they would punish him?) No. (How come?) It's not really doing anything bad. (Why isn't it bad?) Because, like, if he was breaking a window, and he kept on doing that, they could punish him, because you're not supposed to break windows. But if you want to, you can play with dolls, but people don't really like you if you play with dolls. (What's the difference between breaking windows and playing with dolls?) Well, breaking windows you're not supposed to do. And if you play with dolls, you can, but boys usually don't. (How come they don't?) Because they think they're like, too dainty and stuff. If he plays with dolls the guys will think that he's a nut and doesn't play with cars and trucks like us. (Do you think he has a right to wear a dress to school?) Yeah. (How come he has a right?) Because he could do whatever he wants to do, and all the other kids can't tell him what to do and boss him around. But if he wore the dress, he probably wouldn't wear it again, because everyone would laugh at him and he'd get embarrassed. (p. 263)

Of course, these children are unusually articulate, but their views are typical and illustrate the changes that take place with age in children's ideas about right and wrong. At first, children equate right with whatever they want to do. At the next stage, children make no distinction between what is morally right and what other people expect and approve: Playing with dolls or wearing a dress is just as wrong for a boy as breaking a window or stealing a toy. Children in this phase of development are uncompromisingly stereotypical in their sex-role attitudes and will ridicule other children without mercy if they detect deviation from their rigid standards of sex-appropriate behavior. Beginning at about age nine, however, children begin to make distinctions between social rules that are merely conventions and those that have genuinely moral force. They distinguish between what is right and what is customary, and they begin to understand that exceptions to rules of custom can be made, while moral rules carry a deeper obligation (see Turiel, 1975, for amplification of this distinction). No sex differences have been found in children's rate of progress through this developmental sequence. (For further discussion of the growth of understanding of moral right and wrong, see Chapter 8).

Older people with more flexible sex-role attitudes are inclined to see six- to eight-year-olds as highly "sexist." An often-quoted example: The daughter of a successful female physician is likely to insist that girls grow up to be nurses and only boys can be doctors. No wonder some parents feel a certain despair over the ineffectiveness of their efforts to raise their children in an egalitarian mode. These parents are inclined to cite television or school textbooks as sources of heavy counterinfluence. Another factor may be at work, however: Children may simply be exaggerating sex roles in order to get them cognitively clear. Perhaps cognitive clarity helps children establish their own sex identity firmly, and only after this identity is established, can they become more flexible and less sex-bound. From this point of view, the sex-stereotyped attitudes of the early school years represent a developmentally useful phase that children pass through—something they may outgrow if an egalitarian environment is provided. At the moment we cannot say whether this evaluation of the situation is valid. We do know that (1) children go through a highly stereotyped, intolerant phase in their understanding of sex roles, (2) many children become less rigid as they grow older, and (3) these changes are closely linked with other aspects of conceptual development—particularly with understanding of concepts of right and wrong.

VARIATIONS IN DEGREE OF SEX TYPING

Six-year-old girls know quite clearly that they are girls and will grow up to be women. Nevertheless, some girls of this age play with dolls, worry about their appearance, disdain the rough play of boys, and insist on wearing dresses even when their mothers want them to wear jeans. Other girls prefer play clothes, don't mind getting dirty, like to play with boys, and have little interest in dolls. Boys also vary in how closely they conform to stereotypically masculine behavior patterns and interests.

A first question of interest is whether, on the average, one sex is more strongly sex-typed than the other. Boys of preschool age are somewhat more likely to choose strictly masculine toys and play activities than girls are likely to choose feminine ones. This difference is clearly seen when the children are offered an opportunity to play with materials appropriate for the opposite sex. In this situation boys avoid playing with a lipstick and mirror, hair ribbons, a handbag, or nail polish, and girls avoid a shaving kit, a necktie, a gun, or a cowboy hat. But boys show more avoidance than girls. And surprisingly, when the adult experimenter goes out of the room, boys will experiment with the feminine objects while for girls the presence or absence of the experimenter makes little difference (Hartup and Moore, 1963). It is as though boys are interested in these things but know that they must not play with them when anybody is watching—a clear sign that they have learned to expect negative reactions for showing such interests.

But what about the differences in degree of sex typing *within* each sex? Can we identify certain boys who are more masculine than other boys, certain girls who are more feminine? The consistency of individual children's sex typing is not very great (Mischel, 1966). Children respond with some consistency to pictured toy preference tests, but they do not show much consistency in play behavior. A girl who spends most of one day in the doll corner is quite likely to play in neutral areas the next time she is observed (Sears, Rau, and Alpert, 1965). As children grow older, their behavior depends increasingly on context. Thus, adolescents on a date are more likely to act in sex-typed ways than when they are at home. Yet at the extremes certain consistencies can be found. Certain boys have little interest in sports and rough play and maintain bookish and esthetic interests not shared by most other boys. Certain other boys consistently spend much time in stereotypically masculine activities. Similarly, certain girls prefer boys' games during a considerable span of their childhood and spend little time with other girls, while other girls are centrally involved in girls' social activities. What we do not know is the implications of these childhood differences for adult masculinity or femininity. Stereotypes about what constitutes masculine or feminine behavior are not the same for adults as they are for children, and the adult definitions are changing fast. At the moment there is no good reason to believe that highly sex-typed children become highly sex-typed adults. The matter remains open for further study.

An individual can have some of the stereotypical characteristics of *both* sexes. A number of writers have argued that masculinity and femininity are not opposites—that there is considerable overlapping in the qualities regarded as characteristic of a given sex (Bem, 1974; Brim, 1958; Ferguson and Maccoby, 1966; Sears, Rau and Alpert, 1965). When these researchers assessed feminine and masculine sex typing independently, they found that some individuals rated high and some rated low on both sex's characteristics, although the majority of people had more same-sex than cross-sex characteristics. Bem has used the term *androgynous* for people who achieve high scores on both masculinity and femininity scales.

CAUSES OF SEX-TYPED BEHAVIOR

We have seen that a young boy's fear of being a sissy is more intense than a girl's fear of being a tomboy. Why is this so? And why is some children's behavior more sex-typed than others'? We have clearer answers to the first question than the second.

Social pressure

Parents provide distinctive environments for boys and girls. They give them different toys and clothing and decorate their rooms differently (Rheingold and Cook, 1975). They respond negatively to more obvious forms of cross-sex behavior. A very young boy who tries on his mother's high-heeled shoes or puts on a dress or lipstick may be regarded with amused tolerance or gently ridiculed, but such behavior in an older child is regarded as outrageous rather than funny. Fathers react especially strongly to any such signs of feminine tendencies in their sons. For example, a father who was asked whether he would be upset by signs of femininity in his son said: "Yes, I would be. Very, very much. Terrifically disturbed—couldn't tell you the extent of my disturbance. I can't *bear* female characteristics in a man. I abhor them." (E. Goodenough, 1957, p. 310). A possible interpretation of such reactions is that many men experience emotional revulsion over signs of homosexuality in other males. They may interpret certain kinds of feminine interests or actions as signs of developing homosexual tendencies in their sons and react to these tendencies in the strongest terms.

Little girls are allowed more latitude for cross-sex interests and play, but they too are pressured to behave in sex-appropriate ways—again primarily by their fathers. Many fathers react warmly to signs of femininity in their daughters: They like to see them dressed neatly in dresses and hair ribbons; they protest if their wives want to cut a girl's long hair; they often describe their little daughters as "a little flirt," "cuddly," or say "she certainly knows how to flatter her dad"—all of which the fathers quite evidently enjoy (Goodenough, 1957).

Recent studies by Langlois and Downs (as yet unpublished) confirm the crucial role of fathers in exerting pressure for sex-appropriate behavior. These studies examined adults' and children's reactions to sex-appropriate and sex-inappropriate play. The experimenters asked young children to play with a sex-typed set of toys. The feminine set of toys included a dollhouse with furniture, a large stove with pots and pans, and women's dress-up outfits consisting of dresses, hats, purses, shoes, and a mirror. The masculine set included an army game with soldiers and war vehicles, a highway tollbooth with cars, and cowboy outfits including hats, guns, holsters, and bandanas. When one of the boys' sets was present, the child was instructed: "Play with these toys the way boys do." With a girls' set, the instructions were to play as a girl would. Once each child had begun to play, the child's mother, father, or a same-sex playmate was ushered into the room. The experimenters then compared the parental and peer responses to sex-appropriate and sex-inappropriate play.

Both positive reactions (joining in the play, helping, showing interest and approval) and negative responses (interfering with the play, showing expressions of disgust or disapproval) were recorded. Figure 6-5 shows the negative reactions. Clearly, it is the fathers who are most concerned about the sex-appropriateness of their children's play. Furthermore, fathers react more negatively to their sons' than their daughters' sex-inappropriate play. Mothers' negative reactions to sons are not affected by the type of toy with which the child is playing. With daughters, mothers show slightly more disapproval for cross-sex play than they show for sex-appropriate play, but even when their daughters are playing with boys' toys the level of mothers' disapproval is low. Girls seem to have no objection to other girls playing with boys' toys. Boys, on the other hand, do put extra negative pressure on other boys when they see them engaged in girls' activities. We know little about the sex-typing pressure exerted by peers but can guess (judging partly from the interviews reported by Damon) that among boys it is considerable. Interestingly, a common feature in the early histories of transsexuals is isolation from same-sex playmates. Perhaps the fact that they are not subjected to this highly potent

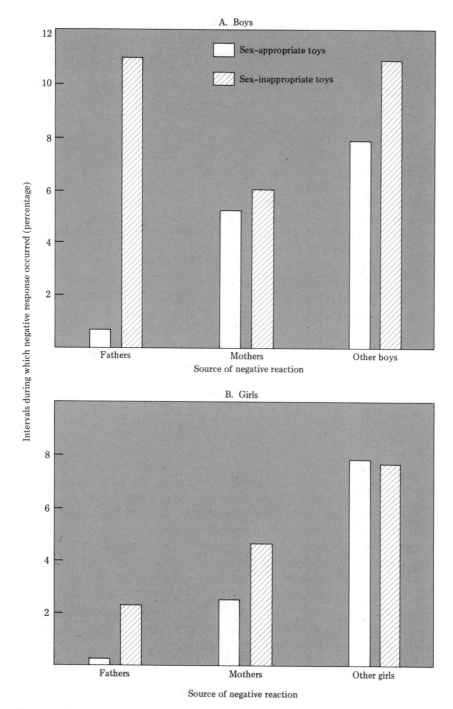

Figure 6-5. Sex-typing pressures on play. Differences between mothers' and fathers' negative reactions to child's play with sex-appropriate or sex-inappropriate toys. Note that boys are under greater pressure, especially from their fathers and other boys. (Adapted from Langlois and Downs, unpublished data)

source of sex-typing pressure is related to their failure to assume their prescribed sex identity.

The importance of fathers in the development of children's sex-typed behavior is further underscored by Hetherington's (1967) studies of the relationship between parents' attitudes and attributes and children's characteristics: She found that preschool and kindergarten girls who were most stereotypically feminine had fathers who were warm and assertive, liked women (particularly their wives!), and approved of feminine behavior in their daughters. Boys who were most highly sex-typed had fathers who were dominant (in the sense that they tended to win when there were differences of opinion with their wives). Thus, the fathers' attitudes and behavior had an effect on the degree of sex typing in both boys and girls, although each sex was influenced differently. The mothers' attitudes and behavior, by contrast, showed little relationship to sex typing in children of either sex.

Are there domains of behavior other than play activities and dress in which parental pressure to behave in sex-appropriate ways is different for boys and girls? Probably so, although the evidence is not so clear. Block (in press) finds that both parents and grown children believe that boys are under more pressure than girls not to show their softer feelings. Most especially, boys are expected not to cry. No doubt they experience similar or perhaps stronger pressures from peers.

Having emphasized social pressure, we should not overestimate its power. Society allows each individual a surprising amount of flexibility in playing out his or her sex role without incurring strong social sanctions. A tomboy does not encounter serious opposition from her parents or her playmates. A quiet boy who does not enjoy rough body-contact play can still find friends and will not be considered feminine as long as he avoids explicitly feminine mannerisms, dress, and play activities.

Imitation and identification

Children learn a great deal from observation, of course. And a widely held view suggests that children acquire their preference for sex-appropriate activities by imitating the same-sex parent. Research on imitation has shown that children tend to imitate persons who are available for observation, powerful (or dominant), and warm and nurturant toward the child. Both parents generally have these qualities vis-à-vis their children, so the conditions promoting imitation by children are amply present within the family.

But why should a boy preferentially imitate his father or a girl imitate her mother? The answer appears to be that children—at least under the age of six—do not. A review of the evidence (Maccoby and Jacklin, 1974) found very little relationship between parents' own sex typing and that of their children, and recent work confirms this conclusion (Smith and Daglish, 1977). On the average, the most "masculine" fathers do not have sons who are more masculine than other men's sons, and the same applies to the femininity of mothers and daughters. Hetherington (1967) found that children of both sexes imitate and have personality characteristics that are similar to the parent who is dominant, but this need not be the same-sex parent. In addition, Hetherington found little relationship between children's femininity or masculinity and their tendency to imitate either parent. These facts contradict earlier theories of the origins of sex-typed behavior, suggesting that (1) sex-typed behavior patterns are not acquired through preferential imitation of the same-sex parents and (2) parental social pressure to behave in sex-appropriate ways will not necessarily lead to adoption by the child of the same-sex parent's own sex-typing style.

We saw in Chapter 1 that Freudian theory of sex typing assumed that the parents' repression of the child's aggression and sexuality would lead the child to identify with the same-sex parent. The child would strive to pattern her- or himself after the same-sex parent's characteristics—including any distinctively masculine or feminine behaviors—and a sense of sex-role identity would then develop. The findings on imitation cited previously are not consistent with Freud's view, nor are the results of a study of preschoolers by Sears, Rau, and Alpert (1965), which was carefully designed to test the theory. These researchers reasoned that if a child's same-sex parent was an especially strong model (that is, was the more nurturant or the more dominant parent) the child would be more strongly sex-typed. This hypothesis was not confirmed. The Sears group did find, however, that if parents were especially repressive toward their children's sexual and aggressive impulses, both their daughters *and sons* were more feminine than other children of the same sex. Hetherington (1967) confirmed this relationship for girls, but not for boys. Thus, Freud was partly correct: Repression of aggression and sexuality is related to sex typing, especially for girls. But, since repression of these impulses does not seem to cause children to identify with or imitate the same-sex parent, it seems likely that parental practices affect children more directly than Freud imagined.

Biological influences

Does social pressure account for all the sex differences that were discussed at the beginning of the chapter? Does it account for all the variations in masculinity among boys or femininity among girls? Probably not. Social influences have not yet been shown to be a primary factor in the greater tendency of boys to be aggressive, to engage in rough-and-tumble play, to congregate in large rather than small groups, and to attempt to dominate other children and adults. Our evidence is not as good on these matters as it is for choice of sex-typed play materials. Since researchers cannot arrange fights or bouts of rough play in order to observe parents' reactions, it has been necessary to rely on parents' (usually mothers') reports of how they deal with such behavior. Surprisingly, parents say they dislike boys' fighting as much as girls' fighting and say that they discourage it with equal firmness unless the child is being teased or bullied by other children, in which case they encourage their children of both sexes to fight back (see Chapter 4). In the rare cases where fathers as well as mothers have been interviewed, the results are the same (Sears, Rau, and Alpert, 1965).

The higher incidence of boys' aggression, rough-and-tumble play, and attempts to dominate is closely paralleled by similar behavior among monkeys and apes. And we can certainly assume that the subhuman primate infants are not being deliberately trained by their parents in accordance with sex-role concepts. This evidence makes us take more seriously the possibility that something other than adult pressure underlies these sex-typed behaviors. We should be aware, however, that even among monkey mothers, a certain amount of differential socialization takes place. For example, they administer more punishment to male than female young, just as human parents do.

We face a chicken-and-egg problem in many of these matters. Fathers play more roughly with their sons than with their daughters. Do these games develop because boys enjoy and seek them? Or do fathers teach their sons to like rough play—and do boys then continue this behavior when interacting with their friends? This is the kind of question we raised when attempting to understand why parents more often enter into mutually coercive cycles of interaction with their sons. Does this kind of conflict develop because boys become more angry when punished and do not yield to mild pressures, so that parents are forced to use stronger disciplinary measures? Or do boys become more angry and aggressive because their parents react to them more negatively? In both cases the influence probably runs in both directions.

Some evidence from studies of animals and human children does suggest that a biological element helps to start some of these circular processes. As we have noted, masculine styles of play are typical of males in species lower than man. And if females of these species receive extra dosages of male hormones prior to birth, they too play in a male way. Human girls who are *prenatally androgenized* (receive excess male hormones) tend to be tomboys. These girls like rough outdoor games and sports and playing with boys, and they are less interested in playing with dolls than their normal sisters (Ehrhardt and Baker, 1974). All this does not mean that the hormones present prior to birth directly cause a child to be aggressive or rough in play. Prenatal hor-

mone levels may simply establish a predisposition to learn certain behaviors readily, so that rough-and-tumble play, for example, seems
more interesting (or less frightening). Some presetting of this kind
probably characterizes most normal boys. The strength of the presetting undoubtedly varies from child to child, and the child's social experience, of course, quickly begins to influence the child's interests and
activity preferences. Social experience and biological presetting are
probably interwoven. A given experience can have a different effect
on one child than it has on another, depending on biologically influenced temperamental factors.

Is there a biological element in the tendency of women and girls
to be especially interested in infants? The issue is in dispute. Frodi
and Lamb (1978) investigated it by monitoring the heart beat (and
other indicators of emotion) of individuals as they watched a videotape of a crying infant and listened to the child's cry. These reactions
were then compared to reactions when the tape showed a quiet or actively happy infant. While girls and women in this kind of experiment
are more likely than males to *say* that they find the infant's cry distressing, the physiological reactions of the female subjects were no
different from those of the male subjects. These findings, they believe mean that a female's greater responsiveness to infants is social,
not biological, in origin. However, increased stress is not the only possible biological reaction to an infant's cry. For example, many women
who are breast-feeding their infants find that the infant's cry stimulates the flow of milk, a reaction that helps to bring the mother to the
child and that obviously does not occur in men! However, such a reaction would not explain why women and girls who are not lactating
have heightened interest in babies. Once again, it is likely that biological and social factors are intricately interwoven.

Self-regulation by rule

We have suggested that children's sex identity and boys' avoidance of interests and activities that have overtones of femininity develop early in childhood and are largely the product of social shaping.
We have also suggested that the distinctive play styles of the two
sexes, which also develop during the preschool years, are less clearly a
product of social pressure and probably have a biological "push" behind them. These influences on sex-role development are reinforced at
about the beginning of the school years (and earlier in some children)
by a third factor: the emergence of a conceptual understanding of the
implications of being male or female. A boy of four avoids playing
with a doll because he has discovered that his father and/or his playmates don't like it and may punish or avoid him if he engages in this
behavior. By the age of seven, he thinks of himself as a boy who is a

member of the group *boys*, and he wants to do what boys do. Understanding sex constancy is an important element in the development of sex-typed rules of conduct, but many other conceptual acquisitions are important as well, particularly a growing understanding of the sex-linked roles and scripts that govern the interactions of men and women, boys and girls.

How does this understanding of these rules of conduct develop? Children use their observations of the behavior of the two sexes as the raw material for their concepts and as the basis for inferences about social rules. Variations in extent of sex typing, then, reflect different degrees of conceptual maturity: Preschoolers and young school-age children who are unusually advanced cognitively tend to be more fully sex-typed than less-advanced children of the same age (Conner and Serbin, 1977; Kohlberg, 1966). The findings are not entirely consistent, however. The most we can say at present is that a child's general intellectual level probably does play a role in sex typing—both in helping to determine how quickly a child will achieve sex constancy and in influencing the child's level of understanding of the social expectations linked to sex. These understandings are important because they guide children's efforts to monitor and shape their own behavior.

Ideas about sex-appropriate behavior are picked up from many sources—from observing adults, from television, and probably most commonly from playmates and older children. Like other aspects of social development these ideas change predictably with age and depend as much on children's cognitive capacities as on the availability of sources of information. The subtleties of sex-roles and the variety of acceptably masculine or feminine behaviors are likely to escape the notice of young children in the early stages of the formation of sex-role concepts. Consequently, early attempts to behave in sex-appropriate ways are based on concepts that are highly stereotyped. But children's sex-role concepts do become more differentiated. Perhaps the views and behavior of parents become more influential at this later time. The point to be emphasized is that during the first few years of school children are engaged in elaborating the basic sex identities formed early in childhood. This process is part of the formation of the social self, the topic to which we now turn.

SUMMARY AND COMMENTARY

The chapter began with a brief overview of some of the ways in which the development of boys and girls differs. We noted that many aspects of the behavior of an individual child cannot be predicted merely from a knowledge of the child's sex and that a great deal of individual variation exists within each sex. In some respects, however, the average boy behaves somewhat differently from the average girl:

1. In their social play girls and boys tend to segregate themselves by sex. Their tendency to play more actively and more comfortably with children of the same rather than the opposite sex is apparent before the third birthday.

2. Boys' play is rougher and includes more playful rough-housing, more fighting, and more attempts to establish dominance by one child over another.

3. By nursery-school age girls are somewhat more likely to set up rules of procedure (for example, turn-taking) to avoid conflicts during social play.

4. Boys are somewhat more resistant and challenging toward their parents, and discipline is more likely to be an issue for them than for girls, who more often develop a cooperative relationship with their parents.

The establishment of sex identity is a gradual process:

5. By the age of three children can label people according to sex. They make their judgments primarily on the basis of hairstyles and clothes and do not understand that an individual's sex cannot change when appearance changes. *Sex constancy* is usually achieved several years after children use sex labels accurately.

6. Children almost always comfortably accept the sex identity that is assigned to them. In the rare cases where a child has been mistakenly assigned the wrong sex at birth, so that a reassignment is necessary, the children have accepted reassignment without residual problems as long as it took place before the age of three. After that age, evidence is contradictory concerning the psychological effects of reassignment.

Many adult roles such as truck driver and nurse are closely linked to sex (that is, persons of one sex are more likely to occupy them). In the process of developing an understanding of sex roles, children learn about the probable behavior that goes with a given role. Children also learn that certain sex-linked expectations pervade the performance of a range of roles—for example, wherever they are and whatever occupation they have, women are expected to be gentler and men more assertive. Most people have strong social expectations concerning the toys, play, dress, and so forth, that are considered appropriate for children of the two sexes. Throughout childhood, children are acquiring an understanding of these social expectations, and the development of their ideas about sex-appropriate behavior follows a fairly predictable course.

7. Children's first ideas about sex roles are quite stereotyped.

8. They begin by believing that sex-inappropriate behavior is

wrong, and they are quite ruthless in their reactions to other children's deviations from what they consider proper.

9. After about the age of nine, children begin to make distinctions between what is right and what is customary; requirements for sex appropriateness in behavior no longer seem to have strong moral force, and children become less insistent on conformity to a narrow set of sex-role standards.

The sexes differ in how closely they conform to conventional standards for the behavior of their own sex.

10. Boys are more likely to avoid "sissy" behavior than girls are to avoid being tomboys.

The reasons for this are fairly clear:

11. Boys receive more pressure from their fathers and their peers to behave in sex-appropriate ways than girls do. Thus, boys are ridiculed if they play girls' games or dress in girls' clothes, while girls can cross the sex-typing lines more safely. But social pressure is probably not the whole explanation for sex differences.

12. Biological dispositions (perhaps mediated by sex hormones present prenatally or in very early infancy) may contribute to boys' greater aggressiveness and interest in rough play.

13. Cognitive maturity also affects children's self-regulation of their behavior. Children conform to what they understand, and in the early stages of the formation of sex-role concepts, their understandings are narrow.

Children of the same sex and the same age vary in how closely they conform to the stereotypes of sex-appropriate behavior. But our knowledge about the conditions that determine these variations is still fragmentary. Surprisingly, the differences are not usually related to the parents' own masculinity or femininity. The rate of cognitive development has some causal relationship to both girls' and boys' sex typing. But, the factors producing femininity in girls are more clearly understood than the factors producing masculinity in boys. For girls, having a warm, strong father who reacts positively to signs of femininity (in his daughter as well as adult women) promotes the development of stereotypically feminine behavior. Repression of little girls' aggression and overt sexuality also seems to make them more stereotypically feminine. Parental reactions do not seem to make as much difference in the development of boys' masculinity. Apparently, forces outside the home play a larger role for boys.

CHAPTER 7

The Sense of Self

IT HAS OFTEN been said that infants have no sense of self—that they cannot distinguish themselves from other people. It is also said that an infant merges herself or himself with the mother, not knowing where one body ends and the other begins. On the face of it, this assumption seems implausible. Considering the complex distinctions that infants are capable of making, they ought to learn quite soon to tell the difference between their own bodies and other peoples'. They have ample basis for making this distinction—their own fingers hurt when bitten; they experience no such sensation when biting a rattle or the mother's fingers. We do not know precisely when infants begin to associate the feelings that come from their own bodily movements with the sight of their own limbs and the sound of their own cries. But it is reasonable to expect that, quite early in life, these sense impressions are bound together into a cluster that defines the bodily self. Of course, a rudimentary understanding of the limits of and the sensations that emanate from one's own body does not necessarily lead to an understanding of the existence of other similar bodies. And therefore, young children may not truly distinguish themselves from other selves, even when some initial features of a self-concept are present. If we ask "Do infants have or do they not have a sense of self?" we are asking the wrong question. A sense of self is not achieved in a single step; it is not something that is either present or absent; it develops by degrees and is a product of more and more complex understandings. We might more reasonably ask how the understanding of self grows and changes through a lifetime, and how far a given child has progressed along the path to a mature concept of self.

251

Philosophers and anthropologists have long sought to identify the characteristics that make human beings unique and distinguish them most clearly from lower species. Some theorists have focused on the use of tools, others on language. But probably the most basic difference between humans and other creatures is the human capacity for self-consciousness. While animals may have consciousness, *self*-consciousness requires a much more complex level of functioning. The self-conscious individual not only thinks, but also is able to take the self as an object of thought. Young children may know their own names and understand the limits of their own bodies, but be unable to think about themselves as coherent entities. And so the development of *self*-consciousness is something that it is important to trace.

The concept of self is a very elastic thing. It can be invested in or identified with a wide range of other people, material objects, and social entities such as a football team, a business organization, a church, a country. Nearly a century ago, William James (1896) discussed an adult man's consciousness of self in the following terms:

> In its widest possible sense, a man's *self* is the sum total of all he can call his, not only his body and his psychic powers, but his clothes and his house, his wife and children, his ancestors and friends, his reputation and works, his lands and horses, and yacht and bank account. All these things give him the same emotions. If they wax and prosper, he feels triumphant; if they dwindle and die away, he feels cast down. (p. 291)

While we no longer include horses or yachts in lists of self-identifying possessions, James's point is still valid: The self is not just a physical entity bounded by the skin; it is a psychological construct in which the concept of *me* and the concept of *my* are blended. But to define *self* any more exactly than this is a tricky process. Nearly as many definitions exist as there are people who have written and thought about the problem. Bannister and Agnew (1976) point out that the personal construct of self is intrinsically bipolar—that is, having a concept of the self also implies a concept of the *not*-self. In fact, the clearest view of the self grows out of contrasts with other entities. Each self has access to a set of separate, unique, and private experiences and related memories that produce a sense of personal continuity and a sense of separateness. Each self also includes a private knowledge of its own intentions and expectations. "We possess our biography and live in relation to it; we entertain a notion of ourselves as causes, we have purposes, we intend, we accept a partial responsibility for the effects of what we do" (Bannister and Agnew, p. 102). When we think of ourselves in these terms, we can begin to work by analogy toward an understanding of what other people must be like in the privacy of *their* own subjective experience. We begin to react to other people at least partly in terms of what we think their selves must be like, making inferences from what we know of their histories and about what we believe their intentions are.

William James made a special point of distinguishing our private, psychological selves from our social selves. In fact, he said that we usually have several social selves, in the sense that we try to project different images of ourselves to different people. James pointed out that a man will present a different self to his customers than he does to his employers, a different self to his drinking companions than he does to his children. In order to tailor our presentations of self to specific audiences, we must be able to understand that other people have an image of us and that different people may have different images. In other words, we must be able to think of ourselves from a variety of different perspectives, and we must be able to imagine how other people's images of us will be affected by what we do or say. Such processes are obviously quite complex and sophisticated; it would not be surprising if they came rather late in the series of steps that children take in achieving a self-concept.

Less research has been undertaken on the development of self-concepts than on the topics taken up in previous chapters. Nevertheless, developmental psychologists have devoted some attention to the study of several aspects of the growth of children's concept of self. They have been interested in self-recognition: how children learn to know their own faces. They have also been interested in self-definition: how children learn personal pronouns like *I* and what they mean when they use these words, how children come to understand the self as separate from other people, how children come to identify the self with other people, how children develop an ideal self—a sense of what they ought to be—and how children learn to take the perspective of others. Finally, they have been interested in the development of self-esteem, and in *locus of control* (whether the individual's actions are attributed to internal or external causes). These topics will all be taken up, with some speculative elaboration concerning aspects of the self-concept that have not yet been systematically studied. Throughout, we shall be interested in how children's understanding of themselves is affected by increasing cognitive and social maturity, and how the developing self-concept serves as an organizer of behavior. As Sarbin (1959) states, some of the postulates on which our analysis of self is built are:

1. Behavior is organized around cognitive structures . . . the self is one such cognitive structure or inference.

2. The self is empirically derived . . . it is the resultant of experience.

3. The self (in common with other cognitive structures) is subject to continual and progressive change, usually in the direction from low-order inferences about simple perceptions to higher-order inferences about complex cognitions. (p. 12)

SELF-RECOGNITION

We constantly see others' faces but never our own. How, then, does a child recognize his or her self in a mirror or in a photograph? How early does the child know that this image is not the picture or reflection of another child? Obviously, these questions are difficult to answer. Before the age of eighteen months or two years a child may not answer correctly when shown a mirror and asked "Who is that?" But being unable to respond correctly may merely reflect a poor command of language. Perhaps children recognize their own image at an earlier age but cannot tell us so. Fortunately, questions about self-recognition have been posed in relation to animals, and ingenious nonverbal methods have been devised to explore them—methods that can be used with children as well. Gordon Gallup's (1977) work with chimpanzees is an excellent starting point.

Self-recognition in monkeys

Gallup was interested in whether subhuman primates could learn to recognize their own image in a mirror. Working with several pre-adolescent wild-born chimpanzees, he began by placing a full-length mirror on the wall of each animal's cage. At first, the chimps reacted as though another animal had appeared: They threatened, vocalized, or made conciliatory gestures to the image in the mirror. Such behavior rapidly declined, however, and by the end of the third day was almost totally absent. Instead, the animals now began to use the mirror to explore themselves. A chimp might pick a bit of food from a place on its face that it could not otherwise see, or it might watch itself blow bubbles. After ten days' exposure to the mirror, each chimpanzee was anesthetized. While the animal was unconscious, a bright red spot was painted with an odorless, nonirritating dye on the uppermost part of an eyebrow ridge and another spot was painted on the top of the opposite ear. On recovery, each animal was returned to its cage, from which the mirror had been removed. Observers then recorded the number of times it touched the marked portions of its body. When the mirror was put back in the cage, the results were clear: Each chimp immediately began to explore the marked spots with its hands. In fact, these animals made over twenty-five times more efforts to touch the marked portions of their bodies than they had without the mirror.

To make absolutely sure of the meaning of these reactions, Gallup used the anesthetizing and marking procedure with several animals that had never seen themselves in a mirror. When these animals recovered and were given an opportunity to look in a mirror, they did not touch the marked spots. Instead, they reacted as if they were seeing an unfamiliar chimpanzee. Thus, it was clear that the first group had learned to recognize themselves in a mirror during their prior ten days of mirror exposure.

Now the most fascinating discovery of all. Among animals tested so far, only the most highly evolved of the great apes have been able to recognize themselves! Monkeys cannot do it. Neither can olive baboons or gibbons. Gallup gave a wild-born, preadolescent macaque monkey over 2,400 hours of mirror exposure during a period of five months, but it never showed any signs of self-recognition. Chimpanzees, in contrast, will begin to show such signs after only a few hours of such exposure. The monkeys' inability to use a mirror in this way is especially surprising since they can use a mirror to locate food that is out of their direct line of sight and will turn directly toward the food instead of trying to find it in the mirror itself. Clearly, their problem does not reflect an inability to process a mirror image. Gallup believes that the difficulty goes deeper and reflects the absence of a concept of self-identity. The image that the animal sees must be mapped onto such a concept, and among animals, only the great apes have this capacity.

If an ape has a concept of identity that permits it to solve the self-identification problem, how does this concept develop? In addressing this question, Gallup made a considerable leap and drew upon the theories of Cooley (1902) and Mead (1934), early social philosophers who speculated on the origins of the self. These writers referred to the *looking-glass self,* meaning that people's understanding of their own identity represents a reflection of how they are regarded and responded to by others. They regarded the self as an internalization of others' viewpoints. In other words, the self develops out of reflections in a social mirror. If these ideas were valid, Gallup reasoned, then chimpanzees reared in social isolation should lack the sense of self-identity that would enable them to learn to recognize themselves. And true to the prediction, when chimpanzees raised without contact with other animals were anesthetized, marked, and tested with a mirror, they did not touch the marked portion of their faces, nor did they show any increase in their interest in the animal in the mirror. Their behavior was the same as before the marking: They responded to the image as if it were another animal (see Figure 7-1). Thus, in these great apes social experience appears to be a prerequisite for self-recognition. This is doubly remarkable, considering that looking into a social mirror does not tell one much about the appearance of one's own face. Presumably, it is other aspects of the self that are reflected.

Self-recognition in human infants

What about self-recognition in human children? When do children first understand the significance of their own reflection? The

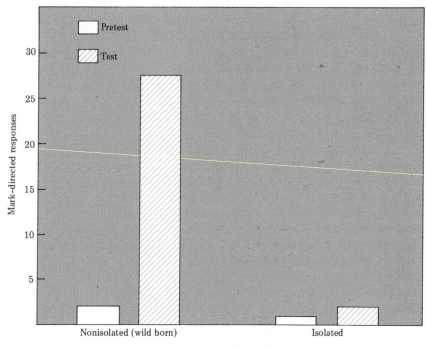

Figure 7-1.   Self-recognition in chimpanzees. Note that animals raised without contact with other members of their species do not increase their
frequency of touching the marks painted on their faces. This response is interpreted to mean that they do not recognize their own image in a mirror.
(From Gallup, 1977)

technique worked out with monkeys and apes seems very promising
for studying preverbal children, except of course that no one would
run the risk of anesthetizing children without medical necessity. Two
teams of researchers have used a modified form of the Gallup technique to study children ranging in age from six to twenty-four months
(Lewis and Brooks, 1974; Bertenthal and Fischer, 1978). In these experiments, the mother applies a dot of rouge to her child's nose as unob-
trusively as possible. During a pretest period, an observer keeps a
record of how frequently the infant touches his or her nose. Then the
infant is seated in front of a mirror, and observers note whether the
frequency of nose-touching increases. The results of the two studies
are consistent: At about the age of eighteen months children show by
greatly increased nose-touching that they recognize their own image
and coordinate the image they see in the mirror with the motions of
touching their own body.

   Bertenthal and Fischer also studied the sequence of developmental
milestones that were reached before the infants passed the nose-dot

test. They found that as early as six months children would reach out and touch some part of their mirror image. By about ten months they usually passed the hat test. In this test the mother dressed the child in a special vest. Attached to the back of this vest was a wooden rod with a hat on top. Whenever the infant moved, the hat also moved. Without a mirror the infant could not see the hat. With a mirror infants as young as ten months quite quickly looked up at the real hat or reached out for it. This response indicated that the child understood (1) that the movement of the object was in some way connected with the movement of the child's own body and (2) how to use the mirror to locate the place where the movement was occurring. Another task involved seating the child in front of a mirror and then lowering a toy from the ceiling slightly behind the child's head. The toy could be seen in the mirror but was not in the child's direct line of sight. This task was harder for the infants than the hat task. Infants did not look up at the real toy after seeing the descending toy in the mirror until fourteen to sixteen months of age.

The self-recognition that is implied by nose-touching is the culmination of several prior developmental steps. Almost no children in the study understood the meaning of the dot until after they were able to pass the hat test and the descending toy test. This finding means that the first step in self-recognition is being able to coordinate mirror-imaged movements with the spatial location of objects that are out of line of sight. But if a ten-month-old infant can locate the hat, why can't the infant find the red dot? Both move when the child moves. Why is dot-recognition delayed until so much later? Because, say Bertenthal and Fischer, children must build up an image (a *schema*) of how their own face ought to look in a mirror before they can notice the discrepancy produced by the red dot. In the same vein, Gallup says that an animal must have previously developed a concept or schema of certain aspects of its identity before it can understand the meaning of an unusual facial marking. Great apes can do this. So can human children, at least by the time they are eighteen months old. Of course, these experiments do not tell us how fine a distinction children can make between their own face and the faces of other children. If we could somehow show a child a mirror image of a different face with a nose-dot, how would the child respond? We can only assume that previous experiences with mirrors would have taught the child that no one else's face looks exactly like the child's and that no one else's face makes movements exactly coordinated with the bodily sensations coming from the child's own movements. Thus, self-recognition in a mirror does indeed require the building up of a quite specific schema of one's own face and no other.

The growth of the ability to recognize the image of the self in a mirror closely parallels other aspects of a child's intellectual development, giving further weight to the belief that self-recognition is a conceptual matching process. Specifically, the ages at which children take each of Bertenthal and Fischer's steps in self-recognition almost exactly coincide with the ages of achieving each of a series of graded steps in understanding *object permanence*—that is, understanding that objects exist when out of sight and where they ought to be when their containers are moved. The two accomplishments are not obviously connected, unless we think of self-recognition as a task requiring the child to use the mirror to locate an object that is known to exist even though hidden from direct view. The main point, however, is that even as early as eighteen months of age, the *self* is a concept, and the way children think about themselves is closely linked with the thought processes they use to understand other aspects of their world.

SELF-DEFINITION

The concept of the self receives further elaboration and refinement as children achieve mastery of language. An indicator of the child's growing sense of separateness from others is the acquisition of the pronouns *I, me,* and *you.* As we shall see, understanding these words is more difficult than learning the meaning of such words as *clock* or *chair.* Indeed, the proper use of personal pronouns may call for some ability to take the perspective others take toward the self.

Understanding I and you

The proper use of the pronouns *you* and *I* requires an inversion of point of view. The child must realize that when adults use *you,* the child's self is being taken as an object. One part of the problem is illustrated in an episode related by Epstein (1973):

> A little girl named Donna who was two years old was seated at the table with some relatives who were visiting. She was asked to point to Aunt Alice, which she did correctly. Everyone then entered into a game in which they asked Donna to point to various other people whom they named. Donna and her parents were delighted at how skillfully she could do this. Then someone said: "Point to Donna." She was confused and began to point at random. Her mother said: "You know who Donna is. Point to the little girl everybody calls Donna." At this, she evidently had an insight, for she pointed unhesitatingly to herself.

Donna had just achieved an essential step in sorting out the meaning of *I* and *you*. But a further problem must be solved: The child must realize that she is *you* to others and not *you* to herself. Her parents' use of different names will add to the confusion. Sometimes they will call her Donna; sometimes they will speak to her or about her as *baby;* and sometimes they will simply say *you.* The young child just learning to speak will follow the parents' lead. Sometimes the child will say "no Donna milk" (meaning Donna has no milk, or Donna does not want milk, or that's not Donna's milk), or she will say "baby bye-bye" when leaving the house. She may even say "you eating" when she means "I am eating." A number of children do exactly this. Here is dialogue between a mother and a child, just under two years old, who is getting ready for bed:

Mother: What do you want?
Nigel: Daddy toothbrush.
Mother: Oh, you want Daddy's toothbrush, do you?
Nigel: Yes. You want to put the frog in the mug. (you = I)
Mother: I think the frog is too big for the mug.
Nigel: Yes you can put the duck in the mug . . . make bubble, make bubble. (you = I)
Mother: Tomorrow. Nearly all the water's run out.
Nigel: You want Mummy red toothbrush. . . . yes, you can have Mummy old red toothbrush. (you = I) (Halliday, 1975, p. 132)

When a child has reversed the meaning of *I* and *you* in this way, the problem usually extends to the use of *my* and *your* as well. For example, a child who wanted to climb up on a chair which was being used as a footstool by an adult said: "Take my leg up!" (meaning "move your leg").

Surprisingly the majority of children do not invert the meaning of *I* and *you.* Most children use *I* (along with *me, my,* or *mine*) as their first personal pronoun. They use the word interchangeably with their own name or *baby* and do not seem to be confused by other people's use of *I* to refer to themselves. Most children's second pronoun is *you;* this word requires the child to decide on a working rule of usage. The problem, as Clark (1976) points out, is one of shifting reference: *I* sometimes refers to the child's mother, sometimes to father, sometimes to other people, depending on who is using it or who is being addressed. Clark suggests that children may adopt one of two hypotheses to work out this puzzling problem of reference: (1) *I* means an adult who is speaking with a child while *you* means the child; or (2) *I* means whoever is speaking and *you* means whoever is spoken to. The child who adopts the first hypothesis has overlooked the shifting reference.

While some children accept the incorrect hypothesis and then abandon it after several months, most children take up hypothesis 2 directly. We do not know why some children have more trouble than others in understanding the shifting reference. We may speculate that, as in the case of Gallup's apes, correct usage rests on some rudimentary ability to regard the self as an object—to take the perspective of others toward one's self and to understand that the self can be a *you* to others in the same way that the others are *you* to one's self. This line of thought suggests that children use a social mirror to achieve the required perspective taking, and that something about their early social experience facilitates the necessary inferences. We do not know what social experiences are most helpful in achieving this result, but we do know that the correct distinctions are usually mastered early and easily.

Where is the self?

When children recognize themselves in a mirror, we know that they are developing an understanding of what their own faces and bodies look like. When they use *I, me,* and *you* properly, they can distinguish between the self and others and are thinking of themselves as both agent and object. But what do they mean by *I* or *me*? Are they thinking of self as being anything other than a physical entity enclosed by an envelope of skin? We do not know what the two-year-old perceives the *self* to be. By the age of three, however, we have reason to believe that children are beginning to develop a sense of the *psychological self*—an inner, private, thinking person hidden from the purview of others—and that children can distinguish this psychological self from the bodily self that other people see.

Young children sometimes seem to believe that when they close their eyes other people can't see them. If this were true, the assumption might simply reflect what Piaget calls *egocentrism*—children's belief that other people see what they see and their inability to imagine that other people have perspectives different from their own. John Flavell (1978) suggests another hypothesis: that children may think of their eyes as the "windows of the soul." Perhaps young children believe that when people aren't looking directly into their eyes, they aren't seeing the child's real self. To check both possibilities, Flavell gave two-and-a-half to five-year-old children a series of tests designed to discover what they think other people can see. The experimenter and child sat on opposite sides of a small table on which a Snoopy doll had been placed. In the simplest procedure the child was asked to close or cover both eyes. The experimenter would say: "Now your eyes are closed and my eyes are open" and then would ask a series of questions: "Do I see you? Do I see Snoopy? Do I see your head? Do I see your arm?" Children younger than three-and-a-half years old quite often said that the experimenter did not see them. Without exception, however, they believed that the experimenters could see Snoopy. Most also believed that the experimenter could see their head or arm. Thus, the egocentric explanation was ruled out: These young children did not believe that the experimenter was unable to see just because they themselves were unable to see. However, young children often gave different answers than older people to questions about their visibility. When a child was hidden behind a screen so that only the child's eyes could be seen through two eyeholes, the youngest children usually answered "yes" to the question "Can I see you?" while older children doubted that they were visible unless quite a substantial part of their bodies could be seen.

Did the youngest children have a concept of a private, thinking self that was not visible to others? Further questions were directed toward this issue. The experimenter placed a doll on the table in front of the child and explained that dolls are like people in some ways: They have arms, legs, heads, and so forth. (In explaining this, the experimenter would point to the corresponding parts on doll and experimenter.) Then the child was asked how dolls are different from people, whether dolls know their names and think about things the way people do. Most of the children said that a doll does not know its name and is not able to think about things, but that people can do these things. The experimenter then asked: "Where is the part of you that knows your name and thinks about things? Where do you do your thinking and knowing?" The questions were difficult for some of the children, but fourteen out of twenty-two children did give a fairly clear localization for the thinking self, most often saying that thinking and knowing go on in their heads. The experimenter then looked directly into the child's eyes and asked: "Can I see you thinking in there?" Usually, the child thought not. Here is an example of an interchange:

> (Can I see you thinking?) "No." (Even if I look in your eyes, do I see you thinking?) "No." (Why not?) "Cause I don't have any big holes." (You mean there would have to be a hole there for me to see you thinking?) Child nods. (Flavell, 1978, p. 16)

Another child said his thinking processes could not be seen "cause the skin's over it." These answers suggest that children as young as three years of age have a rudimentary concept of a private, thinking self that is not visible even to someone looking directly into their eyes. They distinguish this self from the bodily self, which they know is visible to others, although their definition of what is meant by the visible self differs with age. Flavell suggests that the face is necessary to the child's definition of the bodily self and that this conception derives from adult training. He points out that when adults say, "Look at me," they usually want the child to meet their gaze. Indeed, if the child does not, the adult may turn the child's face and say "Look at me when I talk to you." It is not surprising, then, that children come to believe that adults are referring to the face when they use personal pronouns. In contrast, when adults use *you*, they are more likely to mean the whole physical body or any part of the body that can be recognized. Thus, "I saw you downtown yesterday but you didn't see me" can mean that the speaker saw and recognized the other person's silhouette from the rear and perhaps from some distance. With this kind of experience children come to broaden their conception of what is meant by one person seeing another.

For our present purposes, however, the point is that children can distinguish between an outer self that is visible to others and an inner psychological self. Evidently, by the age of three-and-a-half to four, children have begun to have some conception of a private, thinking self that is not accessible to the observation of others.

Distinguishing the private self

As Vygotsky (1934) pointed out many years ago, three-and-a-half to four years is the age at which children begin to distinguish between "speech for self" and "speech for others." Often during the first year or two after children have learned to talk, they speak out loud to themselves while playing. At first, this speech is very much like their comments to a listener, but as they grow older, the self-directed dialogue is heard less often. Vygotsky suggested that it becomes internal—that is, speech for self becomes thought. Before children stop talking to themselves, however, their dialogue acquires a distinctive quality: The child may say "this" without specifying the referent; while in speech directed to another person, the meaning of "this" would be spelled out. In talking to listeners, of course, children are often not very skillful in guessing what the listener needs to know, and so their interpersonal speech does not always specify the details needed for clear communication. Nevertheless, they do begin to elaborate their speech for others and truncate their speech for self. The increase in the cryptic quality of speech for the self is another example of the fact that the child is beginning to function in terms of a self that has a private fund of knowledge.

Children do not always know which of their experiences are private and which are shared by others. Consider the reaction of a highly verbal two-year-old child who has been offered a glass of milk. She prefers her milk to be quite cold. She takes a sip and says to her mother "It's too warm." The mother says: "Oh, no, honey, I just took it out of the frig!" The child looks intently at her mother, takes another sip, and says "See? It *is* warm!" The child evidently believes that her own taste experience can be shared directly by her mother. A similar problem arises in the case of dreams. The child may say "Remember? The big dog? It wanted to bite me? And then it ran away?" and be upset when a parent does not "remember." Through continued insistence on the parent's part that it was only a dream, the child learns to distinguish personal images and fantasies from external events that are perceptible to others.

We cannot say when the idea of having a separate, private consciousness first becomes explicit. For some children, the process is undoubtedly quite gradual. For others, a critical incident may cause the idea of the separate self to crystallize. Bannister and Agnew (1976) asked several adults to write essays on their first memories of consciousness of *self* in childhood. The instructions were: "Think about how you became aware of yourself as an individual when you were a child. Write an account of any experience or experiences (events, situations, ideas) which significantly contributed to your developing a feeling of being a separate individual, a 'self,' during your childhood" (p. 116). Here are some of the themes that emerged from the written accounts:

The feeling of separateness. "I was playing blindman's buff . . . and the lost feeling when I had been blindfolded seemed to set up a very much I-Them situation. The isolation of what I felt as a lost feeling made me aware of what it was like to be outside of, or in a sense 'not belonging to,' the group. . . . With this feeling of separateness came a feeling of power and independence." (pp. 116–17)

The privacy of consciousness. A. "The first time I had been away from home alone . . . I very easily remembered thinking, after a couple of days, that I had done all sorts of odd things which, even if my mother was thinking of me, she wouldn't know until I had told her." (p. 117) B. A man recollects that at the age of three, he was riding in an empty barrel which was on a wheelbarrow being pulled by his brother. "At some point in the journey my brother met a man he knew and stopped to talk to him. I was crouched down in the barrel and suddenly realized with great clarity that I could hear this man speaking but he didn't know I was there, he didn't know I could hear him, and that I was able to know about him without him knowing about me. In some way this sticks in my mind as one of the times I realized that I was an individual, that I was a self. It was the knowledge that I could observe someone without them knowing that I was observing them. It was to do with being secret and in myself." (p. 121)

Possessions—the meaning of "mine." "Perhaps the first time I remembered that I had a vague feeling of self was when playing with one of the children and we exchanged toys. On returning home, the distinction between my toys and the toys belonging to others was pointed out, and it became obvious that life was not so simple as it had appeared. There was a difference between what others had and what I had, and there was therefore a distinction between them and me." (p. 118)

Being a causal agent. One writer described an experience at age 5, when she was to take part in a school play and was overcome with stage fright and couldn't go on stage: "Panic stricken, I bawled my eyes out and my sister took me backstage to Miss W. She came up to me and almost pleadingly asked would I do it (i.e., go on stage) and I remember the feeling that I could say yes or no. I could decide as me, not just what I was told to do. This lady was asking *me*, not my sister, who was usually volunteered into pacifying me at school. I felt very surprised and also felt that I had been treated as a person and somehow felt a person." (p. 118)

Realization of how one appears to others. One man describes being mocked by his father because he could not correctly wire up a radio he had been given for Christmas. "It was from incidents like this that I learned I was a stupid and ignorant person." (pp. 121–22).

In the last example, the child not only recognized how he was seen by a significant other but adopted this evaluation of himself—an excellent example of the looking-glass self! Some of the writers, however, reported being frustrated that others did not see them as they really were. They experienced a discrepancy between their public and private images and did not adopt the public image as their own self-concept. A child can sometimes take pleasure in the secret knowledge of being different from what others believe, but a child may also be disturbed over the discrepancy and relieved when the difference is resolved, even though the process may not be flattering:

Another memory of a discovery of a separate "me" was the day when I deliberately tripped my younger brother and then pretended to my parents that this silly child kept falling. My deceit was discovered, and this seemed to be the first appreciation that I wasn't just the "good little girl" which seemed to be an imposed character; she had a nasty side too. Though it wasn't pleasant to have this nasty bit made known, there was a positive side and that was that this was definitely "me" and not what others saw me as. It seems that it was important for me to differentiate myself from my brother in the eyes of my parents. (p. 119)

Of course, adult recollections of childhood reactions cannot be taken as definitive evidence of what actually occurred. However, certain themes are worth noting and making use of in future work with children. Bannister and Agnew identify two such themes: (1) the self comes to be defined primarily in terms of how it is differentiated from other selves, rather than in terms of any absolute properties it may possess *per se*; and (2) an important developmental milestone occurs when children achieve *reflexivity*—that is, when they become able to think about their own definition of self and compare this with the way they believe they are seen and defined by others. Both of these achievements require children to develop some understanding of other selves and to develop hypotheses about other people—what they must be like, what they know, what they must be thinking, and what will influence them.

We should recognize that not all aspects of the self-concept are dependent on differentiation from other selves or on being able to take an outside perspective toward the self. Before these steps are achieved, a simpler kind of self-awareness is needed: the limits of the body, recognition of the appearance of the face, and the classification by sex (at least at the first, most rudimentary level). Bannister and Agnew point to aspects of the self-concept that follow these earliest achievements and that transform the self-concept in a way that places the self in a social context.

Defining the private self

Given that children come to realize that the psychological self is unique, how do they define and recognize this self? Bannister and Agnew have traced some interesting changes that occur between the ages of five and nine. They studied children's changing ability to recognize the things that they had previously said, and the changing bases for arriving at decisions about whether an utterance represents their own selves speaking. First the researchers asked the children to answer a series of questions, such as: "What do you do at school? What do you want to do when you grow up? What is your best friend like? What is the most frightening thing you know? What do you like best on television? What sort of boy (girl) are you?" The children's answers were recorded word for word, and then a tape was made of an adult reading several children's answers. (All clues to the identity of the original speaker, such as proper names or references to father's occupation were eliminated.) Several months after the initial interview each child heard a tape of the child's own answers mixed in with the answers of five other children (all six were spoken in the same adult voice). The tape was played through twice, and then the children were asked to identify their own responses given several months before. The children improved with age in their ability to identify their own answers, but improvement was greater on some kinds of questions than on others. Questions such as "What is your teacher like?" or "What is your best friend like?" can be called *psychological questions,* in that they call upon the subject to make some sort of assessment of the personality attributes of another person. Questions such as "What games do you play?" are less psychological in this sense. The children's improved ability to recognize their own statements occurred primarily on the psychological questions.

The nature of the age change in self-recognition is further indicated by an analysis of the reasons children gave for deciding that an answer was or was not their own. Some children simply depended on memory; others referred to specific activities that they normally engage in and that they were able to recognize. For example, one taped answer to the question "What do you like best on television?" was "I like to watch matches." A boy said this statement could not have been his own " 'Cos I hardly ever watch matches." Older children, however, would reject an answer to this question on the basis of a psychological *disposition*. For example, when asked whether she had said "I like to watch cartoons" a girl said no, " 'Cos cartoons, for instance, are not my style. I can watch them for five minutes and get bored."

We see here a developmental progression in how the self is defined. Initially children think of themselves in terms of appearance and activities (for example, "I am a person who has brown hair and goes to Lincoln School"). In addition, as we saw in Chapter 6, children soon include their sex as an element in self-definition. Children also include their likes and dislikes. And gradually they begin to conceptualize themselves more abstractly.

Good me, bad me, not me

The discussion thus far has implied that the growing child develops a single, coherent concept of the self. The psychiatrist Harry Stack Sullivan (1953) took the opposite view; he proposed that different views of the self can exist side by side. In his view, the self grows out of social experience, with the crucial figure in this experience being the "mothering one." One part of the self-system, the *good me*, grows out of experiences in which this mothering person increases her tenderness toward the child when the child does things that are pleasing to her. *Good me* is the part of the self to which the child is usually referring when saying "I." However, the mothering person also expresses disapproval when the child does not meet her requirements and this disapproval induces anxiety. *Bad me* is the part of the self-system that is made up of the impulses, wishes, and actions that have elicited moderately disapproving responses. These impulses and actions create anxiety, but the anxiety is not strong enough to drive them out of consciousness, and therefore the *bad me* is still part of the self-system. However, when the mothering one has shown very strong revulsion over something the child has done (such as doing real injury to a sibling or eating feces) any thoughts or feelings connected with such events cannot be accepted as part of the self. These feelings are split off and become the *not me*. The existence of the *not me* can be inferred only indirectly from nightmares or from unintended verbalizations or actions. Most children, Sullivan believed, experience "uncanny emotions": reactions of awe, horror, loathing, or dread over actions or feelings whose very nature is poorly grasped. Thus, each individual's self includes a set of rather primitive and strongly unpleasant emotional reactions that cannot be modified by rational thought because the origins and even the existence of these feelings are denied, repressed, and defended against. The *not me* is very private, and while the emotional reactions associated with this part of the self may not occur very often, Sullivan believed that these feelings persist over many years.

Sullivan's claims about the power and persistence of unconscious anxieties are difficult to prove. However, his views remind us that: (1) children's definitions of themselves include both what the self is and what the self is not, (2) the characteristics accepted as part of the self can be evaluated by the self as either good or bad—although the good elements usually predominate, and (3) very powerful emotions attend the self-definition. The self is not merely an intellectual construct.

Emergence of the social self

We have seen that self-definitions change as children develop increased understanding of the distinctions between the self and others. In other words, the self is progressively differentiated as the child develops. But a parallel process is also taking place, and it is the opposite of differentiation. Increasingly the self is invested in or extended to other individuals and groups of people. The self comes to be defined in terms of the groups or individuals with whom the person's fate has become intertwined. In answering the simple question "Who am I?," an adult man might say: "I am the foreman of an oil-rig crew; I am a Catholic; I am the father of Jim and Emily; I am a Democrat; I am a member of the Knights of Columbus." The adult would seem to be saying: "The social groups I belong to are part of my identity." The adult concept is similar to the one William James expressed when he said that a man's wife, children, and fellow club members are part of his self—that the self felt diminished or enhanced as the fortunes of these other people waned or prospered. Kuhn (1960) has shown that children are less likely to define themselves in terms of identification with others. He tested many hundreds of individuals age seven through twenty-four by asking them to make twenty statements answering the question "Who am I?" He found that the youngest subjects referred to less than six groups when giving their twenty answers, while the oldest subjects averaged eleven. This difference no doubt reflects the widening range of social opportunities available to children as they grow older. A seven-year-old child's primary social contacts are at home and school, while young adults have usually entered the world of work and formed the additional social relationships that this entails. However, the point remains valid: Children tend to answer "Who am I" questions in such terms as: "I am a person who has a bicycle; I live on Oak Street; I am almost five feet tall" and only gradually shift toward defining themselves in terms of their relationships to persons and groups.

Ziller (1973) has also looked at the development of social identity and social obligations in his studies of what he calls *self-other orienta-*

tion. He starts by assuming the existence of a certain amount of inevitable conflict between the interests of the self and the interests of others, that can be resolved by forming coalitions. If the individual adopts the same values as the social group—seeks the same goals and identifies with their interests—then their gain is also a gain for the self and there is little conflict. In such a situation a trusting relationship with shared goals and values is established. People can begin to predict one another's behavior and adapt themselves to one another's actions; shared enterprises can be accomplished smoothly. The expectations shared by people who are engaged in cooperative activities constitute the cement that produces stability in social relationships. The social self, then, develops as the individual learns (1) to let his or her plans and intentions be known to others, (2) to be predictable, and (3) to live up to others' expectations about what the self will do. Ziller presents some evidence that children feel closer to others as they grow older and more tied to a social network. At the same time he reports that older children feel more *individual* than younger children. That is, with increasing age, children come to have a stronger feeling of being a distinct and different self.

We have been discussing the development of the social self in very optimistic terms. We have claimed that a sense of group membership, built up through shared expectations and cooperative activities, is a source of stability and smoothness in social relationships. We should not overlook the fact that when children and their families are members of groups that are looked down upon by the rest of society, the development of a sense of group membership carries some drawbacks as well as some assets. For nearly all children, there are some painful elements in their social selves, but for some, their families' position in the social structure tends to make these problems especially great.

Of course, people vary greatly in the degree to which they feel socially isolated from or close to other people. The range goes all the way from complete alienation to excessive identification and complete reliance on others for values and a program of activities. However, most individuals can balance privacy and social involvement and can extend the boundaries of the self to encompass other individuals without a loss of individuality. Thus a parent who is not particularly interested in shells but who is aware of a child's intense interest in a shell collection can create opportunities for the child to collect shells, help to classify them, and empathically share in the child's pleasure over an exceptionally good find, without adopting shell collection as a hobby. In other words, an individual's social self can include a relationship with another person and the behavioral obligations toward that other person, without breaking down the distinctiveness of their separate identities.

The more important point, however, is this: In order to enter into a cooperative, mutually trusting relationship with other people, children must learn to monitor their own behavior, asking themselves how their behavior looks to other people and how it fits in with others' expectations. The child must learn to ask, at least in some rudimentary way, "Does mother know what I am planning to do? Will it be O.K. with her? Will she have to change her plans if I do it? What if I don't do what I agreed to do—will she be upset? What will she think of me?"

The process of self-monitoring can become quite complex as the child enters a variety of social situations with a variety of partners, since the partners will vary in knowledge or expectations about the child. Here we return to William James's point about multiple social selves. And while the various social selves may be quite similar, the requirements of some stituations may necessitate presenting different selves to different people and keeping certain social spheres quite separate. The young man who plays tough guy to his male friends and tender guy to his girlfriend will be embarrassed if the girlfriend overhears discussions with his friends that were not intended for her ears. Weinstein (1969) points out that maintaining social interaction in a group requires agreement among all the participants concerning the kind of behavior that is expected. Goffman (1959) refers to this as the "working consensus of an interaction" and points out that this consensus differs considerably from one situation to another. Furthermore, the consensus can be negotiated. Thus, self-presentation may depend on the claims an individual wishes to make on the other people involved in a given situation. If a man wants to be treated as someone who needs help, he may exaggerate aches and pains or even limp a little. However, if he wants to assert leadership and be respected, he will conceal any weaknesses in order to be awarded the desired identity by the others in the group. Goffman says that consensus is achieved through a process of "identity bargaining" in which all the persons involved call attention to the aspects of themselves that they think will help establish their desired role.

All this seems quite Machiavellian, and it is obvious that young children will find it hard to tailor their behavior deliberately to create certain impressions. They will have only a dim idea about what roles can be played in a new situation, what roles they might reasonably aspire to, and what kinds of self-presentations are compatible with the roles they want to achieve. But these are skills that can be learned and the acquisition of social competence involves, in part, the mastery of just these skills.

No individual is a total chameleon, however, and there is some continuity in the presentation of self to different audiences. The consistent core grows out of self-monitoring in which the actions of the self are judged in terms of the self's own standards and values, rather than in terms of what others want one to be.

The ideal self

Children not only build up a concept of themselves—what their own personalities are like and how they are seen by others—but they also construct a concept of what they would prefer to be like. Some children's ideal self is very similar to their concept of their actual self, and they do not aspire to be more than what they believe they already are. For other children the ideal self (sometimes called the *ego ideal*) is a distant goal, something to be worked toward. It may be modeled on one or several admired persons. Sometimes the ideal self is realistic; sometimes it is almost pure fantasy.

What does it mean if the ego ideal is very different from the child's actual self? Clinical psychologists have suggested that a very large discrepancy between the real and ideal selves is an unhealthy sign. A child who feels avoided by other children but wants very much to be popular surely experiences a state of considerable tension compared to either a contented loner or a sociable child with a secure place in a group of friends.

Katz and Zigler (1967) and Katz, Zigler, and Zelk (1975) have challenged this view, suggesting that a gap between the ego ideal and the real current self is a sign of maturity rather than disturbance. They asked groups of children in grade school and junior high school to respond to a series of statements such as "I get along well with other people" and "I feel unsure of myself." First the young subjects rated the statements in terms of their actual self (the scale ranging from very true to very untrue) and then in terms of their ideal self (the scale ranging from "I would like this to be true" to "I prefer that this is *not* true"). Each subject's answers concerning the real self were combined into a single score, the same was done for the ideal self, and then a difference score was obtained. The ideal-self score was always higher than the real-self score, but the difference was much greater for some children than for others. In two studies conducted with fifth-grade through eighth-grade children older children had higher discrepancies.

Katz and Zigler also investigated the question of whether a large discrepancy is associated with psychological disturbance. Working in a school system that had separate classes for emotionally disturbed children, they compared the children in these classes with those in normal classes. The disturbed children had *lower* discrepancy scores. This finding was particularly true of children who had *externalizing* symptoms—that is, children whose problems included frequent fighting or stealing and inability to settle down and pay attention in class. Thus, setting a high standard for the ideal self is associated with impulse control. Other disturbed children were classified as *internalizers*; these children suffered from anxiety, depression, or social withdrawal. Although they did not have quite as large a gap between their real and ideal self-images as normal children, the internalizers were more similar to the normal children than the externalizers were.

By what process do children come to differentiate between the actual self and the wished-for self? How does a discrepancy between these selves develop? The theory of the looking-glass self, mentioned earlier, suggests that experience in role taking—skill in taking the perspective of others—helps the child to develop a realistic self-concept. Following this lead, Leahy and Huard (1976) tested children's ability to take the perspective of others. They used a story procedure (adapted from Flavell) in which the child was given a series of nine cartoon-like pictures, one at a time, and was asked to tell the story as the sequence unfolded. Partway through the story a bystander appeared who could not know about the earlier episodes. The child was asked to retell the story from the standpoint of this poorly informed bystander. Some children were able to understand that the first part of the story was privileged information not available to the bystander; they told the story from the bystander's point of view. Other children were unable to do this; they assumed the bystander must somehow have access to whatever information they possessed. They could not take the perspective of a person with different experience than their own. The experimenters also asked Katz and Zigler's self-image questions and found that the children with the greatest discrepancy between the real and ideal selves were the ones who were the most successful in taking the bystander's perspective. Thus, these findings suggest that role-taking skill *is* involved in a child's capacity to develop differential concepts of an actual and an ideal self.

During the latter part of the grade-school years, then, most children develop a concept of the kind of person they would like to be. In normal children, this image is truly *ideal*, in the sense that it has more positive qualities and fewer negative ones than the children think they currently possess. We do not know the precise function of the ideal self-image. But children probably try actively to shape their own behavior toward this ideal. The formation of an ideal self-image probably helps children develop the kind of impulse controls that were discussed in Chapter 5. Children whose aspirations do not include an ideal self that is in some ways better or more mature than the current self seem to remain impulsive longer than normally developing children.

SELF-ESTEEM

We have seen that during the first ten years of their lives, children develop a complex set of concepts about themselves. They come to know how they look. They come to understand that their own fund of information and memories is unique and not accessible to others. They begin to define themselves in terms of their own skills and preferences and in terms of the psychological traits they attribute to themselves. They begin to understand how they are seen by other people. They may develop more than one social self, in the sense that they try to create different impressions for different people. However they also evaluate their own behavior on the basis of a set of self-accepted standards, and if their evaluation is favorable, we can say that they have high (or at least positive) *self-esteem*. But, self-esteem is only one element in the complex network of attitudes and beliefs that make up the self-concept. Unlike the descriptive components we have been discussing thus far, self-esteem refers to the evaluative component. Thus the descriptive statement "I have brown hair" is part of the self-concept but is not necessarily relevant to self-esteem; the statement "I am good looking," on the other hand, clearly is.

Self-esteem in relation to aspirations

William James pointed to the subjective nature of self-esteem. We invest our self-esteem in a limited number of endeavors, and we judge ourselves against high standards of competence only in areas in which we have chosen to complete. James (1896) said that our self-satisfaction is a ratio of what we accomplish to what we have set out to accomplish:

> We have the paradox of a man shamed to death because he is only the second pugilist or the second oarsman in the world. That he is able to beat the whole population of the globe minus one is nothing; he has pitted himself to beat that one, and as long as he doesn't do that nothing else counts. . . . Yonder puny fellow, however, whom everyone can beat, suffers no chagrin about it, for he has long ago abandoned the attempt to "carry that line" . . . . With no attempt there can be no failure; with no failure, no humiliation. (p. 310)

The child faces the task of staking out the territory in which the self will be invested. In choosing activities to master, the child runs certain risks, since aspiring to certain kinds of success creates the possibility that self-esteem will be lost through failure. But only by incurring some degree of risk can any significant amount of ego-enhancement be obtained. Once self-investment does occur, the child works to defend and maintain the areas that have been selected as central to self-esteem. We saw in Chapter 4 that a change in the nature of the triggering conditions that will make a child angry takes place at about the age of six or seven. For younger children the usual instigation is another child taking a toy or invading play space. But after this age the instigation is likely to be an insult. Taunts such as

"Hah hah—you're a scaredy-cat" or "You're a sissy" or "You're a great big stupid" will evoke anger if a child's ego is invested in being brave, masculine, or smart. A boy of six or seven is not likely to be taunted by his playmates with "Hah hah—you got mad at your mother!" They know full well that the boy is much more interested in maintaining a tough social self than an obedient or considerate self. The important point, however, is that only when a child's self-definition consists of having certain traits can self-esteem be linked to having these traits (for example, being smart) and not having others (for example, not being a sissy). Only when the child comes to define him- or herself based on these traits will he or she be aroused to defensive maneuvers when especially valued traits are challenged.

On the basis of extensive interviews with children and adults, Coopersmith (1967) concludes that people assess their own success in terms of:

1. *power*—the ability to influence and control others,
2. *significance*—the acceptance, attention, and affection of others,
3. *virtue*—adherence to moral and ethical standards,
4. *competence*—successful performance in meeting demands for achievement.

Each of these areas can be subdivided: A child can choose to aspire to success in sports but not in academic performance; a child may long for the approval of a parent or special friend. Just who is significant at what age has not been traced in detail, but the identity of these people whose approval is closely bound up with self-esteem probably does shift during childhood from parents, to prestigious age mates, to the girlfriend or boyfriend with whom the adolescent is in love.

Success helps to determine children's choices of areas for self-investment. Children who do well in school are more likely to define themselves as smart and establish high standards of academic excellence for themselves. And only the strong boy who is quick with his fists and wins his early fights is likely to develop into the man, described by James, whose self-esteem rides on becoming a champion boxer.

Differentiation of attitudes toward the self

Considering that self-definitions become more complex as children grow older, it would be reasonable to expect that, instead of becoming more or less satisfied with themselves in an overall sense, children would become more differentiated in their self-attitudes. That is, they would begin to be satisfied with certain aspects of themselves and less satisfied with others.

Mullener and Laird (1971) provide some evidence of increasing differentiation in self-esteem with age. Their subjects were seventh-graders, high school seniors, and evening college students whose ages averaged in the upper twenties. (The groups were reasonably comparable with respect to IQ.) The subjects were asked to use a six-point scale running from "very true" to "very untrue" to rate themselves on forty characteristics (for example, "I think I am good at mathematics"). The statements were chosen to represent five different areas: achievement traits, intellectual skills, interpersonal skills, physical skills, and social responsibility. When measures of individual variation among the five areas were computed, older subjects were found to vary more than younger ones. That is, older subjects might rate themselves very high on intellectual skills and very low on interpersonal skills or physical skills, while children in the seventh grade would be more likely to rate the five areas of competence similarly. However, even the youngest children varied considerably from one area to another.

There are several ways to think about the fact that self-esteem seems to become increasingly differentiated as children grow older. Mullener and Laird suggest that a single global self-concept breaks down into several distinct ones, and that the single global concept ceases to exist. Let us consider the responses of a fourth-grade girl who was asked to make several statements in answer to the simple question "Who am I?" (Kuhn, 1960). Here are her replies (with the original spelling):

I boss to much.	I fidde around
I get mad a my sisters.	I am careless at times
I am a show off	I forget
I interupt to much	Sometimes I don't do what mother tells me to
I talk to much	
I wast time	I tattle on my sisters
Sometimes I am a bad sport	Sometimes I am unkind (p. 41)

This child appears to have a quite pervasive feeling of being unworthy and incompetent. If Mullener and Laird are right, we can expect that in a few years she will begin to think of herself in more positive terms in some areas of her life while continuing with a negative self-image in other areas. There are alternative views about what will happen with development, however. Brim (1976) and Epstein (1973) say that each individual has a theory of self, organized in the same way as other theories and consisting of major premises, postulates and axioms, and hypotheses. Hypotheses go in search of evidence and will change on the basis of new information, but major premises are not so open to this kind of change. As people grow older, their theories become more complex, but a person may be able to maintain a basic premise throughout a lifetime. Thus, the premise "I am a worthy person" might be maintained, while certain conclusions flowing from it—such as "therefore I can easily get other people to like me"—might undergo considerable elaboration and change with increasing life experience. Bem and Allen (1974) and Bem and Funder (1978) offer another view, namely that some people organize their lives on the basis of a global, overall self-assessment, while other people do not make such a global self-assessment, or if they do, seldom call upon it in their decision processes. Perhaps such individual differences become more pronounced with increasing maturity. At this time we do not know which of these formulations best describes the changes that take place during middle and late childhood.

Meanwhile, if we think about the self-statements of the fourth-grade girl quoted above, a number of questions come to mind. Is she merely making verbal statements in order to show the experimenter that she is not conceited, or does she really believe what she is saying? Assuming these statements do represent genuine feelings, is she likely to continue having such a negative view of herself, or is this something that changes considerably in individual children over time? How did she come to have this negative self-image? How important is this image? Does it make any difference in how she lives her life?

Stability of self-esteem

Coopersmith (1967) has conducted an extensive study of the origins and stability of self-esteem and its relation to personality and behavior. Working primarily with children in the fifth and sixth grades, he asked them to fill out a Self-Esteem Inventory, made up of fifty-eight items such as the following:

	like me	unlike me
I'm pretty sure of myself	——	——
I often wish I were someone else	——	——
I'm easy to like	——	——
I find it very hard to talk in front of the class	——	——
I'm proud of my school work	——	——
I'm popular with kids my own age	——	——
My parents usually consider my feelings	——	——
I give in very easily	——	——
I can usually take care of myself	——	——

I don't care what happens to me   _____   _____

My parents understand me   _____   _____

Kids usually follow my ideas   _____   _____

Things usually don't bother me   _____   _____

SOURCE: Selected from Coopersmith (1967), pp. 265–66.

The items were chosen to represent the children's self-attitudes in regard to peers, parents, school, and personal interests. The latter presumably encompass the more global self-estimates required by such items as "I don't care what happens to me" or "I'm pretty sure of myself." Coopersmith found that the children's self-attitudes in all areas were closely enough related to make it possible to construct an overall index of self-esteem for each child. He also found that the self-estimate is very stable at this age. When a group of children were retested after an interval of five weeks, the correlation of their scores on the two occasions was very high (0.88). More impressive, retesting after a lapse of *three years* yielded a stability correlation of 0.70. These figures mean that individual children have maintained consistent levels of self-esteem over the three-year period—keeping approximately the same position in the self-esteem distribution relative to other children.

The behavioral implications of high and low self-esteem

Coopersmith administered the Self-Esteem Inventory to hundreds of fifth and sixth-grade children. He also asked their teachers to rate them on such behaviors as reactions to failure, self-confidence in new situations, sociability with peers, and need for encouragement and reassurance. He then chose five groups, with seventeen children in each group, for intensive study: a High-High group (in the top one-fourth of their class on both self-esteem and their teachers' ratings); a Medium-Medium group (both ratings within the middle half of their class's scores); a Low-Low group (both ratings in the lowest one-fourth of the class); a group with ratings of high self-esteem, but a negative evaluation by the teacher; and a group with low self-esteem, but a high rating by the teacher. For our present purposes, we will concentrate primarily on his analysis of the three high-agreement groups. The children included in these groups were white, middle-class, male, and free from any obvious emotional disorders. (On the average, boys and girls did not differ in the initial large sample. The decision to study only boys was based on the desire to eliminate other sources of unwanted variance that might be associated with sex.)

These children were assessed in depth using clinical tests and observation of their behavior in a variety of situations. For example, they were tested to determine how readily they would yield to group influence in a situation where their own judgment was actually superior. This was done by subjecting them to the Asch test, wherein each child is asked to judge the length of some lines, first alone and then with a group of other children who give biased judgments. The effect of the biased judgment on the subject's judgment was assessed. The young subjects were also given tasks that were either very difficult or very easy in order to determine whether their interest in working on a task was sharpened or weakened by success and failure. They were tested for creativity and were asked how they usually behaved in real-life situations that called for assertiveness. Finally, their classmates were asked to choose the other children in the class whom they would like to have for friends, and a record was kept of how often each child in the self-esteem groups was chosen. On the basis of this broad assessment battery, Coopersmith gave the following description of the "experiential world and social behavior" of children with high self-esteem:

> [They] approach tasks and persons with the expectation that they will be well received and successful. They have confidence in their perceptions and judgments and believe that they can bring their efforts to a favorable resolution. Their favorable self-attitudes lead them to accept their own opinions and place credence and trust in their reactions and conclusions. This permits them to follow their own judgments when there is a difference of opinion and also permits them to consider novel ideas. The trust in self that accompanies feelings of worthiness is likely to provide the conviction that one is correct and the courage to express these convictions. The attitudes and expectations that lead the individual with high self-esteem to greater social independence and creativity also lead him to more assertive and vigorous social actions. They are more likely to be participants than listeners in group discussions, they report less difficulty in forming friendships, and they will express opinions even when they know these opinions may meet with a hostile reception. Among the factors that underlie and contribute to these actions are their lack of self-consciousness and their lack of preoccupation with personal problems. Lack of self-consciousness permits them to present their ideas in a full and forthright fashion; lack of self-preoccupation permits them to consider and examine external issues. (pp. 70–71)

This assessment of the effect of self-esteem on behavior is consistent with therapists' clinical observations of depressed patients. Depressed people contrast almost perfectly with people having high self-esteem: They lack confidence in their perceptions and judgments, expect that they will fail at new tasks, do not expect to be able to influence other people, and hence hesitate to express their opinions.

Returning to our questions about the little girl who made so many negative self-statements, Coopersmith would probably say that she will continue to have a negative self-image at least over the next several years and that this self-appraisal will make a difference in many aspects of her functioning. Our earlier question, then, is especially important: How does a child develop a negative self-image? Understanding the relevant life conditions should put us in a better position to work out a strategy for change.

The origins of self-esteem

Reviewing the writings of personality theorists on the conditions that affect the development of self-esteem, Coopersmith identifies two factors that are especially important:

1. the amount of respectful, accepting, and concerned treatment that an individual receives from the significant other people in his or her life
2. the individual's history of success and failure, including the objective status and social position the individual has achieved.

However, these factors do not act directly on behavior but are interpreted in terms of the individual's values and aspirations. As we have seen, an objective achievement that represents success to one individual may mean very little to another, depending on the extent of ego investment in the activity. Also, people erect defenses against loss of self-esteem. They may simply fail to notice objective evidence of failure or they may refuse to accept other people's judgments.

Coopersmith found that an objective basis for self-esteem did exist among children in his sample: Those with high self-esteem were doing better in school and were more often chosen as friends by other children than the low-esteem children. Their current status was consistent with their history. Low-esteem children were more likely than high-esteem children to have been loners during earlier periods of their childhood, and they more often had a variety of problems—from bedwetting and thumb-sucking to academic difficulties. However, he found no difference between the groups in other objective factors, such as the incidence of major illnesses, accidents, separations, or birth traumas.

Coopersmith devoted primary attention to the child's treatment by significant others. Here we return again to the concept of the looking-glass self. Since family members are the significant others whose attitudes matter most when children form their own self-concept, Coopersmith investigated in depth the child-rearing practices employed by his subjects' parents. He focused on the following aspects of parenting: acceptance of the boy and affection shown toward him; the kind and amount of punishment used; the level of achievement demands placed on the child; the strictness and consistency with which rules were enforced; the extent to which the child was allowed to participate in family decision making; the extent to which the child was listened to and consulted when rules were being set and enforced; and the extent to which the child was allowed independence (as distinct from being overprotected). Information was obtained through questionnaires filled out by the mothers (the PARI Scales), in-depth interviews in which the mothers were asked how they dealt with their sons in a variety of circumstances, and interviews in which the sons were asked how their parents raised them. Some clear relationships between the child-rearing patterns employed by the parents and the self-esteem of their sons were evident. Parents of boys with high self-esteem more often had the following characteristics:

1. *Accepting, affectionate, involved.* They frequently showed affection to their children. They took an interest in the children's affairs and were acquainted with their children's friends. They indicated that they believed parents should concern themselves with their children's problems—even unimportant ones—and they believed in the meaningfulness of these problems.

2. *Strict.* They believed that it was more important for children to meet high standards than just to enjoy themselves and that children are happier under strict training. They enforced rules carefully and consistently, exercised a fairly high level of control (establishing many rules for a wide range of behaviors), and were firm and decisive in telling the child what he might or might not do.

3. *Favored noncoercive kinds of discipline.* They used relatively little physical punishment and relatively little withdrawal of love. They punished their children by using denial of privileges and isolation. They tended to discuss with the children the reasons why certain actions are good or bad.

4. *Democratic.* They allowed the children to set their own bedtime. They indicated that they believed in their children's right to express their own opinions, to "have their own way" some of the time, and to participate in making family plans. They indicated that they would not discourage their children from questioning the parents' point of view.

In Coopersmith's results we find some confirmation for the idea of the looking-glass self: Parents are a child's social mirror, and if children see that parents regard them with affection, respect, and trust, then they come to think of themselves as worthy of affection, respect, and trust. But there are some surprises in the results. Why is firm, strict control related to high self-esteem? Coopersmith offers several explanations:

1. Firm management helps the child develop firm inner controls. When parents give children a clear idea of the right way to behave, they are providing clues that maximize successful interactions and minimize anxiety about parental response. When children experience a predictable, ordered social environment, it is easier for them to deal with their environment and hence to feel in control.

2. Clear, firmly enforced rules help children to establish clear self-definitions. Children are compelled to acknowledge forces outside themselves and to recognize the needs and powers of other people. They are given an opportunity to learn the difference between wish and reality and the distinction between self and others.

3. Parental restrictions may irritate children on occasion, but children also see them as proof of parental concern about the children's welfare. The parent who says "Do whatever you like, just don't bother me" is conveying a message that the children are not worthy of concern.

Significantly, Coopersmith found that parents can be both strict and democratic and that this pattern, rather than strictness and autocracy, is associated with high self-esteem.

We have been interpreting Coopersmith's findings as if parental practices directly produced high self-esteem, but the causal linkages can also go the other way. Many of the high self-esteem boys said that when they were punished, they usually deserved it and that they usually agreed with the views of their parents. Mothers of these children reported that punishment was usually effective in correcting the children's misbehavior, and that they had good rapport with their sons—implying mutual trust and a willingness of each to accommodate to the other. The high self-esteem boys are relatively easy to live with, self-confident, and competent in school and in their social relationships. They share their parents' values and accept their discipline. Surely such children are very easy for parents to accept, love, and respect. Perhaps these parents seldom use coercive, punitive methods with these children because they don't need to—the children yield to reasoning. We cannot be sure whether the parents' firm, loving, and democratic treatment of these boys has led to their high self-esteem or whether the boys' competence, trustworthiness, and cooperative attitude toward their parents has enabled their parents to be loving, firm, and democratic. Probably the influences run both ways. For the present, the major point to keep in mind is this: A fifth or sixth-grade boy who has high self-esteem is one who has established a good relationship with his parents—a relationship that undoubtedly has a long history of mutual trust. And when parents establish reasonable rules (taking the child's point of view into account when deciding on the rules) and enforce them firmly, the child's sense of self-control and competence is not diminished. On the contrary, it appears to be enhanced.

In considering Coopersmith's findings, it should be noted that his more intensive work was done with white, middle-class boys in a fairly narrow age range. We cannot be sure that the same results would have been obtained if his studies had included girls or children from a wider range of ethnic and social backgrounds. It also would be useful to know whether changes take place with age in the way parental methods relate to children's self-concepts. Nevertheless, the Coopersmith work is remarkably informative.

THE LOCUS OF CONTROL

We saw earlier that an important element in the development of the sense of being a separate self is children's realization that they can make decisions—can make things happen or refuse to let them happen. Knowing that their actions and environment can be controlled, however, has even broader implications. Coopersmith suggests that people evaluate themselves in terms of their ability to control events and that their self-esteem rests to some extent on the feeling that they have this power. Seligman (1975) has assembled impressive evidence in his book on helplessness that people (or animals) become passive—initiate little activity and lose motivation—when placed in situations where outcomes are unaffected by their behavior. Even when these individuals do succeed in influencing events they seem unable to believe that they have done so. They continue to think that they are simply pawns of external circumstances. In extreme cases, individuals with a history of having very little control over their life circumstances become severely depressed. They walk slowly, withdraw from contact with other people, feel unable to make decisions—in short, they seem to give up any effort to cope with even the most ordinary daily tasks.

Students of personality (for example, Rotter, 1954) have found some consistent differences among normally functioning individuals with respect to their sense of control over their own lives. Certain individuals characteristically feel that they are helpless—that the things that happen to them are a result of luck or fate. Others feel that outcomes are a result of their own actions—that they have the power to determine what happens to them and are responsible for their own success or failure. The first group are said to have an *external* locus of control, the second group an *internal* locus. Locus of control is a personality dimension that has been of special interest to educators because of the repeated finding that children with an internal locus of control do better academically (for example, Nowicki and Segal, 1974).

Learning to control the environment

In order to understand the development of a child's sense of control we must first ask how the understanding of cause and effect begins—how early do infants learn that they have the power to produce an outcome? There is reason to believe that very young infants do not process contingencies in cause-and-effect terms (Watson, 1977). Piaget has examined the early development of infants' understanding of causality. His detailed observations of his own three infants indicated that it is not until about the age of five or six months that children show awareness that their own actions can bring about an effect. (This is the stage of the so-called secondary circular reaction, when the infant repeats a movement that is associated with an interesting external event, looking at the locus of that event, presumably to see if it will happen again. See Flavell, 1977, for a summary of the Piagetian stages.) However, Piaget does not believe that this behavior is yet intentional or goal directed. Intentional behavior appears between the ages of eight and twelve months, approximately. Between twelve and eighteen months infants expand their understanding of cause-and-effect relationships by experimenting with new ways of producing familiar effects. Therefore, according to Piaget's theory, twelve months or a little earlier is the approximate age at which children should first begin to distinguish between the events that are caused by their own actions and those that are not.

Gunnar's (1980) examination of the fear-reducing effects of allowing an infant to control an unfamiliar stimulus highlights these early developmental milestones. Working with infants of six, nine, and twelve months, her procedure was to have the infants come with their mothers to a laboratory room and to seat them in a child-sized chair equipped with a tray. She placed an attractive toy merry-go-round on a table in front of the child—close, but out of reach. The tray in front of some infants was equipped with a panel that could be pressed to activate the motor-driven toy. The children were trained to press the panel, to make the merry-go-round turn and play its music box. The mother would demonstrate the panel. Nearly all the children readily learned the task. (The few who did not were excused from the experimental session.) Then a monkey holding a pair of cymbals, a toy that often frightens children of this age, was substituted for the merry-go-round. When activated, the monkey would clash its cymbals together and flash its eyes. The child could activate the monkey by pressing the panel.

A second group of infants did not have a panel on the tray. The experimenter activated their toys using a remote control switch. Each child in this group was *yolked* to one of the children in the panel group. That is, the experimenter turned on the toy as often and at the same intervals as the yolked partner turned it on. The only difference between the two groups was who controlled the toy.

Records were made of the children's reactions to the monkey (while they were in the chair), including the number of times the children who could control it turned it on, whether they smiled and showed pleased interest in the toy, or whether they sobered, stiffened their bodies, drew back, cried, or otherwise indicated distress or fear. After a limited number of opportunities to see the monkey activated from the vantage point of the chair, the children were lifted out of the chair and put down on the floor next to it. The experimenter observed their movements toward the toy, and whether they attempted to touch it and examine it more closely or withdrew to their mothers.

The results of the experiment are shown in Figure 7-2. At the age of six months, being able to control the onset of the toy did not have a significant effect on the children's fear. At nine months, being in control of the toy made the infants *more* afraid. At twelve months, control

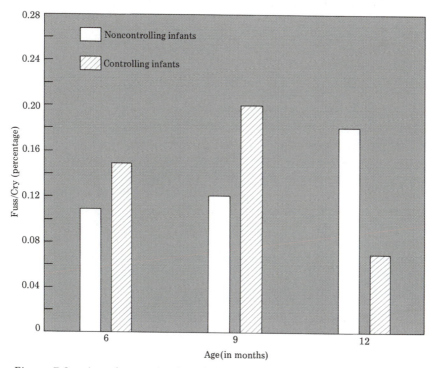

Figure 7-2. Age changes in the relationship between fear and control. Note that being able to control a frightening toy reduces fussing only in the oldest group. (Adapted from Gunnar, 1980)

made them considerably less afraid. The results for the twelve-month-old infants are consistent with two earlier infant studies in which Gunnar showed that twelve-month-old children were less afraid when they could activate the toy than when they could not. The earlier studies suggested that the reduction in fear that comes with control was greater for male than female infants.

Gunnar suggests the following interpretation of the age changes. Six-month-old infants do not know that their own movements are the causal agent activating the toy (this is true despite the fact that almost all the infants tested at this age were easily able to learn the contingency between pressing the panel and activating the toy). At nine months they do know that their own actions start the toy's motion, but they do not know that by *refraining* from pressing the panel they can *prevent* the toy from being activated. Hence, the fact of being in control does not sooth them; it increases their certainty that the feared toy will go on and does not make them feel that they can avoid it. By the age of twelve months they understand both aspects of being in control—that they can make the event occur, and that they can also prevent its occurrence. This knowledge alleviates fear.

The results with the nine-month-old infants remind us that being able to predict an event is not the same thing as being able to control it. In a separate experiment with twelve-month-old infants, Gunnar (1980) gave them preparatory warning signals when the toy was about to be activated. Even though they clearly understood the warning signal, their fears were not moderated. Control was the crucial factor that alleviated fear. This is not to say that predictability is not important in achieving control. Knowing the conditions under which an unpleasant event is likely to occur often makes it possible to find ways and means to avoid or at least minimize unwanted effects. But under the restricted conditions of the Gunnar experiment, the children who could predict the activation of the toy had no means of using this information to avoid the potentially frightening event.

At about the age of one year, then, children begin to understand that they can have an impact on their environment by responding and by not responding. They begin trying out their new-found powers on their caretakers ("If I grab her glasses she'll yell at me; if I don't grab them, she won't."). After a certain amount of time passes—we do not know exactly how much—children discover that withholding compliance may also provide them with a certain amount of power over their caretakers. Once this discovery has been made, the famous negativistic period is ushered in.

What determines the locus of control

Some important age changes must take place in children's ability to perceive when they are being manipulated although this has not received the attention of researchers. Even very young children can easily understand when their parents are using physical punishment or physical restraints to force them to do something against their own wishes. But parents can also control more subtly—for example, they can arouse the child's interest in what they want the child to do. Thus, instead of "Now, David, I want you to pick up your blocks," the parent might try: "Hey—let's throw all these blocks into the box here: Oh! What a nice noise they make! Isn't this fun?" Although researchers have not documented this, we can be sure that the children begin to see through these maneuvers as they grow older, and praise and reward—welcome as they are under certain circumstances—come to be seen as manipulation. No doubt, this dawning awareness is one of the causes of Lepper and Greene's (1975) finding that reinforcement can have a negative motivational effect. Starting with activities in which children showed an initial, spontaneous interest, they rewarded these activities and found that the children subsequently lost interest in performing them spontaneously. (This work is discussed more fully in Chapter 10.) Various explanations have been offered for this reverse effect. One reasonable interpretation is that the children feel they are no longer doing the activity because *they* want to but because someone else wants them to. Their own control is weakened, and the result is the predictable one stressed by Seligman: a loss of motivation.

We have seen that very young children do not see other people as selves with motives and traits different from their own. They also do not readily take another's perspective, and so we would not expect them to think of themselves as objects of other people's manipulations. Nevertheless, the Lepper effect can be detected in children of four or five (the youngest subjects thus far tested), and the effect probably becomes stronger as children grow more sophisticated in detecting adults' attempts at deliberate manipulation.

The cumulating experiences of the first several years of life ought to provide children with an understanding that they have the power to do certain things and that control of many other activities rests with others. Children's sphere of power should gradually widen as parents trust them to make more and more choices. Differentiating between what can and cannot be accomplished should be relatively easy, and children indeed seem to learn to make many such discriminations. However, we would hardly expect individual children to develop any overall sense of either control or lack of control, and yet, this seems to happen. We have seen that some children develop a pervasive internal locus of control. They believe that they can choose their friends, determine by their own efforts how well they do at school, and keep unpleasant things from happening by adequate foresight. Other children see their place in the world very differently. They feel they are at the mercy of fate or luck and that their own actions make very little difference in the outcomes that are important to them. It is as if these beliefs about the extent of their control had become one of the major premises in their theory of the self (see Brim, 1976, and Epstein, 1973)—and a fixed assumption at that, as a child's assumptions about the locus of control over its life have become quite stable by the third grade (Crandall, Katkovsky, and Crandall, 1965; Nowicki and Strickland, 1973).

What determines which kind of theory of control a child will develop? Judging from the studies reported by Seligman, a sense of control develops when the things that happen to the child are contingent on the child's own actions. From the standpoint of the parent-child relationship, this translates into a simple proposition: Infants and young children develop a sense of being in control when their parents are responsive. Responsiveness toward infants was discussed quite fully in Chapter 3. We saw that some mothers offer the next bite in the intimate process of feeding according to their own rhythm while others adapt themselves to the infant's rate of chewing and swallowing. This example is only one of the multitude of instances in which a parent may or may not notice the infant's signals and take them into account in interacting with the child. We saw in Chapter 3 that responsiveness in a parent seemed to foster the development of a secure attachment and that secure attachment in its turn was associated with the child's being willing to explore new situations, approach strange persons, and so forth. It seems reasonable to assume that the development of a sense of control is an important element in this sequence of events. We are probably seeing here the beginnings of a functional relationship in which development of a range of competencies depends in part on prior opportunities to influence both physical and social events.

Implications for child rearing

As the child grows out of infancy, parents must decide not only how responsive they should be, but also how responsive they expect their children to be. Children make an increasingly wide range of demands; some are reasonable and some are not. As we saw in Chapter 5, they develop the capacity to wait at least briefly while other people's needs are served. And of course, they also learn how to do many things for themselves that previously required adult assistance. Thus, the parent becomes able to make demands on the child. Influence flows in both directions.

In the interaction between parent and child, two people's loci of control need to be considered. If the child is allowed to become a tyrant and control the sequence of events in every particular, then presumably the *parent* will begin to feel helpless, manipulated, and depressed. If the parent attempts to break the child's will, never yielding to the child's demands, then presumably the child will develop the helplessness syndrome which Seligman has shown to be so damaging. In Chapter 10 we will return to how several interacting individuals maintain a balance of control. For the present we merely point out that a parent can choose alternatives, short of yielding up control of their interaction entirely to the child, that will foster the development of an internal locus in the child.

A study of locus of control by Loeb (1975) provides an excellent illustration. Loeb administered a locus of control scale to large numbers of fourth- and fifth-grade children and selected two groups of boys: an internal group scoring in the top 10 percent of the internality scale and an external group scoring in the bottom 10 percent. A session was conducted in each subject's home in which the boy was seated at a table with one of his parents. (The procedure was repeated later with the other parent.) The boy was blindfolded and asked to build a tower out of irregular-shaped blocks. The parents were told that they could help the boy as much or as little as they wished. The kind of control exercised by the parents was rated by the observer according to whether it was primarily *directive* or primarily *suggestive*. If the parent said "Why don't you try a flatter piece" this was considered suggestive, while "Here, use this block" was rated directive. The observations were made by people who did not know how the boy had scored on the locus of control scale. The ratings showed that the parents of internal boys more often used a suggestive style in directing their sons, while the parents of the external boys issued directive orders.

Bee (1967) almost exactly paralleled these results in her study of the child-rearing correlates of children's ability to focus attention in the presence of potentially distracting stimuli. Bee asked children in a school setting to do arithmetic problems while wearing earphones over which a voice was solving different arithmetic problems. Two groups of children were selected: a distractible group whose performance deteriorated markedly when the distracting voice was present and a group who appeared to be able to shut out the distraction quite effectively. During a home visit the children were asked to work on a series of tasks in the presence of their parents, and the parental style of helping the child was noted. When the child was working on anagrams, for example, and trying to spell as many words as possible from a given set of letters, some parents would make suggestions such as "Why don't you try spelling backwards some of the words you've already got?" Other parents would say simply: "Try g-o-a-t." Parents of the distractible children more often used a directive style. The children who had been able to resist distraction had parents who suggested strategies but did not give them solutions directly.

Thus, we see that parents who leave the actual solution finding to the child have children who are more likely to (1) have an internal locus of control and (2) resist distraction. Although the connection between these two findings has not been proven, we suggest the following: In the Bee study the distracting voice on the earphones made the task more difficult; the child had to be more highly motivated to keep trying to do as well as possible on the arithmetic problems. Children whose interaction with their parents have led them to have an internal locus of control are more likely to maintain a strong task motivation in the face of difficult conditions. A link may be inferred between internal locus of control and the various aspects of impulse control discussed in Chapter 5.

The nature of self-attributed causes

Repeatedly, we have seen that children's motivation is intimately linked to the amount of *agency*—the power to effect outcomes—that they attribute to themselves. Actually, attributing causality to the self does not always imply that one has the power to change things. Consider, for example, the perceived causes of failure. Certain children may have an internal locus in the sense that they believe failure is their own fault and is not due to back luck. But in some cases they believe the problem lies in their own stupidity, while in other cases they believe they simply did not try hard enough. Effort, of course, is seen as being much more under the individual's control than ability. Thus, an internal causal locus sometimes frees a child from a sense of helplessness, but sometimes it does not.

A series of studies by Dweck and her colleagues (Dweck, 1975; Dweck and Bush, 1976; Dweck and Gilliard, 1975; Dweck and Reppucci, 1973; Dweck et al., 1978) have demonstrated that when children attribute their failures to stable, uncontrollable factors in themselves, such as lack of ability, their task performance deteriorates following failure. If they believe, however, that their failures are due to lack of effort, they often show increased effort and improved performance after failure. In several studies Dweck has found that girls are more likely than boys to suffer from the kind of learned helplessness that comes from attributing lack of ability to themselves. Boys tend to believe, when they do not do well, that they have not worked hard enough. These sex differences are especially interesting in view of the fact that the two sexes perform very similarly on achievement tests. Dweck's observations in classrooms have revealed that one source of these attributional differences is direct training by teachers. When boys turn in poor work, teachers are likely to scold them for lack of effort, for not paying attention, for sloppiness. The message is: "If you would only stop fooling around and get down to work, you could do very well." Teachers seem to make the assumption that girls are already trying as hard as they can. When a girl makes a mistake, the feedback from the teacher is "You didn't get it right even though you tried," and the implication is that the girl can't get it right—that she lacks ability.

The Dweck group set up experimental conditions that paralleled their classroom observations (Dweck et al., 1978). One group of boys and girls were treated the way girls normally are treated in the classroom. When they did poorly on an anagram task, they were simply told: "You didn't do very well that time; you didn't get it right." Another group of children were treated as boys are usually treated. Following failure they were sometimes given the girl-type criticism focused on the incorrectness of their answers, but such criticism was mixed with criticism aimed at nonintellectual aspects of the work—for example, that they hadn't written the answers neatly enough. The boy-type feedback caused most girls and boys to believe that their failures were due to lack of effort and led to increased effort after failure for both sexes. The girl-type feedback resulted in subjects of both sexes believing that they simply did not have the ability to do the task and made the children give up more easily after failure.

The implications here for parental treatment of children may seem paradoxical. A parent who scolds a child for laziness may be building a self-confident stance toward problem solving! (Unless, of course, a mother says: "You were *born* lazy; you'll be a lazy bum all your life, just like your father!") The child is likely to share the parent's assumptions. If the parent assumes that the behavior is under the child's own control and that the child can learn to do what is expected, and if the parent helps to create the conditions that facilitate success, the chances are lessened that the child will acquire a helpless attitude.

In our discussion of the role parents play in the development of their children's self-concepts and self-esteem, several themes have emerged. To summarize: Children's sense of self-worth is closely related to their parents' view of them as lovable and worthy of respect. We have found much support for the proposition that children's self-concepts are to a great extent reflections of the way they are viewed by others. If adults treat children as if any shortcomings can be remedied by the children's own actions, children are likely to share this optimism about their problem-solving competence and to behave accordingly.

Affection, acceptance, and respect (as shown by democratic child-rearing practices) are not the only parental attributes that are associated with a child's sense of self-worth. Parents who have these characteristics but are also rather strict in enforcing rules, and who demand rather high levels of performance from their children, are likely to have children with an especially positive view of themselves. We can only hypothesize that this fact, too, may point to the looking-glass nature of the self. A child who is allowed to control the interaction with parents and whose parents do not exercise reciprocal control is likely to have parents who are resentful—who feel manipulated and exploited. When the child looks into its social mirror—the parents' eyes—the child does not necessarily see a pretty picture. But if firm control by the parents results in the child's behaving according to the parents' standards, then the child will read approval in the parents' eyes.

A cautionary note is needed now. We have identified some parental behaviors that have an impact on children's self-esteem. But our account is surely not complete. Many other aspects of parenting, not yet studied, must also make a difference. Also, many people other than the parents have an impact on self-esteem, and the values and viewpoints of these others may sometimes conflict with the values of the parents. When this occurs, the child's self-esteem is vulnerable no matter how skillful the parents have been in supporting the child's ego.

Some poorly understood issues

Students of development have given little attention to the fact that different social mirrors reflect different images. A boy of eight or ten may perceive that the other boys in the play group respect him when they see him defy adults; he is also aware that his mother and father are disappointed in him when he does this. As G. H. Mead said many years ago, children's own evaluations of themselves will probably ultimately incorporate the views of all the significant others in their lives—a composite that the children construct and that becomes the self-accepted standard against which they evaluate themselves.

The self-evaluating functions are not the only significant functions of the self. As Bandura (1978) has noted, the self-regulation of behavior includes a number of component processes: People observe themselves and compute the quantity, quality, and originality of what they have done; they consider their own performance in terms of the importance of the activity to their own goals; they compare the performance to a set of standards that are usually based on a chosen reference group (the professional ballplayer compares his performance with the League's leading hitter, but the Sunday softball player compares his performance with others in the neighborhood games). The individual evaluates the self's performance using these standards and then may go on to administer rewards or punishments to the self. Bandura's contention is that we have concentrated on self-evaluation (self-esteem) and neglected the other aspects of self-regulation that make up the more comprehensive picture of the functioning of the self.

The issue of the investment of the self in possessions, persons, or institutions remains an intriguing one that has not yet been adequately explored. The child's extensions of his or her self to include friends and family members and the development of the feeling that their interests are the child's interests is also not fully understood. During childhood profound changes undoubtedly take place in the child's extensions of his or her self to include others. Surely family members are the first persons with whom the child identifies so fully as to experience defeat or success vicariously when the other people's fortunes wane or prosper. Later, certain teachers or playmates may be selected for this kind of ego investment; we do not know what determines a child's choices, nor how the identification progresses. But extending the ego to other persons seems to be an important step in the growth of children's willingness to be bound into a social network and to behave in ways that promote the interests of others, as well as the interests of the self.

Finally, we may have exaggerated the extent to which the self is merely a reflection of others' views. For when the child is old enough to have developed a set of self-accepted moral standards, violation of these standards may well result in guilt feelings and loss of self-esteem regardless of whether other people know and disapprove of what the child has done. These considerations lead us to the topic of the next chapters: moral development.

SUMMARY AND COMMENTARY

We have traced the development of the cluster of assumptions, beliefs, and hypotheses that become organized into the "theory" that each individual holds about the self. Children begin with the task of distinguishing themselves from others. Major steps are:

1. Self-recognition. Within the animal kingdom only the great apes can learn to recognize themselves in a mirror. Human children can recognize themselves by about the age of eighteen months. This accomplishment seems to depend on the viewer's ability to form a mental representation of his or her own face.

2. Achieving an understanding that one's own experiences and memories are private and often not shared by others.

3. Defining the characteristics of the self. Initially, children's self-definitions are based on external characteristics—how they look, where they live, what activities they engage in. Later—after about the age of six or seven—they begin to define themselves in terms of psychological traits. With increasing age, group membership takes a more important place in self-definition.

The growing ability to take the perspective of others toward the self is important in clarifying the self-concept. Young children have difficulties in this regard—they are sometimes confused about whether other people can see them, and also they are often unaware of the impressions their actions make on others. A major developmental change is:

   4. Children learn to anticipate how others will react to what they do, and they begin to tailor their actions for different audiences, depending on the nature of the social self that they wish to project. At this point they become more guarded in the nature of their self-disclosure to others.

With accumulating experience children begin to limit their choices of activities and their aspirations for achievement. In consequence:

   5. The self-concept becomes differentiated. Children begin to think of themselves as having certain skills and not having others and as being virtuous in some respects and not so virtuous in other respects.

   6. The areas that are important to the self evoke strong emotions. Children will react very vigorously to keep their self-image intact.

   7. An ideal self emerges. Children form a concept of the kind of person they would like to be. School-age children who aspire to a self that is more virtuous or more competent than the present self have been found to have better impulse control and more freedom from emotional disturbance than children who do not conceptualize such an ideal self.

Children evaluate themselves using the ideal self as a basis for comparison. Most children develop a basic attitude about their self-worth; one child may experience a profound sense of worthlessness, while at the opposite extreme another child may have a sense of being a valuable, competent person worthy of the esteem of others.

   8. By about the age of eight to ten, self-esteem has become quite stable, remaining constant over periods of several years.

   9. Self-esteem has pervasive implications for behavior. Children with high self-esteem have confidence in their own judgments, are not greatly influenced when others disagree, and approach new tasks optimistically. In social interactions they are assertive and make friends easily. They seem free to approach new situations with zest and interest.

How do some children develop high self-esteem while others do not? Studies show that children with high self-esteem:

10. Have a history of success in enterprises they have under-taken.

11. Are accepted and approved of by their parents, who are both strict and democratic (in the sense that they involve their children in family decision making and respect their opinions). When discipline is necessary, these parents tend to use reasoning or withdrawal of privileges rather than physical punishment or withdrawal of love.

We must be cautious about deciding what is cause and what is effect in these relationships. Perhaps the children's competence and good adjustment enable their parents to treat them in rational and approving ways and permit the children to think highly of themselves; thus their self-esteem need not be an outcome of parental acceptance. Nevertheless, the weight of evidence supports the view that children's self-concept and self-esteem reflect to some extent the way they are seen by significant others in their lives.

An important element in the self-concept is the *locus of control*— the sense of either being in control of one's life or being at the mercy of luck or fate. The conditions that determine which kind of orientation a child will develop are not well understood, but there is reason to believe that an internal locus of control will be fostered if:

12. Parents respond to their children's signals contingently rather than in terms of the parents' own needs and time schedules.

13. Parents suggest problem solutions to their children but do not give detailed directions, leaving some of the problem solution in the children's hands.

If children believe that their failures are their own fault but think the problem lies in their own lack of ability, their internal locus is associated with negative consequences—a reduction in and loss of interest in tasks. If children come to believe that they *can* do things if they try, failures are followed by increased effort. Thus motivation, persistence, and effort in problem solving depend not only on the locus of control but also on the assessment of competence.

CHAPTER 8

Moral Development I:

Moral Thought

W E have followed the child from the early symbiotic relationship with the mother or other principal caretaker to the
emergence of the sense of self as a coherent entity. We now
turn to an examination of the child's acquisition of the rules that govern behavior in the social world. In particular, we are concerned with
the development of the sense of right and wrong—how the child
begins to understand the values that guide and regulate behavior
within a given social system.

Of course, morality is not merely a matter of acquiring an intellectual sense of society's rules. Children—and adults, for that matter—do
not always do what they know to be right. We need to consider both
moral thought and moral behavior. In the present chapter we examine
the development of children's understanding of moral issues. In
Chapter 9 we turn to the emotional and behavioral aspects of moral
development.

The first section of the present chapter defines morality in general
terms, but with special focus on the issues that generate the rules most
societies teach to their children. We then look at stages of moral
thought: what individuals at various levels of development mean by
such things as misbehavior and lying. Finally, we examine the cognitive processes underlying the ability to make moral judgments, paying
particular attention to the role of perspective taking.

THE SOCIAL MEANING OF MORALITY

In a theater in a small city in the English Midlands, attached to the backs of many of the seats is a small rack that once contained opera glasses. The racks were coin-operated: the insertion of a shilling released the opera glasses from their holder. At the end of a performance, the user would return the glasses to the rack, which locked automatically. The glasses would then be ready for a member of the next audience. The glasses were small, and in the darkness a user could easily slip them under a coat or into a pocket and carry them out of the theater without being seen. But for many years almost no one took them. The rate of theft was so low that the intake of shillings covered the losses and yielded a profit to the management. In the 1960s the rate of theft began to rise and reached the point where the management could no longer afford to replace the stolen glasses. So the system fell into disuse; only the empty racks remained to remind the theater-goer of a convenience made possible by the honesty of an earlier generation.

We may speculate about social changes in the Midlands (and elsewhere in the industrialized world) in the late 1960s. But more important for our present concerns is the fact that many social arrangements depend on the willing compliance of large numbers of people with social rules or customs that run counter to their immediate self-interest. The sight of the empty racks forcibly draws attention to the fragility of social arrangements fostering well-being or convenience. We can no longer take it for granted that these arrangements will be maintained.

In a sense the example of the opera glasses is trivial—a mere convenience that is easily dispensed with. But other arrangements can be vital to the survival of a group and its way of life, and these practices are less likely to be abandoned in a drift toward noncompliance. In a culture that depends upon both corn and cattle for its food supply, all members of the society must close the gate that keeps the cattle out of the corn patch. And in a nomadic desert tribe every member must cooperate in conserving and protecting the precious water supply. No child can be allowed in a playful moment to pull the corks from the goatskins that carry the water. Social arrangements differ, then, in how vital they are to the survival and optimal functioning of the group and in the degree of compliance the society expects. A group adrift in a lifeboat cannot tolerate one single deviant who proposes to bore a hole in the bottom of the boat. A modern nation can tolerate a certain number of thieves or murderers, but it must keep theft and murder at a low rate or the social fabric will disintegrate.[1]

---

[1] Terms such as "a society must keep" or "a society will tolerate" are being used loosely here. Of course, societies do not "need" or "intend" in the sense that individuals do.

Efforts by social scientists to examine human societies and to identify universal themes have a long and honorable history. Some problems seem to arise in all societies, and societies solve these problems in ways suited to their ecological niche (see Goldschmidt's *Man's Way;* Malinowski's *Science, Magic, and Religion;* Sumner's *Folkways*). All or nearly all societies have developed rules and norms to deal with these problems, applying socialization pressures as they teach them to their children. A sampling of the kinds of issues that generate social rules in most societies follows.

1. *Endangering self or others.* The safeguarding of food and water supplies has already been mentioned. Children are also trained not to set fires, to exercise care in the use of dangerous tools or weapons, and not to interfere with the driver of the family car.

2. *Health.* The specific training depends on the society's theory of disease. Societies that attribute disease to contact with bodily wastes teach their children to dispose of their feces so others will not come into contact with them. In cultures that are aware of the transmission of germs by mouth, children are taught to cover their mouths when they cough, not to put soiled objects into their mouths, not to spit on sidewalks, and not to put a used handkerchief or tissue down on someone else's dinner plate. As knowledge concerning pollution and its effects is disseminated, social pressure is mounting against individuals who release contaminants into the air or public water supply.

3. *Property.* Although societies differ in how much property is communally owned and how much is assigned to individual ownership, all known societies (with the possible exception of a recently discovered Stone-Age tribe in the Philippines) have some individual property. Children are taught to identify those objects they have the right to control and dispose of and those that belong to others. They are taught the implications of ownership: borrowing and lending, asking permission for use, and the meaning and consequences of theft. When property is communally owned, strong values are attached to proper care of this property and regulations usually govern its use.

Analyses of the functions served by customs or institutions set teleological traps for the unwary. The intention here is not to impute actual motives to societies, but simply to draw attention to some of the social regulations that promote social cohesion and to remind the reader that socialization pressures on the young are geared to these regulations.

4. *Control of aggression.* Societies place strict limits on the individual's right to inflict pain on others in the group. Such rules usually apply primarily to a specific group: members of one's family, tribe, or religious sect. In many instances individuals receive approval for or are even required to inflict damage on their group's enemies. The inhibition of aggression within the group usually extends to damage to the self-esteem or possessions of other people, as well as to physical injury.

5. *Control of sex.* All societies have some way of regulating their members' sexual lives. Rules specify with whom and under what conditions sexual intercourse is considered legitimate. The incest taboo is the best-proven example of a cultural universal. In addition all societies probably have a concept of rape and take measures to prevent or punish it. Most of the social customs surrounding sexual behavior have evolved during periods when contraception was unavailable or ineffective and when sex was likely to lead to child bearing. Most of these customs seem designed to assure that children will be born into a social setting where certain adults will clearly bear (and will be able to carry out) the obligation to care for them.

6. *Self-reliance and work.* Mature individuals are expected to contribute to their own support and that of the social group. They must not grow up to drain the resources of their society. Children are therefore taught to ask for help only when necessary, to help with chores when they are old enough, and to learn skills that will contribute to their self-support (and support of their children) when they are grown.

7. *Telling the truth and keeping promises.* Societies differ with respect to their reliance on the spoken word to maintain social arrangements. In industrial societies, which call for an intricate coordination of the time schedules of many different people, individuals are censured if they agree to an appointment with others and fail to keep it. In simpler societies promises regarding time schedules may be less important, but other verbal agreements—for example, to pay a given number of cows as a bride price—are regarded as solemnly binding. Thus, although societies vary in the value they place upon promise keeping or truth telling, they do have certain requirements that stem from the need to maintain interpersonal trust.

8. *Respect for authority.* Most social groups are hierarchically organized, although the complexity and nature of the authority structure vary greatly form one society to another. Extended families traditionally have a head; tribes have chiefs; nations have leaders or rulers; armies have officers; orchestras

have conductors; classrooms have teachers. Maintaining certain hierarchical systems is necessary for achieving group goals, and children are trained to show some degree of respect or deference toward persons in authority, which can take the form of respectful terms of address, respectful gestures, or immediate compliance to demands. While societies differ in terms of how rigidly they enforce observance of authority relationships, almost all exact some forms of deference from children toward their parents and toward certain authority figures outside the family.

Such rules exist because human beings are social animals and each person's capacity to act—and indeed, each person's welfare and safety—depends upon the actions of other people. Each individual's behavior, then, must be integrated into a network of social arrangements.

The social utility of some rules of conduct is so obvious that little effort is required to exact compliance. New drivers accept without resistance the rule that they must stay on the right side of the road in the United States and the left side in England. The learner's own self-interest obviously coincides with that of all the other drivers. The individual benefits of rules that help to maintain an authority structure are not nearly so obvious, and some social requirements (for example, the obligation to risk one's life for others) are *not* in the individual's immediate self-interest. Nevertheless, societies must exact acceptable social behavior from their members, whether the personal benefits to the individual are obvious or not. The simplest method of control—rewarding prosocial and punishing antisocial behavior—cannot be relied on exclusively or even primarily for economic reasons: No society can afford enough policemen or monitors to impose social behavior by force. (To say nothing of the difficulty of maintaining the behavior of the policemen and monitors!) Social rules must be accepted by the members of a social group because (1) they feel the "rightness" of the rules as guides for their own behavior or (2) they feel that by conforming they can keep the respect of others whose good opinion they value. Thus, group functioning depends on the existence of a set of shared social values, and a central task in the socializing (or civilizing) of each new generation is to transmit these values. Of course, simply transmitting a preformed set of values is not sufficient for maintaining social cohesion in times of rapid social change. Young people must somehow acquire the capacity to join others in adapting old values to new conditions and inventing new social agreements as needed.

Only a brave (even foolhardy!) person would attempt to define morality. To some true morality can only be gained through accepting a specific religious creed. To others a system of personal ethics can be valid without the ratification of any external institution or supernatural being and without making it part of a spiritual life. In all the writings about morality, however, three themes are paramount:

1. Moral values are social values. The Ten Commandments (except for those specifying religious duties) and the Golden Rule deal with individual behavior in relation to fellow human beings.

2. The fully moral person behaves in accordance with a system of values that are self-accepted and self-enforced. Mature morality implies attempting to be good at all times—not only when a policeman is in view or when actions will be monitored by those who have the power to reward and punish.

3. Moral persons see themselves as part of a social network in which all have mutual responsibilities. Thus, moral values are not rules imposed by one person on another, but rather reciprocal agreements that balance the individual's obligations to others against others' obligations to the individual.

Some people argue that a moral person has a higher duty to himself or herself than to society and that a moral person must live in accordance with the principles of conscience, even if society says these rules are wrong. This kind of behavior is exemplified by the martyr or saint who goes to jail or faces death to defend a set of higher values that conflict with law or custom. Yet these higher principles are social—that is, they reflect the individual's obligations to a social order. The person who goes to jail in defense of the right to exploit other people for personal gain is not considered a martyr or saint.

The developmental psychologist adds a fourth theme to the definition of morality: Moral values and moral conduct develop systematically during childhood and are linked to other aspects of development. Adults can distinguish between social rules that are merely customs or conventions and rules that have moral force. Young children do not always understand this difference. For many young children the rules against eating with one's fingers or a boy wearing a skirt seem to have the same moral status as rules against stealing. For older children, however, the primary basis for the distinction is whether other people's rights and interests are violated. Eating with one's fingers hurts no one, while taking property does injure someone else. A morally socialized child has been taught to resolve the conflict between self-interest and the interests of others. A balance of individual rights must be struck. Thus, the individual's refusal to be vaccinated on grounds of religious principle must be balanced against the 95 percent level of vaccination that may be needed to prevent the spread of a particular disease.

John Rawls (1971) contends that individual rights must be defined in a context of justice for all. Justice is fairness. Social rules are just if they represent rational decisions stemming from an original position of equality:

> We are to imagine that those who engage in social cooperation choose together, in one joint act, the principles which are to assign basic rights and duties and to determine the division of social benefits. Men are to decide *in advance* how they are to regulate their claims against one another. . . . In justice as fairness, the original position . . . is that no one knows his place in society, his class position or social status, nor does anyone know his fortune in the distribution of natural assets and abilities, his intelligence, strength and the like. . . . The principles of justice are chosen behind a veil of ignorance. . . . Since all (persons) are similarly situated and no one is able to design principles to favor his particular condition, the principles of justice are the result of a fair agreement or bargain. (pp. 11–12) (Italics are mine.)

In other words, a social rule would be just if all those affected by it agreed to it at a point when they did not know what position they were going to occupy when the rule was enforced. In the case of the right not to be vaccinated the just rule would be one considered fair by people who did not know whether they would be among the minority with religious scruples or the majority whose health needed protection. Rules imposed on one group by another group at a time when the rule-makers have only their own interests in mind may be suspected of being unfair.

We cannot expect, of course, that a young child will understand the Rawls principle for determining what is just or fair. Such a concept is the outcome of a lengthy developmental process, and most adults never reach this level of sophistication. We now consider the "steps" that children go through when acquiring moral understanding.

THE DEVELOPMENT OF MORAL UNDERSTANDING

Certain items of moral knowledge are acquired fairly early in life. Most six-year-olds will say that it is wrong to tell a lie or steal or commit murder, and they will continue to assert these basic moral truths as they grow older. However, children's capacity to comprehend the meaning of these statements undergoes great changes. Only gradually do they begin to understand what kind of statements are lies, how borrowing differs from stealing, or that there are different degrees of culpability for murder. Two-year-olds, who are just beginning to talk and who have only the dimmest understanding of the causal sequence of events, are incapable of being either moral or immoral. As they grow older, they become capable of moral reasoning. But the nature of this reasoning undergoes a number of transformations before the individual is capable of truly mature moral understanding.

Piaget on moral judgments

Piaget was the first to attempt a systematic tracing of these transformations in children's moral reasoning. His book, *The Moral Judgment of the Child* (1932), was a landmark in developmental psychology. Starting with the assumption that a sense of justice and respect for the rules of the social order are the two central elements in mature morality, he studied (1) how children understand the rules of games and the basis of their validity, (2) what children mean by lies or truth telling, and (3) children's concepts of authority and what constitutes a legitimate basis for anyone to assume authority. Piaget not only provided the first systematic account of the development of these concepts, but he also evolved a method of questioning children that has been used (with some modifications) by most of the researchers on moral judgments who followed him. To illustrate Piaget's approach, we will consider his method of assessing children's thinking about the role of *intent* in moral judgments. Piaget worked with a substantial number of Swiss children in the age range six to twelve (including children from a variety of social backgrounds). He told them pairs of stories about childish transgressions, in each case asking the child to tell him which action was naughtier and why. He was more interested in the reasons his subjects gave for their choices than in the choices themselves. One set of stories follows:

> A. There was once a little girl who was called Marie. She wanted to give her mother a nice surprise, and cut out a piece of sewing for her. But she didn't know how to use the scissors properly, and cut a big hole in her dress.

> B. A little girl called Margaret went and took her mother's scissors one day that her mother was out. She played with them for a bit. Then, as she didn't know how to use them properly, she made a little hole in her dress. (1965, p. 122[2])

Younger children usually insisted that the girl in Story A was naughtier because she had made a bigger hole in her dress. Did they come to this conclusion because they did not understand that she was trying to be helpful? Piaget found that even when they *did* understand this, the younger children still based their decision on the amount of damage that had been done.

Piaget calls this type of moral reasoning *objective responsibility,*

---

[2] First published in English in 1932; citation refers to the First Paperback Edition.

meaning that actions are judged on the basis of their material out-comes, rather than their intent. Perhaps it should be noted that most of Piaget's stories do not compare intentional with accidental damage. Usually one accident occurs while the child is trying to help, and the other while the child is misbehaving. Armsby (1971) has shown that if children are asked to compare a small amount of deliberate damage with a larger amount of accidental damage, even children as young as six usually say that the deliberate damage was naughtier. However, their answers do depend to some extent on the amount of the acciden-tal damage. In comparing the deliberate breaking of one cup with the accidental breaking of a new television set, 40 percent of six-year-olds and less than 10 percent of ten-year-olds said damage to the television was naughtier. Armsby's work suggests that young children can un-derstand intent in the sense of recognizing deliberate naughtiness. They are also aware that damage to valued objects is something to be avoided. Children do have difficulty, however, weighing the relative importance of these factors, and they sometimes have trouble inferring other people's intents.

Judgments about intent are, of course, only one small element in the larger picture Piaget painted. His studies led him to believe that a major transition occurs as children move from what he called *heteronomous morality* (sometimes called *moral realism* or the *morality of constraint*) to *morality of cooperation* (sometimes called *autonomous mo-rality*). He believed that the first view grows out of children's rela-tionship to adult authority. Because they are subordinate to adults, they come to believe that rules emanate from sources outside them-selves and that wrongness is whatever adults forbid or punish. When children begin to free themselves from adult authority and interact on an equal basis with age mates, Piaget thought, they begin to under-stand that rules are social agreements accepted by all members of a group as a basis for cooperative action. It is not possible in this brief space to do justice to Piaget's findings or concepts. Many others have built on his work, and we turn now to some of the more recent re-search, recognizing its Piagetian roots.

Stages of moral judgment

Kohlberg (1969, 1976) has studied the development of moral thought in adolescents and young adults, as well as in younger chil-dren. Initially, Kohlberg compared groups of children of different ages, assuming that if the groups differed consistently, it must be true that individual children move from one stage to the next as they grow older. Later, however, he carried out longitudinal studies, following the same children from the age of ten into adulthood. The consisten-cies between the cross-sectional and longitudinal studies give him a firm basis for claiming that differences among age groups do reflect individual development.[3]

Kohlberg presented his subjects with moral dilemmas embodying a conflict between several contending claims for justice. He was interested in his subjects' reasoning, rather than in their substantive decisions. The most famous of Kohlberg's dilemmas concerns a hypothetical person, Heinz, whose wife is fatally ill with cancer. A drug that may save her is invented by a local druggist. The price is very high. Heinz does not have enough money to buy it. He borrows part of what is needed and offers to pay what he has and try to pay off the rest later. The druggist refuses to sell, saying that he put many years of work into his invention and deserves to be adequately compensated. Heinz, in desperation, breaks into the drugstore to steal the drug for his wife. The question is: Should Heinz have done this?

Clearly, the story presents issues that do not reflect the real-life moral conflicts faced by children. Even so, most children understand the problem well enough to discuss it, and as they grow older, the nature of their reasoning clearly changes. Consider the responses of Joe, who was interviewed several times:

> At age 10. (Why shouldn't you steal from a store?) It's not good to steal from a store. It's against the law. Someone could see you and call the police. (1976, p. 36)

> At age 17. (Why shouldn't you steal from a store?) It is a matter of law. It's one of our rules that we're trying to help protect everyone, protect property, not just to protect a store. It's something that's needed in our society. If we didn't have these laws, people would steal, they wouldn't have to work for a living, and our whole society would get out of kilter. (p. 36)

> At age 24. (Why shouldn't someone steal from a store?) It's violating another person's rights, in this case, to property. (Does the law enter in?) Well, the law in most cases is based on what is morally right, so it's not a separate subject, it's a consideration. . . . (What does "morality," or "morally right" mean to you?) Recognizing the rights of other individuals, first to life, and then to do as he pleases as long as it doesn't in-

[3] Longitudinal studies are undertaken to demonstrate that individual children progress from stage to stage and also to investigate the possibility that differences between age groups have other causes. For example, a cross-sectional study of the attitudes of young people in 1969 might have revealed that twenty-year-olds as a group were more hostile toward adult authority and adult institutions than thirty-year-olds as a group. We might interpret this to mean: (1) that the older group was probably more radical when younger and the younger group will become more conservative with age or (2) that the twenty-year-olds were alienated by the Vietnam war and have attitudes different from those of previous or subsequent groups of twenty-year-olds. Indeed, as adults they might remain more alienated than groups that preceded or followed them. The latter type of findings are called *cohort effects*. Differences between successive age groups can be caused either by age changes, by cohort effects, or by a combination of both. The only way to make sure that real developmental change is occurring is to study the same group of children at more than one age.

terfere with somebody else's rights. . . . (returning to Heinz) It is the husband's duty to save his wife. The fact that her life is in danger transcends every other standard you might use to judge his action. Life is more important than property. (Suppose it were a friend, not his wife?) I don't think that would be much different from a moral point of view. It's still a human being in danger. . . . (Should the judge punish the husband?) Usually the moral and legal standpoints coincide. Here they conflict. The judge should weigh the moral standpoint more heavily but preserve the legal law in punishing Heinz lightly. (pp. 37–38)

On the basis of his analysis of many statements by children and young adults, Kohlberg developed the following model of the growth of moral thought:

Level 1: Preconventional Morality. (The level of most children under nine, many adolescents, and many adult criminal offenders.) Social rules and expectations are felt as something external to the self. The individual conforms to social rules on the basis of fear of punishment or expectation of personal reward. This level can be divided into two stages:

> *Stage 1: Punishment and obedience orientation.* Obedience is considered important for its own sake, the individual recognizes the superior power of authority and conforms to avoid punishment.
>
> *Stage 2: Self-interested exchanges.* The individual obeys rules in order to get the best deal possible in a world where other people also have their own interests. A person is good or kind so that others will do things that the self needs or wants them to do.

Level 2: Conventional Morality. (The level of most adolescents and adults.) The individual now understands, accepts, and upholds social rules and expectations, especially those that emanate from authorities. The rules are internalized—felt to be right. This level has two stages:

> *Stage 3: Maintaining good interpersonal relationships.* The individual wants to be seen by others as a good, well-intentioned person and also wants to feel this way about her- or himself. Being good requires the individual to live up to the expectations of important others, especially parents and friends, and to maintain mutual trust, loyalty, respect, and gratitude. A hallmark of this stage is the experience of shame when seen in an unflattering light by significant others.
>
> *Stage 4: Maintaining the social system, including authority relationships.* The individual agrees to a set of social duties and

obligations which are seen as justified because they keep the social system functioning (e.g., "If everyone did that, everything would fall apart"). This stage has sometimes been referred to as *law and order morality*. Individuals at this stage believe in upholding the law, except in extreme cases where it conflicts with other clear social duties. They believe that authorities have the right to punish infractions. They feel people have a duty to live up to accepted obligations and they feel guilt over failure to do so.

Level 3: Postconventional Morality. (A level reached by only a minority of adults, and then seldom until the age of twenty or later.) Society's rules are accepted, but these individuals develop and internalize their own formulation of the basic moral principles that underlie the rules. When the person's own principles conflict with social rules, the individual is guided by the principles. The two stages are:

Stage 5: Morality of social contact and individual rights. Social rules are seen as relative and capable of being changed by mutual agreement among those affected. To be acceptable, rules must be arrived at by democratic procedures and must be impartial. Individuals conform to obligations for the sake of maintaining their own self-respect and the respect of a rational community of equals—in the interests of "the greatest good for the greatest number."

Stage 6: Morality of universal ethical principles. As a rational person, the individual recognizes the validity of universal ethical principles—for example, the right to life and the right to as much liberty as social functioning will allow. The individual has a sense of personal commitment to these principles. Compliance is based on the individual's personal conscience, not on external pressure or even social contract. An individual at this stage may choose a prison sentence rather than violate personal beliefs.

The three levels of morality, according to Kohlberg, reflect three different social orientations. Preconventional people have a concrete *individual* perspective. Conventional people are taking the point of view of a *member of society*. Postconventional people are taking a *prior-to-society* perspective. In other words, the postconventional level is the only one at which individuals have any grasp of the Rawls principle. Only at this level do people ask themselves what kind of social regulations a society would have to develop if it were starting from scratch and on what basis a society could insure that social regulations would be impartial.

Kohlberg's work stands as a monumental contribution to our understanding of moral thought in children and youth. He has been able to show that there is an ordered progression in the development of moral reasoning. Nevertheless, certain criticisms have been made: First, the situations in Kohlberg's story dilemmas were not familiar to most of his subjects, and his critics suggest that children might have employed more mature reasoning if they had been asked about issues relevant to their day-to-day experiences. A second question concerns whether a given individual functions at the same level of moral reasoning regardless of the kind of moral issue that is involved or whether moral thought on different issues may develop at different rates. With these questions in mind, William Damon (1977), working with considerably younger children, has analyzed the development of moral thought in four different areas: concepts of friendship and the mutual rights and obligations that friendship entails, concepts of justice or fairness, concepts of obedience and authority, and social rules and conventions. We will consider some of these concepts below.

Concepts of justice

A child of five or six may complain "That's not *fair!*" and seem to be intensely outraged when another child receives a larger share of something that is prized. Yet the same child may not consider it unfair if the other child gets the smaller share. How do children conceive of what is fair or unfair?

Damon asked four- to eight-year-olds what they considered a fair division of candy, money, or toys among several children. He used several hypothetical situations (illustrated with pictures). In one story a visitor to the school, who liked bracelets—especially bracelets made by children—asked four children to make her some. The children worked together. One child made the most and the prettiest bracelets. One child was bigger than the others. One was younger and couldn't work as well or as fast as the others. The visitor, receiving the set of bracelets, offered ten candy bars to be divided among the four children. The child being interviewed was asked to describe the fairest division of the candy. In a similar story a group of children had to divide money earned through joint effort in making objects for sale at a fair. One of these children was said to be poorer than the others and didn't get any allowance.

Damon was able to document a clear age progression, within the rather narrow age range studied, in the nature of children's thinking about fairness. The youngest children hardly differentiated between what they wanted and what would be fair. Often they would not recognize the fact that their wishes might conflict with others' wishes, and in ignoring this possibility, they evaded the need for making any moral decision. In the next phase (at about age five to six) the children advocated simple equality. Following this, the children began to incorporate the idea that some people were more *deserving* than others— that rights had to be earned and that people should be paid back for doing good or bad things. During the early phase of thinking about this kind of reciprocity, however, children usually took only one kind of claim into account. A little later (after about age eight), many children said that several different kinds of valid claims could exist, and they undertook the more difficult task of balancing competing claims.

Authority and obedience

In analyzing children's thought about moral issues, Piaget studied children's understanding of rules—where they come from, who has the legitimate authority to make them, and under what conditions one is obliged to obey them. As we noted earlier, Piaget argued that some time during the preadolescent years most children change quite drastically in their orientation toward rules. At younger ages they believe that rules are outside themselves, originating with authorities whose right to make rules is taken for granted (heteronomous morality). Later children come to believe that rules are something that exist among equals, are agreed upon by the parties concerned, and can be changed by mutual agreement (autonomous morality). Piaget assumed that children's relationship with their parents was by necessity authority-bound, so that changes could not be expected in attitudes about the nature of authority until children began to spend much of their time away from home in the company of playmates. Thus, Piaget saw the peer group, not the family, as the architect of more mature concepts about authority and its legitimacy.

Damon studied the development of children's understanding about the nature of authority and their obligations to people in authority. He asked his young subjects about the limits of parental authority and peer authority (for example, team captains), and also about the basis on which people have a right to exercise authority.

Damon used the familiar story-dilemma procedure and noted age change in the children's answers. His stories were illustrated with picture cards, and he chose situations that reflected dilemmas familiar to and appropriate for the children being studied. Here is an example of one of Damon's situations:

> This is Peter (Michelle for girl subjects), and here is his mother, Mrs. Johnson. Mrs. Johnson wants Peter to clean up his own room every day, and she tells him that he can't go out and play until he cleans his room up and straightens out his toys. But one day Peter's friend Michael comes over and tells Peter that all the kids are leaving right away for a picnic. Peter wants to go, but his room is a big mess. He tells his mother

that he doesn't have time to straighten his room right now, but he'll do it later. She tells him no, that he'll have to stay in and miss the picnic. (p. 174)

Damon asked each child a series of questions about the story: What should Peter do? Why? Was his mother being fair? What if he could sneak out and not get caught? Damon traced the following developmental changes from the children's answers:

First level. The child does not distinguish between what the authority figure demands and what the self desires.

> Child (aged 4 yrs. 2 mos.): (What do you think Peter should do?) Go to the picnic. (Why should he do that?) Because he wants to and all his friends are going. (But what if his mother says "No, Peter, you can't go until you clean up your room first"?) He would do what his mama says. (Why should he do that?) Because he likes to. (What if Peter really wants to go on the picnic and he doesn't want to clean up his room at all because if he does he'll miss the picnic?) His mama will let him go out with his friends. (But what if she won't let him?) He will stay home and play with his sister and clean up all his toys in his toy box. (Why will he do that?) Because he wants to. (p. 182)

Second level. The child recognizes the potential conflict between the authority figure's commands and the self's wishes and obeys in order to avoid trouble. Authority is legitimized by physical attributes (for example, size) of the person in authority.

> Child (aged 4 yrs. 10 mos.): (Who is right [the mother or the son]?) The mother. (How come?) Because she has the right to tell him. (Who has the right?) The mother. (How come?) Because she's a grown-up. (What difference does it make being a grown-up?) Being bigger than another person. (What difference does being bigger make?) You can reach higher for other people's stuff. (Does Peter ever have the right to tell his mother what to do?) No. (Why not?) 'Cause she's a grown-up and he isn't. (p. 185)

> Child (aged 5 yrs. 11 mos.): (Suppose that Peter could sneak out to the picnic, would that be OK?) No. (Why not?) He'd get in trouble. (Why would he get in trouble?) Mothers can punish you. (Suppose that the door was open and his mother was taking a nap and she couldn't find out. Would it be OK then?) If he was going to the picnic and his mother was cleaning, then he should run down the stairs and out the door so that his mother can't see him. (p. 185)

Third level. Obedience is based upon the child's respect for the authority figure's social or physical power, both of which invest the figure with an aura of omnipotence and omniscience.

> Child (aged 5 yrs. 10 mos.): (If Michelle's mother tells her that she has to stay in even after she's cleaned up her room, is that fair?) Yes. (How come?) Whatever mothers tell their kids to do, they have to do. (Why is that?) If you don't you'll get in trouble. (What

if you don't get in trouble; what if you don't get caught?) It's still not right. (Why not?) Because she'll find out. (How will she find out?) She'll ask her friends to tell her, or she would find out anyway she could find out. (Well, let's pretend she just never does find out, what then?) You don't get in trouble. (Is it OK then not to do what your mommy says?) No. (Why not?) 'Cause you're not supposed to. (Why aren't you supposed to?) Because your father would punish you even if your mommy didn't. (p. 189)

Fourth level.   Obedience is based on an exchange: The child obeys because the authority figure has done things for the child in the past. Authority is legitimized in the eyes of the child by the figure's superior qualities.

Child (aged 7 yrs. 1 mo.): (What should Peter do?) He should miss the picnic. (How come?) Because if his mother told him to do something he should do it. (Why?) Because if you were sick and asked her for a glass of water she would do it for you. But if you won't do something for her she won't do it for you. (p. 191)

Child (8 yrs. 8 mos.): Well, after all she's done for him, it just doesn't seem fair that he wouldn't do what she says. (p. 192)

Fifth level.   Authority is understood as a relation between fundamentally equal persons who have equal rights but who have different amounts of training and experience. Authority is legitimized by the figure's specific ability to lead or command.

Child (8 yrs. 5 mos.) (Why does Peter's mother have the right to tell him what to do?) 'Cause she knows what's best for him. (Why is that?) Because she's had experience and everything. (Suppose it's something that Peter knows more about than his mother, like camping, should he give the orders then?) No, but he could suggest and tell her what's right to do. (Does she have to do what he says?) No, but she should listen. (How come he can only suggest and she can order?) 'Cause she's bigger, first of all, and just because she's bigger she knows more and everything, and she might know something about camping. (p. 194)

Child (9 yrs. 5 mos.) (Does Peter's mother have the right to tell Peter not to go out just because she's cranky?) No, she doesn't have that right, because she's promised him and she can't break that promise. (What should Peter do?) Obey his mother. So he won't get in trouble. (What if he knows he won't get caught? Then is it okay if he sneaks out and plays with his friends?) Yes, because if she said something like that the other day and then she breaks the promise, he can do that because she already made the promise. (But the first thing you said was that he should obey his mother.) Well, if he's afraid he'll get in trouble and he doesn't want to, he'll stay home. But he doesn't have to, 'cause she already told him he can go out. . . . (p. 195)

Sixth level.   Authority is viewed as a shared, consensual relation between parties that is adopted temporarily by one person for the welfare of all. Obedience is situation-specific rather than a general response to a superior person.

> Child (9 yrs. 1 mo.) (Why does Peter have to listen to his mother?) Because she knows what's best for him. (Is that why she's telling him to clean his room?) Well, she knows its best for him to learn to do stuff like that. (How does she know that?) 'Cause she's a mother and has learned a lot about how to raise kids. (What if it were something she didn't know about? Like, suppose the whole family went on a camping trip, and nobody knew about camping, nobody had gone camping before, except Peter?) Then they should all listen to Peter and he should tell them what to do. If he knows the most about camping. (Why should they?) He knows what to do, he should lead the way, and his mother and father better listen. (p. 198)

The level of children's thinking about authority and obedience was closely associated with their age, although (as may be seen from the examples) age was not a perfect index of level of functioning. Does the correlation with age mean that individual children move from level to level as they grow older? Probably, but it is also possible that certain social or cultural conditions made more of an impact on some of these age groups than on others—the cohort effect discussed previously. To make sure, Damon retested a group of children after a one-year interval. He found frequent upward changes in the children's thinking during the year and almost no downward changes. Thus, Damon has shown that there is a true developmental progression, and that between the ages of four and ten most children (at least in the cultural groups represented in his study) may be expected to develop increasingly mature attitudes toward authority. We must not take the ages shown in the examples too literally, however. Many researchers have shown that children's behavior in real-life situations employs more sophisticated reasoning than they are likely to display when talking with an unfamiliar adult about a hypothetical event. Sometimes, on the other hand, they employ *less* sophisticated reasoning in real-life situations if their self-interest is involved. Damon's findings, therefore, may not reflect accurately the age at which the various levels are reached in children's real-life relationships. Certainly, individual children differ in rate of progress through the levels. In addition, we cannot assume that children who accept the legitimacy of parental authority will necessarily obey the authority figure. Frequently, children accept parents' right to make certain demands and know that they *ought* to obey, but conflicting pressures and urgent immediate desires stand in the way of obedience. Finally, Damon's analysis focuses on the intellectual aspects of children's acceptance of parental authority.

No doubt, strong emotions such as love and respect or fear and anger have an important influence on the outcome of real-life situations where authority is at issue. These matters will be taken up more fully in Chapters 9 and 10.

What is a lie?

As we saw in analyzing Kohlberg's levels of moral thought, maintaining mutual trust is an issue of concern for children at the conventional level of morality. But before children can understand the subtler distinctions that govern mature trustworthiness, they must learn the meaning of truth telling and promises. Adults understand that telling the truth and keeping promises are necessary to maintain trust, but that this principle must be interpreted flexibly. For example, most adults recognize the difference between a white lie, which is told to save face or to avoid hurting another person, and a malicious lie, which is told to damage or manipulate the other person. And many adults will excuse a broken promise if the promise was exacted under duress.

Piaget was one of the first to ask what telling a lie means to a young child. He reported that children under about age eight believe that a lie is equivalent to a misstatement of fact. The farther the statement is from the objective truth, the bigger the lie. Thus, if two people are asked to estimate someone's age, and one person guesses thirty-eight and the other twenty-eight, while the true age is thirty, the young child would assert that both had lied and that the first person had told a worse lie. Piaget presented children with pairs of stories about children who had said something that was not true and asked them to say which child had told the worse lie. Here is one pair of Piaget's stories:

> A. A little boy (or a little girl) goes for a walk in the street and meets a big dog which frightens him very much. So then he goes home and tells his mother he has seen a dog that was as big as a cow.
>
> B. A child comes home from school and tells his mother that the teacher had given him good marks, but it was not true. The teacher had given him no marks at all, either good or bad. Then his mother was very pleased and rewarded him. (1965, p. 148)

Piaget found that younger children (those below about eight) did not take the intent of the teller into account, and, strangely, considered the lie worse if it was not believed. Here are the answers of a six-year-old to the stories:

> (Which of these two children is naughtiest?) The little girl who said she saw a dog as big as a cow. (Why is she the naughtiest?) Because it could never happen. (Did her mother believe her?) No, because they never

are. (Why did she say that?) To exaggerate. (And why did the other one tell a lie?) Because she wanted to make people believe that she had a good report. (Did her mother believe her?) Yes. (Which one would you punish most if you were the mother?) The one with the dog, because she told the worst lies and was the naughtiest. (pp. 150–51)

A seven-year-old says:

> The naughtiest is the one who saw a dog as big as a cow. It is naughtier because his mother knew [that it was false or impossible]; whereas the other one, the mother didn't know. If you say something that mother doesn't know, it is less naughty, because his mother might believe. If the mother knows it isn't true, then it's a bigger lie. (p. 152)

Some children went so far as to say that if the mother punished the child, that automatically meant that the child had told a big lie!

According to Piaget, after the age of seven or eight, a turnabout takes place in the children's evaluation of the intent and consequences of lying. For example, a child of ten says the naughtiest child is the one:

> . . . who deceived his mother by saying that the teacher was pleased. (Why is he the naughtiest?) Because the mother knows quite well that there aren't any dogs as big as cows. But she believed the child who said the teacher was pleased. (Why did the child say the dog was as big as a cow?) To make them believe it. As a joke. (And why did the other one say that the teacher was pleased?) Because he had done his work badly. (Was that a joke?) No, it was a lie. (pp. 157–58)

To the older children, then, a lie is worse if it is deliberately intended to deceive. And it is worse if it *does* deceive.

Lickona (1976) studied American first graders' evaluations of lies. He found that, unlike Piaget's subjects, most of the American children did take intent into account. Thus, the children thought that a boy who tried to get out of shoveling snow by telling his father he had a headache was naughtier than a boy who said the snow reached over his head when it actually reached only to his knees. However, the six-year-olds had more difficulty when they were asked to compare an intentional misstatement that has benign consequences (for example, a boy unsuccessfully tries to trick his sister by telling her the wrong time) with an unintentional misstatement that does some damage (for example, a boy accidentally tells his brother the wrong time, and the brother misses the bus). Faced with this kind of choice, younger children chose these alternatives with equal frequency (much as the Swiss children had done); older children weighted intentions more heavily. Thus, while young children are not insensitive to the moral meaning of intentional lies, they are highly sensitive to the amount of damage that results from their actions, whether the actions are intentional or not. Younger children believe that accidental damage is *wrong* in the same sense that lying is wrong, while older children distinguish between accidental injuries for which the doer has no moral responsibility and injuries that are deliberate. Indeed, older children understand that it is the intention to injure that is wrong and that the success or failure of the action is irrelevant.

Lickona's findings thus support Piaget's view that making judgments solely on the basis of intent is a more difficult task (and hence presumably one that comes later developmentally) than making judgments on the basis of consequences. Nevertheless, children of all ages cannot be indifferent to the consequences of their actions, including their verbal actions. However, younger children focus their attention on the objective consequences of a misstatement (for example, getting a reward that should have been withheld), while older children consider the impact of falsehoods on the maintenance of mutual trust in their relationships.

What is a promise?

A parallel evolution takes place in the child's understanding of the meaning and value of promises. Robert Selman (1976) presented children with dilemmas involving promises. One story concerned a little girl, Holly, who was the best tree-climber in her neighborhood. One day she fell from a lower branch, and although she did not really hurt herself, her father saw the accident and was worried that she might get hurt. He asked her to promise not to climb trees any more. Holly promised. Later that day a friend asked her to climb a tree to get a kitten that was stuck in the high branches. The kitten couldn't get down and might die unless rescued. Holly was the only person in the neighborhood who could climb well enough to get the kitten. But she remembered her promise to her father. After telling children this story, Selman would ask what she should do. One six-year-old girl answered as follows:

> (What do you think Holly will do—save the kitten, or keep her promise?) She will save the kitten because she doesn't want the kitten to die. (How will her father feel when he finds out?) Happy, he likes kittens. (What would you do if you were Holly?) Save the kitten so it won't get hurt. (What if her father punishes her if she gets the kitten down?) Then she will leave it up there. (Why?) She doesn't want to get in trouble. (How will she feel?) Good, she listened to her father. (p. 303)

At this age, the child does not experience genuine conflict because she cannot simultaneously keep in mind two conflicting values: maintaining the father's trust and getting the kitten. She answers on a purely hedonistic basis: how best to stay out of trouble. Older children do experience conflict. They want to save the kitten, but they also recognize that they have an obligation to keep their promise and that the father would expect them to do so. They often solve the dilemma by counting on the father's ability to see their point of view: They believe they would not be punished (or would be punished lightly) because the father will understand that this was an exceptional situation, one in which disobedience can be justified. Thus, they expect to be absolved from the promise. Older children are concerned about the consequences of breaking a promise—that is, what it would mean if the father could no longer trust them.

COGNITIVE PROCESSES UNDERLYING DEVELOPMENTAL CHANGE IN MORAL JUDGMENTS

How do these developmental changes in children's moral thinking come about? What processes control them? One tempting view would be that children are simply gradually learning the adult system of values and that they learn because they are being taught. If, for example, all societies scold and punish their children for stealing from members of the social group, we should not be surprised if the children gradually come to understand what stealing means and that stealing is wrong. Older children might hold this belief more strongly and behave more consistently than younger children because they have had more experience with the unpleasant consequences of stealing. However, this explanation is too facile and does not cover all the facts. Developmental change in moral thought is not merely an intensification of belief in the values being advocated by adults. The change takes place in children's ideas about the *basis* for avoiding wrongdoing. When they are quite young, they simply believe that they should not misbehave because they will be caught and punished. As they grow older, they shift from this concern with external consequences to an internalization of social rules and contracts—an acceptance of the obligation to be bound by such contracts without external pressure. What explains this change? It does not seem to be produced by adults teaching children new concepts as the children grow older: Rather, the cognitive developmental theorist maintains that the parents' teaching remains fairly constant as the child grows, but that what the child learns does not. The motor that drives the growth of moral thought is the process of cognitive development itself. Older children are capable of a different sort of inference about social relationships than younger children are. Even if adults preach the same moral doctrine to children of all ages, children of different levels of cognitive maturity derive different messages from an encounter with an adult teacher.

We now consider the evidence for the cognitive-developmentalist's position.

The role of general cognitive development

Children's thinking about moral issues changes with age. So do general mental abilities. The fact that the two kinds of growth occur concurrently does not prove that one depends in any way on the other. Many things change with age, including stature and number of teeth. Clearly, only selected aspects of development are functionally related to changing conceptions of morality. How can we determine whether certain mental achievements permit the progress of moral thinking to occur? A common approach is to study a group of same-age children who differ in the mental abilities that may be relevant. Holding age constant permits us to rule out factors such as physical growth that change with age but are not relevant to the study of moral judgments. The most common way to study the effects of intellectual level, while holding age constant, is to use intelligence quotient (IQ) scores, since this score describes a child's intellectual status in comparison with other children of the same chronological age.

There is good evidence that children with higher IQs have more mature levels of moral reasoning. The studies which document this relationship have been summarized elsewhere (Lickona, 1976; Mischel and Mischel, 1976), and the details need not be recapitulated here. It has been suggested that the relationship may be very superficial. For example, children who have good vocabularies and good sentence comprehension (and who therefore obtain high scores on IQ tests) probably understand the experimenter's questions more easily. But high-IQ children bring more than test-taking ability to these tasks. After all, moral judgment is a process of reasoning, and it must call upon some of the same judgmental skills that a child employs in reasoning about other matters.

Kohlberg (1976), Selman (1976), and Damon (1977), among others, have analyzed the particular aspects of intellectual competence that ought to affect moral judgments. Drawing upon Piaget's analysis of the development of cognitive processes, they have looked at the utilization of these processes in moral reasoning. Damon, in particular, draws attention to children's skills in classifying and grouping and their understanding of the way in which the change in one dimension compensates for a change in another dimension (revealed in Piaget's classic conservation tasks). He argues that these cognitive skills ought to help children to balance competing justice claims and also to understand the notion of *reciprocity* ("I help her because she helps me"). He has been able to show some modest relationships between the Piagetian levels and levels of moral judgment.

Clearly, however, many people who are above average in intelligence do not think in mature ways when presented with moral dilemmas. Interestingly, the reverse is seldom true: If an individual's moral reasoning is mature, the individual is almost certain to be advanced on tests of cognitive level (Kohlberg and DeVries, 1969; Kuhn, Langer, and Kohlberg, in preparation). Thus, well-developed intelligence seems to be a necessary but not sufficient condition for mature moral reasoning. In addition to intelligence, what moves an individual from the early stages of egocentric reasoning about justice to more advanced levels? The word *egocentric* is the key. According to the cognitive-developmental theorists, the morally advanced individual must be able to take the perspective of other persons.

The role of perspective taking [4]

A child's progress through the developmental levels of moral judgment requires an increasingly sophisticated understanding of other people's wants and needs. In Chapter 7 we noted that a mature self-concept requires the ability to stand off and look at the self objectively, as the self would be seen by others. Objective self-assessment is also necessary in making moral judgments. For example, adequate functioning at Kohlberg's stage 3 (the child is anxious to be seen as a good, well-intentioned person) requires a fairly clear conception of what will be regarded by others as good behavior.

While we have chosen to discuss perspective taking in connection with moral development, the process has implications for many aspects of social development discussed in earlier chapters. We saw in Chapter 2, for example, that the nature of the child's attachment changes when he or she becomes able to conceive of the caretaker as a separate person who has her or his own feelings and motives. Similarly, the nature of aggression changes qualitatively when children learn how to judge the intent of another person's hurtful action and how to get revenge on their opponents (action that requires understanding of what other people value). And even more basic to all aspects of social behavior is the role of perspective taking in facilitating children's ability to communicate effectively and to cooperate with others. Both of these activities depend on an assessment of what other people already know and what they need to know about the task or situation at hand.

---

[4] Many writers use the term *role taking* for the processes to be discussed in this section. I have chosen to use *perspective taking* because it is more general. *Role* refers to a position in a social structure (see Chapter 6). Children may be able to understand another's perspective without knowing anything about the person's role. They may have a very good idea of what a person who is sitting in a different position sees, even if it is hidden from their own view. Their understanding does not depend on whether the other person is an adult or a child, an employer or an employee. Thus, their understanding is based on taking the other person's perspective, not the other person's role; on the other hand, some perspective taking does involve understanding others' roles.

Seeing things as others see them

Piaget was the pioneer in focusing attention on developmental changes in children's ability to take the perspective of other people. In one of his best-known experiments a child was seated at a table on which a three-dimensional model of a Swiss landscape had been placed. The child's task was to determine how the scene would look to someone seated at a different side of the table than the child's own. Piaget tested the children in several ways. One procedure required the children to look at pictures of the scene taken from the four different sides of the table and to pick out pictures that showed how the scene looked from their own position and from the positions of dolls seated to the right, the left, and on the opposite side of the table. He found that the youngest children tested (ages four to six) did not seem to understand that there *were* perspectives different from their own. Children of six or seven were aware that different perspectives existed but had very poor ability to understand just what another person might be seeing. After this age, the ability to describe other people's perspectives gradually developed.

As we noted in Chapter 7, Flavell's work has shown that even children as young as three are aware that perspectives can differ. They understand that closing their own eyes has no effect on other people's ability to see. So rudimentary knowledge about the way the world looks to other people is present earlier than Piaget thought.

Understanding things as others understand them

Studies by Flavell on the development of communication skills as they involve knowledge of others' viewpoints have confirmed Piaget's idea that there is a fairly uniform developmental progression in perspective taking. Flavell asked children to explain such things as the rules of a game to various listeners. He wanted to see whether his young subjects would take listener characteristics into account in their explanations. One ingenious procedure contrasted the child's explanation to a person who was blindfolded with his or her explanation to a sighted listener. The game included many visual elements (for example, a cube with different-colored faces, colored counters, and a playing board with squares that matched the colors on the cube). As might be expected, the youngest children were less skillful in explaining the game, regardless of whether their listener was blindfolded. Often, for example, they would describe how to roll the cube without explaining the relationship between the throw and the movement of the counters on the board. More important for our present purposes is the fact that the youngest children (second-graders) seldom took account of whether their listeners could see. For example, they might say to a blindfolded listener: "You have to go to the closest color on your side," or "Shake the block in the glass and whatever color it is . . . ." without realizing that their blindfolded listener could not detect colors. They also used gestures: "You put *this* red one *there* (pointing)." Older children, by contrast, might guide a blindfolded listener's hand to the correct object and place. Older children seldom said "this" or "there" to a blindfolded listener, and they used more detailed verbal descriptions when gestures could not amplify meaning. By the mid-high-school years subjects were equally competent in giving information to blindfolded and sighted listeners.

Flavell varied listener status in other ways. One method was to ask children to communicate to a listener much younger than themselves. Another approach varied the amount of information the listener had about a joint task. He found that younger children tended to assume that their listeners knew everything about a situation that they themselves knew. Older children understood when their listeners did not have access to certain necessary pieces of information and would adjust their communications accordingly. These findings suggest that while second-graders have begun to understand that others have perspectives different from their own, an enormous improvement takes place between the ages of seven and sixteen in the ability to appreciate the implications of these differences and to use this knowledge in communication. Young children have to learn to consider another person's perspective when trying to explain something to a listener; they often have difficulty *maintaining* this stance and easily slip back into an egocentric perspective. Of course, keeping another's perspective in mind is not enough. This information must be used to construct a message that is well adapted to the listener's point of view—a process that takes considerable skill. These skills undergo major improvement in the middle-childhood years, with improvement being much greater for some children than others.

Experiencing things as others experience them

Selman (1976) has used his Holly and the kitten story and other moral dilemmas to study a different aspect of age changes in perspective taking: namely, children's understanding of other people's *personalities*—their desires, feelings, expectations, probable reactions, and probable social judgments. Working with children ranging from preschool age to adolescence, he has distinguished the following levels of perspective taking:

> *Stage 0: Egocentric role taking* (about ages four to six). The child knows that other people are different from the self and that others can think and feel. But the child assumes that others have

thoughts and feelings more or less identical to the child's own. Thus, in responding to the story of Holly, a child who concentrates on getting the kitten down from the tree is likely to assume that the father is thinking about this too. Although children of this age can distinguish between happiness and sadness and understand the various emotions that other people display, they have difficulty tracing the *reasons* for another person's feelings when these feelings are different from their own. In other words, four- to six-year-olds have very little understanding of other people's motives. They react mainly to the external cues and do not make inferences about other people's thinking.

Stage 1: Social information role taking (about ages six to eight). The child now recognizes that two different actors may have different interpretations of the same social situation. However, the child has great difficulty in simultaneously maintaining both perspectives. A child may focus on Holly's desire to get the kitten down or on her father's expectation that she will keep her promise. The conflict between the two is not salient and may not be perceived. Children at this level have begun to think about intent. They can distinguish between intentional and unintentional actions, and they know that other people also make these distinctions.

Stage 2: Self-reflective role taking (about ages eight to ten). Realizing that other people have their own values and purposes, and that these are quite often different from the child's own, the child is for the first time a relativist. Children at this level understand that their own perspectives are not necessarily the only right or valid ones, that others are making judgments of the self's behavior and motives, and that the self is being judged in the same terms that the self judges others. Thus, the child begins to think about the conclusions others may come to when they observe and interpret the child's actions.

Stage 3: Mutual role taking (about ages ten to twelve). The child now not only takes the other's perspective but also can understand that the other can take the self's point of view. Responding to the Kohlberg story about Heinz and the stolen drugs, when asked how the judge will react, the child may say that the judge knows it is wrong for Heinz to steal but, on hearing Heinz's side of the story, will understand his motive and mitigate the sentence. Children at this level also believe that the judge will understand Heinz's self-reflection, will know that Heinz was doing what he thought was right. Thus, they understand that each member of an interacting pair is aware of the self-reflection process in the other.

Stage 4: Social and conventional system role taking (about ages twelve to fifteen and older). The adolescent is able to go beyond individual perspectives and take a third perspective: that of society. An example of this kind of thinking, taken from an answer to the dilemma of Heinz, is as follows:

> (What do you think the judge would do in Heinz's case?) I'm afraid he'd have to convict him. When Heinz stole the drug, he knew it was wrong from society's point of view. He also knew that if he were caught, he'd be convicted because he'd realize the judge would have to uphold the law. (Why?) The judge has to think about the way it would look to everybody else. If they see Heinz getting no punishment, they might think they can get away with stealing. Heinz should realize this and take some form of punishment. (Would the judge think Heinz was right or wrong to do what he did?) The judge is not supposed to be a philosopher. Even if the judge thought Heinz was morally right, from the legal point of view the judge has to consider the law of the people. (Selman, p. 307)

The changing levels of perspective taking imply that children of different levels will have very different understandings of the same moral injunction. For example, young children may misconstrue the Golden Rule thinking that it means: "Do unto others what they do unto you" and use it to justify hitting back if they have been hit. A few years later, children understand that the Golden Rule means putting one's self in the place of the other and imagining what the other would want. Later still, the child or young adult will think of both parties putting themselves in the other's place—understanding that the Golden Rule can operate mutually, reciprocally.

Before we accept Selman's account fully, we must consider the fact that his levels are based on an analysis of children's responses to questions. Children know many things that they cannot verbalize in an interview. Simplifying the kinds of indicators we look for, so that children can show us what they know in actions rather than words, might enable us to detect signs of perspective taking at a much younger age than Selman's results would imply. Rubin and Pepler (1980) have reviewed both their own and others' work on children's play with this question in mind, and they do find such signs. For example, they present Garvey's (1976) case of a pair of preschool children who were playing that one of the children (Child A) was sick. Child B took up a toy telephone and pretended to call the doctor. Child A pretended to answer the phone. Child B protested "No, you're not the doctor, you're sick." Such an incident certainly implies that a four-year-old is capable of understanding the role expectations that impinge on another person. Some startling observations even suggest that children as young as two have some perspective-taking ability. Hoffman (1976) gives an example:

> Marcy, aged twenty months, was in the playroom of her home and wanted a toy that her sister Sara was playing with. She asked Sara for it,

but Sara refused vehemently. Marcy then paused, as if reflecting on what to do, and then began rocking Sara's favorite rocking horse (which Sara never allowed anyone to touch) yelling "Nice horsey! Nice horsey!" and keeping her eyes on Sara all the time. Sara came running angrily, whereupon Marcy immediately ran around Sara directly to the toy and grabbed it. (p. 129)

A child of two must have a very limited grasp of others' motivations, and yet Marcy's actions do indicate at least a rudimentary awareness of at least one of her sister's characteristics. Some potential for perspective taking must therefore be present. Laboratory tests of role taking that call for very simple responses from children (Flavell, 1968; Liben, 1978) also reveal potential in children of preschool age or younger. On the basis of evidence of this kind, Rubin and Pepler conclude that while Selman is quite right about the nature of the developmental changes that occur—his description of successive levels is accurate—the ages that he attaches to each level are conservative. In fact, each level is anticipated in children's behavior (at least occasionally) by as much as several years. An exact age range cannot be associated with each level; a given child's functioning will fluctuate a great deal from one occasion to another. Thus, children do not always perform at the level of their most advanced insights, but their most complex level of functioning does advance with age.

Different aspects of perspective taking also develop at different rates. For example, a child who can take another's perspective for a moment may fail to do so if the task requires maintaining the other's perspective for a longer period. And a child who understands the perspective of familiar people in familiar situations may be much less skillful when the person or situation is unfamiliar. Nevertheless, inferences are made from familiar situations so that the child comes to understand, for example, that strangers also have motives, make inferences about the child's self, and so forth.

Perspective taking and moral judgments: implications for child rearing

Selman (1971, 1976) also studied how the growing ability to take the perspective of others affects morality, and he has found that it does make a difference in the child's ability to make mature moral judgments. In a group of children of the same age and level of general intelligence, the children who had reached the higher levels of perspective taking on his scale were more likely to have reached the higher levels of moral reasoning when discussing Kohlberg's dilemmas. But the relationship is one sided: While individuals at the postconventional level of morality are almost all skillful perspective takers, individuals with excellent perspective taking abilities are not necessarily highly moral. In other words, knowing what other people want, feel and believe is not enough to make individuals believe that they *ought* to behave in considerate, prosocial ways. But without such knowledge an individual cannot develop a mature understanding of mutual rights and obligations.

It follows that if parents can foster children's perspective-taking skills, they will have helped the children along the road to moral maturity. They will not have guaranteed the children's progress in this respect, but they will have provided one of the necessary ingredients. Of course, children can learn a great deal about perspective taking without being deliberately taught. But we may ask, nevertheless, what kinds of parenting behavior are related to children's acquisition of perspective-taking abilities.

With this question in mind Bearison and Cassel (1975) investigated the kinds of discussions parents have with their children when disciplinary issues arise and the relationship of these discussions to the children's perspective-taking ability in a communication game. Mothers of first-graders were questioned about typical disciplinary situations:

> Suppose you thought it was time for Judy to go to bed but she started to cry because she wanted to watch something on TV? What would you say to Judy?

> Imagine that one day Frank says that he doesn't want to go to school. He's not sick or anything, but he just doesn't want to go. What would you say to Frank to get him to go to school? (p. 31)

The name of the mother's own first-grade child was used in each question. Her answers were analyzed to determine whether she engaged in *person-oriented* or *position-oriented* discussions with the child.[5] Person-oriented appeals were defined as regulatory statements which express the feelings, thoughts, needs, and/or intentions of either the mother, the child, or a third person who is affected by the child's behavior (e.g., the teacher). An example would be "If you stay home, later on today you'll be sorry, because you'll miss your friends and you'll sit here wondering what's going on in class," or: "Your dad will be disappointed in you." Position-oriented appeals referred to rules, e.g., "Eight-thirty is your bedtime"; or "All children have to go to school."

In a separate session, each child was tested for the ability to take the perspective of another person, using the Flavell (1968) task, in which the child is asked to explain the rules of a game to a blindfolded person. Bearison and Cassel found that children whose mothers used person-oriented appeals were more skillful in adjusting their com-

---

[5] This distinction comes from the work of Bernstein (1972).

munication style to the state of the listener. Thus, there is evidence that when parents frequently call attention to and explain other people's perspectives, children learn to be sensitive to these perspectives. On the basis of Selman's work, we can infer that children with person-oriented mothers would be more advanced than their peers in ability to make moral judgments.

Further questions

Rousseau thought that reasoning with young children about moral questions was useless. In *Emile* he invented an imaginary dialogue to illustrate the futility of such an approach:

Master: You must not do that.
Child: Why not?
Master: Because it is wrong.
Child: Wrong! What is wrong?
Master: What is forbidden you.
Child: Why is it wrong to do what is forbidden?
Master: You will be punished for disobedience.
Child: I will do it when no one is looking.
Master: We shall watch you.
Child: I will hide.
Master: We shall ask you what you were doing.
Child: I shall tell a lie.
Master: You must not tell lies.
Child: Why must I not tell lies?
Master: Because it is wrong, etc. (1763, p. 54)

Nowadays, we would question the nature of the "reasoning" being used here. The adult was presenting a rationale based on what Kohlberg would call a punishment-and-obedience orientation, and this, as we have seen, is an immature orientation. Also from Bearison and Cassel's standpoint the adult is using a position-oriented rather than person-oriented argument. Thus, the adult is not helping the child build perspective-taking skills—skills that are needed for advancing to more mature levels of moral reasoning.

Yet we must not dismiss Rousseau's position too quickly. He was saying that young children cannot understand the moral reasoning of adults because they have not yet accumulated the necessary real-life experience. Without this experience, adult reasoning falls on deaf ears because children learn only what they are advanced enough to understand. In this respect Rousseau's view is fully consistent with the basic premises of present-day cognitive-developmental theory.

The proponents of cognitive-developmental theory have succeeded in establishing certain facts that support Rousseau's point: (1) young children do not think about matters of justice and right and wrong in the same way older people do and (2) individual children progress along a predictable path from one level of thought to another as they grow older. Some theorists argue for distinct stages, believing that a rather fundamental reorganization of moral thought takes place at several points in development. Other theorists think that the changes are more gradual. Since individual children of a given age often use different levels of reasoning in different situations, it seems unlikely that the stages have sharp boundaries. The upward progression exists nonetheless and we can take it as established that mature moral thinking is different from immature moral thought and that young children are *incapable* of mature moral thought.

The efforts to understand why and how these developmental progressions take place have raised some puzzling questions. We have seen that the age changes in moral thinking are linked to general cognitive development and depend to some extent on the growth of children's perspective-taking abilities. Yet moral thinking often lags behind the other cognitive capacities. And many people who have highly developed problem-solving and perspective-taking skills never reach a level of principled morality. Cognitive developmental theory does not give us much insight into the reasons for this discrepancy. The theory does not account for clever, amoral people—individuals who clearly understand the effect of their actions on others and who nevertheless heartlessly exploit them. Such individuals may know quite well how their actions may be judged by others, and they may go to great lengths to manipulate others' judgment of their actions. While they may create a socially acceptable (and false) facade, underneath it all their self-accepted morality is preconventional: They are trying to get the most they can for themselves while managing to avoid punishment. Their answers to moral judgment questions derive from this immature perspective and have the theme: "I know the rules of social behavior, but I'll only conform if it's to my own advantage." Such people are markedly different from individuals who take other people's needs and rights into account in guiding their own behavior. The difference must lie, at least in part, in the realm of feeling. Morally mature people have learned to *care* about others' welfare, as well as to *know* about their welfare. Cognitive-developmental theory is a "cold" theory, in that it gives relatively little attention to the strong emotions that influence moral responsibility in both its mental and behavioral aspects.

So far, we have been considering the development of moral thought, and the factors that influence the rate of this development. But this is only half of the story of moral development in children. We also need to consider moral *behavior*. Many questions come to mind: Do developmental changes in moral behavior parallel changes in moral thinking? What factors influence children's ability to resist the temptation to do something they know is wrong? Under what conditions will a child sacrifice personal gain in order to give aid or comfort to someone else? We will consider these questions in the next chapter. In so doing, we will be concerned with the *moral emotions*—fear, guilt, and love—and we will approach moral development from a theoretical perspective very different from the one highlighted so far. Moral behavior, like other behavior, has been studied from the standpoint of both behaviorism and psychodynamic theory. Researchers influenced by the former have emphasized experimental studies of human learning, while those influenced by the latter viewpoint have stressed moral emotions, particularly the importance of early relationships within the family in producing the developmental shift from external to internal systems of control. These two perspectives will therefore loom large in the next chapter.

SUMMARY AND COMMENTARY

All societies have moral rules that individual members are expected to obey. But the child's task in learning to be moral is not merely one of learning what the rules are and conforming to them. Children—or at least, a majority of children in any society—must accept the rules and regulate their own behavior in accordance with them.

Very young children are neither moral nor immoral; they understand neither conflicting claims of several people nor the basis on which a just balance can be reached. Legal systems take this fact into account when they insist that a child must be old enough to know right from wrong before the child's actions can be subject to legal sanctions. But morality is not achieved all at once or at some fixed age of reason:

1. The acquisition of moral understanding is a gradual process that takes a predictable developmental course. Age changes in moral thought are similar in children from different societies.

2. Children's views about what is fair or just move from the hedonistic stance of the preschooler—"what is fair is what I want"—to an advocacy of simple equality for all, to a more complex balancing of claims based on what each person deserves.

3. Concepts of right and wrong also show an upward progression. Young children are oriented toward external authority. They believe that authority defines what is right and that obedience is a value in its own right. When asked about their behavior, young children say that one should obey to avoid punishment. Later, virtuous behavior is viewed as a bargaining chip, enabling the individual to exchange favors with

other self-interested persons. Most children move on to acceptance of society's rules as part of their own values and to conformity with these rules in order to keep the approval of people they admire. From their point of view law and order are necessary for a smoothly functioning society and the authority figures have the *right* to punish infractions. As some children approach adulthood, they move on to a level of principled morality in which social contracts and individual rights are understood.

4. Maintaining mutual trust becomes important to most children in middle childhood, at which point their understanding of the reasons for avoiding lies and keeping promises is considerably sharpened.

Individual children of any given age differ in the level of maturity of their moral thinking. Several factors have been shown to be associated with the extent of their progress:

5. High achievement on tests of general intelligence and on measures of Piagetian cognitive stages are associated on the average with more mature levels of moral thought.

6. Children who are skillful in taking the perspective of others—in understanding what others see, what others know, and how others react to their actions—tend to be advanced in moral thought, compared to other children of the same age.

7. Both intelligence and perspective-taking ability appear to be necessary but not sufficient conditions for the development of high levels of moral thought. Almost all people who reach the higher levels of moral thought are intelligent and good perspective takers. However, not all individuals who are intelligent or who have a good understanding of other people's perspectives have mature levels of moral understanding.

Parents play a role in determining how skillful a child will be at taking the perspective of others.

8. In discussing with children the reasons why they must do what is expected of them, some parents simply state rules (for example, "Children have to go to bed earlier than grownups"). Other parents stress the effects of the child's behavior on other people or on the child's relation to other children (for example, "How could your teacher manage the class if the children all came to school at different times?"). Children whose parents use the latter type of reasoning tend to have advanced perspective-taking skills. We may assume then that the person-oriented approach helps equip children with some of the reasoning skills necessary for mature moral thought.

Moral Development II:

Moral Emotions

and Moral Behavior

MORALITY is fundamentally a matter of respecting the rights of others. We have traced the ways in which children come to understand what others' rights are and how competing rights are balanced and negotiated. But knowing the principles of right and wrong is not enough. The moral individual must also feel *obligated to respect others' rights*—must avoid doing things that hurt others and must do things that will promote others' welfare or relieve their distress.

Clearly children who are too young to have internalized moral values or to monitor their own conformity to standards can nevertheless learn to avoid injuring others. Through human history punishment has probably been the principal means of controlling young children's mischievous or hurtful impulses. But punishment is only partially effective. Children do not always remember why they have been punished, nor can they always inhibit their actions out of fear of punishment. More important, being controlled by fear of punishment represents an immature stage of morality. A popular theory of moral development suggests that children move from fear of punishment by others to fear of punishment by the self. They develop a conscience or "inner voice" that tells them that they have done wrong; the emotion they then feel is *guilt* rather than fear. We need to consider whether this assumed transition is a real one, and if so, how it comes about.

The first part of this chapter deals with the avoidance issues, considering the role of both punishment and guilt in the inhibition of forbidden actions. The second part of the chapter deals with prosocial or altruistic behavior and the conditions that foster its development. For just as young children can learn to avoid wrongdoing, so can they also learn to help others, share with them, and offer them comfort. We will draw in both sections on a body of research with theoretical perspectives very different from the cognitive-developmental view. The work on guilt has grown primarily out of psychoanalytic theory and reflects the Freudian emphasis on the intense emotional relationship between the child and significant others in the child's early life. Most of the research on avoidance of forbidden actions (resistance to temptation) and altruism is the work of social learning theorists. A major assumption underlying their work is that moral behavior is learned in the same way as any other behavior: (1) through experiencing the consequences of one's own actions and (2) by observing what other people do and what consequences *their* actions provoke. Unlike the cognitive theorists, social learning theorists make no assumptions about regular developmental progressions or sets of steps that must be taken in any particular order; however, they do expect to find evidence of cumulative effects if consistent training continues over long periods of time. As we discuss the effects of punishment and reward, however, and the example set by models, we will note at several points that these effects change as children mature cognitively and develop the ability to interpret external events in terms of their developing sense of self and their growing understanding of moral concepts. In the final section of the chapter we address the question of how moral actions and feelings are related to the stages of moral judgment outlined in the preceding chapter.

INHIBITION OF FORBIDDEN ACTS

As we have seen, a hallmark of moral development in children is the achievement of control over their own behavior in situations where no outside agent is present to enforce the rules. Cultures vary in the freedom they permit young children. In some cultures children are almost never unsupervised, while in others children spend most of their time with playmates, and adults are rarely present. However, children in every culture have at least occasional opportunities to engage in forbidden but desired activities. In Western society, for example, children may be tempted to sneak a piece of candy before dinner, cheat on a test, watch a forbidden television program, push or pinch a sibling, and so forth. What determines whether a child will be able to resist the temptation to do these things?

The effectiveness of punishment

If a child has been punished for a given action or rewarded for not performing it, the child will frequently refrain from repeating the action even if no controlling person is nearby. (See Johnston, 1972, for a review of the research with human children and adults on punishment and its effects.) A possible explanation for this consistent behavior pattern is that children are not sure whether they will be caught. Children frequently believe that they have privacy but discover later that they have been watched. A little girl who believes she is playing out of her mother's sight may suddenly hear her mother call out a warning from the kitchen window. A boy who has sneaked a bit of candy may be caught with chocolate on his face. So children may come to believe that the punishing agent is somehow omniscient—a belief that has the effect of inhibiting action even when the child is alone.

Even if a child is sure of being unobserved, however, a fairly automatic conditioned fear response may serve to deter a previously punished action. Many years ago Pavlov showed that stimuli that previously did not elicit a response could be made to do so if the stimuli were repeatedly presented at the same time the response was made to occur in some other way. His most famous experiments involved conditioned salivation or paw-lifting in dogs, but his methods proved to have more general applicability. An extensive body of research with human as well as animal subjects has shown that emotional reactions can be conditioned with Pavlovian procedures. Thus, a child who is upset when his or her hand is spanked when reaching for an electric outlet will experience emotional distress (fear) at the sight of the electric outlet on later occasions, even though the child's hand is not being spanked at the time. Indeed the very act of reaching toward the forbidden object will elicit conditioned fear. If simple conditioning is the nature of the process whereby punishment has its effects, then the timing of punishment should make a difference. If punishment is administered at the beginning of an action—before the child actually touches the forbidden object—the fear should be associated with the first steps in a chain of action, and the child should interrupt the action sequence almost before getting started. If punishment follows the completion of the act, however, the fear should be most strongly associated with actions and events that *follow* the punished response. The child would not be expected to inhibit the action but might learn to feel upset afterwards. If these assumptions are correct, early punishment should be a more powerful inhibitor of naughty behavior than late punishment.

A number of experiments were carried out in the 1960s to test this reasoning about the relationship between timing of punishment and resistance to temptation (Aronfreed and Reber, 1965; Walters, Parke, and Cane, 1965). In these studies preschool children were presented with two or more toys and punished when they reached for certain of the more attractive ones. The punishment sometimes consisted of the experimenter saying "No!" sharply and taking some candy out of the child's candy bank (a small pile of candy given the child at the beginning of the experiment) and at other times consisted of the sounding of a loud unpleasant-sounding buzzer. Some children were punished just as they reached for the forbidden toy; others were punished after the toy had been picked up. Subsequently, each child was left alone with the attractive toy for about fifteen minutes with instructions not to touch it. Privacy was insured by having the child lock the door as the experimenter left and unlock it only when the experimenter knocked. The children's behavior with the forbidden toy was consistent with the predictions from simple conditioning theory: Children punished before touching the toy were more able to resist touching it than children who were punished afterwards.

In further experiments some children were given reasons for avoiding the forbidden toy, and this procedure turned up some curious effects. Some of the children were told that the toy was fragile and might break or that the toy belonged to another child who did not want them to touch it. Giving children a rationale for their behavior (without any punishment) proved to be considerably more effective than punishment. However, the combination of punishment *and* reasoning was most effective of all (LaVoie, 1970; Parke and Murray, 1971; both summarized in Parke, 1974). When children had a rationale, the timing of punishment no longer made any difference. This finding, which is of great theoretical interest, suggests that punishment alone results in an automatic conditioning process similar to that established in laboratory studies of animals. But with the introduction of a rationale, simple conditioning is superseded by a process that is closer to what we usually mean by self-control.

The early work on resistance to temptation was carried out almost entirely with preschool children. However, Ross Parke's discovery of the importance of introducing a cognitive rationale suggested that children's resistance to temptation might depend on the level of their cognitive development (and therefore on their age). To test this possibility Parke (1974) included somewhat older children (kindergarteners) in some of his studies and found an age difference in rationale effectiveness (see Figure 9-1). Three-year-olds are quite effectively inhibited from touching by telling them the toy is fragile and might

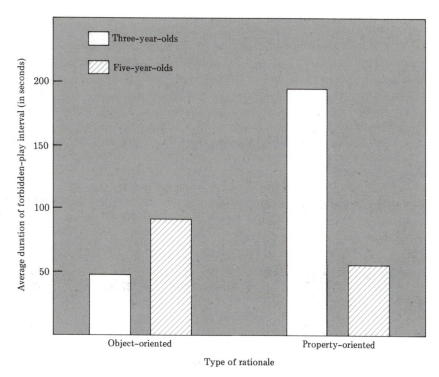

Figure 9-1. Age changes in rationale effectiveness. Note that the younger children's response was inhibited by cautions regarding the fragile object itself, while the older children were more impressed by a rationale based on property rights. (Adapted from Parke, 1974)

break; telling them that the toy belongs to another child has very little effect. Five-year-olds, on the other hand, do respond to appeals based on property rights, indicating that they have come to understand and accept other people's rights to control access to their property.

Studies of resistance to temptation have not generally considered the authority of the person setting up the rules. Yet by the age of about ten children have begun to feel that not all rules—or all authority figures—are equally deserving of obedience (Chapter 8), and older children have undoubtedly begun to question the right of an experimenter to set limits on what they might touch. This failure to take cognitive development into account is another reason why the early, simplistic studies based on animal conditioning do not generalize very widely across successive age groups.

The studies previously described have shown that punishment does influence the likelihood that a young child will resist temptation. However, there is a paradox. Studies of the effects of punishment administered by parents at home have repeatedly shown that parents who use a great deal of physical punishment have children with weak internal controls who have difficulty resisting temptation in a variety of situations. Threats and other forms of power-assertive parental discipline ("You do it because I tell you to, *or else* . . .") also weaken inner controls or hamper their growth. Power-assertive methods of discipline also are associated with delinquency (see Hoffman, 1970, for a review; also MacKinnon, 1938; Maurer, 1974; Bacon, Child, and Barry, 1963). Clearly, while punishment has the immediate effect of suppressing undesired behavior, it often does long-term harm by interfering with the transfer of behavioral control from the adult trainer to the child.

Attributing transgression to the self

We have seen that punishment often has the immediate effect of suppressing behavior that adults have forbidden—presumably by arousing emotions of fear or guilt. These emotions serve as a warning for the child to avoid certain behaviors even when a punishing agent is not present. Richard Dienstbier and his colleagues (1975) have suggested that while emotional distress is a necessary prerequisite for resistance to temptation, it is not enough. They suggest that whether such emotions will lead to self-controlled avoidance of wrongdoing also depends on the child's interpretation of this feeling—on what the child thinks is the *source* of the emotional distress.

Dienstbier had carried out earlier studies with college-age men and women who were given an opportunity to cheat on a vocabulary test. He had reasoned that most people become emotionally upset if they have an opportunity to cheat, and that if they think their emotional upset is due to the fear of cheating, their cheating should be inhibited. If they think their feelings are due to other, unrelated causes, however, their cheating should not be inhibited. He showed that when his college-age subjects thought their upset was due to a vitamin injection given previously, they did cheat considerably more often than students who did not have any such explanation. How the subject interprets emotional arousal thus makes a difference in whether or not the emotional state leads to resistance to temptation.

Dienstbier and his colleagues then carried this reasoning into studies with young children. They compared two conditions: a temptation situation in which children would attribute their emotional arousal to their inner conflict over the forbidden activity itself and a situation in which they would believe they were upset because of the danger of getting caught (an *external* condition). The researchers assumed that a child who is upset over the prospect of carrying out a particular action will handle these feelings by not performing the action, while a child whose fears are based on the possibility of external danger will ask "How can I avoid being caught?" And if the situation is arranged so that the child feels quite sure of not being caught, then emotional excitement (due to previous experiences with temptation) will die out rather quickly and the child will not need to resist temptation in order to deal with the feelings.

The hypothesis was tested in the following way: Second-grade children were asked to monitor the operation of a slot car. They were told that they must not let the car fall off the track because it was old and might break. A signal light flashed if the car went too fast, and a control device enabled the child to slow the car's motion. The researchers had placed some attractive toys elsewhere in the room to draw the child's attention away from the rather boring task. When the experimenter briefly left the room, all the children eventually let their attention wander, at which point a control device in the observation room made the car jump the track. The experimenter then returned, picked up the car, and remarked sadly that it was broken. At this point the children were divided into two groups. The experimenter said to the *guilt* group:

> I bet you feel a little bad now that the car fell off. I've seen other kids feel bad when they weren't able to do exactly what they were supposed to do. . . . But it's important that we do stop the car when the light first comes on, and before it flies off the track, so we'll try again with this new car. You won't feel bad if this car stays on the track. If you've done a good job, you'll feel good, won't you? Have you noticed that when other kids have done the right thing, they feel good? And when they did things they were not supposed to do, they feel bad, don't they? Even if no one ever finds out, they feel bad for not doing what they were supposed to do, don't they? (p. 305)

The *shame* group script was much the same, except that the child's upset feelings were attributed to getting caught:

> I bet you feel a little bad now that I found out the car fell off. I've seen other kids feel bad when somebody found out they weren't able to do what they were supposed to do. . . . But it's important that we do stop the car when the light first comes on, and before it flies off the track, so we'll try again with this new car. You won't feel bad if I find this car still on the track—if I find you've done a good job, you'll feel good, won't you? Have you noticed that when other kids can show people that they have done the right thing, they feel good? And when people find out they did things they were not supposed to, they feel bad, don't they? (p. 305)

Following these discussions the children were left alone with the slot car and the temptingly distracting toys, but this time, when the experimenter left the room, he ensured the children's privacy by asking them to lock the door and commenting that he did not have a key. The results of this strategy were clear: Children who received the shame treatment, which emphasized getting caught, were more easily distracted and spent between 60 and 80 percent more time playing with the tempting toys than the children who received the guilt treatment.

Dienstbier and his colleagues make use of these results to suggest a reason why the punishment in laboratory settings has different effects than real-life punishment by parents. Punishment always focuses the child's attention on external controlling situations. In the laboratory the situation is unfamiliar, the child is uncertain about the chances of getting caught (unless the experimenter goes to great lengths), and so the safe course of action is not to cheat. The severity of the experimental punishment is directly related to the intensity of the child's feelings in the temptation situation, and the greater the fear the greater the likelihood that the child will conform.

The situation at home is different. Here also the use of physical punishment and other forms of power assertion focuses children's attention on external controls—on the danger of getting caught. But children have had a great deal of experience with parental responses and can assess the magnitude of the danger—they know when they can get away with a forbidden activity. When temptation arises and safety from detection seems assured, children feel apprehensive, but they attribute this feeling to the external forces. And knowing that the external forces are not operating, they feel free to cheat. If parents use methods of discipline that focus on the rightness or wrongness of the behavior, resistance to temptation is likely to be maintained, even in situations where the chances of getting caught are realistically low. In short, the child will be more capable of self-control. The nature of these nonpunitive child-rearing techniques will be more fully discussed in Chapter 10.

Observing what other people do

Children learn from their own experience with pleasant or painful outcomes and also by example. The behavior of a model can have a profound effect on what a child will do when tempted. A study by Stein (1967) illustrates the negative effect of a self-indulgent model. Fourth-grade boys were taught to perform a vigilance task similar to radar monitoring. Each boy watched for a light that came on at unpredictable intervals and pressed a lever whenever he saw the light. In another part of the room out of his line of sight a very interesting movie was being shown. Before being put into this situation, the boys in the experimental groups watched an adult model perform the same task. Each child heard the model say, "I sure wish I could watch the movie." Some subjects saw the model actually leave the task to watch the movie, others did not. (The control group did not observe a model.) The children who saw the model yielding to temptation were more likely to leave their assigned task to watch the movie. The children who saw the model remain at his task were more likely to resist temptation than the children who saw a yielding model but did not show any more temptation resistance than the control group who saw no model at all. Thus, the contagion from the model's behavior seemed to work primarily in one direction: A self-indulgent model could influence the children toward yielding to temptation, but a dutiful model did not increase the tendency to be dutiful.

These results are rather discouraging, in the sense that they suggest that efforts to teach children temptation resistance by setting a good example do not have much chance of success. More encouraging results have been obtained by Ross (1971) and Rosenkoetter (1973). Their subjects' temptation resistance increased moderately (compared to a no-model control group) after they were exposed to a nonyielding model. In addition, Wolf and Cheyne (1972) found that a conforming model increased children's ability to resist playing with a prohibited toy—an effect that lasted for a month. The evidence to date, then, indicates that prosocial models do have an effect but that influencing children toward self-indulgent behavior is probably easier than influencing them in the opposite direction.

Guilt and identification: the psychodynamic point of view

Freud was a developmentalist. He believed that structural reorganizations of the personality occur at certain crucial points in development and that these successive stages are universal features in the development of all human beings. Freud saw little children as impulsive creatures who want every wish gratified immediately and who flare into anger and aggression when frustrated. He also believed that children have fairly strong sexual passions. This aspect of his work initially provoked considerable opposition, since his contemporaries believed that children were pure and in need of protection from the corrupting influence of worldly adults. (The reader should be aware of some inconsistencies in the ideology of those times: Children were pure, but they also needed to have their hands tied to the side of the bed at night so that they would not masturbate, had to be punished severely if they were aggressive, and had to have their mouths washed out with soap if they told a lie. In short, puritanical parents reacted as if they greatly feared their children's impulses—impulses whose very existence they usually denied!)

From the Freudian point of view socialization is a process in which children's antisocial impulses are brought under control. Freud, like other writers on morality, saw moral development as a process of internalization in which children move from external behavioral controls (rewards and punishments) to internal self-controls. The transition, he believed, was closely bound up with the feelings that tie children to their caretakers. He assumed that parental pressures toward socialization make children angry and that the thought of expressing anger toward the parents arouses the children's anxiety. They fear the parents' direct punishment, but they fear the loss of the parents' love even more. Children therefore repress their anger and turn it against themselves. They become self-punishing. According to psychoanalytic theory, this process forms the basis for guilt, and guilt becomes a powerful motivating force in the child's moral development.

The term *internalization* has a rather literal meaning in Freudian theory. Children not only take over the responsibility for monitoring their own behavior and enforcing their own rules, but they symbolically incorporate their parents, so that the "still small voice of conscience" is like a parent's voice, telling the child the right thing to do, warning about the consequences of wrongdoing, scolding for infractions, and (sparingly!) giving approval for righteousness. As Freud said: "The institution of conscience was at bottom an embodiment, first of parental criticism, and subsequently, of that of society" (1914, p. 53). It should be noted that in Freudian theory, the *superego*—the structure in the personality that represents the internalized parent—is fairly harsh, punitive, and inflexible. Most important, Freud thought that the development of the superego enabled children to behave morally—to resist temptation—when parents were not present.

Although Freud did not originally propose this theory as an explanation of individual differences, it has been used as a basis for making predictions about what kinds of parenting ought to be associated with the strongest conscience in children. Here are some of the predictions:

1. The parent who puts the most socialization pressure on the child—makes the most demands, restricts the child most—will generate the most anger in the child, thus maximizing the conditions under which internalization ought to occur.

2. If the parent enforces demands with threats of withdrawal of love rather than with physical punishment or the withholding of material rewards, the child will be more likely to repress anger and develop self-punitive reactions.

3. Punishment of any sort administered by a warm and affectionate parent will be more effective in producing internalization than punishment administered by a cold or indifferent parent.

4. Parents who do not allow a child to show aggression toward them and who discourage any open expression of the child's

sexuality in the family context are creating conditions favorable to internalization. These factors are thought to be particularly important for sons, especially when the pressure emanates from the father.

Testing the validity of Freud's theory is extraordinarily difficult—a child's conscience is hard to measure. If children hang their heads and look upset after doing something wrong, are they showing guilt or fear? Measures of the development of conscience always involve some degree of inference. Researchers have measured guilt, for example, by noting whether a child attempts to repair the damage or confesses to an otherwise secret misdeed. Children have also been asked to act out imaginary family scenes, using dolls to show how a child of their own age and sex would feel following a transgression. Self-punishing responses (the naughty child in the story falls and gets hurt) are interpreted as manifestations of guilt feelings. Sears, Rau, and Alpert (1965) studied the development of conscience in a group of four-year-old children, using both indirect measures and direct observation of the children in several temptation situations. Children with considerable conscience development (who were likely to confess misdeeds and show emotional upset over deviation) were no more likely than other children to resist temptation. Thus, the findings do not support the idea that generalized feelings of guilt motivate children to resist temptation. The temptation resisters were less aggressive toward their parents than the other children, although their parents were not doing anything significantly different from other parents to repress the children's aggression. The researchers concluded therefore that learning to resist temptation is part of a more general process of learning to inhibit impulsive behavior (see Chapter 5). Their findings also seem to suggest that the turning inward of aggression toward the self, motivated by fear of parents' strong reactions, does not play the important role that Freud assigned to it in the development of impulse controls.

Working with older children, Hoffman and Saltzstein (1967) also tested the validity of some of the psychoanalytic predictions by determining the relationships between the techniques parents use to discipline their children and several aspects of the children's moral development. The researchers began by distinguishing between *power assertive* and *love-oriented* techniques of discipline (Hoffman, 1970):

1. *Power assertion.* The parent uses physical punishment, deprives the child of material objects or privileges, directly applies force, or threatens any of these actions. In effect, control is exercised by taking advantage of greater physical strength and/or control over the family's resources. This technique relies for its effect on the child's fear of punishment and does not appeal to the child's inner resources—to a sense of responsibility or affection and respect for others.

2. *Love withdrawal.* The parent gives direct but nonphysical expression to anger, disappointment, or disapproval when the child misbehaves. For example, the parent may ignore, isolate, or turn away from the child, refuse to speak or listen, explicitly state negative feelings, or threaten to leave the child. Love withdrawal has a punitive quality.

3. *Induction.* The parent appeals to the child's affection or respect for others. For example, the child may be reminded that someone else will be hurt, inconvenienced, or disappointed by the child's actions.

Hoffman and Saltzstein worked with middle-class seventh-graders and their parents. Parents were classified in terms of child-rearing techniques on the basis of information obtained in interviews. Mothers and fathers were separately asked to discuss four specific situations common to family life: (1) the child delays when asked to do something, (2) the child is careless and breaks or damages something of value, (3) the child "talks back" to the parent, and (4) the parent learns that the child is doing badly in school. The parents were given a list of possible reactions and were asked to choose which reactions they would be most likely to display in these situations. The choices were then analyzed to determine how frequently the three kinds of techniques were used. To determine their level of affection, the researchers also asked the parents about their demonstrativeness and use of approval and rewards.

Five indices of the child's level of moral development were obtained. *Guilt* was measured by asking each subject to create an ending for a story about a transgression committed by a child of the same age and sex. The responses were scored for the number of conscious, self-initiated, self-critical reactions. To obtain a score on *internalized moral judgments,* the children were asked to listen to Piaget-like pairs of stories, to choose which of two children had been naughtier, and to give the reasons for the choice. If a child's choice was based on fear of punishment or hope of reward, the response was called an externalized moral judgment. Responses based on moral principles and reflecting considerations of mutual trust were classed as internalized. A child's tendency to *confess* after doing something wrong or to *accept responsibility* was assessed by asking the teacher and the mother about the child's behavior. And finally, the child's *consideration for others* was determined by asking classmates for ratings.

Table 9-1 shows the relationships that were found between these various aspects of the child's moral development and the socialization techniques employed by the child's parents. Note that the mother's child-rearing practices seem to have more impact than the father's—and this finding holds for both sons and daughters. The findings also suggest that the arbitrary assertion of power by the mother is as-

TABLE 9-1 Relationship between child-rearing practices and children's moral development[1]

TYPE OF CHILD-REARING PRACTICE[2]

ASPECTS OF CHILD'S MORALITY	Power assertion		Love withdrawal		Induction		Affection	
	Mother	Father	Mother	Father	Mother	Father	Mother	Father
Guilt	−				+		+[3]	
Internal moral judgments	−[3]		−[3]		+		+	+
Confession	−	+			+		+[3]	+
Acceptance of responsibility	−	−[3]		+[3]	+			
Consideration for other children		+			+		+	

[1]This table includes only those relationships that were significant for the two sexes combined.

[2]Sources of data are as follows: power assertion and love withdrawal, Tables 1 and 2; induction, Table 3; affection, Table 6.

[3]These relationships were significant only for reports of their parents' child-rearing practices.

SOURCE: Hoffman and Saltzstein, 1967.

sociated with poor development of several aspects of conscience. Contrary to the psychoanalytic prediction, withdrawing love from the child does not seem to promote internalization of morality. Talking to the child about the importance of being considerate and not jeopardizing others' trust does seem to be associated with a variety of manifestations of conscience. Affection also has a positive effect—but on a narrower range of manifestations of conscience.

In subsequent work Hoffman (1970) refined his analysis of children's responses to moral judgment issues. He continued to classify one group of children as having an *external* orientation on the grounds that they make their moral judgments primarily on the basis of the likelihood of punishment or reward. He subdivided those with an *internal* orientation, categorizing them according to which of two kinds of responses predominated:

1. *Humanistic-flexible.* Included in this group are children whose responses primarily emphasized the consequences of an action for others and stressed the importance of maintaining mutual trust. These children also tended to apply moral standards flexibly, taking extenuating circumstances into account.

2. *Conventional-rigid.* These children stressed the strict applications of a moral code having absolute rules.

In examining the child-rearing practices of the parents, Hoffman broadened his definition of induction to include such parental actions as pointing out the probable consequences of the child's actions (including injury to other people, but other consequences as well) and appealing to the child's pride and wish to be grown up. The revised definition of induction comes close to what other studies have called reasoning.

Hoffman's findings are consistent with his previous work: Parents of the *external* group used more power assertion and less affection and induction than parents of children in either of the internal groups. Comparing the two internal groups, however: Parents of humanistic-flexible children (compared with parents of conventional-rigid children): (1) *less* often used withdrawal of love, (2) *more* often used power assertion (gave direct orders and insisted on compliance), and (3) responded to the child's anger by focusing on the original instigation of the anger, rather than on the anger itself. The use of power assertion by these parents, however, never reached levels comparable to the power assertion used by the parents of external children. The parents of the humanistic-flexible children did nevertheless give direct orders and insist on compliance with moderate frequency.

The finding on response to anger deserves some comment. When parents attempt to stop a child from behaving in undesired ways or insist on some desired behavior the child would rather avoid, the parents' demands quite often make the child angry. The parents are then faced with a dual problem: If the child responds with angry words, a temper tantrum, or direct aggression, the parents must deal with this behavior as well as with the original problem. Some parents react by focusing on the child's angry tones or defiant manner and demand that the child maintain an obedient and deferential stance. Other parents, while not ignoring the anger, do not allow it to divert them from the pursuit of the original socialization issue. Interestingly, Hoffman finds that the former response is most clearly associated with conventional-rigid moral judgments in children.

Hoffman has studied the three groups of children quite intensively, inquiring especially into the quality of guilt they feel over misdeeds. He provides some evidence that the conventional-rigid children are likely to experience guilt over arousal of their own impulses, while the humanistic-flexible children will experience guilt when their actions have led to injury of others. Furthermore, the conventional-rigid children are less aware of their own impulses. Hoffman's findings, then, provide empirical support for two of Freud's conceptions: (1) the existence of a punitive, inflexible superego in some children and (2) the origins of this hypermoralistic stance in strong parental suppression of the child's anger, especially by threatening the child with loss of love. Of course, Hoffman points out, an inflexible conscience—one that directs harsh punitiveness toward the self and that grows out of the vigorous denial of forbidden impulses—is not the only kind of internalized morality. There is also a rational morality that has its origins in different socialization techniques and which develops as the child comes to recognize responsibilities to others.

The reader will have noticed the similarity between Hoffman's types of moral orientation and the different developmental levels described in Chapter 8. The external children are at Kohlberg's preconventional level. We cannot be sure exactly where the conventional-rigid and humanistic-flexible children would be classified by Damon or Kohlberg, but the conventional-rigid children would most likely be placed at a lower level. However, the Hoffman-Saltzstein work does not have a developmental orientation. Hoffman does not suggest, as Kohlberg would, that humanistic-flexible children were conventional-rigid a year or two earlier. Hoffman would probably argue (although he does not say so explicitly) that parents' techniques of discipline lead directly to a humanistic-flexible orientation without an intervening period of conventional-rigid morality. While the issue is not settled, the evidence from studies of moral thought (Chapter 8) is strong enough to permit an educated guess about how morality develops. It seems likely that the socialization techniques used by parents of humanistic-flexible children may *accelerate* the children's progress through the moral orientation levels, but we may speculate that they may first go through at least a brief period of conventional-rigid morality. If so, some vestiges of this kind of thinking could probably still be detected. We do not yet know, however, whether a qualitative difference exists between the children who move on quickly to higher morality and those who do not—these differences are not captured in Kohlberg's definitions.

Hoffman assessed children's moral reasoning and their emotional reactions by using cognitive measures such as story completion and also by asking teachers, classmates, and parents about his young subjects' behavior. Hoffman appears to have assumed that both approaches assessed the same characteristic—a child's moral level. And indeed, he found that children rated helpful and cooperative by their classmates were also likely to show humanistic-flexible reasoning in their story completions. Still, a direct correspondence between children's moral thought and their moral behavior may certainly not be taken for granted. Indeed, the nature of this correspondence—or even the question of whether any correspondence exists—is currently a matter of active debate. We turn to that issue in the last portion of this chapter. First, however, we must consider the positive side of moral behavior and emotions—the individual's willingness to take positive action to further the interests of other people, even if the action requires sacrifice of time or immediate self-interested goals.

ALTRUISTIC BEHAVIOR

Altruistic behavior includes helping, comforting, rescuing, defending, or sharing with others. The idea of young children sharing candy or toys in order to comfort or gratify another child seems inconsistent with our previous description of them as impulsive and almost entirely egocentric. And yet altruistic behavior occurs. Consider this example: Jerry is visiting his friend John, who is nearly two. John's mother reports:

> Today Jerry was kind of cranky; he just started completely bawling and he wouldn't stop. John kept coming over and handing Jerry toys, trying to cheer him up, so to speak. He'd say things like "Here, Jerry," and I said to John: "Jerry's sad; he doesn't feel good; he had a shot today." John would look at me with his eyebrows kind of wrinkled together like he really understood that Jerry was crying because he was unhappy, not that he was just being a crybaby. He went over and rubbed Jerry's arm and said "Nice Jerry" and continued to give him toys. (Zahn-Waxler, Radke-Yarrow, and King, 1979, pp. 321–22)

Perhaps this mother credited her son with too much understanding of the reasons for his friend's emotional state. But he was surely affected by his friend's state and he certainly acted altruistically. Since John was much too young to be capable of taking the perspective of another person in the sense that this process was defined and described in Chapter 8, what prompted him to act altruistically? It seems that John was capable of empathic feelings that had some other basis than cognitive perspective taking. In order to discover what the basis of such feelings might be, we first examine the nature of altruistic responding in a group of very young children and consider the child-rearing techniques employed by the mothers of children who frequently show such behavior. Then we consider age changes in the role of empathy in children's altruism. Finally, we present the findings of several studies in which attempts were made to teach altruism by using such techniques as role playing and modeling.

Altruism in very young children

The unfamiliar setting of a laboratory playroom often affects children's behavior and sometimes makes it difficult to determine the limits of their capabilities. A team of researchers (Zahn-Waxler, Radke-Yarrow, and King, 1979) therefore chose to study young children's altruism by asking mothers for careful reports of incidents occurring during the children's normal daily lives. The mothers of sixteen children (those in the younger group were fifteen months old when they entered the study, those in the older group were twenty months old) were enlisted as research assistants and received considerable training as observers. During nine months of study, the mothers tape-recorded descriptions of every incident in which someone in the child's presence expressed painful feelings—anger, fear, sorrow, pain, or fatigue. The mothers indicated the events that preceded and followed the distress and both the child's and their own reactions. Two principal types of incidents were reported: those in which the subject child had been responsible for causing the distress of others and those in which the child was a bystander. The case of John and Jerry is typical of the mothers' reports.

In about a third of child-caused distress incidents the children made efforts at reparation, trying to comfort their victim, offering a toy, giving help, or going to find someone else to help. The rate of altruistic reactions was similar in bystander incidents. But the number of altruistic reactions varied greatly from child to child, prompting the researchers to ask whether the individual mothers' responses made a difference in their children's behavior. They found that the way the mother reprimanded the child was clearly related to the child's rate of altruism. Some mothers frequently used what the researchers called *affective explanations*—moralizing ("You made Doug cry; it's not nice to bite"), prohibition with explanation, statements of principle ("You must *never* poke anyone's eyes"), withdrawal of love. Others used neutral explanations ("Tom is crying because you pushed him"). Others used unexplained prohibition, physical restraint, and physical punishment. Some mothers made use of several kinds of techniques. The use of affective explanations was associated with high levels[1] of altruistic behavior in both child-caused and bystander incidents. Especially powerful were mothers' use of moralizing and statements of principle. Unexplained verbal prohibitions ("Stop that!") and physical punishment were associated with low rates of altruism in the children. Physical punishment, however, did not occur frequently, and its relationship with altruism was of borderline significance. Neutral explanations had little effect either way.

[1] A high level means that the child reacted altruistically a high *proportion* of the times when others' distress occurred.

We see that altruistic behavior occurs with some frequency as early as the second year of life and that the amount of such behavior is related to the way the mother handles other people's distress that occurs in the child's presence. Although the assessment of the children's altruism and the measures of the mothers' reactions were not independent—both came from the mothers' reports—the findings strongly suggest that mothers' emotional reactions do make a difference in how frequently their children offer to help, comfort, or share objects with another person. The mothers of highly altruistic children did not simply offer cognitive clarification of others' distress; they reacted emotionally, sometimes quite strongly, and stated forcefully that socially responsible behavior was expected. Observers gave these same mothers high ratings on *empathic care giving*—that is, they were responsive to their children's needs and skillful at anticipating dangers or difficulties. Thus, the emotionally toned disciplinary encounter between parent and child occurred in a context of dependable support.

Although these mothers were directly teaching their children, the effects seemed to go beyond what was being taught. The researchers investigated the possibility that the mothers were modeling altruistic behavior, but the frequency of such modeling was not associated with the frequency of the child's altruistic behavior (although occasionally a child copied one of the mother's characteristic ministrations when trying to help a playmate). And, while the mothers did give direct commands, such directives as "Don't hit!" would not be likely to foster the sharing of toys or the giving of comfort. It appears that the mothers who effectively produced altruism were making their children aware of other people's emotional states and playing on the children's sympathies. Does this mean that the mothers were teaching the children to feel sympathy? Or were the mothers taking advantage of sympathetic feelings that occur naturally in children? To answer these questions we turn our attention to the acquisition of sympathetic feelings.

Empathy and altruism

Empathy is "the involuntary, at times forceful, experiencing of another person's emotional state" (Hoffman, 1976).[2] As we have seen, even very young children seem able to feel what others are feeling. A child of eighteen months who sees another child fall and start to cry may also cry or look anxious and suck his or her thumb. Such reactions have been called *primitive empathy*—because they occur in the first year of life and may not reflect any real understanding of the other

---

[2] In Chapter 4 distinctions were made between several meanings of *empathy,* including knowledge of others' emotional states and sharing of those states. The latter meaning is used here.

person's state. Such reactions are commonly explained in terms of classical conditioning—the same processes that were invoked to explain children's acquisition of fears. With empathic distress the process would work in the following way: A twelve-month-old has cried on hundreds of different occasions and the sound of crying has repeatedly been associated with the child's own distress. And so by a process of simple association, the sound of crying—anyone's crying—can now evoke feelings of distress and perhaps memories of previous distress and even tears. If the young listener thinks of a way to make the other person stop crying, he or she will feel better. From the standpoint of simple self-interest, then, we should expect children to learn to perform such "altruistic" actions.

Following this line of reasoning, Aronfreed (1969), working with second-grade children, explored the conditions under which children will make sacrifices to relieve another child's distress. He found that children are willing to do this if:

1. They first shared a number of experiences in which their own distress occurred at the same time as their partner's distress.
2. Their partner showed overt signs of distress such as a pained expression. Simply *knowing* about the partner's distress was not enough.

In a parallel experiment, Aronfreed showed that shared experiences and overt displays of happy emotion also motivate children to make small sacrifices to produce pleasant experiences for a partner. This work underlines the importance of actually seeing the signs of the other person's distress or pleasure in motivating altruistic behavior. We need not cite the plentiful evidence that adults as well as children are more likely to do harm to others when at a distance and shielded from direct exposure to their victims' suffering.

The Aronfreed work indicates that responding empathically depends on having attention forcibly drawn to what others are experiencing. His findings help us to understand why some of the two-year-olds studied by Zahn-Waxler and colleagues were more altruistic than others. The mothers of these children seem to have been applying the Aronfreed conditioning principles (no doubt inadvertently!)—that is, their scolding was simultaneously creating distress and drawing attention to the emotional distress of another person. The foundation for altruism was thus laid down. The children needed only to discover that acting to relieve the others' distress would relieve their own and the process would be complete.

Returning to Aronfreed: In an unfamiliar experimental situation children may have to learn *de novo* that other people are experiencing the same emotion that they feel themselves. But in more familiar situations with familiar people, the child can draw on past experience to infer what others must be experiencing. Also, the growth of children's ability to take the perspective of others (see Chapter 8) undoubtedly increases their ability to respond empathically without constant *reconditioning* (pairing of outward signs of others' emotional states with their own directly induced emotions). In many everyday situations we share other people's emotions vicariously without having direct access to information about their emotional states. For example, we may immediately call to offer comfort to a friend we know will be distressed by a piece of bad news. We may do this even if the news does not affect us personally and without seeing the signs of distress on the other person's face. An empathic response of this kind is based on an interpersonal history that enables us to predict and share another's reactions with little new information.

It can be shown, however, that we can react empathically even to a stranger and in the absence of conditioning trials if we have some sense of shared identity with the stranger. Working with young adults, Krebs (1975) monitored the responses of observers who were exposed to the sight of a stranger undergoing either pleasant or painful experiences. Some subjects believed that they had interests, values and personality traits in common with the stranger, and other subjects believed the stranger was different from themselves. Krebs measured the vicarious sharing of emotions by monitoring changes in each observer's heart rate, skin conductance, and other psychophysiological indicators of emotion and also by asking the observers how fully they identified with the stranger. He found more vicarious emotion and more identification among observers who believed the stranger was similar to themselves than among those who believed the stranger was different. Here we see another example of the interrelatedness of cognition and interpersonal emotions. As we saw in Chapter 7, young children are likely to base perception of similarity on objective characteristics ("We live on the same street," "We both have brown hair," or "We play ball together"), while older children can think in terms of shared personality attributes and values. Therefore, while young children are capable of and often show empathic responses, circumstances that will evoke empathy change and broaden with cognitive growth, as the child's perceptions become less tied to immediate life circumstances.

Krebs also showed that individuals not only experience the emotions of people similar to themselves, but also *act on* these feelings. His subjects were given the opportunity to (1) prevent discomfort to a partner by accepting some discomfort for themselves or (2) allow another person to win some money by sacrificing their own monetary gain. A choice maximally favorable to the partner brought maximum penalty to the subject. A choice maximally favorable to the subject brought maximum penalty to the partner. There was a range of possible choices between the two extremes. The subject's role in deciding the outcome was kept confidential from the partner. Krebs found that subjects were most altruistic when they experienced the most vicarious emotion—that is, they were willing to accept more discomfort or forego more money for the sake of the partner if the partner was a person described as similar to themselves. Thus, there is evidence that empathy is translated into altruism.

Krebs's work underscores the universal human tendency to be more altruistic to those who are near and dear and more unfeeling toward strangers. According to moral theorists the essence of mature morality is giving equal weight to all moral claims, regardless of the claimants' relatedness to the person making the judgments. During development many individuals do make considerable progress toward this kind of objective perspective. Yet the claims of those who share one's point of view and states of feeling are hard to set aside. Their interests seem like self-interests. This tendency is so well understood that people in official positions regularly disqualify themselves from making decisions that affect the fate of family members or close associates. Thus, although empathy may strongly promote moral behavior by motivating individuals to act in the interests of others, empathy may also interfere with the development of a truly universal moral creed. Religious teachings attempt to counteract the narrow focus of empathic responses by stressing the universal qualities that make strangers similar to the self—for example, "All men are brothers."

Mood and altruism

Altruistic behavior is also affected by an individual's mood. When people are depressed, they are self-centered, preoccupied with their own problems, and not much inclined to think about needs of others. A person who feels optimistic and self-confident is more likely to notice other people's states, and take the time and trouble to help them if the opportunity arises. Moore, Underwood, and Rosenhan (1973) have studied the effect of mood on willingness to share with others. They conducted a hearing test in which children earned small amounts of money for their participation. The children were given an opportunity to contribute some of their earnings to children who did not have a chance to take part in the research. First, however, one group of children was asked to reminisce about events in their lives that had made them happy, another group thought about events that had made them sad, and a third group thought about events that were affectively neutral. The happy group contributed the most money to the nonparticipating subjects, the neutral group an intermediate amount, and the sad group the least.

In a similar study Isen, Horn, and Rosenhan (1973) found that children who had just succeeded at a task were more likely to contribute anonymously to charity than children who had failed. Cox (1974) reported that a child whose partner had just complied with the child's request was more likely to help the partner when asked. Thus, a positive, self-confident mood can be generated in a number of ways, and such a mood can contribute to prosocial behavior.

Training for altruism

We have already seen that mothers' reactions in the realistic setting of the home make a difference in the amount of altruistic behavior in children as young as one or two years old. Can training programs be developed that will strengthen older children's altruistic tendencies? A number of attempts to teach helpful behavior to children have been reported. In one such project (Chittenden, 1942) a group of children who habitually dominated other children through force and threats of force and rarely played cooperatively with other children were trained over several weeks to use dolls for acting out scenes of conflict between children. The scenarios stressed the negative consequences of fighting and the enjoyable aspects of shared or cooperative play. This training technique proved effective in reducing the amount of aggressive and dominant behavior subsequently shown by the children, but it was only marginally effective in increasing the amount of cooperative behavior. Perhaps the distressing consequences of fighting were simply more dramatic, and therefore more easily remembered by the children. Clearly, the Chittenden approach is a useful first step in moderating negative behaviors, but other techniques are needed if substitute positive behaviors are to be acquired.

The work of Radke-Yarrow, Zahn-Waxler, and their colleagues (Yarrow, Scott, and Waxler, 1973) provides an example of successful training of helpful behavior patterns. The Radke-Yarrow group assumed that the frequency of helpful behavior could be increased by directly praising and rewarding children for such behavior. However since the goal of most parents and teachers is to facilitate helpfulness for the sake of other people's comfort or pleasure rather than for personal gain, the researchers set up a training program using modeling but not direct reinforcement. They also wanted to make their training program as similar as possible to children's normal everyday experiences with other people. Working with children of nursery-school age, they first observed the children during the school day and eliminated from the study the small group of children whose spontaneous helpfulness was already at a high level. The remaining children participated in the following training sessions (called type A training):

> Miniature three-dimensional models had been constructed of
> street scenes, family scenes, or animal scenes, each showing a
> situation in which someone was in distress (see Figure 9-2). For

Figure 9-2. Samples of distress situations. Upper figures are pictures; lower figures are dioramas. (Adapted from Yarrow, Scott, and Waxler, 1973)

example, one animal scene showed a caged monkey trying to reach a banana that was beyond its grasp and another showed a turtle lying helplessly on its back at the edge of a pond. One of the family scenes showed a mother whose string of beads had broken. The scenes were always presented in pairs—that is, two setups of the same or similar scenes. When the child entered the room on the day when animal scenes were being used, the experimenter would say: "We have some animals here today. They need someone to take care of them. I'll have the first turn and the next turn will be yours." For the monkey scene the experimenter would say: "Oh, Mr. Monkey, you must be hungry. You can't reach your food. I'll help you. Here's your banana. Now you won't be hungry." The model always commented explicitly on the victim's distress and her own sympathy for the victim and expressed pleasure over the improvement the helpful action had wrought in the victim's situation. Then the model uncovered the matching scene and told the child to take a turn. If the child got the banana for the monkey, the experimenter would say: "I think the monkey feels better because you gave him his food. He isn't hungry now." In other words the only reinforcement was the child's knowledge of having helped, rather than a reward received personally. If the child did not help, the experimenter expressed no disapproval, but simply turned to the next set of scenes and repeated the procedure for several scenes. The training was similar on the day that scenes of human distress were used. (Adapted from pp. 246–47)

Some subjects also received additional (type B) training: (1) They saw the adult experimenter model helpful responses to a series of pictured scenes. For example, "That boy is falling out of the swing. I hope he doesn't hurt himself. I'll pick him up." (2) In addition, real incidents were staged in which the experimenter took advantage of an opportunity to be helpful. For example, another adult would start to pick up some toys and bang her head against the edge of the table; the experimenter would put her hand on the other adult's shoulder and say: "I hope you aren't hurt. Do you want to sit down for a minute?" (p. 247).

In an additional feature of the experiment, the experimenter established a warm, nurturant relationship with some of the children during a period of two weeks before the experiment began. The experimenter spent the same amount of time with other children but was nonnurturant—that is, she was matter-of-fact and rather reserved, showed little enthusiasm over what the children were doing, often ignored requests for help, gave directions and occasional criticism, and did not become involved in the children's play.

Tests of the impact of these various treatment conditions (using new scenes, pictures, and incidents) were made two days after the end of the training and again after two weeks had passed. The two-week test is in some ways the most interesting. Here each child was brought into a situation completely different from the training session, in a different building with different people, and was offered two opportunities for spontaneous helpfulness: A basket of spools and buttons was "accidentally" spilled onto the floor. Also, a baby was sitting in a playpen, and the baby's toys were on the floor out of the baby's reach.

The major findings were:

1. The children's tendency to make helpful or sympathetic responses to the scenes and pictures was increased by both type A and type B training. Their response to the pictures and scenes did not depend upon how nurturant the experimenter had been.

2. The children's tendency to be altruistic in the realistic encounters (for example, getting the toys for the baby or picking up some of the spilled objects) was increased only if they had received type B training, in which they were exposed to real-life as well as pictorial instances of helpful or sympathetic behavior. Furthermore, the children only followed the experimenter's good example if she had previously established a nurturant relationship with them.

Thus, we see that the symbolic modeling represented by the adults' verbal responses to the pictorial distress scenes did teach the children to take notice of signs of distress and to express helpful intentions. The good intentions did not spill over into action, however, unless additional features were added to the training. It is especially interesting that the child's relationship to the model made a difference in whether the child would *act on* the abstract knowledge gained from observation. We encounter here a psychodynamic theme: Affection makes a difference in whether children are motivated to pattern themselves after adults—that is, identify with them. A further point is obvious but deserving of emphasis: Once a child has identified with an adult model, the model's effect on the child will depend as much (or more) on what the adult *does* as on what the adult preaches.

Training for altruism may also include practice in taking the role of other persons. Staub (1971) has experimented with this process. Working with pairs of kindergarten children, he asked one child to act the part of someone who needed help (for example, trying to carry a chair that is too heavy or standing in the path of an oncoming bicycle) and the other child to act the part of a helping person (that is, to think of appropriate helpful actions and act them out). Then the children changed roles. A week after training, helpfulness was tested by giving the children: (1) the chance to go to the aid of a distressed child who was crying in the next room and (2) the chance to share candy with another child. The trained children were then compared with children who had enacted scenes that did not involve helping. Staub found that the children who had undergone the reciprocal role training were more likely to be helpful to another child than the children who had not had this training. We do not know whether the practice in being helpful or the practice in being helped was important in promoting the children's subsequent altruism. Very likely, both aspects of the training contributed to the effect. If the experience of acting out the role of a person needing help creates a sense of being similar to such a person ("There but for the grace of God go I"), it should foster empathy and hence altruism.

Other factors besides opportunities for reciprocal role playing can make a difference in how altruistic children will be. Staub (1970b) explicitly assigned responsibility to kindergarten and first-grade children. When the young subjects were told that they were "in charge of things" by a departing adult, the probability was increased that they would go to the aid of another child who was heard crying in the next room. The effect was especially clear for the first-graders.

In contrast, situations that promote competition between children lessen altruistic behavior. A study by Stendler, Damrin, and Hines (1951) illustrates the point. These investigators asked seven-year-olds to paint murals and awarded group prizes for excellence at some sessions and individual prizes at other sessions. Friendly conversation, sharing, and helping one another were commonly seen during the group-reward sessions, but not under the competitive individual-reward condition. A similar result was obtained by Kinney (1953), who compared the social behavior of children taught by competitive methods with the behavior of children taught in small cooperating (not "ability") groups. Under the latter conditions fewer children were socially rejected by other children in the classroom.

We have experimental evidence, then, that altruistic behavior can be taught. Cross-cultural work by John and Beatrice Whiting (1973, 1975) makes the same point but gives a broader view of some of the real-life social conditions that foster helpfulness in growing children. Working in small communities in Kenya, India, the Philippines, Okinawa, Mexico, and the United States (New England), their observers took systematic time-sampled observations of the behavior of children between the ages of three and six and of other children between six and ten. The children were individually scored for the frequency with which they spontaneously exhibited the following behaviors:

1. *Altruistic behavior—offering help* to another (including feeding and assisting in carrying out a task), *offering support* to others (including offering comfort and reassurance), and *suggesting responsibly* (giving someone directions or suggestions that are meant to protect the person, or further his or her interests or the group's interests rather than the actor's interests).

2. *Egoistic behavior*—seeking help, attention, or to dominate another (in the service of the actor's own goals).

Taking the set of six cultures as a group, some fairly systematic changes with age were observed in the frequency with which altruistic and egoistic behaviors occurred. Seeking help became less frequent as the children grew older and giving help became more frequent, but this change was statistically significant only in certain cultures and certain sex groups. Seeking attention increased with age most dramatically among the boys of the Mexican village sample. In all the cultures *suggesting responsibly* increased with age—most notably among the boys, who in early childhood had lagged substantially behind the girls. The cultures differed considerably in rates of altruism, with the American children lowest on all three measures of this behavior. The highest rates of altruistic behavior were found in cultures in which:

1. *Children are assigned many tasks.* Specifically, responsibility for the care of younger children is associated with high altruism scores (helpfulness was observed even in non-baby-sitting situations). Also, the requirement that children help with the production and processing of food is associated with altruism. However, assignment of housecleaning chores is not.

2. *Mothers have considerable work responsibilities outside of the home and family size is large.* The crucial variable in these

families apparently is the consistent and strict enforcement of parental demands for obedience, especially when children are helping with child care and food-producing chores. An additional factor is the requirement that children show a high level of respect for parental authority.

The Whitings believe that children become more helpful to others when they live in cultures in which (1) their work makes a genuine contribution to the family's welfare, (2) these tasks *must* be done, and (3) parents and children are aware of the importance of the tasks to the family's safety, health, and comfort. When this situation prevails, parents (often assisted by others in the culture) will see to it that the child learns a helpful way of life, and this helpfulness will show itself in spontaneous altruism when no authority figure is present.

A number of questions come to mind when thinking about this work. How much did the children's altruism depend on an invisible network of control being exercised by all the members of the community? Did their helpfulness to others mean that they *wanted* to be helpful or only that they were afraid of the consequences if they were not? The data do not tell us. We only know that helpful behavior, regardless of its motivation, occurs more frequently in certain kinds of cultural settings. Interestingly, the personality characteristics of individual mothers, as scored from interviews and observations, had relatively little bearing on the altruism of their children.

As noted earlier, most of the work on resistance to temptation and on altruistic behavior represents the approach taken by social learning theorists. These workers have assumed that children learn what they are taught—that is, that moral behavior is usually acquired in piecemeal fashion, depending on the particular conditions set up by parents and teachers: A child may learn to avoid certain temptations and not others or to help some people and not others; a child may learn to offer help to a person in distress and then refuse to share candy with this same person. In other words, social learning theorists do not support the idea of any sort of general behavioral cluster called moral character. They believe that while training in the home might generalize to similar situations outside the home, the generalization would probably break down quite quickly if the contingencies (rewards and punishments) in the new situations were different from the ones the child was accustomed to. In general, social learning theorists have rejected the notion of overarching personality characteristics that (1) bring about behavioral consistency across many situations and (2) change with age in a systematic way. Of course, they would say that as children grow older, they learn more. And if what they are learning is prosocial behavior, then they will become more moral with age. But they are not saying (as a cognitive-developmentalist or a psychodynamic theorist would) that development has certain laws of its own and that all children change in similar ways although perhaps at different rates, as they grow older. Is there any way to reconcile the two points of view? More important, is there any way to create a consistent picture of the development of morality out of the evidence generated by the advocates of these different positions?

Students of moral judgments have been primarily concerned with developmental changes in thinking and problem solving, while those interested in moral behavior have been concerned with the conditions under which a child of a given age is likely to behave in a particular way. In effect, the focus of study reflects the theory: The developmentalists believe that behavior is controlled by inner conditions, while the learning theorists believe that behavior is primarily a function of external conditions. Surely both conditions are important. The way children act *must* have something to do with the way they think, as well as with the situations in which they find themselves. We now consider the relationship of moral thought to moral behavior.

THE RELATIONSHIP BETWEEN MORAL THINKING AND MORAL BEHAVIOR

The empirical connections

Are children who have an advanced understanding of moral issues more likely to resist temptation or behave altruistically than less advanced children in the same age group? Some rough correspondences have been reported. Kohlberg (1969) reported that juvenile delinquents display low levels of moral judgment on moral problem-solving tasks—lower levels than are found among law-abiding young people of the same age and intelligence. In addition, people who achieve higher moral levels on Kohlberg's dilemmas are more likely than low-scorers to offer direct help when they witness another's distress (Huston and Korte, 1976). Furthermore, relationships have been found between attitudes on social-political issues (which are related to behavioral indicators such as voting) and levels of moral judgment (Lockwood, 1970, 1976). But, on the whole only weak associations have been found between Kohlberg's levels and whether a child will (1) cheat on a test, (2) yield to temptation when put into a laboratory situation where there is an opportunity for self-gratification if an adult prohibition is disobeyed, or (3) behave altruistically toward another person if doing so requires some sacrifice of the child's own interests (see Mischel and Mischel, 1976, for a review of the evidence).

The implications of age changes

In attempting to identify thought-behavior correspondences, we immediately encounter a major problem: Unlike moral thinking, moral behavior does not seem to follow a predictable developmental course. Some early work on children's cheating by Hartshorne and May (1928) illustrates the point. These researchers provided children with opportunities to raise their scores on a test by peeking at an answer key or completing additional items after time had been called or erasing an incorrect item and substituting a correct one. (Methods were devised for detecting any cheating that occurred.) Opportunities were also provided for cheating on a test of athletic ability and on tests of strength. (Children recorded their own scores, and the experimenter, who was not present, knew with reasonable accuracy each child's possible range of scores.) In other contrived situations the children had opportunities to pocket some small change illicitly. The researchers also measured the children's tendency to tell lies in order to present themselves in a favorable light. Table 9-2 shows the percentage of children at each age who cheated in three of these situations. Cheating on tests actually increased somewhat over the age range studied, particularly between the ages of nine and ten. Cheating on measures of athletic ability did not change with age.

TABLE 9-2   Age differences in percentage of children who cheated on each test

AGE	CLASSROOM ACHIEVEMENT TEST	CLASSROOM SPEED TEST	ATHLETIC ABILITY MEASURES
9	23.1	19.0	—
10	34.4	34.2	45
11	33.1	35.8	49
12	37.2	40.7	36
13	37.4	46.0	43
14	—	—	44

SOURCE: Adapted from Hartshorne and May, 1928.

The frequency of the children's lying was also measured by asking such questions as "Do you always do today things that you could put off till tomorrow?" or "Did you ever break, destroy, or lose anything belonging to someone else?" A child who said that he *never* procrastinated or *never* broke or lost someone else's belongings was scored as telling an untruth. The frequency of lying, as so measured, decreases somewhat with age, perhaps because the child comes to realize that he will not be believed.

In a similar vein, Staub (1970a) failed to find any systematic increase with age in children's willingness to help another child in distress. In the age range from kindergarten through the sixth grade, this form of altruism first increased and then decreased. Once more we must ask: Why does the advancing level of maturity in moral reasoning not carry moral behavior along in its wake?

The Staub work provides one clue. His older subjects expressed concern about whether they were allowed to go into the next room—some thought it might be a teacher's room that was out of bounds to the school-children. The older children also wondered whether the distressed child would *want* them to intervene—something the younger children seldom mentioned. The older children were also concerned about what their age mates would think if they saw them interfering. In other words, the older children, unlike the younger children, considered all the possible implications of their action. Sometimes their more mature thinking led to altruistic action, sometimes it did not.

Varying actions with similar reasoning

Staub's findings illustrate an important fact: A number of possible courses of action are open to a child at a given level of thought. Preconventional children will cheat if they think they can get away with it and be honest if they think they are being watched; both courses of action are consistent with the fear of punishment that is a principal motivation at this level of moral thought. Similarly, conventional children at Kohlberg's stage 3 will try to do what other people consider good but will define *good* in terms of the expectations of people they respect. When stage-3 children move from one respected group to another—from the family to a gang of peers, for example—their behavior may shift accordingly. Since the differences in behavior reflect the values of the two groups, the stage-3 children are acting in a way that is consistent with their conventional orientation.

Kohlberg explicitly states that a given level of moral thinking does not dictate a single course of action. In solving the dilemma about Heinz and the druggist (see Chapter 8), individuals at stage 5 might conclude either that Heinz ought to steal the drug or that he ought not. In either case, however, they would make the decision after thinking about overarching moral values such as the value of human life and would weigh these against the importance of maintaining social regulations and social institutions.

Variation in reasoning from one occasion to another

The level of moral judgment on which a given child may draw in discussing moral dilemmas is not fixed. Usually, the child functions at several levels: One type of thinking predominates and a scattering of elements are drawn from the next-higher or next-lower level. Thus, if a child who is predominantly at stage 3 is faced with a real-life dilemma, we cannot assume that he or she will use stage-3 thinking. Children (and also adults) do not always consider all the items of information that are relevant to a decision. They would know how to use the facts properly if they remembered all of them. This *production deficiency* is illustrated in a moral dilemma study by Bearison and Isaacs (1975). Their first-grade subjects sometimes judged another child's naughty action on the basis of outcome rather than intent—an immature response, according to Piaget's scale. However, when the story was rewritten slightly to bring the actor's intent strongly to the child's attention, the first-graders were quite capable of taking the actor's intent into account in making a moral judgment. In other words, their decisions were quite mature when certain story elements were made salient and immature when these elements were not. In a real-life situation children may not notice or remember relevant information either because they are distracted or because the information is not highlighted. This variability in what information is immediately salient may explain some of the variation in moral behavior—variation which reduces the correspondence between behavior and moral judgment.

Self-interest

Of course, whether relevant information is recalled and considered is not just a matter of chance. Sometimes oversight is motivated. Children (and adults too) will sometimes ignore information that, if taken into account, would lead to more mature moral behavior—particularly when self-interests are at stake. This discrepancy is clearly illustrated in Damon's (1977) work. Earlier, we described his studies of children's judgments of "fairness" in several hypothetical situations. He compared these judgments with their judgments in real-life situations. Groups of four children were assigned to work together on a product and work was stopped at a point when one child had produced more of the joint product than the others. The children were then rewarded with ten candy bars and asked to divide them among the group.

In private interviews Damon asked each child to suggest and give reasons for a fair division of the candy and also to actually divide the ten candy bars among the members of the group. The group was also asked to arrive at a joint decision. Under these real-life conditions, with the candy temptingly nearby, the children's reasoning was less mature than when the situation was posed to them hypothetically. Children who had suggested giving the most candy to the person who produced the most when the situation was hypothetical were likely to say that everybody should share equally when the situation was real—especially if the child being questioned had been a less productive member of the group. Children who had advocated equal division in the hypothetical situation might simply ignore the issue of fairness when dealing with real candy and might demand the largest share. When children's real-life judgments differed from hypothetical judgments, the real-life judgments were usually about one level lower on Damon's maturity scale. Some correspondence was found between the children's reasoning and the actual division of the candy bars. Children at the lowest level of maturity in their thinking about justice were more likely than the more sophisticated children to give a larger share of the candy to themselves. No correspondence was found, however, between whether children distributed real candy equally or on the basis of merit and whether they advocated doing so when asked the hypothetical question. This study, then, provides moderate support for a linkage between moral thought and moral action. When the two fail to correspond, the pressures of immediate self-interest seem to be preventing children from taking full advantage of their reasoning capacities.

Plainly, the children's failure to divide up the real candy in accordance with abstract principles of justice is an excellent illustration of the problem of postponing gratification—the difficulty of weighing future gains against present ones—that was discussed in Chapter 5. If the children had been willing to sacrifice a larger share of the candy, they would presumably have gained a sense of mutual trust and group cohesion that would have fostered many of each child's long-term goals. Yet these values seemed pale in comparison with the lure of the seeable, touchable, smellable, about-to-be-tasted candy bar.

Does morality change with age?

We have seen that as children grow and change, they increasingly come to understand the moral implications of their actions and they become capable of more effective impulse control. And, returning to Dienstbier's argument, they begin to attribute emotional arousal in temptation situations to themselves—that is, to their own behavior (planned or actual) rather than to external controls. These changes are not surprising. After all, coercive parental treatment, such as physical punishment, becomes less frequent as children grow older. Children begin to manage their own lives. Actions increasingly reflect the child's own goals rather than external requirements. As children grow older, then, there ought to be an increasing range of situations in which they resist temptation, behaving according to their own standards of right and wrong. And the increasing morality ought to reflect the growth of internal controls, especially as the child constructs a more coherent *self* to whom actions can be referred. Why, then, have several studies not shown an age progression in moral behavior?

The moral behavior of children may actually improve with age, even though studies have not yet documented this fact. There are several possible reasons: (1) the same temptations are offered to all subjects without taking account of age and (2) the temptations consist of arbitrary requirements imposed by an external authority, so that the attention of both older and younger subjects is drawn to external factors as the cause of their apprehension. Consider the first point: In studies of cheating, such as Hartshorne and May's, the subjects are being tempted to try to get a better grade on a test or a better score on a measure of skill or physical prowess than they have actually earned. Assuming that during grade school children increasingly become convinced of the importance of outstanding performance on such tests, then the fact that older children cheat at least as often as younger children could reflect the joint actions of (1) their better resistance to temptation and (2) their stronger motivation to cheat. The second point may be more important. If laboratory studies of resistance to temptation are to give older children a chance to show better powers of self-control than younger children, the studies must provide conditions in which children can attribute their emotional arousal to internal causes. We suggest, therefore, that the existing research on age changes in resistance to temptation (or the absence of such changes) has not provided the definitive answer to questions about developmental change. The correspondence between the cognitive and behavioral levels of development may be closer than we have yet detected.

We have been considering instances in which children's moral thinking becomes more morally mature while their behavior does not seem to—cases in which older children do not behave as morally as their level of moral thought might lead us to expect. There is an opposite kind of case, one in which children behave in a morally proper manner when they are much too young to be capable of mature moral thought. Sometimes their behavior can be explained simply as a reflection of their fear that they will be punished if they misbehave. But altruistic acts are less easily explained. Such behavior provides clear evidence that prosocial behavior can grow out of processes other than the acquisition of moral understanding and the improvements in perspective taking that occur with increasing age. Perhaps these other processes, such as a primitive form of empathy that is based on simple affective conditioning, do not change with age, while other processes affecting moral behavior do.

Even for the processes that do change with age, development is not automatic. Clearly, the kind of training children receive matters a great deal, both in how children think about moral issues and in how they behave. Moral maturity in behavior and thinking is enhanced by child-rearing techniques that: (1) build children's perspective-taking skills, enabling them to understand how their own actions will be experienced by others and to take account of others' needs, information, and expectations; (2) foster children's empathy, making possible both the understanding and the sharing of emotions; (3) give children a reasonable amount of control over their own actions and emphasize that they *have* this control; and (4) avoid using discipline that leads children to conclude they are ruled by arbitrary, external forces.

We have shown that patterns of family interaction are important in the development of attachment, aggression, self-esteem, impulse control, sex typing, and moral thought and behavior. It is time now to draw some of these themes together and consider parent-child interaction in its own right, looking for any overall principles that apply to a wide range of behavioral domains.

SUMMARY AND COMMENTARY

We have discussed two main aspects of moral development: Children's ability to inhibit actions that are socially disapproved (*resistance to temptation*) and their ability to take positive action to help, comfort, or gratify other people (*altruism*). How do children learn to resist temptation?

1. Children can learn such inhibition simply out of fear of punishment. However, as children become skilled in judging when they are likely to get caught, fear alone becomes less of a deterrent when they are free from surveillance. Punishment works fairly well to inhibit undesired behavior in the short run, but in the long run it interferes with the internalization of values and achievement of self-control.

2. Children become upset when they do something wrong. Often it is not clear (to others or to the children themselves) whether they are afraid of being punished or upset because they have violated their own standards. If children are told that their upset is due to transgressing against their own values, their ability to resist temptation on future occasions is strengthened.

3. Children are influenced by whether they have seen someone else resist or yield to a temptation. However, modeling is more likely to produce disinhibition (that is, influence a child in the direction of yielding to temptation) than to strengthen inhibition.

4. The Freudian view that children achieve self-control by forming an internalized representation of the parent (the superego) and punishing themselves (through guilt) for their own misdeeds has not stood up well to empirical test. For example, children who most successfully resist temptation do not show any more guilt (or other emotional upset) about wrongdoing than other children.

5. The development of self-control is fostered by parents' use of *induction* (appeals to children's respect and affection for others). Preschool children can be effectively deterred from undesired behavior if prohibitions are supported by explanations. Older children become more responsive to moral arguments regarding the rights of others (Parke, 1974). By junior high school age, children whose parents frequently use induction show the strongest internal controls. These children tend to have *strong* and *flexible* consciences: they behave in a self-controlled way in order to maintain relations of mutual trust with others; they do not rigidly insist on applying rules.

How do children learn helpfulness and concern for others?

6. Children behave altruistically at a surprisingly early age. In their second year children quite often offer help or comfort when someone else is distressed. Frequency of this behavior varies considerably from child to child, with the highest rates found among children whose mothers talk to them about how other people feel and at the same time express strong feelings of indignation and disappointment when the child causes distress to another.

7. The principles of classical conditioning can be used to explain early altruism. Experiments have shown that children are more likely to help another person (even at some cost to themselves) or share with the other person if they have a common experience of distress or pleasure and if these feelings have been *visible* on the face of the partner. No doubt, the affective explanations used by the mothers of altruistic two-year-olds (point 6) provide occasions for such conditioning.

8. A number of experimental programs for increasing children's altruism have demonstrated that children become more al-

truistic if: (a) they are put into a good mood and (b) they are given practice in helping and being helped, taking turns with an adult who models altruistic responses.

Thus, we have good evidence that altruism can be directly taught. Yet some curious findings and some curious gaps in the findings raise questions about the important elements in the training process. First, the role of the model is not straightforward: While models can draw children's attention to others' distress and show them how help and comfort can be given to others, children are not likely to use this knowledge in real-life situations unless they have an affectionate relationship with the model. Second, the role played by direct reinforcement is unclear: Praise or reward ought to make children more altruistic, and yet, as Radke-Yarrow has pointed out, being helpful in order to get a personal reward is almost a contradiction in terms. Parents and teachers want children to be helpful without the thought of personal gain or even at some sacrifice of personal goals. Thus the Radke-Yarrow group made an effort to train children in altruistic behavior while carefully avoiding direct reinforcement. As we shall see in Chapter 10, direct reward sometimes undermines the very behavior it is intended to strengthen. So while direct reinforcement undoubtedly plays *some* role in moral development (perhaps especially with very young children), its possible advantages and disadvantages are not yet fully understood.

Is there a relationship between the regular developmental changes in moral thinking and children's moral behavior and its accompanying emotions (fear of punishment, empathic concern about others' distress or pleasure)?

9. While clear progressions occur with age in the nature of moral thought, a similar progression in moral action is by no means established.

10. Children know a good deal more about what they ought to do than they show in their actions. Part of the problem is simple self-interest: Children often do what is immediately self-gratifying even if they know they should give others' interests more weight.

11. Certain techniques of child rearing seem to foster both the development of mature moral thinking and the ability to behave morally. Paramount among these is the emphasis on the needs, rights, and feelings of other people. The arbitrary assertion of parental power, on the other hand, appears to have negative effects on both moral reasoning and moral behavior.

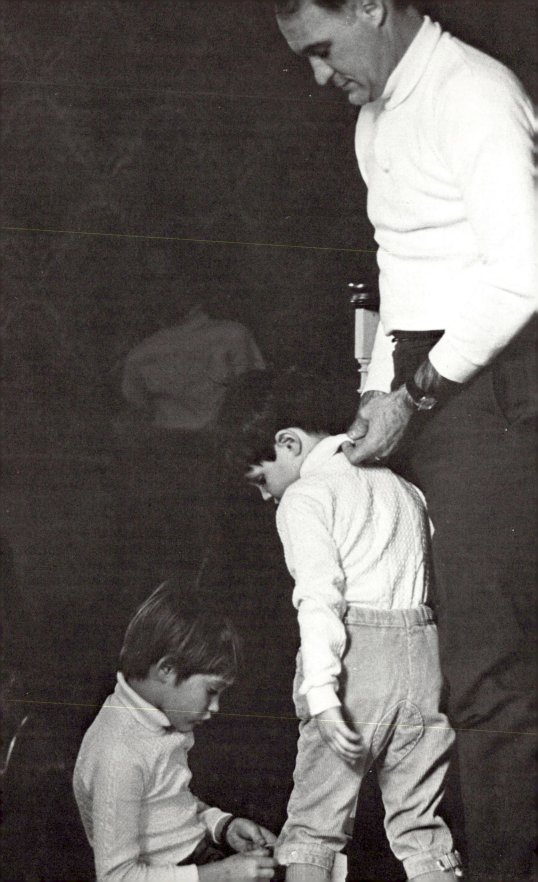

CHAPTER 10

Child-Rearing Practices
and Their Effects

W<small>E</small> have followed the child from the emergence of attachment during early infancy through the development of the more mature forms of social affiliation. We have examined aggressive behavior and discussed the changes in the ways children express and control anger as they grow older. We have traced the shift from impulsivity to a higher level of organization in which impulses are inhibited at least temporarily and integrated into a more planful life that permits the pursuit of long-range goals. We have examined the development of the sense of self and considered the role played by knowledge of self and knowledge of others in the maturing of social behavior. We have found that social knowledge and empathic emotions are primary factors in moral development.

We have emphasized the strong developmental thrust in all these realms of behavior. The process of growing up has its own intrinsic energy, and we cannot understand socialization by merely examining child-rearing techniques. Children grow physically, intellectually, socially, despite anything that parents do. And indeed, these growth processes impose certain requirements and limitations on parents—on what methods they can use and how effective these methods will be with children at different developmental levels. Nevertheless, parents' child-rearing practices do have an impact on outcome—that is, on their children's social behavior.

367

We now attempt to integrate what we know about the effects of different styles of child rearing on the whole range of social behavior. First, we review several important studies that—unlike the work we have been discussing—focus on more than one behavioral domain. These studies contrast the child-rearing practices of parents whose children readily develop good competence in a number of respects with the practices of parents whose children have been slow to acquire age-appropriate competencies. We then present a summary of findings, drawing on studies presented in earlier chapters as well as those discussed in this chapter. Finally, we briefly consider what makes parents behave the way they do—the conditions that influence the strategies parents use to carry out their child-rearing responsibilities.

CHILD REARING AND THE GROWTH OF COMPETENCE

Two classic studies of child rearing—one from the early 1940s by A. L. Baldwin and his associates (Baldwin, Kalhorn, and Breese, 1945) and the other from the 1960s by Diana Baumrind (1967, 1971, 1973)—come to somewhat different conclusions about how children are affected by parenting styles—specifically, the effect of close control. We first describe the studies and their findings and then attempt to reconcile their differences in the light of other research.

Democratic child rearing

During the 1940s Baldwin was associated with the Fels Institute, which was conducting a long-range study of children's development. Families entered the study at the time of a child's birth and remained as part of the research sample until the child was grown. Parents were interviewed at several times during the child's growth and observers visited the home many times, taking detailed notes on the parent-child interaction. Children were also observed at school (including nursery school) and at camp. The kind of information obtained from home visits is illustrated in Baldwin's description of a farm family, the Dugans (the name is fictitious). The parents were married young, and in their late twenties seem much older—sober, industrious, conservative, not given to spontaneous expression of feelings. Baldwin describes interactions with their son Sam as follows:

> Parental policy set rigid boundaries, required a minimum of contact with the child, and let the parents off in the easiest fashion commensurate with their obligations to the child so that they could devote them-

selves to the more important work waiting for them. A visitor reports that "at eleven months, his mother was dressing him at the kitchen table, holding him on her lap like a small baby and thrusting him into his clothes." No opportunity was given for any degree of self-help because that would have been time-consuming. At the same age, on the other hand, he was already being given sharp slaps to teach him not to get into things.

An observation at 17 mo.: "He saw my (observer's) book, and dove for it, jabbering unintelligibly. He slapped at my book, and his mother said 'don't do that.' He took my ankle in his hand and his mother told him not to do that. He went over to the couch and pulled at a pillow, to which his mother said "Now leave that alone."

As Sam grew older and could more nearly be trusted to conform, the relationship became more inert, with Mrs. D. ignoring his activities until a disciplinary crisis would arise. The fact that Mrs. Dugan rarely forestalls a crisis by acting ahead of time can, in part, be attributed to her lack of attention to the child—there is practically no interaction between her and Sam *except* when he has done something irritating or "Wrong." . . . In the school area, as in others, Mrs. Dugan's only concern is with success or failure, conforming conduct or troublesome mischief. (Baldwin, 1945, pp. 493–94).

In many other Fels families the interaction between parents and children was frequent, lighthearted, and full of good humor—seemingly enjoyed by all parties concerned.

The researchers identified two major dimensions on which the families in the study showed considerable variation: *democracy* and *control*. These two dimensions were defined as follows:

1. *Democracy*. Parents received a high rating if: (a) verbal communication between parent and child was at a high level; (b) the child was consulted about policy decisions, offered explanations of reasons for the family rules and answers to questions; (c) the child was given a choice in as many decisions as possible and was allowed the maximum freedom compatible with safety and the rights of others; (d) self-reliance was encouraged by withholding help when the child could do (or learn to do) without help; (e) restraint was placed on excess emotionality; the children were viewed objectively.

2. *Control*. Parents received a high rating if: (a) restrictions on the child's behavior were emphasized; (b) these restrictions were clearly conveyed to the child (whether arrived at democratically or autocratically); (c) friction over disciplinary decisions was rare.

The two dimensions were not independent: Families with a democratic child-rearing style were also above average in demanding and obtaining control. However, the dimensions were also not identical—democracy and control had somewhat different effects.

The longitudinal study continued for many years, and as new families were recruited into the sample, the correlation between parents' characteristics and children's behavior was studied for successive "waves" of families. The results sometimes varied from sample to sample. As an example of the kinds of relationships that were obtained for one sample, we examine the results of an analysis of observations of sixty-seven four-year-olds in nursery school (Baldwin, 1948).

The researchers rated these children on such characteristics as friendly play, bossing other children, asking help, curiosity, and lack of emotional control. When the parents' scores on the democracy factor were correlated with the characteristics of the children, the children of highly democratic parents were found to be above average in ability to plan, fearlessness, leadership, aggressiveness (and seldom being the victims of other children's aggression), and cruelty.

In another report Baldwin (1949) amplified his description of the children of democratic parents by indicating that these children tended to be bossy, and successfully so—that is, they managed to control other children without letting the other children control them. They were also physically vigorous and active, highly socially involved (forming alliances with other children quite readily), somewhat less likely than other children to offer help to others, and not much involved in exploring the physical environment on their own. We see, then, that democratic child rearing appears to produce socially interactive children who effectively use both verbal persuasion and physical force to gain their own ends but are not especially sensitive to others' needs nor susceptible to their influence. While generally constructive, these children were sometimes coercive to the point of cruelty in obtaining what they wanted.

The children of highly controlling parents were found to be obedient, suggestible, fearful, and lacking in tenacity. They were not quarrelsome, resistive, nor aggressive. And interestingly the children of parents who were *both* undemocratic and controlling—a combination that implies an authoritarian style of child rearing—were obedient and suggestible and lacking in curiosity, fancifulness, originality, and displays of affection. They were not quarrelsome, resistive, aggressive, or cruel.

We must remember that a key factor in a rating of high control was the absence of friction over disciplinary issues. In some cases this lack of friction did in fact reflect the parents' use of authority—they simply did not allow the children to talk back. In other cases, however, the parents had good control over their children because the children *accepted* parental directives without fuss and without being pressured. Thus, the obedience and lack of resistiveness at nursery school may have reflected the child's preexisting cooperative disposition and was not necessarily an outcome of parental control. Of course, some earlier aspects of the parent-child relationship may have been responsible for the children's cooperativeness.

Baldwin thought that while authoritarian control of children might be effective in getting children to conform to cultural demands, it placed too many restrictions on the child's personal freedom. Baldwin believed that children should have (1) a voice in family decision making, (2) few restrictions on their activities, and (3) the widest possible range of self-determination and choice. He acknowledged that a child who received such an upbringing might be somewhat resistant to the requirements of adult society. But he believed that the democratic approach would support the child's curiosity and independence of mind and was therefore to be preferred to the authoritarian approach.

Several problems with the Fels studies probably limit their generality. First, the democratic parents were considerably better educated (and more prosperous) than the parents who adopted more authoritarian methods of child rearing. Their better education and higher social position rather than their child-rearing methods may therefore explain two of the findings: (1) the tendency of these basically permissive parents to apply acceleratory pressure when it came to the mastery of certain skills, particularly school-related skills and (2) the fact that their children were more bossy, sociable, and planful than the children of authoritarian parents. In addition, the same pattern of relationships was difficult to find in different samples of children, and thus the overall conclusions were not clear-cut. Nevertheless, the findings were influential, providing support for the permissive philosophy of child rearing that was being advocated by many family relations experts and that was gaining considerable public acceptance at the time.

The child-rearing correlates of competence

More recently, researchers have focused on different aspects of child rearing. Families have been identified and grouped on bases different from those Baldwin used. And the effects of permissiveness (nonrestrictiveness) have been separated from the effects of open, rational discussion between parent and child. Baumrind's (1967, 1971, 1973) studies of the relationship between parents' behavior and children's characteristics started with the assumption that children's behavior is organized and that it is possible to identify consistent patterns or clusters of behavior. She examined the child-rearing practices associated with these clusters rather than attempting to find correlates of single, isolated traits, assuming that important distinctions among parental behaviors would begin to emerge only through studies of combinations of characteristics.

In her first major study, published in 1967, Baumrind set out to identify children who had certain combinations of scores on the following dimensions: self-control, approach-avoidance tendency, self-reliance, subjective mood, and peer affiliation. By approach-avoidance tendency she meant the extent to which a child reacts to novel, stressful, exciting, or unexpected stimuli by approaching them in an exploratory or curious way. Subjective mood referred to the amount of pleasure or zest shown by the child in the course of daily activities. A child who scored low on this dimension may have been either fearful, bored, subdued, or angry. Of course, no child is happy and zestful all the time, and individual children vary from one situation to another in how much self-control or self-reliance they show or in how eager they are to play with other children. However, certain children will display a given pattern of behavior quite often and across a variety of situations, so that this characteristic can be seen as a dominant feature of the child's personality.

Baumrind and her colleagues spent fourteen weeks observing 110 nursery-school children between the ages of three and four. Each child was rated using a Q-sort, a technique in which the rater works with a long list of specific behavior attributes, such as "impetuous," "wants to be alone when hurt," "sets difficult tasks for self," "accepts blame," and so forth, and then selects the attributes which more clearly describe the dominant behavior patterns of each child being observed. Other attributes are also selected which are most *unlike* the child. In addition, the researchers also observe some of the children in situations set up to elicit strategies for coping with frustration. It was possible to identify small subgroups of children who clearly displayed the following patterns:

1. *Competent* children (pattern I) were rated high on mood (generally happy), self-reliance, and approach or self-control (N = 13).
2. *Withdrawn* children (pattern II) were rated low on peer affiliation, mood (generally sad), and on approach tendencies (N = 11).
3. *Immature* children (pattern III) were rated low on self-reliance and self-control or approach (N = 8).

The researchers intensively studied the interactions between the three subgroups of children and their parents. They evaluated four dimensions of parental behavior that Baumrind believed should have important effects on the children's development:

1. *Parental control.* High ratings meant that parents were willing to exert influence over the child, able to resist pressure

from the child, and consistent in enforcing directives. Controlling actions were defined as parental attempts to modify the child's expressions of dependent, aggressive, or playful behavior, or to promote the child's internalization of parental standards.

2. *Maturity demands*. High ratings meant that parents were willing to pressure children to perform up to (or beyond) their ability in social, intellectual, and emotional spheres. These parents also insisted on independence, including giving children leeway to make their own decisions.

3. *Parent-child communication*. High ratings meant that parents used reasoning to obtain compliance, asked the child's opinion, and attempted to find out how the child felt about the issue under discussion. These parents also were willing to engage their child in arguments, listen to the child's reasons, and allow themselves to be influenced by sound reasoning. Low ratings were obtained by parents who acceded to crying and whining and who were not open about control efforts, manipulating the child by distraction or otherwise disguising the fact that control was intended.

4. *Nurturance*. High ratings were obtained by parents who were able to express love and compassion by acts and attitudes and to promote the child's physical and emotional well-being and who were able to express pride and pleasure in the child's accomplishments.

Baumrind's observers (who did not know whether the children were competent, withdrawn or immature) made two visits to the home, on one occasion remaining from just before dinner until the child was put to bed. They did not interact with family members but remained in the background as much as possible, recording all instances in which one member of the family attempted to influence another and the outcome of these influence attempts. Here are two typical examples:

1. Family is at the dinner table. Boy gets up.
   Father: "Hey, sit down!" (Yells, but good naturedly.)
   Boy sits and finishes milk. Boy gets up.
   Father: "What do you say, Todd?"
   Boy: "Excuse me, please."
   Father: "What?"
   Boy: "Excuse me please."
   Father "O.K."
   Boy: (on way out) "Tomorrow I'm not going to say it because I said it two times." (1967, pp. 65–66.)
2. Mother and son are in kitchen.
   Boy: "Can I go out?"

> Mother: "Yes. Oh, no, I guess you can't. I didn't realize how late it was."
>
> Boy: "*Please*, mother." Crying, beseeching, pleading. "I never get to go down the street."
>
> Mother: "I'll tell you, you can ride your bike on Fall Street."
>
> Boy: "On Spring Street."
>
> Mother: "Just once."
>
> Boy: "Why just once?"
>
> Mother: "You don't really want to go out."
>
> Boy leaves. (p. 66)

Many such sequences were recorded and scored. The father in the first sequence would receive a high score on control, for example, because he was willing to exert influence over the child and was consistent in enforcing his rules about leaving the table. The mother in the second sequence would receive a low score on control (at least for this particular sequence) because she did not resist pressure from the child and was inconsistent in enforcement. She would probably also be scored low on communication because she did not state clearly what she wanted the child to do (or not do) but kept shifting the nature of her demand. Furthermore, she allowed the child to use emotional pressure to change her mind. These particular vignettes would probably not be scorable on nurturance.

Interactions between the mother and child were also studied during a structured observation session in a laboratory playroom containing toys, a mouse in a cage, and a work table with a child-sized chair and an adult chair. During the first part of the session the mother was asked to teach her child number concepts. In the second part of the session the mother was told that the child could play with the mouse, keeping it in the cage or on the child's lap, but off the furniture or floor. The mother was also asked to have the child help tidy up the room before leaving. Magazines were provided so that the mother could play with the child or read. These instructions were designed to create situations in which the mother would have to try to direct the child—to keep working on number concepts, to keep the mouse off the floor, and to help clean up.

The behavior of both parents during the home visits and the behavior of the mother during the structured observation were scored and the scores were combined to yield measures of control, maturity demands, communication, and nurturance. The parental scores were then computed for the families of the competent, withdrawn, and immature children (the three groups originally selected). The results are shown in Figure 10-1.

Both the home visits and the structured observations yielded similar findings. The children who were happy, self-reliant, and able to meet challenging situations directly (pattern I) had parents who exercised a good deal of control over their children and demanded re-

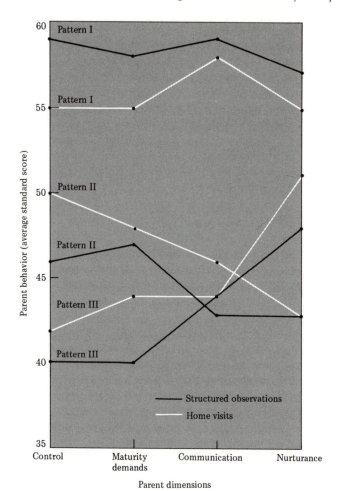

Figure 10-1. Differences in parents' behavior patterns. Note that parents of the competent children (pattern I) score highest on all parenting dimensions. Parents of the immature children (pattern III) seem to expect less of their children than parents of competent or withdrawn (pattern II) children. (Adapted from Baumrind, 1967)

sponsible, independent behavior from them but who also explained, listened, and provided emotional support. The parents of children in the other two groups had lower scores on all four dimensions than the parents of the competent children. The parents of withdrawn children (pattern II) tended to be somewhat more controlling and demanding and somewhat less warm than parents of the immature children (pattern III). The parents of the immature children were moderately nurturant but conspicuously low in exercising control. These findings are, of course, based on very small samples of children who clearly fit a particular behavioral pattern. We are given no information about the many children who had mixed patterns—were competent in some respects but either immature or withdrawn in others.

The Baumrind research group has since extended its work to new samples of parents and children (Baumrind 1971, 1973). The original findings have been supported in almost all respects. In the more recent work, a different approach was taken; the first step was to define clusters of parental behaviors. Then the characteristics of children in different types of families were studied. Three patterns of parenting were identified: authoritarian, authoritative, and permissive. Once more, we should note that no parent fits a given category all the time—no one was always permissive or always authoritarian. These categories are simply dominant patterns that reliably distinguish certain parents from one another. These three types of parents can be described as follows:

1. *Authoritarian.* Parents who fit this classification were likely to: attempt to shape, control, and evaluate the behavior and attitudes of their children in accordance with an absolute set of standards; value obedience, respect for authority, work, tradition, and preservation of order; discourage verbal give and take. These parents sometimes rejected their children.

2. *Authoritative.* Parents who fit this classification were likely to: attempt to direct the child in a rational, issue-oriented manner; encourage verbal give and take, explain the reasons behind demands and discipline but also use power when necessary; expect the child to conform to adult requirements but also to be independent and self-directing; recognize the rights of both adults and children; set standards and enforce them firmly. These parents did not regard themselves as infallible but also did not base decisions primarily on the child's desires.

3. *Permissive.* Parents who fit this classification were likely to: attempt to behave in an accepting, positive way toward the child's impulses, desires, and actions; use little punishment; consult the child; make few demands for household responsibility or order; allow the child to regulate his or her own activities as much as possible and avoid the exercise of control; attempt to use reasoning but not overt power to achieve objectives.

Children of these types of parents differed behaviorally in a number of ways, especially:

1. Authoritarian parents had children who showed little independence and who obtained middle-range scores on social responsibility.

2. Authoritative parents had independent and socially responsible children.

3. Permissive parents had children who conspicuously lacked social responsibility and who were not especially independent.

While these general outcomes held true for boys and girls, some sex differences in the effect of parenting patterns were observed. Authoritarian parenting seemed to be more damaging to boys than girls, in the sense that the sons of these parents were less likely than the other children to have developed independent, self-reliant behavior; also they were more likely to be angry and defiant. (Curiously, permissive parenting also seems to have had this same effect on boys.) Authoritative parenting seemed to be more strongly associated with self-reliance and achievement orientation in girls than boys, and these girls were often resistive toward parents and domineering toward age mates. In boys, authoritative parenting seemed to be associated with being friendly and cooperative.

A group of the Baumrind subjects (forty-two girls and fifty-six boys) who had been studied as preschoolers were reevaluated at the age of eight to nine during free-play periods at school, while working in the classroom, and during family interaction sessions (the child and the two parents were asked to agree on some moral dilemma problems). Baumrind (1977) no longer used the term *competence* to describe the child; she now focused on *agency*—the tendency to take initiative, assume control of situations, and make efforts to deal with the daily problems that arose. She rated the children according to social and cognitive agency:

1. *Social agency* was rated high if the child participated actively and showed leadership in group activities, was bold in approaching and interacting with other children, and was not anxious or apprehensive in peer interactions.

2. *Cognitive agency* was rated high if the child had a clear sense of identity, set standards and strove to meet them, liked and responded positively to intellectual challenges, and showed originality in thought.

In both the cognitive and social spheres, *agentic* children were distinguished from passive, helpless, dependent children—those who wait for others to solve their problems and tend to withdraw from challenges and social encounters.

After many hours of observation it was found that children could be reliably rank-ordered from high to low along these two dimensions. The early and later interactions with their parents were then analyzed to see what types of parental treatment were associated with high agency. Table 10-1 summarizes the results:

TABLE 10-1 Relationship between parental practices and children's social and cognitive agency

PARENTAL PRACTICES	CHILDREN'S CHARACTERISTICS AT AGES 8–9	
	Boys	Girls
At preschool age:		
Authoritative	Fairly high cognitive and social agency	Very high cognitive and social agency
Authoritarian	Mid-level social, low cognitive agency	Mid-level cognitive and social agency
Permissive	Low social, very low cognitive agency	Low cognitive and social agency
At ages 8–9:		
Firm rule enforcement		High social and cognitive agency
High demand for self-control	High cognitive agency	
Authoritarian	Low social and cognitive agency	

SOURCE: Based on Baumrind's findings (1971, 1973, 1977).

Clearly, the children who are self-confident and oriented toward achievement at the age of eight or nine do not usually have highly permissive parents. And at this age the children continue to show the positive effects (if one values agency, that is!) of their parents' authoritative behavior when the children were preschoolers. Furthermore, agency was enhanced if the parents continued to demand mature behavior and enforce rules firmly as the child entered school. A sex difference in the effect of certain parental patterns was again observed. Girls—but not boys—were more agentic, and contributed more of their own ideas to family discussion if the nature of their interaction with their parents was rather argumentative and abrasive (Baumrind, 1977). Boys were more likely than girls to show a loss of interest in achievement and to withdraw from social contact during their early school years if their parents had treated them in an authoritarian way.

Mothers' exercise of control and children's self-reliance

Baumrind's sample of children was initially drawn from thirteen nursery schools in the San Francisco Bay area in California. Some of the schools were private cooperatives, some were public school cooperatives, and some were operated by universities in the area. Thus, while the cultural background of the subjects was fairly broad, the results are not necessarily applicable to children in different regions and from different socioeconomic backgrounds. However, some evidence confirming Baumrind's findings is available from Emmerich's (1977) work with 596 preschoolers from low-income families, who lived in three widely separated cities. All the children were eligible for Head Start programs and a majority of the children were black. An intensive assessment program was undertaken with these children, but only a small segment is relevant to our present concerns. The children were observed twice, once in the fall and once in the spring of their first preschool year and each child was given a score on autonomous achievement. Children with high scores frequently took the initiative in carrying out various tasks, tried to pursue difficult tasks, exhibited persistence, completed activities without asking for help, exhibited goal-directed activity as distinct from aimless wandering, showed planning when pursuing activities, and corrected or modified performance to meet the child's own standard. This cluster of behaviors is similar to Baumrind's competence or agency, especially cognitive agency. However, autonomous achievement is related to *social* competence in the sense that high scores on this cluster of attributes are positively correlated with interpersonal friendliness and cooperativeness and negatively correlated with withdrawal or hostility.

Is autonomous achievement related to the way preschoolers are treated by their parents? In order to answer this question Emmerich interviewed the children's mothers (not their fathers) about their child-rearing styles and observed them helping the children learn a task. In the first situation the mothers were asked to describe the instructions they would give their child on the first day he or she went to school. Some of the mothers said they would simply tell the child how to act ("Don't holler," "Mind the teacher," and so forth). Such instructions were coded as *imperative communications*. Other mothers amplified their instructions by giving reasons for what should be done or not done and said they would discuss what to expect from the teacher, how the teacher and other children might react to certain actions by the child, what kind of help the child could expect, and so forth. Such answers were called *instructive communications*. Each mother was given a score that reflected the proportion of imperatives in her total discussion. In the second situation the mother was asked to help the child sort some materials simultaneously on two dimensions—a difficult conceptual task for a preschool child. First, the mother was shown how the sorting was supposed to be done, and then she was asked to teach the task to the child. Observers noted the mother's teaching strategy and the amount of help she gave the child.[1]

[1] This task was originally developed by Hess and Shipman (1967)

Some mothers explained the objective of the exercise; others would simply say, "Put this one there." The mothers also differed in terms of control and a control score was obtained that was based on: (1) number of different control strategies used, (2) number of responses to child inattention, (3) number of criticisms, and (4) variation between positive and negative responses—that is, difference in emotional tone of approving or disapproving responses.

The clearest results were obtained by combining the mothers' scores on control and on imperativeness. When a mother was both imperative and controlling, her son tended to be *low* in autonomous achievement striving. No relationship was found between these aspects of mothers' behavior and their daughters' achievement striving. Thus we again see a sex difference: Certain forms of restricting, controlling, and demanding parental behavior are more damaging to the development of a self-reliant, problem-solving orientation in boys than in girls.

Baumrind and Emmerich worked with fairly young children and their families. The patterns of parental behavior they have described might have a different effect on children approaching adolescence. Alternatively, the effect of parental behavior in later childhood and adolescence may depend on the groundwork already laid: Perhaps permissive parenting works well with adolescents who have been treated authoritatively in earlier childhood. These issues are currently being studied in longitudinal research, but for the moment they remain important but unanswered questions.

MAJOR DIMENSIONS OF CHILD REARING

Almost infinite variations can be found in the way parents carry out their child-rearing functions. Some variations are related to the cultural setting in which the family lives and other variations are related to the economic resources that are available. Even within a fairly homogeneous cultural group, differences can be found in parental practices. A number of studies have suggested that parents differ from one another in terms of two major dimensions:

1. *Permissiveness-restrictiveness.* Some parents exercise close, restrictive control over many aspects of their children's behavior; others give the children almost complete freedom; many find a balance somewhere between the two extremes.

2. *Warmth-hostility.* Although almost all parents feel affection for their children, they vary in how openly or frequently their affection is expressed and in the degree to which affection is mixed with (or even outweighed by) feelings of rejection or hostility.

The second dimension is not controversial, in the sense that few would doubt that children benefit from parental affection, although they may disagree about precisely what the benefits are and how they come about. The first dimension is much more controversial. Through the centuries considerable disagreement has existed concerning optimal levels of control and restriction of children's behavior. More recently, studies of parents and children have not yielded consistent conclusions on the effects of high levels of control. For example, Baldwin concluded that parental restrictiveness is harmful to children, while Baumrind sees positive outcomes from firm parental control. In the sections that follow, we take up these two major dimensions of parenting. As we summarize information on the effects of various patterns of parenting, it is well to remember that only trends or averages are being described. Exceptions to the generalities are plentiful, and many aspects of parenting have not yet been described or understood. Every family is unique, and in analyzing group trends, we must remember that variation among families within a given group is still very great.

PARENTAL CONTROL

Definitions of control and methods of measurement have varied greatly from one study to another. Control has variously meant: (1) restrictiveness—setting rather narrow limits on the child's range of activities, (2) demandingness—expecting a high level of responsibility for the child's age, (3) strictness—enforcing rules and not yielding to the child's attempts at coercion, (4) intrusiveness—interfering in the child's plans and relationships, or (5) arbitrary exercise of power—"You do it because I said so!" We will consider these various aspects of parental control separately, since they clearly have different effects.

Consistent enforcement of demands and rules

When parents consistently enforce their rules and demands and do not let their children's noncompliance or resistance divert them, their children have been found to be:

1. Able to control aggressive impulses and not coercive toward parents (Patterson, 1976, Chapter 4[2]);
2. Adequately controlled (as distinct from undercontrolled or overcontrolled) (Block, 1971, Chapter 5);

---

[2] Chapter designations refer to the chapter in this book where research is presented.

3. High in self-esteem at age ten or eleven (Coopersmith, 1967, Chapter 7);

4. Competent and agentic—that is, able to approach new situations with confidence, to take initiative and persist in tasks once begun—generally positive in mood and not withdrawn or immaturely impulsive (Baumrind, 1967, 1971, 1977, Chapter 10).

An important element in enforcement of demands and rules is parental vigilance: Parents must notice whether children have complied. Yet, children become remarkably skillful at escaping notice; removing themselves from sight and earshot quickly, they hope that by the time they reappear parental demands will have been forgotten. And many parents do forget. In addition, parents may not notice when rules are broken. A child may pinch or push a younger sibling while the mother is talking on the phone or climb on a newly cleaned piece of furniture while the mother is watching television. Some parents find it hard to do several things at once—to carry out other activities while keeping detailed track of what their children are doing. Some parents are perceived by their children as being uncannily vigilant; others are known to be easily distracted and unobservant. Only the reasonably vigilant parent can enforce rules firmly and consistently.

High expectations and training to meet them

Parents differ in the number and type of demands they make. And the level of their demands can be quite independent of the level of enforcement—that is, parents can make many demands but enforce few of them or make few demands but firmly enforce the ones they do make. A demand is a goal that the child is expected to meet, and goals vary: Some parents expect help with household tasks, or some ask for help with child care, others demand politeness and consideration in interpersonal relationships. When parents make few demands they may be underestimating the child's capacities and maturity level or they may be so disinterested and preoccupied that they find it easier to do things themselves than to get the child to do them. Sometimes parents have a permissive philosophy of child rearing that makes them feel they do not have the right to make demands or that restrictions or commands will compromise the child's sense of well-being. Whatever the reason, some parents make few demands and others make many. And different levels of demands seem to result in different outcomes. When parents impose fairly high levels of demands, their children have been found to be:

1. Low in aggression (boys) (Edwards and Whiting, 1977, Chapter 6);

2. Altruistic rather than egoistic (Whiting and Whiting, 1973, 1975, Chapter 9);

3. Above average in competence and agency (Baumrind, 1967, 1971, 1977, Chapter 10).

Low demands, on the other hand, have been found to be associated with:

1. High aggression (Sears, Maccoby, and Levin, 1957, Chapter 4);

2. Undercontrol of impulse (Block, 1971, Chapter 5);

3. Immaturity (Baumrind, 1967, Chapter 10).

The level of demands imposed by Baldwin's democratic parents is not known, but in view of their emphasis on freedom, it seems likely that their demands were not high. The tendency (at least in one sample) of these children to be egoistic, as well as above average in aggression is, then, consistent with the evidence cited above.

Assigning duties to and expecting mature behavior from children appears to have positive effects. Of course, demands are only helpful if the children are old enough and have sufficient skills to carry them out. But how do children develop adequate skills? A theme that has emerged repeatedly is the importance of *training*: Children can be trained to inhibit quarreling (Chittenden, 1942), to tolerate frustration (Keister and Updegraff, 1937), and to be helpful to others (Yarrow, Scott, and Waxler, 1973, Chapter 9; Staub, 1971, Chapter 9) by calling to their attention the signals that action is needed and showing them the kinds of actions that will accomplish the desired ends without generating new problems. Sometimes a very specific motor skill (for example, how to tie shoes) must be taught before the child can respond to a parental demand (for example, to get dressed without help). Clearly, the positive outcomes of high demands—especially a sense of competency—can only be expected if the child has the necessary skills to meet the demands. Indeed, the salutary effect of high parental demands probably results primarily from the learning necessitated by the demands. The children of demanding parents acquire a wide range of skills on which they can subsequently draw for their own enterprises outside the parents' home. In other words, high parental demands that are appropriate to the child's age and are accompanied by training can provide a steppingstone to self-reliance.

Restrictive parenting

Demands require that the child do something he or she does not want to do. Restrictions prevent the child from doing something the child does want to do. In Baldwin's (1955, Chapter 10) study the Fels mother, Mrs. Dugan, was a restrictive parent. She primarily responded to her seventeen-month-old son by saying "Don't do that" or "Leave that alone" or "Stop that." She provided little indication of what she did want him to do. Restrictive parenting takes additional forms, of course, as the child grows older and more independent. At the age of four or five, children begin to ask for permission to explore the neighborhood and play at other children's houses. Sears, Maccoby, and Levin (1957) found that mothers of five-year-olds allowed different degrees of freedom to roam:

> Mother A: I don't want him to leave our own little area. I spent a whole summer chasing him and licking him, and putting him to bed, and we have accomplished it. He must come right home from school and play around here; that is one thing I do enforce. I think that is perhaps the most important thing, because I have had the police looking for the children at times, and what I have been through has taught me to do it. (p. 276)

> Mother B: We live very closely together (neighboring houses), and the children are apt to be all here or all there, and it bothers my mother [child's grandmother] dreadfully. Sometimes she will say to me "You don't know where she is," and I say, "Oh, she's around someplace," and Mother says, "But you're not sure." (p. 277)

Parents also impose many other "don'ts": restrictions on noise-making, touching walls, getting clothes dirty, interrupting adults. Few studies have evaluated the effects of these and other restrictions. We know that children of restrictive parents tend to lack empathy (Feshbach, 1974, Chapter 4). Baldwin's early work (1945, 1948) reported that high parental emphasis on restrictions was associated with obedience, orderliness, and lack of aggression. However, the children of restrictive parents also appeared to be paying a price: They were timid and not tenacious in pursuing their goals. The price appeared to be particularly heavy if the parents were both restrictive and undemocratic, a point to which we will return. In an early review of a number of studies of child-rearing effects, Becker (1964) stresses that the effect of restrictiveness depends on certain other parental attitudes. If parents are warm and accepting, as well as restrictive, the child is likely to have the obedient, polite, and unaggressive character Baldwin has described. However, if parents are not only restrictive, but hostile, the children have difficulty developing normal relationships with age mates and tend to be withdrawn.

Arbitrary power assertion: authoritarian parenting

The authoritarian parent is highly controlling, in the sense that such a parent sets rules, requirements, and restrictions. However, these controls are established by fiat. The message is: "Do it because I said so." Such parents are highly concerned with maintaining parental authority and value obedience for its own sake. They may use fairly severe punishment if the child is defiant. The word "arbitrary" is the key word: The parent's authority is exercised with little explanation and little involvement of the child in decision making. The parent seems to claim the exclusive right to determine the conditions of the child's life and expects that the child will recognize this right. Children of parents who frequently assert power arbitrarily have been found to be:

1. Lacking in empathy (Feshbach, 1974, Chapter 4);

2. Low in self-esteem (Coopersmith, 1967, Chapter 7);

3. Poor in internalization of moral standards; oriented toward external rewards and punishments (Hoffman and Saltzstein, 1967, Chapter 9);

4. Obedient; not quarrelsome, resistive, aggressive, or cruel; lacking in spontaneity, affection, curiosity and originality; low in effective peer interaction (Baldwin, 1945, 1948, Chapter 10);

5. Weak in establishing positive relationships with peers; frequently sad in mood; somewhat withdrawn (Baumrind, 1967, 1971, 1973, 1977, Chapter 10);

6. Lacking independence; mid-level in social responsibility (Baumrind, 1971).

These studies picture the child of authoritarian parents as being quiet, obedient, unassertive, and rather joyless—a girl or boy whose impulses are under control but who lacks the buoyancy, tough self-confidence, and empathy needed for the give and take of peer-group play. But the arbitrary assertion of power is also associated with another kind of child—the aggressive-impulsive boys of Pioneer House and the coercive children (mainly boys) studied by Patterson, 1976, Chapter 4). Both groups of children had been subject to considerable arbitrary power assertion by their parents. The many studies of juvenile delinquents—not reviewed here—tell much the same story. The parents of all these children used discipline arbitrarily, with little explanation and sometimes considerable violence. Clearly, arbitrary power assertion is associated with docile, unaggressive, and constricted behavior only if the parents' power-assertive stance is accompanied by other elements, such as close parental supervision and/or a reasonable level of affection. Without these additional conditions, arbitrary power assertion is associated with both defiant and antisocial behavior.

Open communication patterns

Rules, requirements, and restrictions can also be enforced democratically. As Baldwin described this pattern of child rearing, children had a role in family decision making, with parents and children talking about matters both trivial and important. The children were allowed to voice disagreements with their parents and the parents accepted the obligation of explaining their actions and decisions whenever possible. Baumrind's authoritative parents also had a similar open communication style. The children from these high-communication families tended to be:

1. Competent, independent, cheerful, self-controlled, and socially responsible (Baumrind, 1967, 1971, Chapter 10);
2. Planful, as distinct from being given to aimless wandering; fearless; highly interactive with other children; dominant and fairly aggressive (Baldwin, 1945, 1948, Chapter 10);
3. High in self-esteem (Coopersmith, 1967, Chapter 7).

The content of communication as well as the fact of communication probably also affects children's behavior. While Baldwin and Baumrind would agree that participation in decision making facilitates children's acquisition of social competencies, they do not agree on the value of openly expressing feelings. Baldwin's democratic families were matter-of-fact and not given to displays of excitement, anger, or intense, affectionate involvement—in fact, they avoided the expression of passionate feelings of any kind. Baumrind's authoritative families were more emotionally expressive. Perhaps what we are seeing is the difference between the values held by people living in a Midwestern rural and small-town region in the 1930s and 1940s and the values held by residents of Berkeley, California, in the 1960s and 1970s. Clearly, parents can create a household atmosphere in which the open expression of feelings is allowed or even encouraged, or they can set a much more controlled emotional tone. We know very little about the impact on children of these variations in emotional atmosphere. Clearly, however, open communication concerning mutual expectations and point of view has a positive effect: the facilitation of the child's acquisition of social competencies.

Maintaining the child's sense of control: implications for child rearing

While parents need to be in control of their children—for their own well-being as well as the child's—children must also be able to exercise some degree of control over the events impinging on them. We saw in Chapters 2 and 3 that when mothers are responsive, their infants become more securely attached and subsequently move away from the mother with greater confidence to explore their social and inanimate environment. This finding can be interpreted to mean that the mother's responsiveness allows children to feel in control—that is, to believe that their own signals and responses determine what the mother will do. Since infants are helpless in so many respects, being able to influence the comings and goings of the mother is one of the infant's few means of controlling his or her environment. We also saw that children as young as twelve months of age are less fearful in a situation they can control (Gunnar, 1978). Apparently, a responsive environment—especially a responsive *human* environment—is one of the first requisites for a sense of control. Having such control then helps the child to overcome a fear of novel things. Conversely, if parents respond to their own schedules rather than to the child's signals, the child will suffer a sense of loss of control—what Seligman (1975) has called "learned helplessness." If this situation occurs consistently, the child is likely to become increasingly apathetic, passive, and even depressed.

We mentioned earlier (Chapter 7) that the child's need for being in control poses something of a problem for parents since parents also need to be in control of their lives—including the part that involves their children. They need a responsive child, just as the child needs a responsive parent. We have seen that the enforcement of certain demands for socially responsible behavior fosters an active, sociable, and cheerful orientation in children. Clearly, parental control does not necessarily produce learned helplessness in children. But how can a controlling parent have a child who also feels in control? Perhaps the dilemma is more apparent than real. Perhaps when the parent sets consistent and age-appropriate requirements for the child's behavior and rewards the child for compliance, the child comes to know what to do to satisfy the parents and how to get the reward. Thus, the child is in control of the outcome and at the same time meets parental demands; parent and child are simultaneously in control.

This solution seems simple and satisfactory, but unfortunately there is a problem with it: Children's spontaneous motivation to engage in certain kinds of activities is not necessarily facilitated by the knowledge that someone else wants them to do these things. In fact, if adults set up contingencies for doing the activities, children's interest may be reduced. Lepper, Greene, and Nisbett (1973) demonstrated this unexpected finding in the following way. They worked in a nursery school where the children spent most of their time in a large room with tables on which a variety of toys were arranged (for example, puzzles, clay, picture books, letter games, beads). The children had free choice of activities and were permitted to spend as much time as they wished with each one. For a number of days preceding the experimental sessions, a set of Magic Markers—something that the children had not previously had access to in the school—was put out on one of the tables, and records were kept of the amount of time each child spent in this activity. Then the children were taken individually into an adjoining room where they participated in one of three experimental conditions:

1. The children were seated at a table with a set of Magic Markers. They were shown an impressive "good player award" and were told they could earn the award if they did a very good job of drawing with the Magic Markers. When they had worked for a standard length of time on drawings, they were given the award (Group 1).

2. The children worked with the Magic Markers for a time equal to that spent by Group 1. They were not shown the awards before working on their drawings and nothing was said about a reward for doing a good job. But at the end of the session, they received an award and were told they had done well (Group 2).

3. The children spent an equivalent time working with the Magic Markers but were neither promised nor given an award. (Group 3).

Approximately two weeks after these experimental sessions were completed, the Magic Markers were set out in the classroom again, and the researchers recorded the children's spontaneous interest in the materials. The results were clear: Group 1 children had lost interest in the play materials compared to Group 2 and 3 children (See Figure 10-2). These results have been duplicated with other kinds of rewards and different groups of children by Lepper, Greene, and Nisbett and by other researchers (Deci, 1975).

The sense of being externally controlled may not be entirely responsible for the children's loss of interest, but it is probably at least part of the explanation. Lepper believes that an expected reward robs an activity of its intrinsic interest value and makes it seem like a means to some other end. In support of this interpretation, Lepper was able to show that although children produced more pictures under conditions of promised reward, the pictures were of lower quality—less detailed, thoughtful, and original—than those produced when this incentive was absent.

These findings pose a considerable problem for parents. Apparently, the stipulations that "You must finish your milk before you can leave the table" or "You have to hang up your clothes before you can go out to play" automatically diminish the child's interest in drinking milk or hanging up clothes and enhance the value of leaving

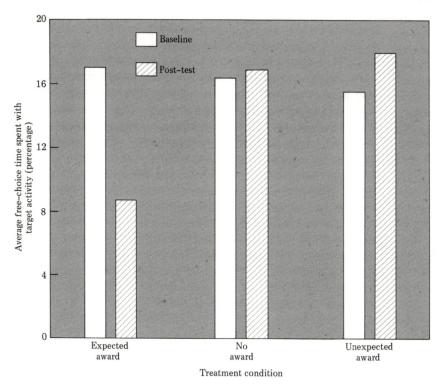

Figure 10-2.   Spontaneous interest in a previously rewarded task. Note that children who were regularly given an incentive to use certain play materials were less likely to play with them when given a free choice. (From Lepper, Greene, and Nisbett, 1973)

the table and going out to play. It would seem, then, that skillful parents must operate within a very delicate balance of forces: They need to obtain compliance to reasonable demands—for the child's, the parents', and the family's sake—without offering bribes and without destroying their children's sense of complying because they choose to, rather than because they are forced to.

A number of studies that we have reviewed offer clues to methods parents can use to help preserve their children's sense of control:

1. *Bee* (1967, Chapter 7) found that parents who used suggestive rather than directive methods of helping their children with problem-solving tasks had children who were better than average at continuing to work on a task in the presence of a highly distracting message.

2. *Dweck* (1975, 1978, Chapter 7) found that when the teacher attributed a child's failures at school to the child's not having tried hard enough, the child's effort was likely to increase on the next chance to do the task. Children who received a direct

or implied message that their failure was due to lack of ability tended to give up and lose interest following failure.

3. *Loeb* (1975, Chapter 7) found that parents who were suggestive rather than directive in interacting with their fourth- and fifth-grade sons had sons who achieved higher scores on a test of inner locus of control.

4. *Dienstbier* et al. (1975, Chapter 9) showed that if children had not complied with an adult instruction (had yielded to the temptation to do something more interesting than the assigned task), they were more likely to resist temptation on the next opportunity if their emotional upset was initially interpreted by an adult as having an internal origin ("You know you did something you shouldn't") rather than an external origin ("You are upset because I caught you").

5. *Staub* (1970b, Chapter 9) found that kindergarten and first-grade children were more likely to venture into another room to try to help a distressed younger child if the experimenter had explicitly left the child "in charge."

6. *Emmerich* (1977, Chapter 10) found that among preschool boys from low-income families, those who were rated highest in autonomous achievement had parents who less often said they would use imperative forms of instruction and who were less controlling while teaching the child a task in a laboratory situation.

Work by Feshbach and Bercovici (1973; not previously discussed) lends support to the findings of Bee and Emmerich that directive control seems to interfere with children's learning. Feshbach compared the mother-child interactions of two groups of first-graders (matched for socioeconomic background): children who were having difficulty learning to read and children who were learning to read quite readily. She found that the mothers of problem readers were more likely to make controlling and directive statements and to "intervene verbally or manually when the child made an error or encountered some difficulty." Apparently, the mothers of problem readers intruded into the child's task and manipulated the materials themselves—that is, tried to solve the problem directly for the child. Mothers of children who were learning well offered helpful suggestions but left the solution to the child—an approach also used by the Loeb and Bee parents. While we have not previously dealt with the very large literature on academic achievement and the family conditions that are associated with it, we introduce the Feshbach study to illustrate the probable linkage between supportive but not intrusive family interaction patterns and the child's (1) sense of being in control, (2) willingness to try a variety of new tasks (including reading), and (3) persistence when difficulties are encountered.

Harmonious families

We have been discussing the variations in the way families work out the issues of control that arise when parents' and child's goals or expectations do not match. Such situations arise in every family. The issues may be resolved in favor of the child (permissive solution), in favor of the adult (authoritarian solution), or a balance may be struck between their competing claims (democratic or authoritative solution). We should be aware, however, that there are families in which issues that need to be resolved in one of these ways very seldom arise. Baumrind found a few families that were neither permissive, authoritarian, or authoritative. The home visitors reported that the parents seemed to *have* control—in the sense that the children cheerfully did what the parents wanted them to do—but that they very seldom *exercised* control. It was as if parents and children agreed that the table needed to be set, clothes hung up, consideration shown by all family members to one another, and so forth. The children seemed to carry out their part in family enterprises spontaneously as if they were doing it of their own accord instead of because their parents demanded it. Baumrind labeled these families *harmonious*. Their existence draws our attention to the differences among families in the extent to which family members are committed to a set of mutually agreed upon values. Religion sometimes plays a strong part in forming these values, but whatever their source, shared values undoubtedly foster a sense that all family members are working together for the same objectives. When this sense of mutual sharing exists, bargaining or dominance of one member's objectives over another's becomes less important in parent-child interaction. Of course, it would be foolish to believe that complete harmony ever exists between the objectives of adults and those of children. Adults must be concerned about matters of health, safety, and economic well-being, balancing immediate goals against long-term goals—objectives which young children can hardly even perceive, much less share. Nevertheless, some children usually want to do what their parents want done, while other children have objectives that are frequently at variance with their parents'. And some parents genuinely enjoy doing what their children want done, while others experience their children's demands as irritating interference with their own primary goals. We know little about the conditions that lead to differences in the motivational match between parents and children. Undoubtedly, issues of control arise less frequently for parent-child pairs whose goals match, and this spirit of cooperation, in turn, improves the stability of the family interaction system—especially as the children reach adolescence.

PARENTAL WARMTH AND AFFECTION

Warmth is difficult to define, and yet the findings from almost every study of child rearing suggest that warmth is an important aspect of parenting. Warmth is closely bound up with several of the aspects of parenting already discussed. A warm parent is (1) deeply committed to the child's welfare, (2) responsive to the child's needs, (3) willing to spend time (within limits) in joint enterprises of the child's choosing, (4) ready to show enthusiasm over the child's accomplishments and acts of altruism, and (5) sensitive to the child's emotional states. Noncontingent acceptance of the child is the characteristic shared by all these aspects of warmth. The message is that nothing—neither the child's naughtiness nor the parent's anger—threatens the parent's basic commitment and enduring love for the child.

Effects of variations in parental warmth

Although parents, on the average, are quite warm and loving toward their children, sometimes they feel less than loving. Within the normal range of families the amount of affection they show their children may vary considerably. In most samples at least a small minority of parents show outright rejection—expressing feelings of dislike for the child, indicating that the child is unwanted, or saying that caring for the child is burdensome. We have seen that children's development is related to how affectionate and loving their parents are. Children whose parents are above average in acceptance and affection tend to have these characteristics:

1. They are securely attached at the age of twelve months (Ainsworth and Bell, 1969; Ainsworth, Bell, and Stayton, 1971; Clarke-Stewart, 1973; Chapter 3). Clarke-Stewart stressed that the open expression of pleasure and affection by mothers is an important factor in building secure attachment. Children of rejecting mothers tend to have an avoidant relationship with their mothers. Carrying these studies further, Matas (1978, Chapter 3) found that once a secure attachment had been formed, children were more "teachable" at a later time—that is, paid more attention to their parents' instructions and learned more readily from them.

2. They are noncoercive and relatively compliant (Patterson, 1976, Chapter 4). Patterson found that when parents could be

induced to begin showing affection and approval (on occasions when it was warranted), the first step toward normal patterns of family interaction had been taken.

3. They are high in self-esteem and when they are disciplined, they generally believe their parents' actions have been justified and fair (Coopersmith, 1967, Chapter 7).

4. They are more considerate of schoolmates and more likely to refer to internalized moral standards (rather than fear of punishment or hope of reward) when they discuss the reasons for conforming to moral rules (Hoffman and Saltzstein, 1967, Chapter 9).

5. They are more altruistic, even at a very young age (Zahn-Waxler, Radke-Yarrow, and King, 1979, Chapter 9).

Warmth as part of a pattern of parenting

In a review paper published in the mid-1960s, Becker (1964) summarized the child-rearing research that had been done up to that time. His objective was to understand the differential effects of restrictive versus permissive parenting. He noted many apparent contradictions—restrictiveness seemed to have different effects in some families than in others. He was able to resolve a number of the contradictions by taking the parents' warmth into account. Restrictiveness, in an overall context of parental warmth, was associated with politeness, neatness, obedience, and nonaggressiveness in children. Restrictiveness, when imposed by hostile parents, was associated with a variety of neurotic symptoms, including withdrawal from social interaction with peers. Similarly, the effects of permissiveness depended on the parents' warmth: Children whose parents were both warm and permissive tended to be socially outgoing, independent, active, creative, and domineering, while children whose parents were hostile and permissive (a combination that is close to neglect) tended to be aggressive or delinquent and noncompliant with adult demands.

The more recent work of Baumrind (1967, 1971) underscores the importance of the cluster that includes the characteristic of warmth. Her permissive parents were relatively warm, but they did not exercise firm control. Their children tended to be impulsive and immature. When parents were authoritative—combining warmth with firm control and open communication—the children were self-controlled and unusually competent (for their age) in the endeavors they undertook.

Finally, when Radke-Yarrow, Zahn-Waxler and their colleagues (Yarrow, Scott, and Waxler, 1973) were teaching altruism to children, they found that by observing a model, children could learn to perceive other people's distress and what might be done to help them.

However, they also found that their young subjects would use this knowledge in real-life situations only if the model had previously established a warm, nurturant relationship with them.

A common theme in these various findings seems to be that parental warmth binds children to their parents in a positive way—it makes children responsive and more willing to accept guidance. If the parent-child relationship is close and affectionate, parents can exercise what control is needed without having to apply heavy disciplinary pressure. It is as if parents' responsiveness, affection, and obvious commitment to their children's welfare have earned them the right to make demands and exercise control.

The fear of love

Some children's lives are littered with broken promises. Witness the comment of a fifteen-year-old boy who was living in an orphanage:

> (Why should a promise be kept?) They aren't. My mother called up and says "I will be up in two weeks," and then I don't see her for eight months. That really kills you, something like that. (Kohlberg, 1976, p. 51)

Not unexpectedly, children who have repeatedly had such experiences develop an attitude of suspicion toward unfamiliar adults who approach them offering affection. When Redl and Wineman (1951, 1952) investigated the early histories of the aggressive, out-of-control boys of Pioneer House, they found that the boys had never experienced continuing affection from a trustworthy adult. When the boys had tried to form attachments, they were repeatedly let down by adults who abandoned them. As a result, they had developed strong defenses against forming new ties. They were shocked when the adults of Pioneer House offered them continuing affection and acceptance (along with control) and when the adults made a special point of keeping the bargains they had made. If the boys felt themselves developing affection and trust they fought against it. A favorite device was to try to goad the adults into violence—if they succeeded, the children could then justify their anger against the world and would not have to feel guilty about their own violence. David Wineman describes as an example the case of Danny, who was especially violent during his first month at Pioneer House. The boy would begin each incident by teasing and insulting various members of the staff. When this did not provoke them into punishment, he would attack physically or smash up furniture or equipment. In order to prevent physical injury or unacceptable destruction, a staff member would have to restrain him physically (by holding, not punishment) until he calmed down sufficiently so that he could rejoin the other residents of the house. Incidents of this kind occurred at least twenty-five times during his first month at the House.

When faced with nonviolent control, one of the boys shouted "Why the hell don't you hit us?" Clearly, the boys were trying to prove that the Pioneer House adults were as abusive as their previous caretakers had been. Their provocations were extreme, and the staff members must have had to exercise enormous self-control to keep themselves from falling into the boys' traps. However they did continue with their control-plus-affection-plus-trustworthiness regime, and when the boys finally were able to reciprocate affection, the treatment program turned a corner—the boys began to exercise self-control. Their work graphically illustrates the importance of affectional ties in the socialization of children.

INFLUENCES ON PARENTS' BEHAVIOR

We have identified some of the important ways in which parents can differ in their child-rearing techniques. We have also shown that these differences affect the development of their children. We now briefly consider the question of why parents behave the way they do. What factors influence the effectiveness with which parents care for and guide their children? While this topic has not received much attention from researchers, we know that certain characteristics of the child and certain social and economic influences on parents have an impact on child-rearing practices.

The child's age

Of course, parents do not and cannot treat a twelve-year-old and a twelve-month-old in the same way. The change in parents' behavior reflects changes in the child's needs and competencies as well as changes in the parents' expectations. During the first year of a child's life, the parent-child interaction moves from a heavy focus on routine caretaking—feeding, changing, bathing, and soothing—and comes to include more noncaretaking activities like play and visual-vocal exchanges. During children's second and third years, parents often handle disciplinary issues by physical manipulation: They carry the child away from a mischievous activity to the place they want the child to go; they put fragile and dangerous objects out of reach; they sometimes spank. But as the child grows older, parents turn increasingly to reasoning, moral exhortation, and giving or withholding special privileges. As children move from infancy to middle childhood, parents show them less physical affection, become less protective, and spend less time with them (Baldwin, 1946; Lasko, 1954).

These changes in parental behavior seem clearly linked to the child's physical and mental growth—to changes in motor skills, language, judgment, and perspective-taking ability. It seems obvious that as the child grows larger and heavier, parents are less likely to resort to physical manipulation. And it seems almost equally obvious that parents are unlikely to reason with a child who doesn't yet talk and who seems to have a limited understanding of other people's speech. But the word *seems* is important here. Parents must function in terms of their perception of their children's abilities; the inferences they make may be more or less accurate. As an example of the nature of parental inferences, consider the attitudes on the topic of stubbornness held by a group of mothers of preschool children. The mothers said that they hadn't minded stubbornness when their children were younger—in a two-year-old, they had found it cute. But now that the children were three-and-a-half or four, their stubbornness was not amusing; in fact, it made the mothers very angry. Why? The answers varied. One mother said, "Now it seems *intentional*." Another said, "I feel I'm being manipulated." And still another said, "Now she knows just exactly what will make me mad." Clearly, the mothers were responding to more than the child's resistiveness; they were attributing intent to their children and responding to the *meaning* of the behavior. We have already seen that two- to four-year-olds increasingly come to understand other people's motives and perspectives, which enables them to manipulate others. The mothers quoted above seem quite accurate in their reading of this developmental change. Of course, some parents are less perceptive, and, failing to notice some of the changes taking place, may either baby their children or attribute to them more maturity than they actually possess.

The fact that parenting changes greatly as children grow older has been interpreted in different ways by different theorists. In explaining the developmental changes that occur in children's thinking about moral issues, for example, Mischel and Mischel (1976) suggest that these changes occur in response to certain changes in parental treatment. They argue that reasoning fosters internal rather than external moral orientations, and that as parents of very young children don't use much reasoning, young children tend to have an external orientation. However, they believe that as soon as the parents judge that the children are old enough for reasoning and induction, they begin to use these techniques and that this usage causes the children to shift toward an internal orientation. The cognitive-developmental theorist would be likely to say that it is the changes in the child's cognitions and improvement in the child's ability to take an internal orientation that cause the parent to shift toward an emphasis on reasoning. The cognitive-developmental view holds that parents tend to use whatever form of discipline and control works best. So parents' behavior is a result rather than a cause of developmental change. The difference between these points of view is unresolved. While we await further research, the most reasonable view is that influence runs in both directions throughout development. Those aspects of cognitive growth that depend only marginally on parental training will determine what parental inputs have what effects. At the same time parental inputs *do* have effects and can shape many aspects of the child's development.

Earlier, we discussed some of the ways in which developmental changes in the way children think about the world, themselves, and other people may influence their interactions with their parents (see especially the work on locus of control and self-concepts, Chapter 7, and on social perspective taking, Chapter 8). One set of concepts that ought to have an especially great bearing on the relationships between parents and children is children's understanding of the nature of authority and the obligations to be obedient toward persons in authority.

Damon's work (1977, Chapter 8) demonstrated that children progress through a series of steps in their understanding of authority. Preschoolers hardly recognize that authority is an issue. Sometimes they express the naive belief that what they want does not conflict with their parents' demands. Children soon become aware of such conflicts, however, and begin to equate parental authority with parental power. They believe that they must obey because their parents are bigger and stronger and have the power to discipline but that they are not obliged to obey if disobedience won't be detected. As children reach school age, they begin to understand reciprocal obligations: They believe that they owe obedience to their parents because their parents have done so much for them in the past. Parental authority is now seen as legitimized by the parents' greater knowledge and experience, as well as by the parents' kindness. At the preadolescent age, children have begun to see authority in a more differentiated way: They believe that adults have a right to demand obedience in areas in which they have greater competence but that obedience is less a matter of a general response to a superior person and more an agreed-upon relationship between equals engaged in a joint enterprise.

We do not know how or why children differ in their progress through these stages; surely, parental exercise of authority makes a difference. But disregarding for the moment the differences and considering only the changes that take place with age, we can speculate that the children's changing attitudes must have considerable implications for the parent-child relationship. The disobedience of very young children is rather innocent. These children are protected by their assumption that their parents don't *really* want a different kind of behavior and won't *really* be upset over disobedience. Soon, however, deliberate, knowing disobedience is in full flower. Dealing with children who feel that disobedience is all right if they can get away with it can be rather tension-producing for parents. Progress to the next level of thought brings parents some comfort, but not much. The parent is still cast in the role of policeman or "bad guy" when children comply out of fear of being caught. At the next level, usually reached at about age seven to nine, truly *willing* compliance begins to be seen for the first time; children accept their parent's *right* to exercise authority and believe that it is to their own long-term advantage to obey. This period of calm is brief, however. Soon parents must be able to justify their claim to authority in terms of superior knowledge and competence, and often justification will not be easy. And so, the child's willing acceptance of parental authority will increasingly be restricted to those areas of the child's activities in which the parents have expertise, and parents will not have control over many aspects of the child's extrafamilial life.

Amount of previous parenting experience

In many animal species, mothers are less skilled in caring for their firstborns than their later-borns. Mother rats with their first litter are slower to retrieve a pup that strays out of the nest; mother monkeys are slower to establish close and continuous ventral-ventral contact with a firstborn infant. Indeed, as we have seen, mother monkeys who have been reared in isolation are highly abusive toward their firstborn infants but behave nearly normally with later-borns. Clearly, subhuman young have great power to "educate" their caretakers. There is reason to believe that the same is true of human young.

One of the most interesting studies of the effect of birth order is Lasko's (1954) analysis of Fels longitudinal data (see the Baldwin work reported earlier in this chapter). She contrasted the treatment of firstborns with that of later-born siblings *observed at the same age.* (Thus none of the firstborns in this study were "only" children.) These comparisons revealed that firstborns were treated differently from their younger siblings. Parents provided their firstborns with a very child-centered environment during the first year or two, with the amount of affection and attention then declining more rapidly than was the case for later-borns. The firstborns also received more verbal stimulation, were expected to behave with greater maturity than the later-borns, and they were the recipients of more restrictive and coercive discipline. The younger children received more babying and protection after the age of three. More recent studies that compared parental interaction with firstborns and later-borns—again, holding age constant—have found additional differences in mothers' behavior:

1. Mothers of firstborns use more complex vocabularies and concepts in talking to firstborns than in talking to later-borns of

the same age. In fact, the language used with firstborns is often too difficult for a young child to understand.

2. Mothers are more *anxiously intrusive* with firstborn children. They interfere more with the child's attempts to solve a problem and they more frequently offer direct help, even when it may not be needed.

3. Mothers of firstborns apply more achievement pressure, especially of a verbal-intellectual kind (Hilton, 1967; Rothbart, 1971).

These findings suggest that with experience mothers become more skilled in adapting their behavior to the developmental level of the child; this enables them to achieve better rapport with their later-borns and have less conflict with them over disciplinary issues (Lasko, 1954). However, having inexperienced parents has some advantages: Firstborns tend to be higher achievers as adults. Of course, the effect of position within the family also depends on the temperaments of the individual children, their sex, and the spacing of the children.

From one standpoint the finding that parents have a more relaxed, less conflicted relationship with later-born children is surprising. After all, with other children to care for parents should have less time available for their later-born children than their firstborn. However, the firstborns in most previously described studies were displaced by the birth of later children, while the later-borns often were not. We know little about the effect of the birth of a new child on parents' behavior. It is reasonable to assume, however, that the requirements of infant care cause parents to apportion their time unequally; they probably devote themselves more fully to the infant than to the older child. Thus, later-borns may receive more favored treatment simply because they are less often competing with an infant for their parents' attention. To check on this possibility, Lasko (1954) studied a group of second-borns, some of whom were displaced by still-younger children, some of whom were the last child in the family. She found that the effect of a third child's birth on parental treatment of the second child depended on the second child's age. If the second child was three years old at the time of the birth of the new infant, the parents' treatment of the three-year-old was much affected: Parents of displaced three-year-olds showed less affection, more anger, less understanding, and made fewer attempts to explain their own actions or involve the child in decision making than did parents with no younger children. Probably as a consequence, the parents of the displaced three-year-olds had poorer rapport with the children and more conflicts over discipline than parents with no children younger than three. When the second child was four years old at the time the new baby was born, the second child received treatment very similar to that received by second-born four-year-olds who had no younger sibling. Thus, both parent and child seem better able to cope with the birth of a new child if the displaced child is well beyond the toddler period.

Apparently, later-born children benefit from their parents' greater experience and their relative freedom from caretaking responsibilities. In addition, parents of later-borns may be more relaxed because the younger children have an older sibling to play with, reducing pressure on the parent to provide a program of interesting activities. (No doubt, this advantage is balanced by the increased requirement for the parent to mediate quarrels!) Firstborns, on the other hand, benefit (if it *is* a benefit) from a more child-centered environment during the years before other children are born. These children receive more early linguistic and other stimulation than later children, and as they grow older, also receive more training in nurturant and responsible behavior toward younger children.

The parents' position in society

Among the most powerful and least understood influences on child rearing are the parents' education, income, and occupation. These three factors are usually related, and since their effects are hard to separate, most studies have used a combined index of *socioeconomic status* (SES). Thus, a high-SES parent is well educated, has a relatively high income, and has a high-status occupation (professional, managerial, business-owner); a low-SES parent is poorly educated, has a low income, and has an unskilled or semiskilled job. A family's classification is usually based on the father's occupation, the income of both father and mother, and the education of the two parents. Certain families are difficult to classify along such scales, of course: young parents in graduate school, whose education levels and income-potential are high but whose current income is low; unemployed persons; successful businessmen who have had relatively little formal education, and so forth. An SES index does describe meaningful differences among the majority of families. Comparisons between high and low SES families have revealed some consistent differences: [3]

1. Lower-SES parents tend to stress obedience, respect, neatness, cleanliness, and staying out of trouble. Higher-SES parents are more likely to stress happiness, creativity, ambition, independence, curiosity, and self-control.

2. Lower-SES parents are more controlling, power-assertive, authoritarian, and arbitrary in their discipline, and they are

[3] These generalizations are distilled from a large body of research, a good summary of which may be found in Hess (1970).

more likely to use physical punishment. Higher-SES parents are more democratic and tend to be either permissive or authoritative (to use Baumrind's terms). They are more likely to use induction (that is, point out the effects of a child's actions on others, or ask the child how she or he would feel in the other's place) and to be aware of and responsive to their children's perspectives.

3. Higher-SES parents talk to their children more, reason with them more, and use more complex language.

4. Higher-SES parents tend to show more warmth and affection toward their children.

These relationships seem to hold across race and culture. Similar social-class differences in child-rearing practices have been found in several different societies and among both black families and white families in the United States (Hess and Shipman, 1965; Kamii and Radin, 1967).

A strange footnote to these findings is that higher- and lower-SES parents may differ more in their treatment of their sons than their daughters. Zussman (1977) reports that lower-SES parents used unqualified power assertion with their sons more frequently than did higher-SES parents with their sons, while the two SES groups did not differ in the amount of power assertion shown with daughters. And in one of the early Berkeley longitudinal studies (Bayley and Schaefer, 1960), it was reported that at two different ages sons were more likely than daughters to be the recipients of maternal irritability, punitiveness, and lack of attention.

Some tricky issues of ethics and values arise in interpreting these findings. Obviously the middle-class pattern of child rearing is associated with what most people would consider "better" outcomes in children: more cheerful mood, more planful and vigorous pursuit of goals, higher self-esteem, better skill at taking the perspective of others, more positive social relations with age mates, and so forth. We must not overlook the possibility that a pervasive bias has influenced all these findings. Most of the research has been done by middle-class people. Can it be that they have defined as "good" the qualities they themselves value and then set up their studies to demonstrate that middle-class child-rearing methods produce these outcomes? This question can hardly be discussed objectively because no one can be entirely free of his or her own class origins.

Of course, a given child-rearing practice could have one effect on a child growing up in a poor family and a somewhat different effect on a child from a well-to-do family. For example, physical punishment may have one meaning to a child who is growing up in a community where it is the most commonly accepted form of discipline and a different meaning to a child who has seldom seen it. However, if there are moderating conditions under which a given practice has different outcomes in different social groups, these conditions have not been identified. At present, available research indicates only that (1) relationships do exist between certain child-rearing methods and certain characteristics of children and (2) those child-rearing methods that have been studied do differ, on the average, by social class.

The phrase *on the average* is important. Families labeled *lower-SES* actually differ very greatly among themselves in many important respects: Some lead reasonably stable and organized lives, others are notably unstable—what social service workers call multi-problem families. In such families one or both parents may suffer from mental illness or drug or alcohol addiction; one or both parents may be involved in a succession of sexual liaisons that may or may not involve marriage. The psychological instability of the parents may be such that they cannot hold a job, with the result that there are frequent changes in employment, frequent moves, and frequent periods of unemployment. Whether the family's poverty is a result of their psychological instability or is a cause of that instability is impossible to determine—the causal web is intricate. Clearly, however, the erratic child rearing seen in such families is part of a larger pattern of instability affecting the family's entire life. If the unstable families just described could be identified and eliminated from social-class comparisons, the child rearing of parents at different SES levels would probably be much more similar.

What factors, other than the inclusion of disorganized families among the lower group, might be responsible for social-class differences in child-rearing practices? A number of possibilities have been suggested (see Hess, 1970, for a review). For example, Kohn (1963) proposes that adults develop certain patterns of behavior that facilitate job performance; these same characteristics are then reflected in the way they treat their children and in the way they expect their children to behave. People in higher-status jobs tend to be self-directed; their success depends on their own skill and initiative; they are more likely to deal with ideas and with interpersonal relationships than with physical objects. Thus, in dealing with their children they are more likely to use reasoning and negotiation—the skills they use in their jobs—and to emphasize self-reliance. Another view (Bernstein, 1961; Hess and Shipman, 1967) suggests that the economic uncertainties of lower-class life create stressful conditions that affect a mother's self-esteem, her modes of speaking and thinking, and her modes of coping with daily situations. These effects of life conditions in impoverished environments are passed on to the child in two ways: The mother's child rearing is directly affected, and the child may learn by observation to use the same modes of adaptation that the parents have adopted.

How does living under conditions of economic insecurity affect parental behavior? Low income usually means that living quarters are crowded and that resources are insufficient for meeting emergencies, such as illness, accidents, or the breakdown of the car that gets the breadwinner to work. Chronic anxieties and chronic feelings of help-lessness must result from living under these marginal conditions. The hypothesis is simply that low-income living is more stressful for parents and stress affects the way the parental functions are carried out. We now examine what is known about the effects of stress on parents' behavior and then consider whether the effects are of a kind that would explain SES differences in child rearing.

The effect of stress on parental behavior

Parents' behavior with their children can be influenced by their emotional state. When tired, worried, ill, or feeling unable to control the events that affect their lives, parents may not be as patient and un-derstanding with their children or as willing to take the time to reason with them as they would be at other times. We have seen that chil-dren's altruism is enhanced if they are in a good mood or if some-one has just complied with their requests. Mood and sense of accomplishment undoubtedly also affect parents' willingness to set aside their own immediate needs in order to respond to their children. Indeed, it has been shown that mothers are more likely to start a friendly conversation with a child or offer to join a child in some inter-esting activity if the child had just complied with the mother's request (Yarrow and Waxler, 1976). But other events, having little to do with the child's behavior, can also affect parent's moods and attitudes to-ward their children.

Understandably, experiments are rare in which parents have been put under stress to see whether and how stress affects their child rear-ing. In one study Zussman (1977) created a mildly stressful situation by asking parents to manage their children in an unfamiliar environ-ment and at the same time work on a second, somewhat incompatible task. Parents were selected from families with both a nursery-school-age child and a toddler. One of the parents (for twenty families the fa-ther, for twenty families the mother) brought the children to a labora-tory playroom that contained a variety of equipment. Several items among the available materials were complex enough for the children to need their parent's help. Other items offered opportunities for the children to get into mischief (for example, a stack of index cards, a filled ash tray, a tippable vase). During part of the session the parent was undistracted and free to interact with the children. During an-other part of the session the parent was asked to work on two ana-grams. No note paper or pencil were provided, so the children had no explicit cues that their parents were preoccupied by a mental task.

Under the distracting conditions, the parents' behavior changed. The parents were less responsive toward the preschool child, and they were less likely to play with them, talk with them, and help them than when they had no competing task. The amount of interaction with the toddlers remained about the same as when the parent was undistracted, but the nature of the interaction changed: The parent became more interfering, critical, and peremptory.

The experimentally produced stress was of course very mild, and the effects were transitory. What are the effects of the more severe real-life stresses that continue over a period of time? Hetherington, Cox, and Cox (1976, 1979) studied the effects of divorce on parents' interaction with their children, as well as on the behavior of the children themselves. They compared forty-eight recently divorced families with forty-eight intact families who had children in the same nursery schools. The children were matched with respect to sex, age, and birth order, and the parents were matched on age, education, and length of marriage. All the divorced mothers had custody of the children; all fathers had visiting rights. Information was obtained from the families two months, one year, and two years after the divorce (with comparable timing for the intact families). On each occasion parents were interviewed, detailed observations were made of the interactions between the child and each parent at home and in a laboratory room, and the child's behavior was assessed at nursery school through observation, teacher ratings, and peer ratings.

Hetherington and her colleagues found a number of major differences between divorced parents and parents with intact marriages:

1. During the year following divorce, both divorced parents were more often anxious, depressed, angry, and self-doubting. The women reported longer periods of emotional distress, on the average, than the men.

2. The divorced parents made fewer demands on their children, showed them less affection, communicated with them less well, and were notably inconsistent in their discipline. They also frequently failed to notice whether the children had complied with their demands.

3. Conflict between the parents and children was frequent during the first year following divorce, especially between mothers and sons. The mothers were more likely to issue peremptory commands, and the children (especially the boys) were less likely to comply. The mothers imposed more punishment and more often refused to accede to the child's demands. In short, the mother's negative control efforts increased, while the actual control decreased.

4. The fathers tried hard to keep the children's affection as they felt their contact slipping away, and so, at the beginning of

the post-divorce period, most fathers were highly permissive and indulgent. During visits with the fathers, as Hetherington puts it, "Every day is Christmas."

5. During the second year following the divorce, the mothers began to show more affection to the children, became less authoritarian, and had more success in maintaining control. The fathers moved toward somewhat more restriction and discipline. In short, normal parent-child equilibrium began to be reestablished. By the end of the second year relationships between parents and children were nearly normal for girls and somewhat restored but still unbalanced for boys.

Wallerstein and Kelly (1975, 1976) have studied the impact of divorce on children. They refer to the post-divorce changes as "diminished parenting." And they, like Hetherington, find that the changes in parenting bear a close relationship to changes in the children's behavior. The children become less affectionate, more resistive, aggressive, and manipulative, and more likely to ignore what their mothers say to them. The stress of divorce, then, is another situation in which it is difficult to separate cause and effect. Does parenting become more coercive because the children are emotionally upset and more difficult to deal with? Or do the children become more difficult to deal with because the parents are emotionally upset and less responsive and affectionate? Once more, we can only say that both of these processes must be active in disrupted families. Fortunately, the downward spiral of the post-divorce period is usually followed by the beginnings of a healing process in the second year. The final outcome for the family, then, depends in large measure on the new circumstances of their lives: whether the custodial parent has an adequate income, whether the housing is adequate and in a safe neighborhood, and whether one or both parents remarry.

Returning now to the question of the relationship between child-rearing styles and socioeconomic status: The changes that take place in parents' and children's functioning when the family is under stress are consistent with the differences in the functioning of high-SES and low-SES families. The similarity in findings, then, supports the view that the greater stress of living under economically deprived conditions is responsible, at least in part, for the child-rearing practices.

CAUTIONARY COMMENTS

We have reviewed a considerable body of research on the influence of child-rearing practices on children's development. In our discussion of this relationship, we have suggested that certain methods of parenting seem to foster more positive development than other methods. It is time now to register some cautions: (1) there is no single "best" way to bring up children, (2) we have overstated the case for parental influence, and (3) the studies we have been reviewing have certain weaknesses that may limit their generality. The following cautionary comments should be borne in mind when considering the implications of these findings for child rearing:

1. The information that has been summarized deals mainly with children in early and middle childhood. Few children have been followed into adulthood, and we therefore know little about the long-term benefits or delayed handicaps that may stem from the early interaction of parents and child. Certain aspects of childhood experience within the family undoubtedly have delayed effects. Alternatively, certain self-corrective processes may permit children to free themselves from the influence of early experience as they enter adulthood. Block (1971), in his thoughtful book *Lives through Time* (one of the few studies in which individuals have been followed over an extensive portion of their life span), has reported that individuals with certain types of personalities undergo periods of disorganization and fairly intense distress early in their lives but become organized and effective as they move into maturity. Much depends on the settings they enter after leaving home and on the qualities of the new people with whom they spend their time.

2. The relationships we have traced are not especially strong. That is, the correlations between parental practices and children's characteristics may be statistically significant, but most are not large, and there is plenty of room for exceptions. Not everything that children do or feel is related to the way they have been treated by their parents. Furthermore, the relevant characteristics of family interaction have not all been identified. For example, we know that authoritarian parenting has many negative consequences for children, on the average. But we must also be aware that if we were to select a group of extremely competent, effective and admirable individuals and then inquire into their early histories, many of those selected would turn out to have been raised by authoritarian parents. Conversely, among a group of people leading unsatisfying and ineffective lives, quite a few might come from families that have qualities that should lead to positive outcomes. No doubt, there are a number of moderating parental qualities usually overlooked by researchers (such as a sense of humor or the lack of it) that can moderate the impact of other aspects of parents' behavior.

3. For purposes of exposition we have discussed both parents and children as if aggressiveness or competency or authoritarianism or permissiveness were a set of fairly fixed traits that characterized most behavior most of the time. Actually, of course, both parents and children vary a great deal from time to time and situation to situation. And some people are consistent with respect to certain characteristics, while others are consistent with respect to different characteristics.

4. A given child-rearing practice may have different impacts on different children. Evidence is accumulating, for example, that girls and boys react differently to certain kinds of parental treatment. Maternal warmth, responsiveness, and close interaction seem to promote boys' later readiness to accept socialization pressures from parents and school teachers. On the other hand, early pressures for independence and self-reliance seem to be especially important for girls; these factors seem to help girls to move away from the protected family environment and cope constructively with new tasks (Baumrind, 1979; Martin, 1980). Other attributes besides sex undoubtedly affect children's response to a given parental treatment. Parents must feel their way with every individual child, looking for clues as to what works best with that child.

5. We have mentioned the final caveat a number of times. When a relationship is found between parental behavior and children's characteristics, we cannot be sure about causality. Does a particular kind of parent shape the child's development in a particular direction or does a particular kind of child induce parents to behave in a certain way? Recent detailed analyses of the sequences of events in parent-child interaction have shown that influence flows in both directions but correlation is not proof and does not tell us which kind of influence is stronger.

SUMMARY AND OVERVIEW

Having warned ourselves about the limits on what we know, let us summarize the implications for child rearing of current research findings. But first let us put this statement in the context of some of the major themes discussed in this book.

The development of social behavior in human children has some instinctual basis. Children are preset for efficient acquisition of attachments to the important adults in their lives, and certain later-appearing behaviors (for example, aggression, sexuality) probably also have built-in features. From the beginning, infants as well as their caretakers contribute to social interchanges. The partnership is initially an unequal one, with the demands coming primarily from the infant. Gradually a more balanced relationship develops: Demands and responses to demands come from both sides. Infants' growing ability to inhibit impulsive action (at least briefly) greatly enhances their ability to mesh their behavior with the ongoing stream of someone else's behavior. Parents must initially do the controlling and planning, but these functions are gradually taken over by the children themselves, as their developing cognitive abilities enable them to anticipate other people's actions and the consequences of their own actions. At all points in this transfer process, the regulation of hostility is important. In some families, children and parents attempt to enforce their demands and resist others' demands by hurtful means. Coercive cycles develop that interfere with mutually satisfying problem solving.

Children who are acquiring self-control pass through several phases. At first, a *self* hardly exists, and whatever control children do achieve is not referable to the self. Gradually, however, children develop concepts of their own characteristics and abilities, what groups they belong to, and how they want to be seen by others. They begin to monitor their behavior to make it conform to their self-image. An important aspect of the self-concept is the child's sex identity. As children begin to infer (from observing the regularities in the way males and females behave) what behavior is appropriate for a person of their own sex, they begin to adopt these behaviors. Initially their concepts are quite stereotyped. No doubt their understanding of the many social roles they may occupy is also oversimplified. An important function of fantasy and play in childhood is the trying on of roles to get them cognitively clear and to discover how they intersect with other roles. Children not only work on self-definition; they also *evaluate* themselves. Their behavior is increasingly organized in terms of their beliefs about their own competency, control, and worthiness.

Initially, children do not understand that other people have perspectives and goals different from their own. However, such knowledge is not a necessary prerequisite for certain early prosocial behavior. Children as young as two can be upset by other people's distress and may offer help and comfort, even though they have little understanding of what made the other person unhappy. But as children come to understand others' perspectives and what others expect of them, they begin to adapt their own behavior accordingly. At first this adaptation is almost purely hedonistic: Children simply want to avoid being punished and to get as much as they can for themselves. Most children move on to a bargaining mode: They recognize that if they do things for others, others will do things for them—that they must give if they expect to receive. Many children then progress to some understanding that social relationships imply a set of rights and obligations based on mutual trust, and they begin to have a sense of commitment to others' welfare.

A number of different learning processes are involved in the acquisition of these understandings. Children probably acquire empathic emotions through simple classical conditioning. They learn adaptive social behaviors partly by experiencing the consequences of their own actions and partly by observing the sequences of interaction engaged in by other people. Some aspects of social behavior are simply a matter of acquiring habits (saying "please" and "thank you," smiling and shaking hands upon being introduced). But as children grow older, their social behavior increasingly becomes a matter of planned sequences, organized in pursuit of short-term or long-term goals. These sequences are seldom simple repetitions of a previously practiced pattern. For one thing, they must be integrated with the enterprises of other people, and other people's behavior is not fully predictable. A child needs a repertoire of social behaviors that can be drawn upon flexibly as circumstances vary. The child also needs a wide knowledge of social scripts as a guide to selecting what previously learned social behaviors are appropriate to a particular circumstance. Most important, a child needs to acquire certain social *motives*. Learning to understand other people's perspectives is important, but it is not enough. To become a socially mature person, the child must also share goals with others, and consider others' perspectives in order to arrive at cooperative plans for pursuing these mutual goals.

What role do parents play in these developmental progressions? As we have seen, no single recipe will make an effective parent, and no parent can support every aspect of a child's development with equal effectiveness. Nevertheless, children's social-psychological development will be fostered if their parents:

1. Are committed to their children's welfare and responsive to their needs.

2. Make age-appropriate demands on their children for socially mature behavior, enforce these demands with consistency and firmness, and do not give in to children's attempts at coercion.

3. Create structure in their children's lives, in the form of reasonably predictable environments and schedules of daily events.

4. Allow the children a role in family decision making, insofar as this is compatible with efficient family functioning.

5. Listen to their children's points of view and explain parental actions in a way that the children will understand. Where possible, avoid imposing restrictions and demands arbitrarily ("because I said so") and avoid relying on simple parental power and authority to enforce decisions. Call children's at-

tention to the effect of their actions on others and on the children's own future relationships with others.

6. Allow children to solve their own problems whenever possible, but set up situations that facilitate success.

7. Show affection; notice and give approval for good behavior.

8. Foster the development of a system of joint values.

We have seen that some parents follow most of these prescriptions most of the time, while others do not. What accounts for these variations? Certain parenting styles are more compatible than others with a given parent's own temperament and background. Furthermore, parents differ in what attributes they want their children to have. Some believe that children need to develop a good deal of toughness if they are to deal adequately with the hard knocks of the adult world. These parents therefore deliberately avoid making their children's lives too easy. Others especially want their children to achieve some form of outstanding success in adulthood, and they apply strong achievement pressure, sometimes at the expense of other values. Whatever the reasons for the variations in the extent to which parents display the characteristics listed above, the differences do seem to be associated with certain identifiable differences in the way their children develop.

We have seen that parents can change. The experience of parenthood itself often results in new attitudes and understandings. For example, as parents become more experienced there is improvement in their understanding of what may be reasonably expected of a child of a given age, and they adapt their child rearing accordingly. In addition, they are less anxious and (perhaps for this reason) more affectionate; they are also likely to exercise firmer, more consistent control. Beyond the effect of experience, the parents' life situation affects child rearing. We have seen that stressful events can result in a deterioration of parenting functions along all the dimensions listed above. It follows that the reverse processes can occur as well: Positive life situations can restore or sustain parental morale and keep parents functioning at a high level—make them less arbitrary, more communicative, more understanding and responsive, more affectionate. Different aspects of parenting skill are called for as children move from one developmental level to the next. Hence the family interaction situation is one in which all participants continue to adapt and readapt to one another as they progress through the life cycle.

References

Ainsworth, M. D. S. *Infancy in Uganda: Infant care and the growth of attachment*. Baltimore, Md.: The Johns Hopkins Press, 1967.

Ainsworth, M. D. S., & Bell, S. M. Some contemporary patterns of mother-infant interaction in the feeding situation. In A. Ambrose (Ed.), *Stimulation in early infancy*. New York: Academic Press, 1969.

Ainsworth, M. D. S., Bell, S. M., & Stayton, D. J. Individual differences in strange-situation behavior of one-year-olds. In H. R. Schaffer (Ed.), *The origins of human social relations*. London: Academic Press, 1971.

Ainsworth, M. D. S., & Wittig, B. Attachment and exploratory behavior of one-year-olds in a strange situation. In B. Foss (Ed.), *Determinants of infant behaviour* (Vol. 4). London: Methuen, 1969.

Alexander, G., & Williams, D. Maternal facilitation of a sucking drive in newborn lambs. *Science*, 1964, *146*, 665–66.

Aries, P. *Centuries of childhood*. New York: Vintage Books, 1965. (Originally published, 1962.)

Armsby, R. E. A reexamination of the development of moral judgments in children. *Child Development*, 1971, *42*, 1241–48.

Aronfreed, J. *Conduct and conscience: The socialization of internal controls over behavior*. New York: Academic Press, 1968.

Aronfreed, J. The concept of internalization. In D. A. Goslin (Ed.), *Handbook of socialization theory and research*. Chicago: Rand McNally, 1969.

Aronfreed, J., & Reber, A. Internalized behavioral suppression and the timing of social punishment. *Journal of Personality and Social Psychology*, 1965, *1*, 3–16.

Ausubel, D. P. *Theory and problems of child development*. New York: Grune & Stratton, 1958.

Bacon, M. K., Child, I. L., and Barry, H., III. A cross-cultural study of correlational crime. *Journal of Abnormal Psychology*, 1963, *66*, 291–300.

Baldwin, A. L. Differences in parent behavior toward three- and nine-year-old children. *Journal of Personality*, 1946, *15*, 143–65.

Baldwin, A. L. Socialization and the parent-child relationship. *Child Development*, 1948, *19*, 127–36.

Baldwin, A. L. The effect of home environment on nursery school behavior. *Child Development*, 1949, *20*, 49–62.

Baldwin, A. L. *Behavior and development in childhood*. New York: The Dryden Press, 1955.

Baldwin, A. L., Kalhorn, J., & Breese, F. H. *Psychological Monographs*, 1945, *58* (3).

Baldwin, J. M. *Social and ethical interpretations in mental development*. New York: Macmillan, 1906.

Bandura, A. Social-learning theory of identificatory processes. In D. Goslin (Ed.), *Handbook of socialization theory and research*. Chicago: Rand McNally, 1969.

Bandura, A. (Ed.). *Psychological modeling: Conflicting theories*. New York: Aldine-Atherton, 1971.

Bandura, A. *Aggression*. New York: Holt, Rinehart & Winston, 1973.

Bandura, A. The self-system in reciprocal determinism. *American Psychologist*, 1978, *33*, 344–58.

Bandura, A., & Mischel, W. Modification of self-imposed delay of reward through exposure to live and symbolic models. *Journal of Personality and Social Psychology*, 1965, *2*, 698–705.

Bandura, A., & Walters, R. H. *Social learning and personality development*. New York: Holt, Rinehart & Winston, 1963.

Bannister, D., & Agnew, J. The child's construing of self. In J. K. Cole & A. W. Landfield (Eds.), *Nebraska Symposium on Motivation*. Lincoln: University of Nebraska Press, 1976.

Barnett, M. A., Matthews, K. A., & Howard, J. A. Relationship between competitiveness and empathy in 6 & 7-year-olds. *Developmental Psychology*, 1979, *15*, 221–22.

Barrett, D. E. A naturalistic study of sex differences in children's aggression. *Merrill Palmer Quarterly*, 1979, *25*, 191–203.

Battle, E., & Lacey, B. A context for hyperactivity in children over time. *Child Development*, 1972, *43*, 757–73.

Baumrind, D. Child care practices anteceding three patterns of preschool behavior. *Genetic Psychology Monographs*, 1967, *75*, 43–88.

Baumrind, D. Current patterns of parental authority. *Developmental Psychology Monograph*, 1971, *4* (1, Pt. 2).

Baumrind, D. The development of instrumental competence through socialization. In A. D. Pick (Ed.), *Minnesota Symposium on Child Psychology* (Vol. 7). Minneapolis: University of Minnesota Press, 1973.

Baumrind, D. *Socialization determinants of personal agency*. Paper presented at the biennial meetings of the Society for Research in Child Development, New Orleans, 1977.

Baumrind, D. *Sex-related socialization effects.* Paper presented at the meetings of the Society for Research in Child Development, San Francisco, 1979.

Bayley, N. Individual patterns of development. *Child Development*, 1956, *27*, 45–74.

Bayley, N. Comparisons of mental and motor test scores for ages 1–15 months by sex, birth order, race, geographical location, and education of parents. *Child Development*, 1965, *36*, 380–411.

Bayley, H., & Schaefer, E. S. Relationships between socioeconomic variables and the behavior of mothers toward young children. *Journal of Genetic Psychology*, 1960, *96*, 61–77.

Bearison, D. J., & Cassel, T. Z. Cognitive decentration and social codes: Communication effectiveness in young children from differing family contexts. *Developmental Psychology*, 1975, *11*, 29–36.

Bearison, D. J., & Isaacs, L. Production deficiency in children's moral judgments. *Developmental Psychology*, 1975, *11*, 732–37.

Becker, W. Consequences of different kinds of parental discipline. In M. L. Hoffman & L. W. Hoffman (Eds.), *Review of child development research* (Vol. 1) New York: Russell Sage Foundation, 1964.

Bee, H. L. Parent-child interaction and distractability in 9-year-old children. *Merrill Palmer Quarterly*, 1967, *13*, 175–90.

Bell, R. Q., Weller, G. M., & Waldrop, M. F. Newborn and preschooler: Organization of behavior and relations between periods. *Monographs of the Society for Research in Child Development*, 1971, *36*.

Bem, D. J., & Allen, A. On predicting some of the people some of the time: The search for cross-situational consistencies in behavior. *Psychological Review*, 1974, *81*, 506–20.

Bem, D. J., & Funder, D. C. Predicting more of the people more of the time: Assessing the personality of situations. *Psychological Review*, 1978, *85*, 485–501.

Bem, S. The measurement of psychological androgyny. *Journal of Consulting and Clinical Psychology*, 1974, *42*, 155–62.

Bernat, T. *Social cognition and social behavior in childhood friendships.* Paper presented at the Conference on Social Cognition and Social Behavior, University of Western Ontario, London, Ontario, 1979.

Bernstein, B. Social class and linguistic development: A theory of social learning. In A. H. Halsey, J. Floud, & C. A. Anderson (Eds.), *Economy, education and society.* New York: The Free Press, 1961.

Bernstein, B. A sociolinguistic approach to socialization, with some reference to educability. In J. Gumperz & D. Hymes (Eds.), *Directions in sociolinguistics.* New York: Holt, Rinehart & Winston, 1972.

Bertenthal, B. I., & Fischer, K. W. Development of self-recognition in the infant. *Developmental Psychology*, 1978, *14*, 44–50.

Blatz, W. E. *Human security: Some reflections.* Toronto: University of Toronto Press, 1966.

Blatz, W. E., Bott, E. A., & Millichamp, D. A. *The development of emotion in the infant.* Toronto: University of Toronto Press, 1935.

Block, J. H. *Lives through time.* Berkeley, Cal.: Bancroft Books, 1971.

Block, J. H. Another look at sex difference in the socialization behaviors of mothers and fathers. In J. Sherman & F. Denmark (Eds.), *Psychology of women: Future direction of research.* New York: Psychological Dimensions, Inc., in press.

Blurton-Jones, N. Categories of child-child interaction. In N. Blurton-Jones (Ed.), *Ethological studies of child behavior.* London: Cambridge University Press, 1972.

Bower, T. G. R. *Development in infancy.* San Francisco: Freeman and Co., 1974.

Bowlby, J. *Attachment.* New York: Basic Books, 1969.

Bowlby, J. *Separation.* New York: Basic Books, 1973.

Brackbill, Y. Extinction of the smiling response in infants as a function of reinforcement schedule. *Child Development*, 1958, *29*, 114–24.

Brackbill, Y., & Adams, G. Arousal level in neonates and preschool children under continuous auditory stimulation. *Journal of Experimental Child Psychology*, 1966, *4*, 178–88.

Bradley, C. Characteristics and management of children with behavior problems associated with organic brain damage. *Pediatric Clinics of North America*, 1957, *4*, 1049–60.

Brandt, E. M., & Mitchell, G. Pairing preadolescents with infants (Macaca mulatta). *Developmental Psychology*, 1973, *8*, 222–28.

Brim, O. G. Family structure and sex role learning by children: A further analysis of Helen Kock's data. *Sociometry*, 1958, *21*, 1–16.

Brim, O. G. Life span development of the theory of oneself: Implications for child development. In H. W. Reese (Ed.), *Advances in Child Development and Behavior*

(Vol. 11). New York: Academic Press, 1976.

Bronson, W. C. Developments in behavior with age mates during the second year of life. In M. Lewis & L. A. Rosenblum (Eds.), *The origins of behavior: Friendship and peer relations.* New York: John Wiley & Sons, 1975.

Bryan, J. W., & Luria, Z. Sex-role learning: A test of the selective attention hypothesis. *Child Development,* 1978, *49,* 13–23.

Buss, A. H. Instrumentality of aggression, feedback and frustration as determinants of physical aggression. *Journal of Personality and Social Psychology,* 1966, *3,* 153–62.

Buss, A. H., & Plomin, R. *A temperament theory of personality development.* New York: John Wiley & Sons, 1975.

Cadogan, W. *An essay upon nursing and the management of children, from their birth to three years of age.* London: V. Roberts, 1749.

Cairns, R. B. Development, maintenance and extinction of social attachment behavior in sheep. *Journal of Comparative and Physiological Psychology,* 1966, *62,* 298–306.

Cairns, R. B. *Social development: The origins and plasticity of interchanges.* San Francisco: W. H. Freeman & Co., 1979.

Cairns, R. B., & Johnson, D. L. The development of interspecies social preferences. *Psychonomic Science,* 1965, *2,* 337–38.

Carr, S. J., Dabbs, J. M., Jr., & Carr, T. S. Mother-infant attachment: The importance of the mother's visual field. *Child Development,* 1975, *46,* 331–38.

Chittenden, G. E. An experimental study in measuring and modifying assertive behavior in young children. *Monographs of the Society for Research in Child Development,* 1942, *7* (1).

Cioffi, V., & Kandel, G. L. Laterality of stereognostic accuracy of children for words, shapes and bigrams: A sex difference for bigrams. *Science,* 1979, *204,* 1432–34.

Clark, E. V. From gesture to word: On the natural history of deixis in language acquisition. In J. S. Bruner & A. Gartner (Eds.), *Human growth and development.* Oxford: Clarendon Press, 1976.

Clarke, A. M., & Clarke, A. D. B. *Early experience: Myth and evidence.* New York: The Free Press, 1976.

Clarke-Stewart, A. K. Interactions between mothers and their young children: Characteristics and consequences. *Monographs of the Society for Research in Child Development,* 1973, *38* (6 and 7).

Clifford, E. Discipline in the home: A controlled observational study of parental practices. *Journal of Genetic Psychology,* 1959, *95,* 45–82.

Cohen, L. J., & Campos, J. J. Father, mother and stranger as elicitors of attachment behavior in infancy. *Developmental Psychology,* 1974, *10,* 146–54.

Collins, B. E., Whalen, C. K., & Henker, B. Ecological and pharmacological influences in the classroom: The hyperkinetic behavioral syndrome. In Antrobus (Ed.), *The eco-system of the "sick kid,"* in press.

Condry, J., & Condry, S. Sex differences: A study in the eye of the beholder. *Child Development,* 1976, *47,* 812–19.

Conel, J. L. Histologic development of the cerebral cortex. In *Biology of mental health and disease.* The 27th Annual Conference of the Milbank Memorial Fund. New York: Hoebar, 1952.

Conel, J. L. *The cortex of the twenty four month infant.* Cambridge, Mass.: Harvard University Press, 1959.

Conner, J. M., & Serbin, L. A. Behaviorally based masculine and feminine activity-preference scales for preschoolers: Correlates with other classroom behaviors and cognitive tests. *Child Development,* 1977, *48,* 1411–16.

Cooley, C. H. *Human nature and the social order.* New York: Charles Scribner's Sons, 1902.

Coopersmith, S. *The antecedents of self-esteem.* San Francisco: W. H. Freeman & Co., 1967.

Cox, N. Prior help, ego development and helping behavior. *Child Development,* 1974, *45,* 594–663.

Crandall, V. V., Katkovsky, W., & Crandall, V. J. Children's beliefs in their own control of reinforcements in intellectual academic achievement situations. *Child Development,* 1965, *36,* 91–109.

Damon, W. *The social world of the child.* San Francisco: Jossey-Bass, 1977.

Darwin, C. A biographical sketch of an infant. *Mind,* 1877, *11,* 286–94.

Deci, E. L. *Intrinsic motivation.* New York: Plenum Publishing Co., 1975.

deMause, L. *The history of childhood.* New York: The Psychohistory Press, 1974.

Dienstbier, R. A., Hillman, D., Lehnkoff, J., Hillman, J., & Valkenaar, M. F. An emotion-attribution approach to moral behavior: Interfacing cognitive and avoidance theories of moral development. *Psychological Review,* 1975, *82,* 299–315.

DiPietro, J. *Rough and tumble play: A function of gender.* Unpublished manuscript,

Psychology Department, Stanford University, 1979.

Dollard, J., Doob, L. W., Miller, N. E., Mowrer, O. H., & Sears, R. R. *Frustration and aggression.* New Haven: Yale University Press, 1939.

Downs, A. C., & Langlois, J. H. *Fathers as socialization agents of sex-typed play behaviors in young children.* Unpublished manuscript, Psychology Department, University of Texas, Austin, Texas, 1979.

Dweck, C. S. The role of expectations and attributions in the alleviation of learned helplessness. *Journal of Personality and Social Psychology,* 1975, *31,* 674–85.

Dweck, C. S., & Bush, E. S. Sex differences in learned helplessness: I. Differential debilitation with peer and adult evaluators. *Developmental Psychology,* 1976, *12,* 147–56.

Dweck, C. S., Davidson, W., Nelson, S., & Enna, B. Sex differences in learned helplessness: II. The contingencies of evaluative feedback in the classroom. III. An experimental analysis. *Developmental Psychology,* 1978, *14,* 268–76.

Dweck, C. S., & Gilliard, D. Expectancy statements as determinants of reactions to failure: Sex differences in persistence and expectancy change. *Journal of Personality and Social Psychology,* 1975, *32,* 1077–84.

Dweck, C. S., & Reppucci, N. D. Learned helplessness and reinforcement responsibility in children. *Journal of Personality and Social Psychology,* 1973, *25,* 109–16.

Edwards, C. P. The comparative study of the development of moral judgment and reasoning. In R. Munroe, K. Munroe, and B. B. Whiting (Eds.), *Handbook of cross cultural human development.* New York: Garland Publishing, in press.

Edwards, C. P., & Whiting, B. *Sex differences in children's social interaction.* Unpublished report to the Ford Foundation, 1977.

Ehrhardt, A. A., & Baker, S. W. Fetal androgens, human central nervous system differentiation, and behavioral sex differences in behavior. In R. C. Friedman, R. M. Rickard, and R. L. Van de Wiele (Eds.), *Sex differences in behavior.* New York: John Wiley & Sons, 1974.

Eichorn, D. H. Physiological development. In P. H. Mussen (Ed.), *Carmichael's manual of child psychology* (Vol. 1). New York: John Wiley & Sons, 1970.

Emmerich, W. Continuity and stability in early social development. *Child Development,* 1964, *35,* 311–32.

Emmerich, W. Personality developments and concepts of structure. *Child Development,* 1968, *39,* 671–90.

Emmerich, W. Structure and development of personal-social behaviors in economically disadvantaged preschool children. *Genetic Psychology Monograph,* 1977, *95,* 191–245.

Emmerich, W., Goldman, K. S., Kirsh, B., & Sharabany, R. *Development of gender constancy in economically disadvantaged children.* Report of the Educational Testing Service, Princeton, New Jersey, 1976.

Epstein, S. The self-concept revisited. *American Psychologist,* 1973, *28* (5), 404–16.

Erikson, E. H. *Childhood and society.* New York: W. W. Norton and Co., 1950.

Fagot, B. I. Sex differences in toddlers' behavior and parental reaction. *Developmental Psychology,* 1974, *10,* 459–65.

Fagot, B. I. The influence of sex of child on parental reactions to toddler children. *Child Development,* 1978, *49,* 459–65.

Fantz, R. L., Fagan, J. F., III, & Miranda, S. B. Early visual selectivity. In L. B. Cohen & P. Salapatek (Eds.), *Infant perception: From sensation to cognition* (Vol. 1). New York: Academic Press, 1975.

Fawl, C. L. Disturbances experienced by children in the natural habitats. In R. G. Barker (Ed.), *The stream of behavior.* New York: Appleton-Century-Crofts, 1963.

Fein, G., Johnson, D., Kossan, N. Stark, L., & Wasserman, L. Sex stereotypes and preferences in the toy choices of 20-month-old boys and girls. *Developmental Psychology,* 1975, *11,* 527–28.

Feldman, S. S., & Ingham, M. On the interchangeability of attachment objects in two-year-old children. *Child Development,* 1975, *46,* 319–30.

Feldman, S. S., & Nash, S. C. The influence of age and sex on responsiveness to babies. *Developmental Psychology,* 1977, *16,* 675–76.

Feldman, S. S., & Nash, S. C. Interest in babies during young adulthood. *Child Development,* 1978, *49,* 617–22.

Ferguson, L. R., & Maccoby, E. E. Intrapersonal correlates of differential abilities. *Child Development,* 1966, *37,* 549–71.

Feshbach, N. D. The relationship of child-rearing factors to children's aggression, empathy and related positive and negative behaviors. In J. de Wit & W. W. Hartup (Eds.), *Determinants and origins of aggressive behavior.* The Hague: Mouton Press, 1974.

Feshbach, N. D., & Bercovici, A. *Teaching style of mothers of successful and problem readers.* Paper presented at the meetings of the American Educational Research Association, New Orleans, February 1973.

Feshbach, N. D., & Feshbach, S. The relationship between empathy and aggression in two age groups. *Developmental Psychology*, 1969, *1*, 102–07.

Feshbach, S. Aggression. In P. H. Mussen (Ed.), *Carmichael's manual of child psychology* (Vol. 2). New York: John Wiley & Sons, 1970.

Feshbach, S. The development and regulation of aggression: Some research gaps and a proposed cognitive approach. In J. de Wit & W. W. Hartup (Eds.), *Determinants and origins of aggressive behavior*. The Hague: Mouton Press, 1974.

Fisher, A. E. *The effects of differential early treatment on the social and exploratory behavior of puppies*. Unpublished doctoral dissertation, University of Pennsylvania, 1955.

Flavell, J. H. *The developmental psychology of Jean Piaget*. New York: Van Nostrand Co., 1963.

Flavell, J. H. *Cognitive development*. Englewood Cliffs, N.J.: Prentice-Hall, 1977.

Flavell, J. H., Botkin, P. T., Fry, C. L., Wright, J. W., & Jarvis, P. E. *The development of role-taking and communication skills in children*. New York: John Wiley & Sons, 1968.

Flavell, J. H., Shipstead, S. G, & Croft, K. *What young children think you see when their eyes are closed*. Unpublished report, Stanford University, 1978.

Fleener, D. E. Experimental production of infant maternal attachment behaviors. *Proceedings of the 81st Annual Convention of the American Psychological Association*, 1973, *8*, 57–58.

Flint, B. *The security of infants*. Toronto: University of Toronto Press, 1959.

Flory, C. D. Ossepus development in the hand as an index of skeletal development. *Monograph of the Society for Research in Child Development*, 1936, *1*, 96–97.

Forest, M. G., Cathiard, A. M., Bourgeois, J., & Genoud, J. Androgenes plasmatiques chez le nourrisson normal et premature relation avec la maturation de l'axe hypothalamo-hypophyso-gonadique. *Inserm*, 1974, *32*, 315–36.

Freud, S. *Three contributions to the sexual theory* (A. A. Brill, trans.). New York: Journal of Nervous and Mental Diseases Publishing Co., 1910.

Freud, S. On narcissism: An introduction. In E. Jones (Ed.), *Collected Papers* (Vol. 4). London: Hogarth Press and the Institute of Psychoanalysis, 1914.

Freud, S. *An autobiographical study* (J. Strachey, trans.). London: Hogarth Press, 1935.

Freud, S., & Dann, S. An experiment in group upbringing. *Psychoanalytic study of the child*. New York: International Universities Press, 1951.

Frodi, A. M., & Lamb, M. Sex differences in responsiveness to infants: A developmental study of psychophysiological and behavioral responses. *Child Development*, 1978, *49*, 1182–88.

Frodi, A. M., Lamb, M. E., Leavitt, L. A., & Donoval, W. L. Mothers' and fathers' responses to infant smiles and cries. *Infant Behavior and Development*, 1978, *1*, 187–98.

Frodi, A. M., MacCaulay, J., & Thome, P. R. Are women always less aggressive than men? A review of the experimental literature. *Psychological Bulletin*, 1977, *84*, 634–60.

Gallup, G. Self-recognition in primates. A comparative approach to the bidirectional properties of consciousness. *American Psychologist*, 1977, *32*, 329–38.

Garvey, C. Some properties of social play. In J. S. Bruner, D. Jolly, & K. Sylva (Eds.), *Play–its role in development and evaluation*. Middlesex: Penguin Books, 1976.

Geen, R. G., & Quanty, M. B. The catharsis of aggression: An evaluation of a hypothesis. In L. Berkowitz (Ed.), *Advances in experimental social psychology* (Vol. 10). New York: Academic Press, 1977.

Gewirtz, J. L. The course of infant smiling in four child-rearing environments in Israel. In B. M. Foss (Ed.), *Determinants of infant behaviour* (Vol. 3). London: Methuen, 1965.

Ginott, H. G. *Between parent and child*. New York: Macmillan, 1965.

Goffman, E. *The presentation of self in everyday life*. New York: Doubleday & Co., 1959.

Goldschmidt, W. R. *Man's way: A preface to the understanding of human society*. New York: Holt, Rinehart & Winston, 1959.

Goldstein, J., Freud, A., & Solnit, A. J. *Beyond the best interests of the child*. New York: Free Press, 1973.

Goodenough, E. W. Interest in persons as an aspect of sex differences in the early years. *Genetic Psychology Monographs*, 1957, *55*, 287–323.

Goodenough, F. L. *Anger in young children*. Minneapolis: University of Minnesota Press, 1931.

Gordon, T. *Parent effectiveness training*. New York: Peter H. Wyden, Inc., 1970.

Gunnar, M. Changing a frightening toy into a pleasant toy by allowing the infant to control its actions. *Developmental Psychology*, 1978, *14*, 157–62.

Gunnar, M. Control, warning signals and distress in infancy. *Developmental Psychology*, 1980, *51*, in press.

Gunnar, M., & Donahu, M. Sex differences in social responsiveness between six months and twelve months. *Child Development,* 1980, in press.

Halliday, M. A. K. *Learning how to mean: Explorations in the development of language.* London: Arnold, 1975.

Halverson, C. F. *Studies in activity level.* Paper presented at Southeastern Conference on Human Development, Atlanta, Ga., 1978.

Harlow, H. F. The development of affectional patterns in infant monkeys. In B. M. Foss (Ed.), *Determinants of infant behaviour* (Vol. 1). London: Methuen, 1961.

Harlow, H. F., & Harlow, M. K. The affectional system. In A. M. Scjroer, H. F. Harlow, & F. Stollnitz (Eds.), *Behavior of nonhuman primates* (Vol. 2). New York: Academic Press, 1965.

Harlow, H., & Harlow, M. K. Effects of various mother-infant relationships on rhesus monkey behaviors. In B. M. Foss (Ed.), *Determinants of infant behaviour* (Vol. 4). London: Methuen, 1969.

Hartshorne, H., & May, M. A. *Studies in the nature of character. Studies in deceit* (Vol. 1). New York: Macmillan, 1928.

Hartup, W. W. Aggression in childhood: Developmental perspectives. *American Psychologist,* 1974, *29,* 336–41.

Hartup, W. W., & Moore, S. G. Avoidance of inappropriate sex-typing by young children. *Journal of Consulting Psychology,* 1963, *27,* 467–73.

Hayes, C. *The ape in our house.* New York: Harper & Row, 1951.

Heinicke, C., & Westheimer, I. *Brief separations.* New York: International Universities Press, 1966.

Henshel, A. M. The relationship between values and behavior: A developmental hypothesis. *Child Development,* 1971, *42,* 1997–2007.

Hess, E. H. The conditions limiting critical age of imprinting. *Journal of Comparative and Physiological Psychology,* 1959, *52,* 515–18.

Hess, R. D. Social class and ethnic influences upon socialization. In P. H. Mussen (Ed.), *Carmichael's manual of child psychology* (Vol. 2). New York: John Wiley & Sons, 1970.

Hess, R. D., & Shipman, V. C. Early experience and the socialization of cognitive modes in children. *Child Development,* 1965, *34,* 869–86.

Hess, R. D., & Shipman, V. C. Cognitive elements in maternal behavior. In J. P. Hill (Ed.), *Minnesota Symposium on Child Psychology* (Vol. 1). Minneapolis: University of Minnesota Press, 1967.

Hetherington, E. M. The effects of familial variables on sex-typing, on parent-child similarity, and on imitation in children. In J. P. Hill (Ed.), *Minnesota Symposium on Child Psychology* (Vol. 1). Minneapolis: University of Minnesota Press, 1967.

Hetherington, E. M. Effects of father absence on personality development in adolescent daughters. *Developmental Psychology,* 1972, *7,* 313–26.

Hetherington, E. M., Cox, M., & Cox, R. Divorced fathers. *The Family Coordinator,* 1976, *25,* 417–28.

Hetherington, E. M., Cox, M., & Cox, R. Stress and coping in divorce: A focus on women. In J. E. Gullahorn (Ed.), *Psychology and women: In transition.* Washington, D. C: V. H. Winston & Sons, 1979.

Hilton, I. Differences in the behavior of mothers toward first- and later-born children. *Journal of Personality and Social Psychology,* 1967, *7,* 282–90.

Hinde, R. A., & Spencer-Booth, Y. The effect of social companions on mother-infant relations in rhesus monkeys. In D. Morris (Ed.), *Primate ethology.* London: Weidenfeld & Nicolson, 1967.

Hoffman, M. L. Moral development. In P. H. Mussen (Ed.), *Carmichael's manual of child psychology* (Vol. 2). New York: John Wiley & Sons, 1970.

Hoffman, M. Empathy, role-taking, guilt, and development of altruistic motives. In T. Lickona (Ed.), *Moral development and behavior.* New York: Holt, Rinehart & Winston, 1976.

Hoffman, M. Sex differences in empathy and related behaviors. *Psychology Bulletin,* 1977, *84,* 712–22.

Hoffman, M. L., & Saltzstein, H. D. Parent discipline and the child's moral development. *Journal of Personality and Social Psychology,* 1967, *5,* 45–47.

Holmberg, M. S. *The development of social interchange patterns from 12 to 42 months: Cross-sectional and short-term longitudinal analyses.* Doctoral Dissertation, University of North Carolina at Chapel Hill, 1977.

Horowitz, L. M., Sampson, H., Siegelman, E. Y., Weiss, J., & Goodfriend, S. Cohesive and dispersal behaviors: Two classes of concomitant change in psychotherapy. *Journal of Consulting and Clinical Psychology,* 1978, *46,* 556–64.

Huston, T. L., & Korte, C. The responsive bystander. In T. Lickona (Ed.), *Moral development and behavior.* New York: Holt, Rinehart & Winston, 1976.

Imperato-McGinley, J., Guerro, L., Gautier, T., & Peterson, R. E. Steroid 5—reductase deficiency in man: An inherited form of male pseudohermaphroditism. *Science,* 1974, *186,* 1213–16.

Isen, A. M., Horn, N., & Rosenhan, D. L. Effects of success and failure on children's generosity. *Journal of Personality and Social Psychology,* 1973, *27,* 239–47.

Jacklin, C. N., & Maccoby, E. E. Social behavior at 33 months in same-sex and mixed-sex dyads. *Child Development,* 1978, *49,* 557–69.

Jacklin, C. N., Snow, M. E., Gahart, M., & Maccoby, E. E. *Changes in sleep patterns from 3–33 months: One aspect of maturation rate in boys and girls.* Working paper, Stanford Longitudinal Project, 1979.

Jacklin, C. N., Snow, M. E., & Maccoby, E. E. Tactile sensitivity and strength in newborn boys and girls. *Infant Behavior and Development,* 1980, *3,* in press.

James. W. *The principles of psychology* (Vol. 1). New York: Henry Holt & Co., 1896.

Jensen, G. D., & Tolman, C. W. Activity level of the mother monkey, Maccaca nemestrina, as affected by various conditions of sensory access to the infant following separation. *Animal Behavior,* 1962, *10,* 228–30.

Johnson, S., Wahl, G., Martin, S., & Johansson, S. How deviant is the preschool child and his family? In R. Rubin, J. Brady, & J. Henderson (Eds.), *Advances in behavior therapy* (Vol. 4). New York: Academic Press, 1974.

Johnston, J. M. Punishment of human behavior. *American Psychologist,* 1972, *27,* 1033–54.

Jones, O. H. M. Mother-child communication with pre-linguistic Downs' Syndrome and normal infants. In H. R. Schaffer (Ed.), *Studies in mother-infant interaction.* London: Academic Press, 1977.

Kagan, J. *Change and continuity in infancy.* New York: John Wiley & Sons, 1971.

Kagan, J. Emergent themes in human development. *American Scientist,* 1976, *64,* 186–96.

Kagan, J., Kearsley, R. B., & Zalazo, P. R. *Infancy: Its place in human development.* Cambridge, Mass.: Harvard University Press, 1978.

Kagan, J., & Moss, H. *Birth to maturity.* New York: John Wiley & Sons, 1962.

Kagan, J., Rosman, B. L., Day, D., Albert, J., & Phillips, W. Information processing in the child: Significance of analytic and reflective attitudes. *Psychological Monographs,* 1964, *78*(1).

Kamii, C. K., & Radin, N. L. Class differences in the socialization practices of Negro mothers. *Journal of Marriage and the Family,* 1967, *29,* 302–10.

Katz, P., & Zigler, E. Self-image disparity. A developmental approach. *Journal of Personality and Social Psychology,* 1967, *5,* 186–95.

Katz, P. A., Zigler, E., & Zelk, S. R. Children's self-image disparity: The effects of age, maladjustment, and action-thought orientation. *Developmental Psychology,* 1975, *11,* 546–50.

Kaufman, I. C., & Rosenblum, L. A. Depression in infant monkeys separated from their mothers. *Science,* 1967, *155,* 1030–31.

Keister, M. E., & Updegraff, R. A study of children's reactions to failure and an experimental attempt to modify them. *Child Development,* 1937, *8,* 241–48.

Kellogg, W. N., & Kellogg, L. A. *The ape and the child: A study of environmental influence upon early behavior.* New York: McGraw-Hill, 1933.

Kenney, M. D., Mason, W. A., & Hill, S. D. Effect of age, objects and visual experience in affective responses of rhesus monkeys to strangers. *Developmental Psychology,* 1979, *15,* 176–84.

Kessen, W. *The child.* New York: John Wiley & Sons, 1965.

Kessen, W. (Ed.). *Childhood in China.* New Haven: Yale University Press, 1975.

Kinney, E. E. A study of peer group social acceptability at the fifth grade level in a public school. *Journal of Educational Research,* 1953, *47,* 57–64.

Klaus, M. H., & Kennell, J. H. *Maternal-infant bonding.* St. Louis: C. V. Mosby, 1976.

Klaus, M. H., Kennell, J. H., Plumb, N., & Zuehlke, S. Human maternal behavior at the first contact with her young. *Pediatrics,* 1970, *46,* 187–92.

Knight, G. P., & Kagan, S. Development of prosocial and competitive behaviors in Anglo-American and Mexican-American children. *Child Development,* 1977, *48,* 1385–94.

Kohlberg, L. Development of moral character and moral ideology. In M. Hoffman & L. W. Hoffman (Eds.). *Review of child development research.* New York: Russell Sage Foundation, 1964.

Kohlberg, L. A cognitive-developmental analysis of children's sex-role concepts and attitudes. In E. Maccoby (Ed.), *The development of sex differences.* Stanford, Cal.: Stanford University Press, 1966.

Kohlberg, L. Stage and sequence: The cognitive-developmental approach to socialization. In D. A. Goslin (Ed.), *Handbook of socialization theory and research.* Chicago: Rand McNally, 1969.

Kohlberg, L. Moral stages and moralization: The cognitive-developmental approach. In T. Lickona (Ed.), *Moral development and behavior.* New York: Holt, Rinehart & Winston, 1976.

Kohlberg, L., & deVries, R. *Relations between Piaget and psychometric assessments of intelligence.* Paper presented at the Conference on the Natural Curriculum, Urbana, Ill., 1969.

Kohn, M. L. Social class and parent child relationship: An interpretation. *American Journal of Sociology,* 1963, *68,* 471–80.

Kotelchuk, M. The infant's relationship to the father: Experimental evidence. In M. Lamb (Ed.), *The role of the father in child development.* New York: John Wiley & Sons, 1976.

Krebs, D. Empathy and altruism. *Journal of Personality and Social Psychology,* 1975, *32,* 1134–46.

Kuhn, D., Langer, J., & Kohlberg, L. *Relation between logical and moral development.* New York: Holt, Rinehart & Winston, in preparation.

Kuhn, M. H. Self attitudes by age, sex and professional training. *Physiological Quarterly,* 1960, *1,* 39–55.

Kummer, H. Two variations in the social organization of baboons. In P. C. Jay (Ed.), *Primates: Studies in adaptation and variability.* New York: Holt, Rinehart & Winston, 1968.

Lamb, M. (Ed.). *The role of the father in child development.* New York: John Wiley & Sons, 1978.

Langlois, J. H., & Downs, A. C. *Mothers and peers as socialization agents of sex-typed play behaviors in young children.* Unpublished paper, Psychology Department, University of Texas, Austin, Texas, 1979.

Lasko, J. K. Parent behavior toward first- and second-born children. *Genetic Psychology Monograph,* 1954, *49.*

Lavoie, J. C. *Punishment and adolescent self-control: A study of the effects of aversive stimulation, reasoning and sex of parent.* Unpublished doctoral dissertation, University of Wisconsin, 1970.

Leahy, R. L., & Huard, C. Role taking and self-image disparity in children. *Developmental Psychology,* 1976, *12,* 509–64.

Leon, M. Pheromonal mediation of maternal behavior. In T. Alloway, P. Pliner, & L. Krames (Eds.), *Attachment behavior* (Vol. 3). New York: Plenum Publishing Co., 1977.

Lepper, M. R., & Greene, D. Turning play into work. Effects of surveillance and extrinsic reward on children's intrinsic motivation. *Journal of Personality and Social Psychology,* 1975, *31,* 479–86.

Lepper, M. R., Greene, D., & Nisbett, R. E. Undermining children's intrinsic interest with extrinsic rewards: A test of the overjustification hypothesis. *Journal of Personality and Social Psychology,* 1973, *28,* 129–37.

Lewis, M., & Brooks, J. Self, other and fear: Infants' reactions to people. In M. Lewis & L. A. Rosenblum (Eds.), *The origins of fear.* New York: John Wiley & Sons, 1974.

Liben, L. Perspective-taking skills in young children: Seeing the world through rose-colored glasses. *Developmental Psychology,* 1978, *14,* 87–92.

Lickona, T. Research on Piaget's theory of moral development. In T. Lickona (Ed.), *Moral development and behavior.* New York: Holt, Rinehart & Winston, 1976.

Littenberg, R., Tulkin, S., & Kagan, J. Cognitive components of separation anxiety. *Developmental Psychology,* 1971, *4,* 387–88.

Locke, J. *Some thoughts concerning education* (Rev. ed.). London: C. J. Clay & Sons, 1884. (Originally published, 1693.)

Lockwood, A. L. *Relations of political and moral thought.* Unpublished doctoral dissertation. Harvard University, 1970.

Lockwood, A. L. Moral reasoning and public policy debate. In T. Lickona (Ed.), *Moral development and behavior.* New York: Holt, Rinehart & Winston, 1976.

Loeb, R. Content-concomitants of boys' locus of control examined in parent-child interactions. *Developmental Psychology,* 1975, *11,* 353–59.

Lorenz, K. Companionship in bird life: Fellow members of social behavior. In C. H. Schiller (Ed.), *Instinctive behavior.* New York: International University Press, 1957.

Luria, A. R. *The role of speech in the regulation of normal and abnormal behavior.* New York: Pergamon Press, 1961.

Luria, Z. Psychosocial determinants of gender identity, role and orientation. In H. Katchadurian (Ed.), *Human sexuality: A comparative and developmental perspective.* Berkeley, Cal.: University of California Press, 1979.

Luria, Z., & Rose, M. *Psychology of human sexuality.* New York: John Wiley & Sons, 1979.

Luria, Z., & Rubin, J. Z. The neonate's gender and the eye of the beholder. *Scientific American,* in press.

Maas, H. The young adult adjustment of twenty wartime residential nursery school children. *Child Welfare*, 1963, *42*, 57–72.

Maccoby, E. E., Dowley, E. M., Hagen, J. W., & Degerman, R. Activity level and intellectual functioning in normal preschool children. *Child Development*, 1965, *36*, 761–70.

Maccoby, E. E., & Feldman, S. S. Mother-attachment and stranger-reactions in the third year of life. *Monographs of the Society for Research in Child Development*, 1972, *37* (1).

Maccoby, E. E., & Jacklin, C. N. *The psychology of sex differences*. Stanford, Cal.: Stanford University Press, 1974.

Maccoby, E. E., & Jacklin, C. N. Waiting room behavior of fathers and 12-month-old infants. Working paper, Stanford Longitudinal Study, Stanford, Cal., 1979.

MacKinnon, D. W. Violations of prohibitions. In H. A. Murray et al. (Eds.), *Explorations in personality*. New York: Oxford University Press, 1938.

Main, M. *Play, exploration and competence as related to child-adult attachment*. Unpublished doctoral dissertation, The Johns Hopkins University, 1973.

Malinowski, B. *Science, magic, and religion and other essays*. Garden City, N.Y.: Doubleday, 1954.

Martin, J. A. A longitudinal study of the consequences of early mother-infant interaction: A microanalytic approach. *Monographs of the Society for Research in Child Development*, 1980.

Marvin, R. S. An ethological-cognitive model for the attenuation of mother-child attachment behavior. In T. Alloway, P. Pliner, & L. Krames (Eds.), *Attachment behavior*. New York: Plenum Publishing Co., 1977.

Masters, J., & Wellman, H. Human infant attachment: A procedural critique. *Psychological Bulletin*, 1974, *81*, 218–37.

Matas, L., Arend, R. A., & Sroufe, L. A. Continuity of adaptation in the second year: The relationship between quality of attachment and later competence. *Child Development*, 1978, *49*, 547–56.

Maurer, A. Corporal punishment. *American Psychologist*, 1974, *29*, 614–26.

Mead, G. H. *Mind, self, and society*. Chicago: University of Chicago Press, 1934.

Mendoza, S. P., Coe, C. L., Smotherman, W. P., & Levine, S. Functional consequences of attachment: A comparison of two species. In W. P. Smotherman & R. W. Bell (Eds.), *Maternal influences and early behavior*. New York: Spectrum Press, 1979.

Messer, S. B. Reflection-impulsivity: A review. *Psychological Bulletin*, 1976, *83*, 1026–52.

Meyer, J. S., Novak, M. A., Bowman, R. E., & Harlow, H. F. Behavioral and hormonal effects of attachment object separation in surrogate-peer-reared and mother-reared infant rhesus monkeys. *Developmental Psychobiology*, 1975, *8*, 425–36.

Miller, G. A., Galanter, E., & Pribram, K. *Plans and the structure of behavior*. New York: Holt, Rinehart & Winston, 1960.

Miller, N. E., & Dollard, J. *Social learning and imitation*. New Haven, Conn.: Yale University Press, 1941.

Miller, S. A., Shelton, J., & Flavell, J. H. A test of Luria's hypothesis concerning the development of self-regulation. *Child Development*, 1970, *41*, 651–65.

Minton, C., Kagan, J., & Levine, J. A. Maternal control and obedience in the two-year-old. *Child Development*, 1971, *42*, 1873–94.

Mischel, W. A social learning view of sex differences in behavior. In E. E. Maccoby (Ed.), *The development of sex differences*. Stanford, Cal.: Stanford University Press, 1966.

Mischel, W. *Personality and assessment*. New York: John Wiley & Sons, 1968.

Mischel, W., Coates, B., & Raskoff, A. Effects of success and failure in self-gratification. *Journal of Personality and Social Psychology*, 1968, *10* (4), 381–90.

Mischel, W., & Grusec, J. Determinant of the rehearsal and transmission of neutral and aversive behaviors. *Journal of Personality and Social Psychology*, 1966, *3*, 197–205.

Mischel, W., & Grusec, J. Waiting for rewards and punishments: Effects of time and probability on choice. *Journal of Personality and Social Psychology*, 1967, *5*, 24–31.

Mischel, W., & Metzner, R. Preference for delayed reward as a function of age, intelligence, and length of delay internal. *Journal of Abnormal and Social Psychology*, 1962, *64*, 425–31.

Mischel, W., & Mischel, H. A cognitive social-learning approach to morality and self regulation. In T. Lickona (Ed.), *Moral development and behavior*. New York: Holt, Rinehart & Winston, 1976.

Mischel, W., & Staub, E. Effects of expectancy on working and waiting for larger reward. *Journal of Personality and Social Psychology*, 1965, *2*, 625–33.

Mischel, W., & Underwood, B. Instrumental ideation in delay of gratification. *Child Development*, 1974, *45*, 1083–88.

Mischel, W., Zeiss, R., & Zeiss, A. Internal-external control and persistence: Validation and implications of the Stanford Preschool Internal-External Scale. *Journal of Personality and Social Psychology*, 1974, *29*, 265–78.

Money, J. Ablatiopenis: Normal male infant sex-reassigned as a girl. *Archives of Sexual Behavior*, 1975, *4*, 65–72.

Money, J., Hampson, J. G., & Hampson, J. L. Imprinting and the establishment of gender role. *A.M.A. Archives of Neurology and Psychiatry*, 1957, *77*, 333–36.

Moore, B. S., Underwood, B., & Rosenhan, D. L. Affect and altruism. *Developmental Psychology*, 1973, *8*, 99–104.

Morgan, G. A., & Ricciuti, H. N. Infants' response to strangers during the first year. In B. M. Foss (Ed.), *Determinants of infant behaviour* (Vol. 4). London: Methuen, 1969.

Morris, J. *Conundrum*. New York: Harcourt Brace Jovanovich, 1974.

Mullener, N., & Laird, J. D. Some developmental changes in the organization of self-evaluations. *Developmental Psychology*, 1971, *5*, 237–43.

Murphy, L. B. *Social behavior and child personality*. New York: Columbia University Press, 1937.

Nelson, K. Structure and strategy in learning to talk. *Monographs of the Society for Research in Child Development*, 1973, 1–2 (149).

Newson, J., & Newson, E. *Four years old in an urban community*. Chicago: Aldine Publishing Co., 1968.

Novak, M. A. Social recovery of monkeys isolated for the first year of life. II. Long-term assessment. *Development Psychology*, 1979, *15*, 50–61.

Novak, M. A., & Harlow, H. F. Social recovery of monkeys isolated for the first year of life: I. Rehabilitation and therapy. *Developmental Psychology*, 1975, *11*, 453–65.

Nowicki, S., & Segal, W. Perceived parental characteristics, locus of control orientation, and behavioral correlates of locus of control. *Developmental Psychology*, 1974, *10*, 33–37.

Nowicki, S., & Strickland, B. A locus of control scale for children. *Journal of Consulting and Clinical Psychology*, 1973, *40*, 148–54.

O'Bryant, S. L., & Brophy, J. E. Sex differences in altruistic behavior. *Developmental Psychology*, 1976, *12* (6), 554.

Olweus, D. Stability of aggressive reaction patterns in males. *Psychological Bulletin*, 1979, *86*, 852–75.

Omark, D. R., & Edelman, M. *Peer group social interactions from an evolutionary perspective*. Paper presented at the meetings of the Society for Research in Child Development, Philadelphia, 1973.

Parke, R. D. Rules roles and resistance to deviation: Recent advances in punishment, discipline and self-control. In A. D. Pick (Ed.), *Minnesota Symposium on Child Psychology* (Vol. 8). Minneapolis: University of Minnesota Press, 1974.

Parke, R. D. Perspectives on father-infant interaction. In J. D. Osofsky (Ed.), *Handbook of infancy*. New York: John Wiley & Sons, 1978.

Parke, R. D., & Murray, S. *Reinstatement: A technique for increasing stability of inhibition in children*. Unpublished manuscript, University of Wisconsin, 1971.

Parke, R. D., & Sawin, D. B. The father's role in infancy: A reevaluation. *The Family Coordinator*, 1976, *25*, 365–71.

Patterson, G. R. The aggressive child: Victim and architect of a coercive system. In L. A. Hamerlynck, L. C. Handy, & E. J. Mash (Eds.), *Behavior modification and families. I. Theory and research*. New York: Brunner-Mazell, 1976.

Patterson, G. R., Littman, R. A., & Bricker, W. Assertive behavior in young children: A step toward a theory of aggression. *Monographs of the Society for Research in Child Development*, 1967, *35* (5).

Piaget, J. *The origins of intelligence in children*. New York: International Universities Press, 1952.

Piaget, J. *The construction of reality in the child*. New York: Basic Books, 1954.

Piaget, J. *The moral judgment of the child* (Marjorie Gabain, trans.). New York: The Free Press, 1965. (First published in English, 1932.)

Rawls, J. *A theory of justice*. Cambridge, Mass.: Harvard University Press, 1971.

Redl, F., & Wineman, D. *Children who hate*. Glencoe, Ill.: The Free Press, 1951.

Redl, F., & Wineman, D. *Controls from within*. Glencoe, Ill.: The Free Press, 1952.

Rheingold, H. L. Maternal behavior in the dog. In H. L. Rheingold (Ed.), *Maternal behavior in mammals*. New York: John Wiley & Sons, 1963.

Rheingold, H. L., & Cook, K. U. The contents of boy's and girl's rooms as an index of parents' behavior. *Child Development*, 1975, *46*, 459–63.

Rheingold, H. L., & Eckerman, C. O. The infant separates himself from his mother. *Science*, 1970, *168*, 78–83.

Richter, C. P. Behavior and metabolic cycles in animals and men. In P. Hoch & J. Zubin (Eds.), *Experimental psychopathology*. New York: Grune & Stratton, 1957.

Roche, A. F. Secular trends in human growth, maturation, and development. *Monographs of the Society for Research in Child Development*, 1979, *44* (3 & 4).

Roedell, W. C., & Slaby, R. G. The role of distal and proximal interaction in infant social preference formation. *Developmental Psychology*, 1977, *13*, 266–73.

Rosenblatt, J. S., & Lehrman, D. S. Maternal behavior in the laboratory rat. In H. L. Rheingold (Ed.), *Maternal behavior in mammals*. New York: John Wiley & Sons, 1963.

Rosenblum, L. A., & Harlow, H. F. Approach-avoidance conflict in the mother surrogate situation. *Psychological Reports*, 1963, *12*, 83–85.

Rosenkoetter, L. I. Resistance to temptation: Inhibitory and disinhibitory effects of models. *Developmental Psychology*, 1973, *8*, 80–84.

Ross, D. M., & Ross, S. A. *Hyperactivity: Research, theory and action*. New York: John Wiley & Sons, 1976.

Ross, E. A. *Social control: A survey of the foundations of order*. Cleveland: Case Western Reserve University Press, 1969. (Originally published, 1901.)

Ross, H. S., & Goldman, B. D. Establishing new social relations in infancy. In T. Alloway, P. Pliner, & L. Krames (Eds.), *Attachment behavior*. New York: Plenum Publishing Co., 1977.

Ross, S. A. A test of the generality of the effects of deviant preschool models. *Developmental Psychology*, 1971, *4*, 262–67.

Rothbart, M. K. Birth order and mother-child interaction in an achievement situation. *Journal of Personality and Social Psychology*, 1971, *17*, 113–20.

Rotter, J. B. *Social learning and clinical psychology*. New York: Prentice-Hall, 1954.

Rousseau, J. J. *Emile or on education*. London: Dent, 1974. (Originally published, 1763.)

Routh, D. K., Schroeder, C. S., & O'Tuama, L. A. Development of activity in children. *Developmental Psychology*, 1974, *10*, 163–68.

Routh, D. K., Walton, M. D., & Pedan-Belkin, E. Development of activity level in children revisited: Effects of mother presence. *Developmental Psychology*, 1978, *14*, 571–81.

Rowell, T. *Monkeys*. Baltimore: Penguin Books, 1972.

Rubin, J. Z., Provenzano, F. J., & Luria, Z. The eye of the beholder: Parents' view on sex of newborns. *American Journal of Orthopsychiatry*, 1974, *44*, 512–19.

Rubin, K. H., & Pepler, D. J. The relationship of child's play to social-cognitive growth and development. In H. Foot, A. Chapman, & J. Smith (Eds.), *Friendship and childhood relationships*. London: John Wiley & Sons, 1980.

Ruble, D. N., Balaban, T., & Cooper, J. *Development of responsiveness to sex-stereotyped information in children: A television study*. Unpublished paper, Department of Psychology, Princeton University, 1979.

Rule, B. G. The hostile and instrumental functions of human aggression. In J. de Wit & W. W. Hartup (Eds.), *Determinants and origins of aggressive behavior*. The Hague: Mouton, 1974.

Rutter, M. Sex differences in children's response to family stress. In E. J. Anthony and C. Koupernik (Eds.), *The child in his family*. New York: John Wiley & Sons, 1970.

Rutter, M. *Maternal deprivation reassessed*. Harmondsworth, Eng.: Penguin, 1972.

Rutter, M. Maternal deprivation 1972–1978: New findings, new concepts, new approaches. *Child Development*, 1979, *50*, 283–305.

Sackett, G. P. Monkeys reared in visual isolation with pictures as visual input. Evidence for an innate releasing mechanism. *Science*, 1966, *154*, 1468–72.

Sarbin, T. R. A preface to a psychological analysis of the self. *Psychology Review*, 1959, *52*, 11–22.

Schachter, F. F., Shore, E., Hodapp, R., Chalfin, S., & Bundy, C. Do girls talk earlier? Mean length of utterance in toddlers. *Developmental Psychology*, 1978, *14*, 388–92.

Schaffer, H. R. *The growth of sociability*. Baltimore: Penguin Books, 1971.

Schaffer, H. R. Cognitive components of the infant's response to strangeness. In M. Lewis & L. A. Rosenblum (Eds.), *The origins of fear*. New York: Wiley-Interscience, 1974.

Schaffer, H. R., & Emerson, P. E. The development of social attachments in infancy. *Monographs of the Society for Research in Child Development*, 1964, *29*.(a)

Schaffer, H. R., & Emerson, P. E. Patterns of response to physical contact in early human development. *Journal of Child Psychology and Psychiatry*, 1964, *5*, 1–13.(b)

Schank, R., & Abelson, R. *Scripts, plans, goals and understanding*. Hillsdale, N.J.: Lawrence Erlbaum Assoc., 1977.

Schlesinger, H. The impact of deafness on the life style. In J. M. Stack (Ed.), *The special child*. New York: Human Sciences Press, 1980.

Scott, J. P., & Fuller, J. L. *Genetics and the social behavior of the dog.* Chicago: University of Chicago Press, 1965.

Sears, R. R., Rau, L., & Alpert, R. *Identifications and child rearing.* Stanford, Cal.: Stanford University Press, 1965.

Sears, R. R., Maccoby, E. E., & Levin, H. *Patterns of child rearing.* Evanston, Ill: Row Peterson, 1957.

Seay, B., Alexander, B. K., & Harlow, H. Maternal behavior of socially deprived rhesus monkeys. *Journal of Abnormal and Social Psychology,* 1964, *69,* 345–54.

Seligman, M. E. P. *Helplessness.* San Francisco: W. H. Freeman & Co., 1975.

Selman, R. The relation of role-taking to the development of moral judgment in children. *Child Development,* 1971, *42,* 79–92.

Selman, R. Social-cognitive understanding: A guide to educational and clinical practice. In T. Lickona (Ed.), *Moral development and behavior.* New York: Holt, Rinehart & Winston, 1976.

Serbin, L. A., Tonick, I. J., & Sternglanz, S. Shaping cooperative cross-sex play. *Child Development,* 1977, *48,* 924–29.

Simonds, P. E. Peers, parents and primates: The developing network of attachments. In T. Alloway, P. Pliner, & L. Krames (Eds.), *Attachment behavior.* New York: Plenum Publishing Co., 1977.

Slaby, R. G. Verbal regulation of aggression and altruism. In J. de Wit & W. W. Hartup (Eds.), *Determinants and origins of aggressive behavior.* The Hague: Mouton, 1974.

Slaby, R. G., & Frey, K. S. Development of gender constancy and selective attention to same-sex models. *Child Development,* 1975, *46,* 849–56.

Smith, P. K., & Daglish, L. Sex differences in parent and infant behavior in the home. *Child Development,* 1977, *48,* 1250–54.

Spencer-Booth, Y., & Hinde, R. A. Effects of brief separations from mothers on behaviour of rhesus monkeys 6–24 months later. *Journal of Child Psychology and Psychiatry,* 1971, *12,* 157– 72.

Sroufe, L. A., & Waters, E. Attachment as an organization construct. *Child Development,* 1977, *48,* 1184–99.

Stacy, M., Dearden, R., Pill, R., & Robinson, D. *Hospitals, children and their families.* London: Routledge & Kagan Paul, 1970.

Staub, E. A. The influence of age and number of witnesses on children's attempts to help. *Journal of Personality and Social Psychology,* 1970, *14,* 130–40.(a)

Staub, E. A. The influence of focusing responsibility on children on their attempts to help. *Developmental Psychology,* 1970, *2,* 152–53.(b)

Staub, E. A. The use of role playing and induction in children's learning of helping and sharing behavior. *Child Development,* 1971, *42,* 805–16.

Stein, A. H. Imitation of resistance to temptation. *Child Development,* 1967, *38,* 157–69.

Stendler, D., Damrin, D., & Hines, A. C. Studies in cooperation and competition: In the effects of working for group and individual rewards on the social climate of children's groups. *Journal of Genetic Psychology,* 1951, *79,* 173–97.

Stone, L. *The family, sex and marriage in England, 1500–1800.* New York: Harper & Row, 1977.

Strayer, F. F. Peer attachment and affiliative subgroups. In F. F. Strayer (Ed.), *Ethological perspectives on preschool social organization.* Memo de Recherche #5, Universite du Quebec, A Montreal, Department of Psychologie, Avril 1977.

Strayer, J., & Strayer, F. F. Social aggression and power relations among preschool children. *Aggressive Behavior,* 1978, *4,* 173–82.

Stumphauzer, J. S. Increased delay of gratification in young prison inmates through invitation of high-delay peer models. *Journal of Personality and Social Psychology,* 1972, *21,* 10–17.

Suomi, S. J. Mechanisms underlying social development: A re-examination of mother-infant interactions in monkeys. In A. Pick (Ed.), *Minnesota Symposium on Child Psychology* (Vol. 10). Minneapolis: University of Minnesota Press, 1976.

Suomi, S. J. Adult male-infant interaction among monkeys living in nuclear families. *Child Development,* 1977, *48,* 1255–71.

Suomi, S. J. Development of attachment and other social behaviors in rhesus monkeys. In T. Alloway, P. Pliner, & L. Krames (Eds.), *Attachment behavior.* New York: Plenum Publishing Co., 1977. (b)

Suomi, S. J., & Harlow, H. F. Social rehabilitation of isolate-reared monkeys. *Developmental Psychology,* 1972, *6,* 487–96.

Sullivan, H. S. *The interpersonal theory of psychiatry.* H. S. Perry & M. L. Garvel (Eds.). New York: W. W. Norton Co., 1953.

Sumner, W. G. *Folkways: A study of the sociological importance of usages, manners, customs, mores and morals.* Boston: Ginn & Co., 1907.

Taplin, P. S., & Reid, J. B. Changes in parent consequences as a function of family intervention. *Journal of Consulting and Clinical Psychology,* 1977, *45,* 973–81.

Taylor, D. C., & Ounsted, C. The nature of gender differences explored through ontogenetic analyses of sex ratios in disease. In D. Taylor & C. Ounsted (Eds.), *Gender differences: Their ontogency and significance*. Baltimore: Williams & Wilkins Co., 1972.

Thomas, A., Chess, S., Birch, H. G., Hertzig, M. E., & Korn, S. *Behavioral individuality in early childhood*. New York: University Press, 1971.

Thompson, S. K. Gender labels and early sex-role development. *Child Development*, 1975, 46, 339–47.

Thompson, S. K., & Bentler, P. M. The priority of cues in sex discrimination by children and adults. *Developmental Psychology*, 1971, 5, 181–85.

Tinbergen, N. *The study of instinct*. Oxford: Clarendon Press, 1951.

Turiel, E. The development of social concepts. In DePalma & J. Foley (Eds.), *Moral development*. Hillsdale, N.J.: Lawrence Erlbaum Assoc., 1975.

Van Leishout, C. F. M. Young children's reactions to barriers placed by their mothers. *Child Development*, 1975, 46, 879–86.

Vaughn, B., Egeland, B., Sroufe, L. A., & Waters, E. Individual differences in infant-mother attachment at 12 and 18 months. Stability and change in families under stress. *Child Development*, in press.

Vygotsky, L. S. *Thought and language*. Cambridge, Mass.: MIT Press, 1934.

Waldrop, M. F., & Halverson, C. F., Jr. Intensive and extensive peer behavior: Longitudinal and cross-sectional analysis. *Child Development*, 1975, 46, 19–26.

Walker, R. N. Some temperamental traits in children as viewed by their peers, their teachers, and themselves. *Monographs of the Society for Research in Child Development*, 1967, 32 (6).

Wallerstein, J. S., & Kelly, J. B. The effects of parental divorce: Experiences of the preschool child. *Journal of the American Academy of Child Psychiatry*, 1975, 14, 600–16.

Wallerstein, J. S., & Kelly, J. B. The effects of parental divorce: Experiences of the child in later latency. *American Journal of Orthopsychiatry*, 1976, 46, 256–69.

Walters, R. H., Parke, R. D., & Cane, V. A. Timing of punishment and the observation of consequences to others as determinants of response inhibition. *Journal of Experimental Child Psychology*, 1965, 2, 10–30.

Ward, W. *Disadvantaged children and their first school experience*. ETS-Headstart longitudinal study. Development of self regulatory behaviors. PR-73-18. Princeton, N.J.: ETS, 1973.

Waters, E., Wippman, J., & Sroufe, L. A. At-

tachment, positive affect, and competence in the peer-group: Two studies in construct validation. *Child Development*, 1979, 50, 821–29.

Watson, J. *Infant perception of "necessity."* Paper presented at the meetings of the Society for Research in Child Development, New Orleans, Spring, 1977.

Watson, J. B. *Psychological care of infant and child*. New York: W. W. Norton & Co., 1928.

Weinstein, E. A. The development of interpersonal competence. In D. A. Goslin (Ed.), *Handbook of socialization theory and research*. Chicago: Rand McNally, 1969.

Weisz, J. R. Choosing problem-solving rewards and Halloween prizes: Delay of gratification and preference for symbolic rewards as a function of development, motivation and personal investment. *Developmental Psychology*, 1978, 14, 66–78.

Werry, J. S. Developmental hyperactivity. *Pediatric Clinics of North America*, 1968, 15, 580–99.

Whiting, B. B., & Edwards, C. P. A cross-cultural analysis of sex differences in the behavior of children aged three through eleven. *Journal of Personality and Social Psychology*, 1973, 91, 171–88.

Whiting, B. B., & Whiting, J. W. M. Altruistic and egoistic behavior in six cultures. In L. Nader & T. W. Maretzki (Eds.), *Cultural illness and health: Essays in human adaptation*. Washington, D.C.: American Anthropological Association, 1973.

Whiting, B. B., & Whiting, J. W. M. *Children of six cultures*. Cambridge, Mass.: Harvard University Press, 1975.

Whiting, J. W. M., & Child, I. *Child training and personality: A cross-cultural study*. New Haven: Yale University Press, 1953.

Witelson, S. F. Sex and the single hemisphere: Right hemisphere specialization for spatial processing. *Science*, 1976, 193, 425–27.

Witelson, S. F., & Pallie, W. Left-hemisphere specialization for language in the newborn. *Brain*, 1973, 96, 641–46.

Wolf, T. M., & Cheyne, J. A. Persistence of effects of live behavioral, televised behavioral and live verbal models on resistance to deviation. *Child Development*, 1972, 43, 1429–36.

Wolff, P. H. The natural history of crying and other vocalizations in early infancy. In B. M. Foss (Ed.), *Determinants of infant behaviour* (Vol. 4). London: Methuen, 1969.

Wolkind, S., & Rutter, M. Children who have been "in care"—an epidemiological study. *Journal of Child Psychology and Psychiatry*, 1973, 14, 97–105.

Yarrow, L. J., & Goodwin, M. S. The immediate impact of separation reactions of infants to a change in mother figures. In L. J. Stone, H. T. Smith & L. B. Murphy (Eds.), *The competent infant.* New York: Basic Books, 1973.

Yarrow, L. J., Goodwin, M. S., Manheimer, H., & Milowe, I. D. Infancy experience and cognitive and personality development at ten years. In L. J. Stone, H. T. Smith, & L. B. Murphy (Eds.), *The competent infant.* New York: Basic Books, 1973.

Yarrow, M. R., Scott, P. M., & Waxler, C. Z. Learning concern for others. *Developmental Psychology,* 1973, *8,* 240–60.

Yarrow, M. R., & Waxler, C. Z., with the collaboration of Barrett, D., Darby, J., King, R., Pickett, M., & Smith, J. Dimensions and correlates of prosocial behavior in young children. *Child Development,* 1976, *47,* 118–25.

Zahn-Waxler, C., Radke-Yarrow, M., & King, R. A. Child-rearing and children's pro-social initiations toward victims of distress. *Child Development,* 1979, *50,* 319–30.

Ziller, R. C. *The social self.* New York: Pergamon Press, 1973.

Zussman, J. S. U. *Situational determinants of parental behavior.* Dissertation submitted to the Department of Psychology, Stanford University, 1977.

Acknowledgments and Copyrights

Cover painting:

Mother and Child by Milton Avery. Private collection. Courtesy of Andrew Crispo Gallery, New York.

Text:

The author would like to thank the following for permission to reproduce material in this book:

GEORGE ALLEN & UNWIN (PUBLISHERS) LTD. For the excerpts from *Four Years Old in an Urban Community* by John Newson and Elizabeth Newson. Reprinted with permission of George Allen & Unwin (Publishers) Ltd. and the authors.

EXECUTOR FOR STANLEY COOPERSMITH ESTATE For the excerpts from *Antecedents of Self-Esteem* by Stanley Coopersmith. Copyright © 1967. Reprinted with permission of the Executor for the Stanley Coopersmith Estate.

JOSSEY-BASS, INC. For the excerpts from *The Social World of the Child* by William Damon. Copyright 1977. Reprinted with permission of Jossey-Bass, Inc.

MACMILLAN PUBLISHING CO., INC. For the excerpts from *Children Who Hate* by Fritz Redl and David Wineman. Copyright 1951 by The Free Press, renewed 1979 by Fritz Redl and David Wineman. For the excerpts from *The Moral Judgment of the Child* by Jean Piaget. First Free Press Paperback Edition, 1965. Excerpts from both books are reprinted with permission of Macmillan Publishing Co., Inc.

STANFORD UNIVERSITY PRESS For the excerpts from *Patterns of Child Rearing* by Robert R. Sears, Eleanor E. Maccoby, and Harry Levin, with the permission of the publishers, Stanford University Press. © 1957 by the Board of Trustees of the Leland Stanford Junior University.

UNIVERSITY OF NEBRASKA PRESS For the excerpts from "The Child's Construing of Self" from *Nebraska Symposium on Motivation* by J. K. Cole and A. W. Landfield, eds. Copyright © 1977 by the University of Nebraska Press. Reprinted with permission of the University of Nebraska Press.

JOHN WILEY & SONS, INC. For the excerpts from *Hyperactivity: Research, Theory, and Action* by Dorothea M. Ross and Sheila A. Ross. Copyright © 1976 by John Wiley & Sons, Inc. Reprinted by permission of John Wiley & Sons, Inc.

Tables:

6-1 Based on data from Feldman, S. S. Reprinted with permission of the author. **6-2** Adapted from Thompson, S. K. Gender labels and early sex-role development. *Child Development*, 1975, 46, 339–47. Copyright © 1975 by The Society for Research in Child Development. Reprinted with permission of the author and The Society for Research in Child Development.

9-1 Reprinted from Hoffman, M. L., & Saltzstein, H. D. Parent discipline and children's moral development. *Journal of Personality and Social Psychology*, 1967, 5, 45–47. Copyright 1967 by the American Psychological Association. Reprinted by permission. **9-2** Adapted from Hartshorne, H., & May, M. A. *Studies in the Nature of Character*. Reprinted by Arno Press, Inc., 1975.

Figures:

2-1 Leon, M. Pheromonal mediation of maternal behavior. In T. Alloway, P. Pliner, & L. Krames (Eds.) *Attachment Behavior*. Plenum Publishing Corporation, 1977, p. 181. **2-2** Kagan, J. Emergent themes in human development. *American Scientist*, 1976, 64, 186–96. Reprinted by permission of *American Scientist*, journal of Sigma Xi, The Scientific Research Society. **2-3** Kotelchuk, M. The infant's relationship to the father. In M. Lamb (Ed.), *The Role of the Father in Child Development*. John Wiley & Sons, Inc., 1976, pp. 333, 335. **2-4** Roedell, W. C., & Slaby, R. G. The role of distal and proximal interaction in infant social preference formation. *Developmental Psychology*, 1977, 13, 269. Copyright 1977 by the American Psychological Association. Reprinted by permission.

3-1 Clarke-Stewart, A. K. Interactions between mothers and their young children: Characteristics and consequences. *Monographs of the Society for Research in Child Development*, 1973, 38 (Ser. no. 153), 78, Fig. 6. Copyright 1973 by The Society for Research in Child Development, Inc. **3-2** Reprinted with permission from *Journal of Child Psychology and Psychiatry*, Vol. 12. Spencer-Booth, Y., & Hinde, R. A. Effects of brief separations from mothers on behavior of rhesus monkeys 6–24 months later. Copyright 1971 by Pergamon Press, Ltd.

4-1, 4-2 Goodenough, F. L. *Anger in Young Children*. Copyright 1931, 1959 by the University of Minnesota. University of Minnesota Press, Minneapolis. **4-3** From Sears, R. R., Maccoby, E. E., & Levin, H. *Patterns of Child Rearing* (1957), with permission of the publisher Stanford University Press.

425

5-1 Kagan, J. et al. Information processing in the child. *Psychological Monographs, 1964, 78* (1), 22, Fig. 8. Copyright 1964 by the American Psychological Association. Reprinted by permission. 5-2 Messer, S. B. Reflection-impulsivity: A review. *Psychological Bulletin, 1976, 83,* 1030. Copyright 1976 by the American Psychological Association. Reprinted by permission.

6-1 Adapted from Forest, M. G., Cathiard, A. M., Bourgeois, J., & Genoud, J. Androgenes plasmatiques chez le nourrisson normal et premature relation avec la maturation de l'axe hypothalamo-hypophyso-gonadique. *Inserm,* 1974, *32,* 321. From International Symposium on Sexual Endocrinology of the Perinatal Period. 6-2 Reproduced with permission from "An Ethological Approach to Social Relations among Young Children," by F. F. Strayer. In T. Foot, H. Chapman, & J. Smith (Eds.), *Friendship and Social Relations in Young Children.* Copyright © 1980 John Wiley & Sons Ltd. 6-3 Jacklin, C. N., & Maccoby, E. E. Social behavior at thirty-three months in same-sex and mixed-sex dyads. *Child Development,* 1978, *49,* 563. Copyright © The Society for Research in Child Development, Inc. 6-4 Emmerich, W., Goldman, K. S., Kirsh, B., & Sharabany, R. *Development of Gender Constancy in Economically Disadvantaged Children.* Unpublished manuscript, pp. 58, 59. Educational Testing Service, Princeton, N.J., 1976. 6-5 Langlois, J. H., & Downs, A. C. *Mothers and Peers as Socialization Agents of Sex-typed Play Behaviors in Young Children.* Unpublished paper, Department of Psychology, University of Texas, Austin, Texas, 1979.

7-1 Gordon, G. G. Self-recognition in chimpanzees. *American Psychologist,* 1977, *32,* 329–38. Copyright 1977 by the American Psychological Association. Reprinted by permission. 7-2 Gunnar, M. R. Control, warning signals and distress in infancy. *Developmental Psychology,* 1980, *51.* Copyright 1980 by the American Psychological Association. Reprinted by permission.

9-1 Parke, R. D. Rules, roles and resistance to deviation: Recent advances in punishment, discipline, and self-control. In A. D. Pick (Ed.), *Minnesota Symposium on Child Psychology* (Vol. 8). Copyright © 1974 by the University of Minnesota. University of Minnesota Press, Minneapolis. 9-2 Yarrow, M. R., Scott, P. M., & Waxler, C. Z. Learning concern for others. *Developmental Psychology,* 1973, *8*(2), 246. Copyright 1973 by the American Psychological Association. Reprinted by permission.

10-1 Baumrind, D. Child care practices anteceding three patterns of preschool behavior. *Genetic Psychology Monographs,* 1967, *75,* 78. 10-2 Lepper, M. R., Greene, D., & Nisbett, R. E. Undermining children's intrinsic interest with extrinsic rewards: A test of the overjustification hypothesis. *Journal of Personality and Social Psychology,* 1973, *28,* 129–37. Copyright 1973 by the American Psychological Association. Reprinted by permission.

Pictures:

Page 2 Lewis W. Hine, Library of Congress. 34 Suzanne Szasz. 80 Suzanne Szasz. 114 George W. Gardner. 160 Joel Gordon. 202 Stock, Boston, Elizabeth Hamlin. 250 Suzanne Szasz. 294 Erika Stone. 328 Woodfin Camp & Associates, Ellen Pines. 366 Photo Researchers, Inc.

Author Index

Subject Index

Ability to organize, development of, 163
Acceptance-rejection (maternal), 87
Accessibility-ignoring (maternal), 88
Achievement, autonomous, 379–80
Activity level, 166–68; sex differences in, 211–12
Adolescents, undercontrolled, 196–98
Affection. *See* Warmth; Attachment
Age of child: and aggression, 118–29, 143–44; and altruistic and egoistic behaviors, 354–56, 358; and changes in moral behavior, 357, 360–62; and cheating, 357; and concepts of authority, 308–12; and concepts of fairness, 307–08; and concepts of lying, 312–14; and consideration of intent, 313–14; and moral understanding, 301–15, 326; and parents' behavior, 395–98; and perspective taking, 318–22; and resistance to temptation, 332–33; and understanding of promises, 313–15. *See also* Developmental trends
Agency, social and cognitive, 377–78, 382, 383
Aggression: and altruism, 150–52; in animals, 115–16, 129–31; aversive consequences of, 127; changes with age, 143–49, 157; by children, 115–59, 382; consequences of, 127; control of by society, 298; definition of, 115–16; directed, 119–21; early development of, 118–32; ego and, 147–49; empathy and, 150–52, 158; encouragement of by parents, 132–33; fairness and, 146; family, 137–42; and frustration, 144–46; hostile, 147–48; and ideology, 143; instrumental, 147–48; intent and, 118, 130–31, 157; in interactive play and, 125–26; noncognitive views of, 129–32; in parents, 380; parental influence on, 132–40; and personality structure, 149–50; positive reinforcers of, 127; school setting and, 142–43; sex differences in, 216–17; unintentional encouragement of, 133–34; unlearned aspects of, 129–31; utility of, 152–54
Agonistic interactions, 128–29
Altruism, 344–56, 363–64; and affective explanations, 345; and aggression, 150–52; cross-cultural comparisons, 354–55; definition of, 344; and empathy, 346–49; and mood, 349–50; and parental response, 345–46, 354–55, 383, 393; and social learning theory, 330, 355–56; training for, 350–56, 363–64; in very young children, 345–46
Anger: directed (*see* Aggression); undirected, 119–21
Aspirations and self-esteem, 272–73
Assertiveness, nonaggressive, 149–56
Attachment, 17, 35–79, 392; abuse and, 65;

avoidant, 84–85, 100, 392; child's role, 91–92; consistency over time, 82–83; consequences of early, 92–102; development of, 35–79; emotional security and, 54–56; familiarity and, 70–71; father-infant, 58–60, 72–73; fear of, 394–95; feeding as a factor in, 63–65, 85–87; in humans, 46–62; insecure, 84–85, 89, 100; intensity of, 41–43, 73–77; in lower animals, 36–40; mother's role in, 85–90; mutual reactiveness and, 47–50, 66–70; objects, 53–55, 58–61; phases in, 62; play and, 72–73; in primates, 40–46; punishment and, 65, 108; in rats, 37–40; reasons for lessening of, 73–77; relationship, transformation of, 74–77, 79; resistant, 84–85, 100; secure, 84–85, 89, 91, 100, 101–02, 111, 392; signal system and, 66–70; in subhuman primates, 40–46; typology of, 83–85
Attention span, 176
Attribution. *See* Causal attribution
Authoritarian parenting, 371, 376–78, 384–85
Authoritative parenting, 376–78, 386
Authority, 298–99, 305–06, 308–12, 326–27, 397–98
Autonomous achievement, 379–80
Autonomous morality, 303, 308
Aversive consequences of aggression, 127
Avoidant infants, 84–85, 100, 392

Basal metabolism rate in children, 167–68
Behavior, organization of, 162–64
Behavioral implications of self-esteem, 276–78
Behaviorism, 12–13
Biological influences on sex typing, 243–45, 248
Birds, attachments among, 36–37. *See also* Imprinting
Birth order, and parents' reaction to child, 398–400
Brain maturation, 209–10

Causal attribution, 288–90, 334–36
Cheating: consistency across situations, 357–58, 361
Child-care functions, 217–21
Child-proofing environment, 191
Child-rearing practices: and aggression, 140–42, 154–56; and altruism, 345–46, 354–56; and attachment, 85–91; children's sense of control and, 386–91; and competence, 368–80; democratic, 368–71; early, 4–8; effects of, 367–410; Locke's views on, 8–9; and locus of control, 286–91, 293; major dimensions of, 380–95; and moral development,